The Red Sox Fan Handbook

Everything you need to know to be a Red Sox
fan . . . or to marry one

Compiled by Leigh Grossman

Swordsmith Books
Pomfret, Connecticut

A Swordsmith Book

Published by
Swordsmith Productions
PO Box 242
Pomfret, CT 06258
www.swordsmith.com

Printing history
First edition published in March 2001

ISBN: 1-931013-03-9

Edited by Jamie Johnson
Copyedited by Wendy Goldberg

Swordsmith Books are distributed by
LPC Group
1436 West Randolph Street
Chicago, IL 60607
(800)626-4330
www.coolbooks.com

Printed in the U.S.A.

10 9 8 7 6 5 4 3 2 1

CONTENTS

    More than 330 of the players who people still talk about, and
    why they're important
    Don Aase • Harry Agganis • Rick Aguilera • Israel Alcantara
    • Dale Alexander • Luis Alicea • Gary Allenson • Larry
    Andersen • Brady Anderson • Mike Andrews • Luis Aparicio
    • Luis Aponte • Tony Armas • Rolando Arrojo • Steve Avery
    • Jeff Bagwell • Bob Bailey • Marty Barrett • Don Baylor •
    Rod Beck • Hugh Bedient • Gary Bell • Stan Belinda • Gary
    Bell • Moe Berg • Dante Bichette • Max Bishop • Greg
    Blosser • Mike Boddicker • Wade Boggs • Lou Boudreau •

Oil Can Boyd • Hugh Bradley • Darren Bragg • Eddie
Bressoud • Ken Brett • Tom Brewer • Mike Brown • Tom
Brunansky • Bill Buckner • Tom Burgmeier • Morgan
Burkhart • Ellis Burks • Rick Burleson • George Burns •
Juan Bustabad • Bill Campbell • Jose Canseco • Bernie Carbo
• Bill Carrigan • Frank Castillo • Danny Cater • Orlando
Cepeda • Ben Chapman • Robinson Checo • Eddie Cicotte •
Jack Clark • Mark Clear • Roger Clemens • Reggie Cleveland
• Michael Coleman • Jimmy Collins • Ray Collins • Billy
Conigliaro • Tony Conigliaro • Gene Conley • Billy Consolo
• Cecil Cooper • Scott Cooper • Wil Cordero • Rheal Cormier
• Jim Corsi • Ted Cox • Doc Cramer • Paxton Crawford •
Steve Crawford • Lou Criger • Joe Cronin • Rich Croushore •
Leon Culberson • Ray Culp • Midre Cummings • John Curtis
• Danny Darwin • Brian Daubach • Andre Dawson • Rob
Deer • Brian Denman • Dom DiMaggio • Big Bill Dinneen •
Joe Dobson • Pat Dodson • Bobby Doerr • John Dopson •
Patsy Dougherty • Dick Drago • Walt Dropo • Joe Dugan •
Mike Easler • Dennis Eckersley • Howard Ehmke • Nick
Esasky • Vaughn Eshelman • Dwight Evans • Carl Everett •
Jeff Fassero • Rick Ferrell • Wes Ferrell • Boo Ferriss • Mark
Fidrych • Lou Finney • Carlton Fisk • Bryce Florie • Mike
Fornieles • Tony Fossas • Rube Foster • Pete Fox • Jimmie
Foxx • Joe Foy • Buck Freeman • Jeff Frye • Denny
Galehouse • Rich Garces • Nomar Garciaparra • Larry
Gardner • Wes Gardner • Rich Gedman • Billy Goodman •
Tom Gordon • Jeff Gray • Pumpsie Green • Mike Greenwell
• Doug Griffin • Lefty Grove • Jackie Gutierrez • Erik
Hanson • Carroll Hardy • Tommy Harper • Ken Harrelson •
Greg Harris • Mickey Harris • Billy Hatcher • Scott
Hatteberg • Dave Henderson • Joe Hesketh • Pinky Higgins •
Butch Hobson • Glenn Hoffman • Harry Hooper • Sam Horn
• Dwayne Hosey • Tom House • Elston Howard • Waite
Hoyt • Long Tom Hughes • Tex Hughson • Bruce Hurst •
Reggie Jefferson • Ferguson Jenkins • Jackie Jensen • "Indian
Bob" Johnson • Earl Johnson • Sad Sam Jones • Eddie Joost •
Ed Jurak • George Kell • Dana Kiecker • Ellis Kinder • Jack
Kramer • Roger LaFrançois • Carney Lansford • Mike Lansing
• Bill Lee • Mark Lemke • Dutch Leonard • Darren Lewis •
Duffy Lewis • Tim Lollar • Jim Lonborg • Derek Lowe •
Sparky Lyle • Fred Lynn • Steve Lyons • Mike Macfarlane •
Mike Maddux • Tom Maggard • Ron Mahay • Frank Malzone
• Felix Mantilla • Josias Manzanillo • Juan Marichal • Mike
Marshall • Pedro Martinez • Ramon Martinez • John

PREFACE

I'm 34 years old now, and I've been a Red Sox fan since 1979, when I was 12. I'm about average aged for the contributors to this book, the oldest of whom saw his first Red Sox game in 1927. What made me a Red Sox fan? At the time, I wasn't even a *baseball* fan. No one in my family played baseball. I lived near Atlantic City, New Jersey, close to eight hours' drive away from Boston. I'd been to a few Philadelphia Phillies games, in sterile Veterans' Stadium, and had come away less than impressed.

My sister was in college in the Boston area, and I came up to visit her one summer. She and a bunch of friends dragged me to a Red Sox game. We sat in the bleachers, section 35. I was bored and being pretty obnoxious. Sometime during the game, something captured me. I don't know if it was Fenway Park, or the crowd, or something magical about the game itself, but by the time Dwight Evans broke open a tie game with a ninth-inning grand slam, I was hooked.

Two summers later I traveled to Boston again, for a week this time. I walked from Somerville to Boston to buy Red Sox tickets, and went to every game I could afford, sometimes walking instead of taking public transit so I could save my money to go to more games. The night before I had to leave town, the Red Sox got into a 19-inning duel with the Seattle Mariners. I couldn't bear to leave, even though the last bus back to Somerville left at 1:00 AM. After the game was finally suspended, I ended up walking back through Boston and Cambridge to my sister's apartment in Somerville, showing up around 3:00 in the morning. She never said anything.

I took to listening to the Red Sox on the radio. From Atlantic City, on a clear night, you can just barely pull in WTIC, AM 1080 from Hartford. I'd go up to the highest point in the house and listen on the ancient clock radio that had the best reception of all the radios in the house—making tiny adjustments to try and preserve the signal when it faded. I still listen to most of the Red Sox games on the radio, even though I live in New England now and could probably watch more of them. But the Red Sox captured my imagination as much as my heart, and listening to games on the radio allows my imagination to do much of the work.

What made me come up with the idea for this book? *The Red Sox Fan Handbook* is the book I wish I'd had when the team first captured my imagination. It's easy to find a book about stats, or a dry analysis of a baseball team's chances. It's much harder to find the folklore of a team—not just who the important players were, but why people still care about them, what brought them to life for other fans watching games last year, a dozen years ago—or a hundred years ago. This is a book about Ted Williams and Babe Ruth and Pedro Martinez and Nomar Garciaparra, but it's also a book about Ed Jurak catching a rat in his glove, and Tom Maggard dying just at the brink of the major leagues. There are stories about more than 330 players in this book—some of them famous, some of them funny, some of them tragic, some of them just about the lives of people that we care about, or that previous generations of fans cared about.

There is a history of the team in this book, but that history is part of an ongoing story of how the team and its fans became what they are today, not just an account of who won or lost or was traded.

There are questions and answers that I wanted when I first discovered the game—answers about the basic strategies of the game, about some of baseball's confusing rules and procedures, and about the Red Sox themselves.

There is an account of Fenway Park—not just how to get tickets or where to park or eat (although that's here) but what the experience of Fenway Park has been for other fans, and why a tiny, outdated facility is so beloved by so many people. There are stories by other fans of what captured their imaginations, in the same way that meaningless 1979 game captured mine.

And along the way there are all of the other things you would expect in a guide for Red Sox fans, new or long-suffering: a list of books and a guide to websites, information about visiting Spring Training or the Red Sox minor league teams.

Whether you read through or browse for favorite players and incidents, whether you are using this book to learn about the team for the first time or to relive a half-century of memories, this book is an attempt to capture the soul of a team that has captured the soul of New England.

The Red Sox Fan Handbook was a team effort, with more than two dozen people participating to some degree. The primary contributors to this book include Lyford P. Beverage Jr., Dave Bismo, James J. Lyons, Robert P. Machemer, Heather Anne Nicoll, Toine Otten, Paul Ryan, Neil Serven, Donald J. Violette, and Edward R. Zartler. Others who contributed valuable counsel or stories include Anna Delilah, Don Fisher, Mario Martinelli, Lesley McBain, Susan Shwartz, Colin Smith, Richard Smith, Jim Tiberio, Val Vadeboncoeur, and Eric Van. Jamie Johnson line edited the book, and Lesley McBain, Wendy Goldberg, and Stacy Cortigiano assisted in the editorial process, as did intern Matthew Peck.

—LEIGH GROSSMAN
January, 2001

WHY TO BUY THIS BOOK

It's early spring, and you've been tossed into a book store up in Boston.
While you eye their great selection
Boyfriend Joe is in the section
where the books discuss the Sox
from Freddy Lynn to Jimmy Foxx.

Your last night's date was not so hot
(he'd cooked you dinner, though he's not
a Paul Prudhomme or Fannie Farmer).
Still, he tried, the handsome charmer!
Date soon went from bad to worse
when you both failed to, well, converse.
"So whaddya think of Kennedy?"
you ask him with amenity,
while thinking of the man named Ted.
But Joe's reply is tainted Red:
"I used to like him well enough
I thought him made of sterner stuff
until I saw him pamper Mo.
By then I wanted him to go."
He pampered more? "More what?" you think.
You start to pour yourself a drink.
"I hated Nixon" you expound
while searching for some common ground.
"He's still quite young," your man replies,
"I like the way he catches flies."
Confused, you rule out politics
and think, "this date is hard to fix!"
You ask him for some more chianti
but instead get "El Tiante." He
talks of him and Tony C,
he quotes the loony Spaceman Lee.
He hints at Hughson and at Harris,

waxes eloquent on Ferris,
on and on (he likes to talk!), he
has mixed thoughts on Thomas Yawkey.
Sammy White to Pumpsie Green!
He lectures you on Bill Dineen.
He talks of Roosters and of Bags
of '83 and no-hit Rags.
He calls Frazee, "A Yankee whore."
He talks of Yaz and Bobby Doerr
and Smokey Joe and Tris and Cy.
You're almost ready now to cry,
for every time you start anew
your date finds ways to misconstrue.
His mind and yours are not in tune
while you are normal, he's a lun-
atic whose main concerns
are baseball-ish. Like Doris Kearns
he seems quite normal, till he sees
the dark blue caps with bright red B's.

Within the store, you spy this book
and, what the hey!, you take a look.
You pick this book up off the shelf
surprising him, also yourself.
Your guy is nutty—sure that's true,
and yet, there's something else there too.
You're kinda moved by how he speaks
of Splinters and of Golden Greeks.
You like this man and how his eyes
light up each time you vocalize
some words like "Monster" and, (how droll!)
some other words like "Pesky's Pole."
You think it's cute to (when you're cozy),
whisper nothings like: "Dwayne Hosey."
It is time you learned the truth
on why the Sox sold G. H. Ruth.
You want to know about LeRoux
and Val and Wakes and Nomar too.
You'll see the heights of Morgan's Magic,
know the lows like Buckner's tragic—
never mind, just pay the clerk,
you'll make this Sox-fan romance work.
Your life with him will turn out great.
You'll be conjoined forever. Fate

decrees that Boston fans all must
stick by their loves till "Dust to dust."
For what else earthly lasts as long?
(8 decades now and going strong).
Through good and bad he'll stand by you.
A Sox fan, if naught else, is true
when good times end and bad times come
through players poor and owners dumb.
He'll stay with you through thick and thin
through good guy's loss and bad guy's win.
So buy this. Read. You'll know your man
(as well as any woman can).
And maybe you'll become good friends
with our great team within the Fens.

Please note the poem's author knows
that women like the Scarlet Hose
as much as men, in cases more,
that men might also, in the store,
be seeking ways to know their mate
for when they're out upon a date.
So gay or straight, no one is banned
from buying this that's in your hand
(not even fans of Yanks or Mets—
I'll take their cash without regrets!)
and maybe soon we'll all give cheer
when "next year" comes. Is this the year?

—*Robert P. Machemer*

A Short History of the Boston Red Sox

1. The Cy Young Years: 1901–1908

In 1901 the Boston Americans were a charter member of the new American League. This first Boston team was largely built from star players stolen from other leagues like the established National League, and was very good. Superstar pitcher Cy Young was lured away from St. Louis, along with his personal catcher, Lou Criger. Jimmy Collins, Buck Freeman, and Chick Stahl (who would die bizarrely a few years later) had been the core of the National League's Boston Beaneaters' lineup before they joined the Boston Americans. Third baseman Collins would be the team's player-manager (a common practice in that period).

The Americans were in first place in August, but eventually faded to a close second behind the Chicago White Stockings (soon to be the White Sox). The Americans had terrific pitching; led by Cy Young's league-leading 33 wins and 1.62 earned run average, the team was second in the eight-team league in earned run average. Collins, Freeman, and Stahl all hit over .300, although the team was only in the middle of the pack offensively. The Americans also led the league in home runs—with only 37 in this dead ball era, when the balls used were almost impossible to hit out of the park. Like all teams at the turn of the century, nearly everyone on the team stole a lot of bases. It wasn't until around 1930 that the Red Sox fabled lack of base-stealers took hold.

Renamed the Boston Pilgrims, the 1902 team was even stronger, although they finished third in the league. The pitching staff, which had been inconsistent besides the veteran Cy Young and 23-year-old George Winter, was bolstered by rookie Big Bill Dinneen (who led the league in losses despite pitching well). Boston was still a middle-of-the-road team offensively, but they now had the league's best pitching. For each of the next three years they would lead the league in earned run average—something the Red Sox would not do in consecutive years again until the Pedro Martinez-led, Joe Kerrigan-coached pitching staffs of 1999 and 2000.

Everything came together in 1903. With the war between the National League and the upstart American League settled, the two leagues agreed to play a 9-game series to determine baseball's championship. Boston led the American League in pitching, hitting, and home runs, and romped to the league championship. Boston won 91 games, while the next-closest team in the league won 77. Cy Young led the league with 28 wins, and Bill Dinneen and Long Tom Hughes both won at least 20. The Pilgrims were underdogs in the first World Series, however, and fell behind the Pittsburgh Pirates three games to one. But Dinneen (two shutouts in the series) and Young carried the team to an astonishing comeback, giving Boston the first World Series victory ever.

Another American League championship followed in 1904, but with it came troubling signs of things to come. New owner General Charles Taylor sold Patsy Dougherty (who had hit .342 and .331 the previous two seasons) and 20-game winner Long Tom Hughes to the New York Highlanders, forerunners of the soon-to-be-hated Yankees. Boston slipped offensively, but the league was increasingly dominated by pitching, and Boston still had the best pitching, with Jesse Tannehill filling Hughes's place on the pitching staff along with Cy Young and Bill Dinneen. Dinneen outdueled Highlanders' ace Jack Chesbro (who set a modern record with 41 wins that year) on the last day of the season to clinch the American League pennant, but there would be no second World Series title that year. Embarrassed by Boston's win the previous year, the National League champion New York Giants refused to play the Pilgrims.

The Pilgrims began to fade rapidly in 1905, and by 1906 they were a terrible team, losing 20 games in a row at one point. The offense, built from established National League stars, dwindled to nothing as those stars aged. The pitching staff, which had been the league's best, faded to average, and was the worst in the league by 1906, when Cy Young—nearly 40 years old—finally began to show his age. Late in the season player-manager Jimmy Collins was replaced as manager by outfielder Chick Stahl, who failed to improve the team as manager and then killed himself the following spring. The team went through 4 more managers in 1907 but kept playing badly. While the pitching improved to slightly above average (bolstered by Cy Young's 1.99 ERA at age 40), the hitters remained awful, batting .234 as a team (league average was .247) and scoring the fewest runs in the league. In 1907 it was decided that a name change might help the club's increasingly chaotic image. From then on, the team would be called the Boston Red Sox, a name that dated back to the original Cincinnati Red Stockings, who eventually ended up in Boston (and became the Boston Braves, who moved to Milwaukee and then Atlanta).

The Red Sox returned to near-mediocrity in 1908 with improved hitting and a miraculous season from Cy Young (21–11 with a 1.26 ERA at age 41). Young had the best earned run average of his

---

Key Players, 1901–1908

Jimmy Collins, 3b-mgr
Lou Criger, c
Big Bill Dinneen, p
Patsy Dougherty, of
Buck Freeman, 1b-of
Long Tom Hughes, p
Chick Stahl, of-mgr
Jesse Tannehill, p
Cy Young, p

career, although not his best season in the increasingly pitching-dominated game (the league *average* was 2.39, which would have been better than all but one pitcher in 2000). This would be Young's last 20-win season, and also his last year with the Red Sox. He was traded to Cleveland after the season ended for two mediocre pitchers and $12,500.

2. Fenway Park: 1909–1913

The Red Sox were firmly committed to a youth movement, and it showed immediate positive results. Boston won 88 games in 1909, and began building the core that would make the Red Sox first a good team and then a great team for the next decade. Like many Boston teams since, the rebuilt Red Sox team was built around a fine outfield and good hitting, with an average pitching staff (as the pitching staff improved, the Red Sox would go from contenders to champions). The Sox would lead the league in home runs for each of the next four years, with dead ball era *totals* of between 20 and 43 homers for the team (102 players hit at least 20 homers by themselves in 2000, and 9 of them hit 43 or more). By 1910 the Red Sox outfield contained future Hall of Famer Tris Speaker in center, rifle-armed Harry Hooper (who also made the Hall of Fame) in right, and cult favorite Duffy Lewis in left. All were good hitters and excellent defensively, with Speaker one of the all-time greats at his position. Pitcher Smokey Joe Wood also joined the starting rotation, although he showed few hints of the extraordinary Red Sox star he would become (for an all-too-brief period).

The 1911 Red Sox fell to 78–75 after first baseman Jake Stahl (not related to the late Chick Stahl) left the team to pursue a banking career. Stahl had led the league in home runs in 1910, and while the Red Sox still led the league in homers without him, his offense was missed on a team that had several other hitting stars but little depth. There were some good signs for the future, however; all three of the Red Sox star outfielders hit over .300, and Smokey Joe Wood emerged as a front-of-the-rotation starter, winning 23 games at age 21. More importantly, though, the team began construction of a marvelous new ballpark just off Kenmore Square in Boston.

The Red Sox moved into newly completed Fenway Park in 1912, with immediate and extraordinary results. With Jake Stahl lured back as player/manager and extraordinary seasons by Tris Speaker and Smokey Joe Wood, the Red Sox won a then-record 105 games. Speaker hit .383 (league average was .265) with a league-leading 53 doubles, 12 triples, 10 home runs (more than a third of the teams's league-leading total), 52 stolen bases, 82 walks, 136 runs, and 98 RBI, and was named league most valuable player. Wood went 34–5 with 10

Key Players, 1909–1913

Hugh Bedient, p
Bill Carrigan, c-mgr
Eddie Cicotte, p
Ray Collins, p
Harry Hooper, of
Dutch Leonard, p
Duffy Lewis, of
Buck O'Brien, p
Tris Speaker, of
Jake Stahl, 1b-mgr
Smokey Joe Wood, p

shutouts and a 1.91 earned run average, leading a pitching staff with two other 20-game winners. The Red Sox met the New York Giants in the World Series, the same team that had refused to play them in 1904 (although no Sox players remained from the 1904 team). The seven-game series (reduced from the best-of-nine series the Sox had played in 1903) came down to the tenth inning of the seventh game. Boston fell behind in the top of the tenth, but scored twice in the bottom of the inning to win the World Series, helped by two Giants' fielding misplays, "the $30,000 muff" by outfielder Fred Snodgrass, and a foul ball that went uncaught by first baseman Fred Merkle—already famous for his 1908 baserunning error, immortalized as "Merkle's boner," that cost the Giants a pennant.

The Red Sox followed their world championship with a season of chaos. With Smokey Joe Wood reduced to a part-time pitcher (by a broken hand and the previous season's overwork) and Jake Stahl retiring as a player at age 33, the team fell back to earth, finishing 79–71. The outfield continued to play well (Speaker hit .365), but without Woods as an anchor, the pitching staff was just average. The team hit only 17 home runs, although they led the league in triples and were close to the league lead in doubles. Stahl was fired as manager halfway through the season and replaced by catcher Bill Carrigan, who would soon lead the team to glory. But in a disturbing sign of the future, the team's ownership was in flux. Jimmy McAleer and Bob McRoy had purchased 50 percent of the club from General Taylor prior to 1912 (Jake Stahl also had a small share of the team), but sold the club to hotelier Joe Lannin after the 1913 season. (Lannin would also buy Buffalo of the Federal League and Providence of the International League.) Further, and disastrous, ownership changes would follow in the next decade—but before those changes would come some of the team's greatest moments.

3. The Coming of Babe Ruth: 1914–1919

The second half of the 1910s marked some of the greatest and some of the most tragic moments in Red Sox history. The team spent years as a powerhouse, built around great pitching staffs and decent (but not great) hitting. But the period would also lay the groundwork for the franchise's lowest moments—when Boston would function as the farm club out of which a great New York Yankee dynasty was built. And when the great team was sold off, the Red Sox would experience a decade and a half of humiliatingly bad teams.

The 1914 Red Sox bounced back from the 1913 fiasco, winning 91 games in Bill Carrigan's first season as manager and finishing second in the American League. (The team was overshadowed that summer by the National League Boston Braves' dramatic pennant chase.) The Sox were clearly built around pitching; although the team hit a lot of doubles and triples the offense was only average, carried by Tris Speaker. The major addition to the team's offense was shortstop Everett Scott, a fine fielder who helped steady the infield for the next eight years—but a terrible hitter.

The pitching, on the other hand, was dramatically reinforced in 1914. Holdovers Dutch Leonard and Ray Collins were joined by new starting pitchers Rube Foster and Ernie Shore, more than making up for a fadeout by Hugh Bedient and Smokey Joe Wood's part-time status. Most importantly, a young lefthanded pitcher bought from the cash-strapped Baltimore Orioles (then a minor league team) joined the Red Sox as well—Babe Ruth. Ruth only played briefly with the Red Sox in his first season; with the Sox pitching already strong, owner Joe Lannin instead sent Ruth to Providence, to help the Providence Grays minor league team that Lannin also owned win the International League pennant. (That Providence team was run by future World War II intelligence head Wild Bill Donovan.)

Ruth moved into the rotation the next year and won 18 games, one of five Sox pitchers to win at least 15 games (including Smokey Joe Wood's last hurrah—he went 15–5 with a league-leading 1.49 ERA despite appearing in only 25 games, 16 of them starts). Ruth also led the team with 4 home runs in only 92 at bats. The rest of the team's hitters combined for 10 home runs, with Tris Speaker, Duffy Lewis, and first baseman Dick Hoblitzell the only decent offensive players. More offense wasn't really needed given the Boston pitching staff, however. The team won 101 games to edge a Detroit Tigers team that won 100 but failed to make the playoffs.

The World Series against the Philadelphia Phillies was one-sided. Philadelphia ace Grover Cleveland Alexander beat the Sox in game one, but the Phillies lost the next four and the series. Strangely, the Red Sox had no real home games in the series; games in Boston were played on the Braves' home field, which had a larger seating capacity than Fenway Park (which has since been expanded). Seating capacity played another role in the series. The Phillies added temporary bleachers in the outfield to fit in more spectators, but lost the deciding game when Sox outfielder Harry Hooper—who had hit only two homers during the regular season—hit a pair of fly balls that carried into the extra seats for home runs.

In 1916 the Red Sox picked up right where they had left off the previous season. The team won nine fewer games, but that was enough to win in a well-balanced American League in which seven of eight teams won at least 76 games. The skew between hitting and pitching grew even more extreme; Boston's only hitting star, future Hall of Famer Tris Speaker, was traded to Cleveland after he refused to take a pay cut from owner Joe Lannin, who complained that Speaker's average had fallen to "only" .322 (Speaker was traded for yet another pitcher, future star Sad Sam Jones). The pitchers continued to excel despite the lack of offense. Babe Ruth won 23 games and led the league with a 1.76 earned run average (Ruth also tied for the team lead with 3 home runs). Four other pitchers won at least 14 games, with the departed Smokey Joe Wood replaced in the rotation by Carl Mays, a capable pitcher who is now remembered mostly for accidentally killing a batter with a pitch in 1920, after he was no longer with Boston. The Red Sox were helped by excellent defense as well. They committed by far the fewest errors in the league at a time when errors were rampant. The 1916 Red Sox were the first American League team ever to commit fewer than 200 errors in a season (they made 183), and they would lead the league in this category for the next six years (at which point the team had been stripped of most of its talent). Again the Red Sox won the World Series in five games, this time against the Brooklyn Dodgers.

A flurry of changes began with the end of the 1916 season. With the team coming off back-to-back World Series victories and its value at its peak, Joe Lannin decided to sell the Red Sox. At the same time, player/manager Bill Carrigan—who was independently wealthy and involved with baseball for the fun of it—also decided to leave. The new owner was underfinanced theatrical producer Harry Frazee. While Frazee would be popular and successful at first, a series of cash shortages in his business empire would soon force him to slowly sell off the team's best players in order to pay his debts (including the notes he owed to Lannin) and keep his businesses afloat.

But the disasters to come were not yet apparent in 1917. Frazee replaced Carrigan as manager with second baseman Jack Barry. The team played about as well as it had the year before, with the hitting still mediocre and the pitching and defense superb. Babe Ruth won 24 games and Carl Mays won 22 to lead the pitching staff. The team won 90 games, one less than in 1916, but the Red Sox found themselves in a distant second place behind a Chicago White Sox team that won 100.

The 1918 season would unexpectedly turn out to be the last hurrah for the Red Sox dynasty, which was soon to be disassembled. Although the Red Sox would finish the season as winners of three of the previous four World Series, they would not have another winning season until 1935. Frazee brought in a new manager for the 1918 season (Jack Barry had enlisted in the Navy), former International League president Ed Barrow, who would later become general manager of the Yankees, joining most of the Boston stars who would be sold to New York.

The season would be shortened by a month because of World War I, and stars Duffy Lewis and Dutch Leonard left the team to enter the military. Babe Ruth, who had recently married, stayed in Boston. Frazee helped reinforce the team somewhat by buying players from the financially troubled Philadelphia Athletics, including first baseman Stuffy McInnis and pitcher Bullet Joe Bush. (Frazee's own financial troubles had not yet become severe.) Manager Barrow was still faced with a shortage of outfielders, however, and a team with almost no offensive punch. He decided to make Babe Ruth, his best pitcher but also the best hitter on the team, his left fielder. Given more playing time, Ruth led the league in home runs (with 11; the rest of the team combined for only four) and hit .300, the only Boston player to do so. He also went 13–7 with a 2.22 earned run average as a part-time starting pitcher. This bold strategy led to a World Series victory against the Chicago Cubs, with Ruth pitching a shutout in game one and winning the fourth game of the six-game series as well—the last time he would pitch in a World Series.

Key Players, 1914–1919

Ed Barrow, mgr
Bill Carrigan, c-mgr
Ray Collins, p
Rube Foster, p
Harry Frazee, owner
Harry Hooper, of
Sad Sam Jones, p
Joe Lannin, owner
Dutch Leonard, p
Duffy Lewis, of
Carl Mays, p
Stuffy McInnis, 1b
Babe Ruth, p-of
Everett Scott, ss
Ernie Shore, p
Tris Speaker, of
Smokey Joe Wood, p

The trouble began in 1919. Ruth got into a contract squabble with Frazee. By now Ruth was clearly the team's best player, and he asked to be paid a comparable salary—$10,000, a lot of money but less than what some other top players were making, and less than Tris Speaker had been paid. Frazee refused, telling Ruth, "I wouldn't pay one of my best actors that much." Eventually Ruth settled for $9,000.

The team never gelled in 1919. Although the players who had been in the military returned, everybody else's stars returned as well. Babe Ruth had an extraordinary season as a full-time outfielder and part-time pitcher, hitting .305 with 101 walks and a then-record 29 home runs, helping usher the dead ball era to a close. The previous American League record had been 16, while the major league record of 27 dated back to the 1880s. No one else in the major leagues hit more than 12 home runs. The rest of the Red Sox team hit only four home runs combined. Although the offense was improved with the return of Harry Hooper and good seasons from Stuffy McInnis and the previously punchless Everett Scott, and the defense remained excellent (leading the league in fewest errors committed and most double plays turned), the pitching staff faded from excellent to average. With Dutch Leonard traded to Detroit, Sad Sam Jones having an off-year, and Babe Ruth in left field most of the time (he did go 9–5 in 15 starts), the pitching depth that had characterized Red Sox teams was no longer there. The Red Sox faded to 66–71 as a team, sixth place in the American League. Worst of all, when pitching star Carl Mays left the team under mysterious circumstances at midseason, Frazee's response was to sell his pitcher to the New York Yankees for $40,000. Few people realized at the time that Mays would be just the first of many to go.

4. The Selling of Babe Ruth and the Dark Ages: 1920–1932

The bombshell exploded in January 1920. Owner Harry Frazee, his financial situation shaky and his notes to Lannin coming due, sold his best player, Babe Ruth, to the New York Yankees. In return, Frazee got $125,000 and a $350,000 loan—secured by a mortgage on the Fenway Park bleachers. Worse was yet to come. Over the next three years, Frazee would sell the rest of his team's talent to the well-heeled Yankees in deal after deal. The remarkable pitching depth—Bullet Joe Bush, Waite Hoyt, Herb Pennock, George Pipgras, and others—all went to the Yankees. So did catcher Wally Schang, shortstop Everett Scott, third baseman Joe Dugan, outfielder Elmer Smith, and other useful players. The Red Sox dropped to last place in the standings; by 1923, the Sox were last in the league in hitting, fielding, and earned run average, and next to last in home runs. That year, the New York Yankees won their first World Series—with 11 former Boston players on their roster.

There is a common misperception that Harry Frazee sold Babe Ruth to the Yankees to finance *No No Nanette*, Frazee's big Broadway hit. However, the connection between the money Frazee got for the Babe and *No No Nanette* isn't that direct. Frazee sold the Babe in January 1920 in order to pay off debts which threatened to end his theater production business. The selling of the Babe was only one of many trades in which Frazee got cash for players, all in the hope of saving his theater business. Frazee eventually sold the Sox in 1923, after having gutted the club to stay in business on Broadway. *No No Nanette* came to the boards in 1925 and was the big hit Frazee had been longing for. So to say that Frazee sold the Babe in order to finance *No No Nanette* isn't really accurate. However, without the sale of the Babe, chances are Frazee would not have been around to finance *Nanette* a few years down the road.

Between 1922 and 1932, the depleted Red Sox would finish last 9 times in 11 seasons. The team's cumulative record in those years was 605–1,081, meaning that the team won barely a third of its games. Attendance fell from over 415,000 in 1919 to less than half that in 1932. By the time he sold the team to a group of investors headed by Bob Quinn in 1923, Frazee had gone from being the saviour of the franchise to one of the most reviled men in Boston. (A few years after selling the Red Sox, Frazee supposedly showed up for a game at Fenway Park. Getting out of the cab, Frazee announced to his female companion at the time that "he had once owned this team." The cabbie asked "Are you Harry Frazee?" When Frazee said yes the cabbie hauled off and knocked him to the ground.)

It would take 11 years, another new owner, and a succession of managers before the Red Sox would again win as many as half their games in a season. Although the talent drain stopped, the Sox did not have much left to build with; too many of their regulars were borderline major-league players. And while Quinn didn't sell players off the way Frazee did, he was nearly as underfinanced, and couldn't spend the money to bring in top-tier players; he ran the team on a tight budget. Boston finished last in the league in both batting average and earned run average in 1923, 1925, and 1926. In fact, it wasn't until 1931 that the Red Sox again finished better than last place in hitting. After manager Lee Fohl had back-to-back 100-loss seasons, Quinn managed to lure manager Bill Carrigan—who had won back-to-back World Series a decade before—out of retirement. The team improved only marginally, losing 103, 96, and 96 games before Carrigan left. His replacement, ex-Sox shortstop Heinie Wagner, lost 102 games in 1930.

The team hit rock bottom two managers later. The 1932 Red Sox lost 111 games and won only 43, finishing 64 games behind the New York Yankees. The Sox were again last in the league in batting (the next-worst team was 15 points better) and earned run average. Attendance fell to fewer than 200,000 fans—about 2,500 a game. Off the field, everything seemed to go wrong as well. Ed Morris, one of the team's better pitchers, was stabbed to death by a jealous husband. The team traded for Dale

Key Players, 1920–1932

Dale Alexander, 1b
George Burns, 1b
Joe Dugan, 3b
Howard Ehmke, p
Harry Frazee, owner
Waite Hoyt, p
Sad Sam Jones, p
Stuffy McInnis, 1b
Ed Morris, p
Buddy Myer, ss-3b
Herb Pennock, p
Bob Quinn, owner
Red Ruffing, p
Earl Webb, of

Alexander, who hit .372 for the Red Sox to win the batting title over future Sox star Jimmie Foxx—only to see Alexander's career ended when a mistreated leg injury turned gangrenous and the leg was almost lost.

The end of the losing was in sight, however. Quinn finally sold the team to a wealthy young industrialist by the name of Tom Yawkey. Yawkey, who had inherited millions while still in his early twenties, would be the well-financed owner the Red Sox had lacked for years. And as it turned out, it would be 60 years before a Red Sox team finished in last place again.

5. Enter Tom Yawkey: 1933–1937

Tom Yawkey had many character flaws, but unwillingness to spend money was not one of them. In his long tenure, the team would experience some of its brightest and most memorable moments—but it would never win the world championship he so desperately craved. The team's failure to win everything would be partly due to bad luck and partly to bad choices or management decisions. But perhaps the biggest factor was Yawkey's inability or unwillingness to overcome the racism that was deeply entrenched in Boston baseball (and, some would say, in Yawkey himself). Arguably Dan Duquette's greatest achievement as the Sox general manager over the last half-decade has been ridding the team of the lingering stigma of racism—the perception that black and Latino players were less welcome, less well treated, and more quickly dumped or traded away at the slightest sign of decline (while the team showed more loyalty and patience with its white stars).

But in 1933, integration of baseball was more than a decade—and another World War—away. Yawkey had bought a talent-thin, uninspired team at the bottom of a long decline. He was determined to reverse the Red Sox fortunes quickly, regardless of the cost. He immediately installed former Hall of Fame second baseman Eddie Collins as general manager, and gave Collins the authority to get the players he needed by whatever means necessary.

In a reversal of the Frazee era, Collins went about *buying* players instead of selling them. He had to buy players if he wanted to improve the team—the Red Sox didn't have players other teams wanted to trade for, and it would take a few years to replenish the team's talent base. He bought future Hall of Fame catcher Rick Ferrell from St. Louis in 1933, and his brother (and arguably the better player), pitcher Wes Ferrell the next year. Infielder Billy Werber, bought from the hated Yankees, would lead the league in stolen bases twice for the Red Sox. He also obtained Lefty Grove and others from the cash-poor Philadelphia A's in 1934. He spent a fortune (in

Key Players, 1933–1937

Max Bishop, 2b-1b
Ben Chapman, of
Doc Cramer, of
Joe Cronin, ss-manager
Rick Ferrell, c
Wes Ferrell, p
Jimmie Foxx, 1b
Lefty Grove, p
Pinky Higgins, 3b
Roy Johnson, of
Bill Werber, 3b

the height of the depression) rebuilding the dilapidated Fenway Park, including building the giant wall in left field that became known as the Green Monster. More improvements were to come. Yawkey wanted to win and he wanted to win in a hurry.

The Red Sox climbed out of last place in 1933. The next year they reached mediocrity. By 1938 they would be good.

In 1935 the Sox added another key player. Boston acquired shortstop Joe Cronin from the Washington Senators, who were sinking at the same time the Red Sox were rising. Cronin was made player-manager, replacing Bucky Harris as manager despite the team's first .500 season since 1918 in Harris's one season with the team. By 1935, the team had a mediocre lineup (a big improvement), but very little power or depth. They finished third in the league in pitching, but this was a little misleading. Boston had two terrific front-line pitchers in Wes Ferrell (who led the league with 25 wins) and Lefty Grove (who led the league in ERA), but not much else on the pitching staff. The next year Yawkey added two more key players from the Philadelphia A's, superstar first baseman Jimmie Foxx and center fielder Doc Cramer. Grove and Ferrell continued to pitch brilliantly, but the team still didn't gel, finishing in sixth place amid a rash of injuries and arguments. Wes Ferrell led a clubhouse faction that wanted Joe Cronin fired. In a game against the Yankees in August 1936, Ferrell stormed off the mound in the middle of a New York rally, making Cronin furious.

After the season both Ferrell brothers were traded to Washington for Ben Chapman (who would have two great years for the Sox) and Bobo Newsom, a serviceable pitcher, in what sportswriters dubbed "The Harmony Deal," because it was meant to reassert Cronin's power and ensure peace in the clubhouse. Billy Werber was sent to Philadelphia for Pinky Higgins, in a trade of third basemen. Boston finished 8 games over .500 in 1937 (although still in fifth place, far behind the Yankees). By this time, the farm system was starting to produce talented players again, having recovered from the overfishing and underfinancing of the Frazee and Quinn years. The Red Sox would never turn into the dynasty that Yawkey hoped for, but they would be good—sometimes great—for most of the next 15 years, with the exception of the World War II years.

6. Ted Williams and the Dynasty that Never Happened: 1938–1942

For the first time in 20 years, the Red Sox had a good team. They weren't good enough to beat the Yankees yet—or even seriously threaten them—but the 1938 Red Sox had good hitting, decent pitching, and finished in second place in the American League with 88 wins. Six of the team's regulars hit over .300 as Boston led the league in hitting with a .299 *team* batting average. Jimmie Foxx had perhaps the greatest season of his great career—hitting .349 with 50 home runs and an astonishing 175 runs batted in, leading the league in batting and RBI and setting club records for home runs and RBI that still stand more than 60 years later. The Red Sox weren't serious contenders yet—the Yankees hit almost twice as many home runs and after the aging Lefty Grove the team's pitchers were average at best—but there were good signs of things to come.

While the core of the team was still made up of players Yawkey and general manager Eddie Collins had bought or traded for, home-grown talent was starting to arrive. The new starting second baseman in 1938 was 20-year-old Bobby Doerr, who would anchor the position for the Red Sox for the next 14 years. And in 1939 The Kid would arrive.

Boston won 89 games in 1939 with 20-year-old Ted Williams replacing Ben Chapman in right field (Williams would move to left field after his rookie year). Again the team's hitting was good and its pitching was indifferent (Lefty Grove won the ERA title for the second year in a row but was only a half-time starter because of his age, and no one else on the staff could pick up the slack). Williams hit .327 with 31 homers and 107 walks, while leading the league in doubles and RBI. Jimmie Foxx was even better, hitting .360 with a league-leading 35 home runs. Bobby Doerr, Joe Cronin, and Doc Cramer also hit better than .300, as did key reserve Lou Finney. It wasn't enough. The Yankees won 106 games.

In 1940 the Sox added yet another kid—Joe DiMaggio's 23-year-old younger brother Dom, who hit .301 in right field. (DiMaggio would move to center field the following year, replacing Doc Cramer.) Eight Sox regulars hit .285 or better, topped by Williams at .344. Five players hit more than 20 home runs, led by Foxx's 36. (Foxx was only 31, but alcoholism was starting to erode his talent and he would have only one more good year.) The team narrowly missed the league lead in hitting, and did lead the league in slugging . The Sox were entertaining, but they still couldn't win. In a year when the Yankees slumped to 88 wins, the Red Sox slumped even further, pulled down to 82–72 by their lack of pitching as the 40-year-old Lefty Grove could no longer carry the staff. Despite an extraordinarily gifted offensive team, no pitcher managed to win more than 12 games, and the Red Sox finished fourth.

The story would repeat itself in 1941, with the pitching-shy Sox finishing a distant second to the Yankees. The Sox wasted one of the greatest offensive seasons in history. In 1941 Ted Williams hit .406 (the last major league player to hit .400) and led the league in home runs, runs, and walks. He had an unprecedented .551 on base percentage—meaning he was on base in well over half his plate appearances. He drove in 120 runs and anchored a team that led the league in batting average, slugging, and runs scored. Just like the team as a whole, Williams ended up in second place, as Joe DiMaggio rode a 56 game hitting streak and the adulation of the press to the Most Valuable Player award. Williams, one of the greatest offensive players in history, was never able to master the media in

Key Players, 1938–1942

Ben Chapman, of
Doc Cramer, of
Joe Cronin, ss-manager
Dom DiMaggio, of
Bobby Doerr, 2b
Lou Finney, of-1b
Jimmie Foxx, 1b
Lefty Grove, p
Tex Hughson, p
Johnny Pesky, ss
Jim Tabor, 3b
Ted Williams, of

the way he mastered hitting. Like many Red Sox stars before and since, Williams was bitterly criticized by the media during his career, and only became an icon after his retirement.

Yet another second place finish followed in 1942, but this time better things seemed to be on the horizon. The Red Sox won 93 games, their highest total since 1918. They led the league in hitting once again, and the pitching was dramatically improved—third in the league in ERA. The team's aging stars were being replaced by young talent as well. Joe Cronin continued to manage but only played occasionally. Jimmie Foxx was shipped off to the Chicago Cubs when his alcoholism finally got the best of him. Young stars Williams, Doerr, and DiMaggio were joined by Johnny Pesky, a 22-year-old shortstop who hit .331 and led the league with 205 hits. Williams won the triple crown—leading the league in batting average, home runs, and RBI (as well as walks and runs scored) but again finished second to a popular Yankee (this time Joe Gordon) in the MVP balloting. Even better, the team had a young pitcher who seemed poised to replace Lefty Grove. Twenty-six-year-old Tex Hughson won 22 games in 281 innings pitched to lead the league in both categories.

But what looked like a dynasty in the making was about to be derailed. By the beginning of the next season, half the team would be at war.

7. The War Years: 1943–1945

Boston's young stars were among the first to enlist in the military for World War II. Ted Williams, Johnny Pesky, and Dom DiMaggio were all gone by the beginning of the 1943 season, as was any hope of contention. While Williams was flying planes for the Navy, the Red Sox were sinking to 68–84, a distant seventh place behind the Yankees. The next year the team was in pennant contention in September when Bobby Doerr, Tex Hughson, and catcher Hal Wagner (who was hitting .332) were all drafted into the military within a three-week period. The team went on a 10-game losing streak and finished well out of the race.

With most of the team's players in the armed services, the Red Sox turned to fill-ins like outfielder Catfish Metkovich, shortstop Skeeter Newsome, and pitcher Mike Ryba—players whose roles would be drastically curtailed (or whose careers would end) as soon as the war was over. Thirty-eight-year-old manager Joe Cronin—who hadn't played regularly in four years—inserted himself into the lineup in 1945 when the draft left the team without a third baseman. Three games later Cronin broke his leg, ending his playing career.

One bright spot did come out of the dismal 1945 season. The Red Sox, with little else going for them, came up with a ringer on the pitching staff. Boo Ferriss's asthma would limit his pitching at times—but it also earned him an early discharge from the military. Joe Cronin made the

Key Players, 1943–1945

Joe Cronin, manager
Bobby Doerr, 2b
Boo Ferriss, p
Tex Hughson, p
Hal Wagner, c

23-year old righthander his ace. Ferriss started 31 games (10 more than any other Sox pitcher) and won 21 of them. He also made four relief appearances, saving two more wins in the process. He threw 26 complete games—over 264 innings in all, putting a lot of strain on a young pitcher's arm.

8. The Return to Glory: 1946–1950

The young Red Sox stars had lost three years of their careers to the war, but they returned as a strong, focused team that finally had the pitching to go with their extraordinary offense. The next four years would be some of the most exhilarating—and the most heart-wrenching—in Red Sox history. Three times in four years the Red Sox would reach the brink of glory, only to fall just short of their goal.

The 1946 team led the league in hitting and played terrific defense. The pitching was solid, with a four-man rotation of Tex Hughson (20–11), Boo Ferriss (25–6), Mickey Harris (17–9), and Joe Dobson (13–7). The Sox weren't deep, but their front line players were terrific: Ted Williams, Johnny Pesky, Bobby Doerr, Dom DiMaggio, and aging star Rudy York, imported from Detroit to play first base. Remarkably, the stars all stayed healthy and in the lineup all year (in a typical season about 70% of players are injured at some point), and Boston dominated the league. The Red Sox finished 104–50, 12 games ahead of their nearest competitor. The Yankees were a distant third, 17 games back.

In the World Series the Red Sox faced a St. Louis Cardinals club with deep pitching and two of the national league's most dangerous hitters, Stan Musial and Enos Slaughter. The series lead swung back and forth repeatedly, with the two teams proving extremely well matched. Boston won the first game, rallying in the ninth inning and winning on a York home run in the tenth. St. Louis came back to shut out Boston in Game 2, led by pitcher Harry Brecheen, who'd been mediocre (15–15) in the regular season, but would be dominant in this series. Boo Ferriss pitched a shutout of his own in Game 3, the fiftieth shutout in World Series history, and the teams continued to trade games. After 6 games, the series was tied, with Brecheen having won both his games for St. Louis.

The deciding Game 7 would hinge on a famous misplay that may not have been a misplay at all. After Boston had tied the game with two runs in the top of the eighth inning, St. Louis had Enos Slaughter on first base when Harry Walker dropped a bloop hit into center field. Slaughter was running from the moment the ball was hit, and never slowed down at third base. Leon Culberson, playing center field for the injured Dom DiMaggio, threw the ball weakly to shortstop Johnny Pesky who checked on the runner coming from first before throwing home. It's unlikely a quicker relay would have caught Slaughter, but all most fans remember is the broadcasters' agonized wail, which became one of the most replayed moments in Boston sports history: "Pesky holds the ball!" St. Louis had taken the lead. In the ninth inning Boston was shut down yet again by Harry Brecheen, who won his third game of the series while pitching in relief.

Things did not go as smoothly the next year. The Red Sox lack of depth, which hadn't been a problem in 1946, now haunted them. When Rudy York began to show his age and Dom DiMaggio missed time due to injury, there was no one to fill the gap. Williams and Pesky were both spectacular again, but in 1947 DiMaggio and Doerr were merely good, which negated the strong season of new catcher Birdie Tebbets, who would solidify a position that had been in flux since Rick Ferrell was traded. The pitching was about average, but here, too, there were troubling signs. In an era when 20-game winners were much more common than today, no Red Sox pitcher won more than Joe Dobson's 18 (although 5 pitchers won at least 11 games). Boo Ferriss and Tex Hughson were both starting to show the results of overwork; they each won only 12 games—and they would combine for only 14 more wins in a Red Sox uniform. The Sox limped to the finish line in third place, 14 games behind the once-again victorious Yankees.

Owner Tom Yawkey made changes after the disappointment of 1947. Joe Cronin—a fixture as manager since 1935—was moved into the front office, and Joe McCarthy replaced him as field boss. Reinforcements were brought in from the St. Louis Browns in the form of pitchers Ellis Kinder and Jack Kramer, and shortstop Vern Stephens, in return for 10 players and a huge amount of Yawkey's ready cash. Johnny Pesky moved to third, and rookie Billy Goodman—who'd played a few games in the outfield the previous year—took over at first base.

Although the team was not dramatically better on paper, the 1948 Red Sox played very well. Pesky's move to third base paid off, filling in one of the gaping holes in the lineup (right field was the other), and Stephens hit 29 home runs out of the short-stop position. Billy Goodman hit .310 at first. The bench played respectably. The team didn't lead the league in batting average or home runs, but *everyone* in the lineup was excellent at drawing walks, so there were constantly runners on base. Four players scored at least 114 runs, as Boston led the league in runs scored by a wide margin. The pitching was a little better than the year before, just a little better than league average. Ellis Kinder, Jack Kramer, and Mel Parnell filled the rotation behind Joe Dobson, taking the place of Tex Hughson and Boo Ferriss, neither of whom was effective. Earl Johnson won 10 games in relief.

The pennant race came down to the final days of the season, with both Boston and the Yankees close behind the surprising and powerful Cleveland Indians (who *did* lead the league in both batting average and pitching). Boston knocked the Yankees out by winning two straight, while the Indians lost two of their last three, leaving Boston and Cleveland tied with 96 wins on the last game of the season.

When two teams tie for the league lead there is a one-game playoff, with the winner moving on and the loser going home for the winter. Cleveland started rookie knuckleballer Gene Bearden, who had gone 19–7 and led the league in ERA. Most fans expected Boston manager Joe McCarthy to start young lefthander Mel Parnell, who had been the team's best pitcher down the stretch. But with four dependable starting pitchers to choose from, McCarthy selected none; he chose journeyman Denny Galehouse, pitching on fumes at the end of his career. Galehouse was shelled and the Indians went on to an 8–3 victory—and to the World Series.

The Red Sox began the 1949 season determined to make up for the near-miss of 1948. The lineup remained largely the same, except for an upgrade in right field, where incumbent Stan Spence was sent to St. Louis (along with some of Yawkey's cash) for Al Zarilla. If the offense had been very good in 1948, it was terrific in 1949 Despite the weak bench, the Red Sox led the league in batting average, runs scored, and home runs, all by a wide margin. Ted Williams and Vern Stephens tied for the league lead in RBI with 159, while Williams led the league in home runs. Four players walked at least 96 times. Four starters hit over .300, and two others hit .290 or better. The pitching was better than it had been—decent, not great—but this year it was led by two developing stars. Mel Parnell led the league with 25 wins (setting a record for a Red Sox lefty), a 2.77 ERA, and 27 complete games; Ellis Kinder was right behind with 23 wins, including 13 in a row going into the season's final weekend.

The Red Sox got off to a slow start, falling 12 games behind the Yankees. But as the pitching of Parnell, Kinder, and Joe Dobson clicked and the offense heated up, the Sox began to close the ground. They overtook the Yankees a week before the season's end, and went into the last two games of the season ahead by one game at 96–56, needing only a single victory to go to the World Series. The Yankees beat Parnell in the first game. In the second game, the Yankees took a 1–0 lead into the eighth against Kinder, who had been unbeatable for weeks. Desperate for runs, McCarthy pinch hit for Kinder (who was not a good-hitting pitcher), but the gamble failed. McCarthy, determined not to repeat his previous mistake of losing with someone who wasn't his best player, brought Parnell—the previous night's starter—in as a relief pitcher. But the exhausted Parnell had nothing left. Tex Hughson, brought in to try and rescue a failing situation, fared little better. The Red Sox lost 5–3. Once again 96 wins left them one game short of the pennant.

In 1950, the Red Sox again came close, despite an elbow injury to Ted Williams that would cost him half a season, and an early season injury to Billy Goodman. Instead of relying on the team's weak bench, minor leaguer Walt Dropo was called up to fill in for Goodman. Dropo responded by hitting .322 with 34 homers and a league-leading 144 RBI, winning Rookie of the Year in what, alas, would turn out to be a fluke season. When Goodman came back from his injury the Red Sox made him a utility player, filling in for injured or resting players at all four infield position as well as the outfield. Goodman thrived in his new position, hitting .354 and scoring 91 runs in only 424 at bats. Amazingly, he was only sixth

Key Players, 1946–1950

Joe Cronin, manager
Dom DiMaggio, of
Joe Dobson, p
Bobby Doerr, 2b
Walt Dropo, 1b
Boo Ferriss, p
Denny Galehouse, p
Billy Goodman, of-1b-2b-3b-ss
Mickey Harris, p
Tex Hughson, p
Earl Johnson, p
Ellis Kinder, p
Jack Kramer, p
Joe McCarthy, manager
Mel Parnell, p
Johnny Pesky, ss-3b
Vern Stephens, ss
Birdie Tebbets, c
Ted Williams, of
Rudy York, 1b

on the team in runs—five players scored more than 100 runs. The 1950 Red Sox were the last team to average .300 as a team, hitting .302 and leading the league in slugging and runs by wide margins. It wasn't quite enough to overcome the thinness of the team's pitching, however. Parnell, Kinder, and Dobson were all solid once again, but no one else on the staff pitched very well. As it turned out, average pitching and extraordinary hitting were enough to combine for 94 wins. Boston finished a close third behind better-balanced teams in New York and Detroit.

It wasn't apparent at the time, but the Red Sox had missed their window of opportunity. It would be 17 years before the team won as many as 90 games again. The game was changing profoundly, but Tom Yawkey and his Red Sox were slow to adjust to that change. In 1947 the Dodgers broke the major league color line by playing Jackie Robinson. Later that year, Larry Doby broke the American League color barrier with the Cleveland Indians. The Sox turned down chances to sign Robinson and Willie Mays. In 2000, Red Sox trustee John Harrington claimed it was not racism on Yawkey's part, but reluctance among the Red Sox minor league teams in the South to play blacks that caused the Sox to wait so long to sign black players. Regardless of whether it was racism or just stubborn resistance to change, the Sox paid and would continue to pay for their unwillingness to draw on the newly available talent pool of black players—while other teams benefited. Twice after the color barrier was broken, the Red Sox fell one game short of the World Series—at least in part because of how thin the team's talent was behind its frontline starters. In 1950 the Red Sox had the best offense in the world—but as those hitters began to age, there would be no one of comparable talent to replace them—and this time, Yawkey's money would not be enough to overcome his failings.

9. The End of the Era: 1951–1960

The Red Sox slide started slowly. The team managed to win 87 games in 1951, finishing a respectable third, but they were nowhere near as good as the previous four years' teams had been. Walt Dropo's batting average fell nearly 100 points, and he dropped from 34 home runs to 11. The hole in right field opened up again, despite one torrid stretch by Clyde Vollmer, who hit more than half his 22 homers in a single month. Catcher Birdie Tebbets was traded, and the Sox tried to replace him with seven different players, six of whom hit less than .203 (the seventh hit a still-woeful .229). The core hitters—Ted Williams, Dom DiMaggio, Vern Stephens, Johnny Pesky, Bobby Doerr, and Billy Goodman—were still very good, but some of them were starting to age. Boston still led the league in runs in 1951, but the margin was no longer very large. The pitching staff had two great players and a bunch of maybes. Mel Parnell had another fine year, but he was the only starter to win more than 12 games. Ellis Kinder, his arm no longer able to take the strain of starting regularly, was converted to relief where he pitched brilliantly, leading the league in games and saves (with 14) and winning another 11 games in relief.

The early signs in 1952 were not good. Ted Williams, the best Red Sox hitter since Babe Ruth, and possibly the best ever, was recalled to military duty. The Red Sox would lose two more years of his career, and be lucky to see Williams again at all—twice in his 39 combat missions over Korea Ted Williams would have to bring a flaming plane down intact. Bobby Doerr, the team's second-best hitter, was forced to retire because of back problems.

As he had in 1947, Yawkey was determined to make changes to keep the Red Sox on top, but this time the changes failed. Joe McCarthy had quit as manager in the middle of 1950. Steve O'Neill, the man who replaced him, was fired after 1951, despite the team's 149–97 record in his season and a half at the helm. His replacement was fading Cleveland star Lou Boudreau, who would serve as player/manager. Johnny Pesky and Walt Dropo were traded. The team turned out to be mediocre in every way—average hitting, an average pitching staff on which only Mel Parnell won as many as 12 games, and a 76–78, sixth place record.

The team seemed to recover a little in 1953. The hitting was just average, led by Billy Goodman—now at second base—and third baseman George Kell. Fan favorite Jimmy Piersall took over for Dom DiMaggio in center field. Mostly, the pitching improved dramatically, with Parnell and Kinder returning to brilliance, and a great season from lefthander Mickey McDermott, who liked to sing in nightclubs in his spare time. When Ted Williams returned at the very end of the season there were great hopes that the team could build on its 84-win finish, and maybe become a real contender the following year. As it happened, they were false hopes. The team wouldn't win more than 84 games again until the Impossible Dream season of 1967.

Those hopes evaporated when Ted Williams broke his collarbone in spring training and Mel Parnell broke his arm during the season. Williams would come back at full strength, but Parnell was never able to handle a full-time starter's load again. The Sox pitching was second-worst in the league, and while the hitting was pretty good—led by Williams, Piersall, newcomer Jackie Jensen, and promising rookie Harry Agganis—the Sox finished a dreadful 69–85, an astonishing 42 games behind the powerhouse Cleveland Indians.

The Sox followed with three turbulent but respectable years before sliding into mediocrity. Lou Boudreau was fired as manager and replaced by Pinky Higgins. Ted Williams announced his retirement, only to be talked out of it a month later. First baseman Harry Agganis, a Massachusetts native and former BU star, died suddenly of a pulmonary embolism. Ellis Kinder and Mel Parnell retired. Billy Goodman was traded. The pitching continued to be mediocre. Through it all, the Red Sox had enough hitting to keep them at 82 to 84 wins a year, led by the outfield of Ted Williams, Jackie Jensen, and

Key Players, 1951–1960

Harry Agganis, 1b
Mike Fornieles, p
Billy Goodman, of-1b-2b-3b-ss
Jackie Jensen, of
George Kell, 3b
Ellis Kinder, p
Mickey McDermott, p
Bill Monbouquette, p
Mel Parnell, p
Jimmy Piersall, of-ss
Pete Runnels, 2b
Frank Sullivan, p
Sammy White, c
Ted Williams, of

Jimmy Piersall. In 1957 the 38-year-old Ted Williams hit .388 to win his fifth batting title. He would win another one a year later—battling throughout the season with Red Sox rookie second baseman Pete Runnels—but the team would drop a notch further, to 79 wins. It would be nine years before another Red Sox team would win as many as half its games.

More turbulence followed in 1959 and 1960. Joe Cronin left the front office to become league president. The Red Sox finally fielded their first black player, utility infielder Pumpsie Green, twelve seasons after the color barrier had fallen elsewhere. Ted Williams was hurt most of the year. Pinky Higgins—who had sworn he would never have a black player on his team—was fired as manager, and replaced by Bill Jurges, who rallied a bad team to a strong second half. The next season Jurges was fired and replaced by Higgins again, who had apparently reconsidered his position somewhat. The team finished 65–89.

Amid the chaos on the field, another era was coming to a close. Ted Williams hit .316 with 29 home runs as a 40-year-old part-time player in 1960, an amazing finish to an amazing story. In his last at bat at Fenway Park that year (which he had announced would be the last at bat of his career), he homered into right field. The moment has become a baseball legend, but only a few thousand people, die-hard fans of a seventh-place team, saw it at the time.

The Jimmy Fund

In 1947 the Variety Club of Boston, a social and charitable club set up by show business people in the Boston area, selected a charity. They decided to help Dr. Sidney Farber establish the Children's Cancer Research Foundation, affiliated with Children's Hospital in Boston. That year Dr. Farber had developed a treatment to enable certain cancer-stricken children to go into remission via chemotherapy. In 1947 the Variety Club raised $47,000 for the project, and early in 1948 they teamed with the Boston Braves to orchestrate a mass market fund raiser.

On May 22, 1948, the radio show *Truth Or Consequences*, hosted by Ralph Edwards, talked to a patient named "Jimmy" in a hospital in Boston and asked him whether he liked baseball, and which team was his favorite. Then he asked the boy who his favorite player was. When Jimmy answered that it was Johnny Sain, Sain walked into the hospital room and greeted the boy. As Edwards asked about other Braves players, they entered, one by one. They brought autographed baseballs, T-shirts, and tickets to the Braves doubleheader the next day, and manager Billy Southworth promised that they'd win at least one of the games. (They ended up winning both.) After the phone conversation, Edwards addressed the national radio audience and explained that Jimmy had cancer, but didn't know it. He asked people to send whatever they could to help Jimmy. Dr. Farber was present at the show and talked to Edwards. When the host suggested that the "Variety Club of Boston's Children's Cancer Research Foundation" was a bit unwieldy, Farber suggested just calling it the "Jimmy Fund." The name stuck. To this day, there are few things in New England with a higher name recognition and awareness than the Jimmy Fund.

10. The Seeds of Rebirth: 1961–1966

Ted Williams's familiar place in left field was taken over by a 21-year-old rookie from Long Island, converted second baseman Carl Yastrzemski. Yaz hit .266 (a little better than league average) with 11 home runs, an inauspicious start to what would be a great career. The Red Sox were still pretty bad. They moved Pete Runnels to first base—turning him from one of the best-hitting second baseman in the game to an average first baseman, given his lack of power. Jackie Jensen soon left baseball, unable to conquer his fear of flying at a time when teams no longer traveled exclusively by train. Frank Malzone was pretty good at third base, but that was about it for hitting. The pitching wasn't very good either. Bill Monbouquette anchored the rotation, followed by a cast of mediocrities. Pitcher Don Schwall was Rookie of the Year in 1961, but his control was so poor that the quick disintegration of his career surprised no one.

When the Braves left Boston following the 1952 season, Braves PR man Billy Sullivan (who later owned the New England Patriots) approached Red Sox owner Tom Yawkey at the league meeting about having the Red Sox take over for the Braves in supporting the Jimmy Fund. Yawkey was initially hesitant but finally agreed. On April 10, 1953, the Boston Red Sox officially announced that they would join the motion picture industry as co-sponsors of the Jimmy Fund. Over the years, the Red Sox have helped to raise millions of dollars to fight childhood cancers. Many Red Sox players have been particularly noteworthy in their efforts. Ted Williams, whose own brother died of leukemia, devoted many hours to the cause. Mike Andrews, the second baseman on the 1967 Impossible Dream team, has been the executive director of the Fund since 1978. John Valentin is known to have spent many hours at the institute, visiting with sick kids.

In 1976 the Children's Cancer Research Institute became the Sidney Farber Cancer Institute, in honor of its founder. In 1983, as a result of many years of support from the Charles A. Dana foundation, it was renamed again, as the Dana-Farber Cancer Institute. That name is now nearly as well known as the Jimmy Fund itself.

There have been Red Sox players who have needed the services of the institute. Bob Stanley's son Kyle fought cancer with the help of Dana-Farber. *Boston Globe* sports columnist Dan Shaughnessy, known for the gloominess and cynicism in his writing, is not a cynic with regards to the Dana-Farber Cancer Institute. His daughter Kate has fought leukemia with the help of the Jimmy Fund.

The Jimmy Fund has become almost as much of an institution in New England as the Red Sox themselves. The two are bound to be intertwined, as the Red Sox are a large part of the reason that the Jimmy Fund has been so successful at raising money for the fight against cancer. To contact the Jimmy Fund, call 1-800-52-JIMMY, write to The Jimmy Fund, 375 Longwood Avenue, Boston, MA 02215, or go online to www.jimmyfund.org/jimmy/contribute/index.shtml

The Red Sox added two talented pitchers in 1962, and an enigmatic first baseman in 1963. Neither improved the club's fortunes much, any more than Yaz's improvement as a hitter did. Dick Radatz was the best relief pitcher in the league, and redefined the way short relievers were used. Before Radatz, most relief pitchers—even the best of them—were broken down starters. But Radatz was purely a reliever, whose role was to come in and put out fires with his intimidating fastball. Until his arm burned out from several years of overuse, he was unhittable.

Earl Wilson was the team's first black pitcher. He was a solid starting pitcher, not a star but a talented player who could be dominant when he was at his best. In 1966 he complained about the unequal treatment accorded black and white players, and was quickly traded to Detroit.

First baseman Dick Stuart was the most one-dimensional on a team of one-dimensional players. A slugging first baseman who was nicknamed "stonefingers" for his fielding ineptitude, he would have two great years with the Sox, averaging 38 homers and 116 RBI in an increasingly pitching-dominated era. In many ways, he was a forerunner of the slugging Red Sox teams of the 1970s—and like many of the players on those teams, he fought openly with his manager and was dumped because of it.

Despite some entertaining players, the Red Sox failed to improve much. They were actually a worse team than their record looked in the early 1960s. Because two expansion teams were added in 1961 and the schedule increased from 154 games a year to 162, the Sox record was inflated by their games against these new teams, which were largely built from minor leaguers and burned out major league retreads.

Pinky Higgins was made general manager after the 1962 season and replaced by longtime Red Sox star Johnny Pesky as field manager. The team had power, but not much hitting or pitching. Despite Yaz's first batting title, Radatz's relief dominance, and Bill Monbouquette's 20 wins, the team finished 76–85 in 1963, essentially the same record as the previous two years.

In the next three years the team went through two more managers (Billy Herman and Pete Runnels) and finished in eighth or ninth place each year. Dick Radatz burned out his arm, and both Earl Wilson and Bill Monbouquette were traded—Wilson after complaining about treatment of black players and Monbouquette after leading the league in losses. Despite eight consecutive losing seasons, however, things were beginning to point in the right direction. Between 1964 and 1966, a core of young players began to take over jobs on a team whose only star in his prime was Carl Yastrzemski.

First, 19-year-old Tony Conigliaro claimed an outfield slot, hitting .290 (league average was .247) with 24 homers as a rookie. The next year he would lead the league in home runs. Rico Petrocelli, a 21-year-old shortstop with power, moved into the lineup in 1965. Pitcher Jim Lonborg, age 22, came up in 1965. Lonborg narrowly avoided the league lead in losses that year, but he showed tremendous potential. George Scott, a 22-year-old rookie

Key Players, 1961–1966

Tony Conigliaro, of
Jim Lonborg, p
Bill Monbouquette, p
Rico Petrocelli, ss
Dick Radatz, p
Pete Runnels, 1b
George Scott, 1b
Dick Stuart, 1b
Lee Thomas, of-1b
Earl Wilson, p
Carl Yastrzemski, of

first baseman, hit 27 home runs in 1966 while sparkling defensively—leading the league in putouts and double plays. Before the 1967 season, the Red Sox hired a manager who they hoped could get the most out of all the team's young players. Dick Williams, winner of two consecutive minor league pennants, confidently predicted that the Red Sox would have a winning record in 1967. At the time, few of the team's dispirited fans agreed with him.

11. The Impossible Dream: 1967

Dick Williams was committed to playing the kids in 1967. Three more rookies played key roles on the team: second baseman Mike Andrews, center fielder Reggie Smith, and relief pitcher Sparky Lyle (who was doomed to become one of the worst trades in Red Sox history). More surprisingly, Williams kept his commitment to winning. Somehow, the perennially losing Boston Red Sox started to win.

In a year in which pitching was king, Boston would win with its bats. The Red Sox had terrific hitting. The average hitter in 1967 managed only a .236 batting average. The Sox were above average at eight positions, and had two key bench players who also hit well. Best of all of them was Carl Yastrzemski, who won the triple crown with his .326 batting average, 44 home runs, and 121 runs batted in. The Red Sox led the league in hitting, home runs, slugging percentage, and runs scored. They were third from the bottom in pitching.

Somehow, no matter what the odds against them were, the Red Sox kept winning. Jim Lonborg was the only pitcher who was able to start more than 24 games, and his ERA wasn't all that much better than average, but he led a charmed life that year, and always seemed to find a way to win. Only one other starting pitcher had a winning record, but the team's deep bullpen (led by John Wyatt, Dan Osinski, and Sparky Lyle) found ways to win even when the starters foundered. In August Tony Conigliaro, who already had 20 homers in the season's first half, was hit in the head by a pitch from Jack Hamilton, ending his season. The Red Sox somehow overcame the loss and kept winning.

The 1967 pennant race was one of the closest in history. Four teams finished within three games of the lead, and all four of those teams still had a chance to win in the season's final days. Already having a great season, Yaz carried the team in the final days of the season, with 23 hits in his last 44 at bats (a .523 average). The Sox finished the season with two games against first place Minnesota, needing to win both games to have a chance at the pennant. Yaz went 7 for 8 in the final two games, and made an extraordinary throw to end a Minnesota rally in the eighth inning of the season's final game—preserving the Red Sox Jim Lonborg's league-leading

Key Players, 1967

Mike Andrews, 2b
Tony Conigliaro, of
Jim Lonborg, p
Sparky Lyle, p
Rico Petrocelli, ss
George Scott, 1b
Reggie Smith, of
Dick Williams, manager
John Wyatt, p
Carl Yastrzemski, of

twenty-second win. After an agonizing wait for the results of the Detroit game (a Detroit win would have meant a tie for first and a one-game playoff like in 1948 and 1978) the good news came in: The Red Sox had won the pennant.

Just like in 1946, the World Series would be a hard-fought, evenly matched battle. Just like in 1946, the series would extend to the full seven games. Unfortunately, the result would be the same as well. Boston faced a St. Louis team built on pitching and speed. Offensively, St. Louis was fronted by leadoff hitter extraordinaire Lou Brock, slugging first baseman Orlando Cepeda, former home run king Roger Maris, and Curt Flood, who would later sacrifice his career in an attempt to win fairer contracts for other players. The Cardinals had a terrific pitching staff, including future Hall of Famers Bob Gibson and Steve Carlton. They had won 101 games during the regular season, nine more than the Red Sox.

The series opened on an ominous note for the Red Sox, who got good pitching from Jose Santiago and still lost to Bob Gibson (Santiago homered for the only Boston run). Game 2 was more of what the Sox had hoped for, with Jim Lonborg allowing only one hit and Yaz hitting two homers. But the deep St. Louis pitching staff held Boston to two runs in the next two games, including a shutout by Gibson. Facing elimination, the Red Sox were again saved by Lonborg, who outdueled Steve Carlton in Game 5, allowing only a Roger Maris home run in the ninth inning. The Boston offense finally got going in Game 6 (setting a record with three homers in the fourth inning) and scored eight runs against a record-setting eight St. Louis pitchers.

Once again it would all come down to a seventh game. Bob Gibson and Jim Lonborg, each with two victories in the series, would face each other. However, Gibson was pitching with his normal three days rest (in the days when teams used four-man rotations instead of today's five), while Lonborg was pitching on two day's rest. Too exhausted to be effective after a league-leading 39 regular season starts and two complete games in the series, Lonborg gave up seven runs in six innings. Gibson threw his third complete game of the series, giving up his second and third runs. He would go on to even greater glory the next year, while the Red Sox got to go home and wonder what might have been.

In some ways the Impossible Dream season was a fluke; the pitching-thin Red Sox played over their heads in that glorious year, and were not serious pennant contenders again for some time. But in another sense, the 1967 season did usher in a sort of golden age. If the Red Sox weren't great, they were good, young, and talented. The Red Sox would have 15 winning seasons in a row beginning in 1967, including another World Series appearance, and several other memorable near misses. They would have consistently exciting—if sometimes flawed—teams throughout the 1970s.

12. Good, But Not Good Enough: 1968–1974

In the 1968 season the pitching dominance got out of hand. The *league average* ERA was 2.98. By contrast, in 2000, Pedro Martinez was the only American League pitcher with an ERA that low. The average hitter managed a .230 mark, and the Red Sox Carl Yastrzemski was the only player in the league to hit .300. (The next best was Danny Cater at .290.) Things got so bad for hitters that the rules would be changed after the season, lowering the pitcher's mound and making alterations in the strike zone to give the hitters a chance.

The Red Sox were still a good team, but while they seemed to ride out every disaster in 1967, in 1968 they weren't as adaptable. The hitting was still pretty good, despite George Scott's inexplicable decline from .303 with 19 homers to .171 with 3 homers. Just about everybody's numbers were worse than in 1967, but that was true for the rest of the league as well, which helped even things out.

Ken Harrelson—picked up for free after he was dumped by the A's for criticizing their owner—hit .275 with 35 home runs and, for that season at least, helped the team handle the loss of Tony Conigliaro in the outfield.

The problem was pitching. In 1967 the Red Sox had decent pitching, led by Jim Lonborg and Jose Santiago. In 1968, Jim Lonborg was ineffective after trying to come back from a knee injury and Santiago went down after hurting his arm. What was left were three average starters—Ray Culp, Dick Ellsworth, and Gary Bell—and one terrific reliever in lefty Sparky Lyle. It wasn't enough, as the Red Sox went a respectable 86–76, but finished a distant fourth to the Tigers.

They were about the same in 1969, the first year of divisional play (the league split into Eastern and Western divisions, with the division winners playing each other for the right to go to the World Series). The Sox led the league in homers, and were a good but not great hitting club. The pitching staff once again had three solid starters, some good relief pitching, and a lot of lesser lights. The team was good, but never in serious contention, with the excitement for the year coming from Tony Conigliaro's successful (at least at first) comeback, the controversial trade of popular short-timer Ken Harrelson to make room for Tony C. (Harrelson didn't want to leave and refused to report to Cleveland at first), and the firing of manager Dick Williams. The team finished with 87 wins, the last five of them for new manager Eddie Kasko.

Between 1970 and 1974 the Red Sox would win between 84 and 89 games each year. They would be good, but not quite good enough, despite a playoff near-miss in 1972. Every year the Sox would have great hitting and a few good pitchers, but never enough pitching depth to seriously contend for the pennant. Adjustments were made to change the composition of the team, including controversial trades of Mike Andrews to Chicago for end-of-the line fielding wizard Luis Aparicio; popular Tony Conigliaro to California; George Scott to Milwaukee for Tommy Harper; and Sparky Lyle to the hated Yankees for the now-ineffective Danny Cater. None of them helped or hurt much in the short run, as the team stayed about the same. (Sparky Lyle became a superstar for the Yankees, but the trade made a certain amount of sense at the time. The Red Sox had traded Scott to Milwaukee with the intention of having minor league sensation Cecil Cooper play first base, but Cooper turned out not to be ready. The Sox needed to trade for a first baseman and felt Lyle was expendable, since Bill Lee was coming off a great year as a lefty reliever as well.)

In 1972 the Red Sox fell half a game short of the American League Eastern Division title, robbed of a chance to win the title. Despite the disastrous Danny Cater at first base and a new center fielder who couldn't play center field (the speedy Tommy Harper, with incumbent Reggie Smith moved to right field) the Red Sox were a good hitting team in another great year for pitchers (league ERA was 3.07), leading the league in runs and slugging percentage. The team's pitching was among the league's worst, despite a magnificent addition to the starting rotation. Luis Tiant, cast off by Cleveland and Minnesota after a disastrous 1969 and an injury-plagued 1970, came all the way back in 1972, leading the league in earned run average with an extraordinary 1.91 and winning 15 games—despite spending only the second half of the year in the starting rotation.

The start of the 1972 season was delayed for a week by a player's strike. When the strike ended, a decision was made not to replay any of the lost games, even though it would leave teams with an unequal number of games played at the end of the season. The Red Sox missed seven games because of the strike, while the Detroit Tigers missed six. The season came down to a final series in Detroit, where the Red Sox lost two of three, to finish the season half a game behind the Tigers—with the margin of error the single extra game that the Tigers got to play (they finished 86–70 to the Red Sox 85–70).

Even in the lost hope of another failed playoff drive, there were signs of good things for the future. Tiant looked like a rotation anchor for years to come. Young catcher Carlton Fisk, born and bred a Red Sox fan, hit .293 with 22 homers and won Rookie of the Year. An outfielder named Dwight Evans with a rifle arm was tearing up the minor leagues, and played a few games for the Red Sox late in the season.

Evans and fellow rookie outfielder Rick Miller both broke into the lineup in 1973. Tommy Harper, mercifully moved to left, had a terrific year, setting a team record with a league-leading 54 stolen bases. Reggie Smith hit .303 with 21 homers despite battling injuries. Orlando Cepeda was imported from Oakland to have one last good year in the first year of the designated hitter, batting .289 with 20 homers. Yaz hit .296 and walked 105 times. The team once again led the league in slugging, and this time the pitching was able to carry some of the load as well. Bill Lee moved into the rotation and won 17 games with a 2.74 ERA (very good in a year when the league ERA was 3.82). Luis Tiant won 20 games, and Roger Moret went 13–2. The pitching staff wasn't exactly good, but it was above average. The Red Sox won 89 games, just enough to finish a

Key Players, 1968–1974

Mike Andrews, 2b
Rick Burleson, ss
Tony Conigliaro, of
Ray Culp, p
Dick Drago, p
Dwight Evans, of
Carlton Fisk, c
Ken Harrelson. of
Darrell Johnson, manager
Eddie Kasko, manager
Bill Lee, p
Sparky Lyle, p
Roger Moret, p
Mike Nagy, p
Marty Pattin, p
Rico Petrocelli, ss-3b
George Scott, 1b
Reggie Smith, of
Luis Tiant, p
Dick Williams, manager
Carl Yastrzemski, of

strong second behind the Baltimore Orioles. Eddie Kasko was fired as manager at the end of the season and replaced by Darrell Johnson.

The 1974 team was built around youth. Luis Aparicio was replaced by rookie shortstop Rick Burleson, who hit .284 while fielding brilliantly. Orlando Cepeda was replaced as designated hitter by Tommy Harper. Reggie Smith was traded to St. Louis in a racially charged deal ostensibly designed to bolster the pitching staff. Dwight Evans moved into the lineup full time, with other young players like Mario Guerrero, Juan Beniquez, and Cecil Cooper given key roles. The team won five fewer games and finished in third place, with Luis Tiant (22 wins), Bill Lee (17 wins) and Kansas City retread Dick Drago the only consistent pitchers on a mediocre staff. But the Red Sox seemed to be a young, promising team. The next season they would be even younger—and would begin to fulfill some of that promise.

13. The Sixth Game: 1975

Two kids would join the team as starters in 1975. Fred Lynn would displace Rick Miller—who hadn't really developed as a hitter—in center field, while Jim Rice displaced Juan Beniquez and others in left field (Yaz had moved to first by then). Both played brilliantly, helping the Red Sox to lead the league in batting average, slugging percentage, and runs scored. As in 1967, the 1975 team seemed to have an ability to overcome misfortune. The season started with Tony Conigliaro's last, failed comeback attempt (he hit .123 in 23 games as the team's DH). Key starters Carl Yastrzemski, Rick Burleson, and Rico Petrocelli all had poor seasons. Catcher Carlton Fisk hit .331—but was injured and unable to play for nearly half the season. Petrocelli and Dwight Evans both also missed significant time to injury. None of the starting pitchers had an ERA below the league average, including the team's ace, Luis Tiant.

Somehow, none of those problems mattered. The Red Sox had a talented, mostly young ensemble cast, and other players filled in the gaps. Young first baseman Cecil Cooper, finally given consistent playing time, hit .311. Infielder Denny Doyle, a .250 career hitter, hit .310 as a platoon second baseman. Juan Beniquez hit .291 while filling in for injured players in the outfield and at third base. Bernie Carbo hit 15 home runs in limited playing time as a backup in the outfield. Light-hitting Doug Griffin, relegated to the bench much of the time by Doyle's hitting, turned into a terrific pinch hitter down the stretch. Roger Moret shuttled between the bullpen and the starting rotation, and somehow went 14–3. Tiant, Bill Lee, and Rick Wise

Key Players, 1975

Rick Burleson, ss
Bernie Carbo, of
Reggie Cleveland, p
Cecil Cooper, 1b
Dick Drago, p
Dwight Evans, of
Carlton Fisk, c
Darrell Johnson, manager
Bill Lee, p
Fred Lynn, of
Roger Moret, p
Rico Petrocelli, 3b
Jim Rice, of
Luis Tiant, p
Jim Willoughby, p
Rick Wise, p
Carl Yastrzemski, of

all stayed healthy and won between 17 and 19 games—pitching steadily if unspectacularly in a hitters' ballpark that could make pitchers pay dearly for their mistakes. Dick Drago moved to the bullpen full time and saved 15 games. Relief pitcher Jim Willoughby pitched very well down the stretch.

More than anything, Fred Lynn and Jim Rice carried the team. Called the "Gold Dust Twins" in the media, the two became inextricably tied together in Red Sox lore: Rice, the working-class product of a segregated South who was inhumanly strong, shattering bats with his checked swing, and who doggedly worked on improving his poor defense in left field; Lynn, the Southern California kid who seemed to effortlessly run down everything in center field and whose marvelous throwing arm was overshadowed by Dwight Evans—with the best arm in baseball—beside him in right field. Rice hit .309 with 22 home runs and 102 runs batted in. Lynn was even better—a lefthanded line drive hitter with a perfect Fenway Park swing, Lynn hit .331 with 21 homers and 105 runs batted in, and led the league with 47 doubles and 105 runs. Lynn would win both Rookie of the Year and the league MVP.

At the season's end, when the Red Sox were nearing the division title over the Baltimore Orioles, their luck, pushed to the breaking point, began to run out. Jim Rice's wrist broke when he was hit by a pitch, and he was not available for the playoffs. It didn't seem to matter as the Red Sox swept the Oakland A's in the American League Championship Series (a sweep for which the A's would more than get revenge for in 1988 and 1990), led by Tiant, who won Game 1, and Dick Drago, who saved the other two games. But Rice's loss would be felt in the World Series.

The Red Sox have long been a New England phenomenon, not just in Boston or even Massachusetts. Our yearly trip to Fenway from central Maine was a pilgrimage of sorts. Parking at Wonderland, Blue Line to Government Center, Green Line to Kenmore. But my most vivid memories are of games on the radio. Lying in bed when Lynn hit three home runs in Detroit. Having the radio on the boat while hauling lobster traps on a Saturday afternoon.

The strangest place that I listened to a game was on a football field. On October 2, 1978, the MCI Huskies JV football team played at Mattanawcook Academy, in Lincoln, Maine. We took the field in about the second inning of the Red Sox-Yankees playoff game. I don't know what the score of that football game was, and I didn't know that day. We were blown out, but nobody really wanted to play—everyone was far more concerned with what was happening 5 1/2 hours south. There was a radio on the sideline, and no one wanted to go in—everyone wanted to remain on the bench so that they could listen to the game. They had a radio playing over the speakers, but you couldn't really hear when you were playing.

I know that the Red Sox were down as we left the field, shortly after the Bucky Dent home run. We raced through the showers, radio blaring in the locker room. I vividly remember sitting on the bus, pulling out of the parking lot, when Yaz, always my all-time favorite, popped out to end the game. That was far more devastating than the thumping we had just taken on the field.

—Lyford P. Beverage

In the World Series the Red Sox faced a similar team to themselves, Cincinnati's Big Red Machine, filled with hitting superstars and with decent but unheralded pitching (6 pitchers had won 10 or more games). The Reds won 108 games during the regular season, the Red Sox 95.

At first it looked like Luis Tiant would singlehandedly lead the Red Sox to victory. He shut out the Reds 6–0 in Game 1. After the Reds won on a ninth-inning comeback in Game 2 and a hitters' duel in Game 3 (there were six homers in the game, three by each team), Tiant came back to win Game 4, throwing 163 pitches to win a 5–4 complete game on a day when he didn't have his best stuff. The Reds then beat Reggie Cleveland in Game 5, pulling within one victory of a World Series win. After two days of rain delays, Tiant was brought back again in Game 6 to try and hold off disaster once more.

The sixth game of the 1975 World Series is considered one of the best baseball games ever played. Certainly it was one of the most exciting. The Red Sox took an early 3–0 lead, but Tiant couldn't hold it. After the Reds went ahead 6–3, the Red Sox came back on a pinch-hit three-run homer by Bernie Carbo in the eighth inning to tie the game. The Red Sox loaded the bases with no outs in the ninth, only to be stopped without scoring by Reds reliever Pedro Borbon (whose son is now pitching in the major leagues). In the eleventh inning, Dwight Evans made a spectacular catch of a seemingly uncatchable Joe Morgan drive, throwing out a startled Ken Griffey at first base when he failed to get back in time (Griffey's son now plays for Cincinnati). The game went on to the twelfth inning, where it finally ended in one of the most enduring images of the Red Sox: Carlton Fisk hitting a long fly, jumping up and down at the plate with his arms raised in the air as if desperately trying to wave the ball fair, and then triumphantly circling the bases with the game-winning home run after it landed just on the right side of the foul pole.

After Game 6, the last game of the World Series was almost anticlimactic, and it would end in controversy. The Red Sox were once again unable to hold a 3–0 lead, but Jim Willoughby—who had pitched extremely well all series—came in to put out the fire, leaving the game tied. With two outs in the bottom of the eighth inning, Willoughby was due at the plate (there was no DH used in the World Series that year), and manger Darrell Johnson sent up Cecil Cooper—mired in a 1 for 18 slump—to pinch hit. Cooper fouled out, and Johnson was forced to use rookie Jim Burton to pitch (the extra-inning game the night before had drained the bullpen). The Reds scored on a Joe Morgan single in the ninth and the Red Sox were unable to respond. Once again they had gloriously overachieved, but fallen just short of the prize.

14. The Years of the Gerbil: 1976–1980

Like the United States as a whole, baseball went through a transitional period in the mid-1970s, and the Red Sox would not handle this transition particularly well. The Red Sox had some extraordinarily talented teams in the 1970s, but those teams had to cope with extraordinary tensions. As a result, they would become another team of near misses, with the most famous near miss of all in 1978.

Longtime owner Tom Yawkey was edging closer to death in 1976, and desperate to win a championship before he died. He took one last shot at winning the way he had thirty years before—turning a good team into a powerhouse by purchasing key players from struggling clubs. Yawkey paid $1 million each for Oakland A's stars Rollie Fingers and Joe Rudi (who much-hated Oakland owner Charlie Finley knew he was going to lose with the advent of free agency). Baseball commissioner Bowie Kuhn voided the sales, however, before Fingers and Rudi ever got to play for the Red Sox, ruling that they were not in the best interests of the game.

Despite good hitting and their best pitching in years, the Red Sox never got off the ground in 1976. Luis Tiant won 21 games, and the rotation was solid, despite the loss of Bill Lee (injured by a cheap shot from Yankee outfielder Mickey Rivers during a brawl that put his arm in a sling for most of the year). But Jim Rice and Fred Lynn, who had been superhuman in 1975, were merely very good in 1976. Cecil Cooper, Denny Doyle, and Carlton Fisk all came back to earth as well. Tom Yawkey died on July 9, leaving ownership of the team in the hands of his widow, Jean Yawkey, but control in the hands of two of the team's limited partners, Buddy Leroux and former Red Sox catcher Haywood Sullivan. Ten days after Yawkey's death manager Darrell Johnson was fired, with the team foundering at 41–45. The Red Sox righted themselves slightly the rest of the way, going 42–34 in the season's second half under their new manager, Don Zimmer.

Zimmer would prove to be a poor fit as manager. His record is certainly not a disaster—his first three teams won 97, 99, and 91 games—but his legacy is not reflected in that record. To most Red Sox fans he is remembered as the man who, when handed a supremely talented team, got into a power struggle with his players and eventually refused to play many of them, leaving the team shorthanded at a crucial moment. Zimmer made some good decisions and some poor ones, but was fated to have the poor ones haunt him forever in Red Sox lore.

Zimmer was a former catcher, an ex-marine who had been wounded fighting in the Pacific during World War II, and part of a conservative old guard trying to forestall changes in baseball. He followed conventional wisdom. He wanted his orders followed without question. Many of his players were products of the 1960s, used to asking questions, testing new ideas, and to a certain extent, challenging authority (although Bill Lee, depicted as the ultimate antiestablishment figure, also served in the military).

The Red Sox in 1977 won 97 games, finishing in a second place tie with Baltimore, just behind a New York Yankees team that won 100. The Sox were an offensive powerhouse, leading the league in home runs and slugging percentage by a wide margin, and narrowly missing the lead in batting average and runs scored. Cecil Cooper was traded to Milwaukee to get first baseman George Scott back—a terrible trade in the long run, but in 1977 Scott hit 33 homers. New third baseman Butch Hobson also hit 30, with Fred Lynn and Carl Yastrzemski not far behind. Perhaps most importantly, Jim Rice had a tremendous breakout season—hitting .320 and leading the league with 39 home runs and a .593 slugging percentage—and for the next three years Rice would be the most dangerous hitter in baseball.

The Red Sox pitching was about average, without a standout in the rotation (and aging Luis Tiant went 12–8) but with six pitchers winning 10 or more games. The leading winner was a reliever—Bill Campbell, the first major signee of the new free agent era. Zimmer rode his top reliever hard; Campbell threw 140 innings—an extraordinary total for a reliever—went 13–9 and led the league with 31 saves. The workload was far too heavy, and Campbell would never be consistently effective again.

Zimmer followed the same pattern with the rest of the team. He had starters and bench players, and the starters rarely rested, sometimes even if they were hurt. Only three bench players batted as many as 100 times during the season, and that was mostly because of injuries to Dwight Evans (costing him more than half the season), Denny Doyle, and Fred Lynn. The next year this would turn into a full-fledged disaster, with overplayed starters getting hurt by midseason and bench players being so rusty they were unable to contribute.

Even more damaging was the open rift between the manager and many of his players. Bill Lee christened Zimmer "the Gerbil," and the nickname stuck. Lee, Ferguson Jenkins (a future Hall of Fame starter for whom the Sox had traded Juan Beniquez to Texas), key reliever Jim Willoughby, and primary outfield backup Bernie Carbo formed the core of a group called the "Buffalo Heads," which openly mocked Zimmer and derided his intellect. Zimmer responded by benching them, or insisting that the team dump them for whatever they could get. His attempt to enforce discipline without gaining the players' respect failed badly, even though Zimmer did get his way. Carbo, Willoughby, and Jenkins were gone by the time they were needed in 1978, and Lee was demoted to the bullpen, leaving the Red Sox without a lefthanded starter.

The damage wouldn't be apparent until midseason. The Red Sox began the 1978 season with an extraordinary run. After trading with Cleveland for hard-throwing young Dennis Eckersley and signing free agent 20-game-winner Mike Torrez away from the Yankees, the Red Sox had a formidable rotation in the season's first half, with Tiant and Bill Lee in the last two spots. Bill Campbell was a shadow of the reliever he'd been the previous year, but much of the slack was filled by Bob Stanley (who went 15–2, mostly in relief) and Dick Drago, in his second tour of duty with the Red Sox. With a powerful offense led by Jim Rice (who would finish the year at .315 while leading the league in triples, home runs, RBI, and slugging percentage), the Red Sox had a 14½ game lead over the Yankees at midseason. At that point, the cumulative effect of injuries and two years of overwork hit the Red Sox

Key Players, 1976–1980

Tom Burgmeier, p
Rick Burleson, ss
Bill Campbell, p
Bernie Carbo, of
Dennis Eckersley, p
Dwight Evans, of
Carlton Fisk, c
Butch Hobson, 3b
Ferguson Jenkins, p
Bill Lee, p
Fred Lynn, of
Tony Perez, 1b
Jerry Remy, 2b
Jim Rice, of
George Scott, 1b
Bob Stanley, p
Luis Tiant, p
Bob Watson, 1b
Jim Willoughby, p
Carl Yastrzemski, of
Don Zimmer, manager

stars. Rick Burleson hurt his knee. Zimmer left him in the lineup as the steady .280 hitter saw his average fall to .248. Dwight Evans was beaned, and began having vision problems. Zimmer left him in the lineup. Evans, a superb fielder, had never dropped a fly ball in the major leagues, but now he did it twice in a week. His average dropped from .287 the previous year to .247. Butch Hobson had bone chips in his elbow that would cause it to lock during games, and made throwing painful. Zimmer left him in the lineup until Hobson finally begged to be taken out, knowing he was hurting the team—but in the meantime Hobson would make a league-leading 43 errors at third base and drop from 30 home runs to 17. For the second straight year, Carlton Fisk played more than 150 games at catcher, the most physically demanding position on the field, and his numbers declined significantly. Thirty-four-year-old George Scott, overplayed in 1977, stopped hitting entirely by the middle of 1978.

The Red Sox foundered at midseason, and in one of the biggest collapses of all time allowed the Yankees to catch and pass them. With Bill Lee banished to the bullpen, Zimmer used terrified-looking rookie Bobby Sprowl in an attempt to stop the bleeding during the so-called "Boston Massacre." The Yankees swept the Sox in a four-game series at Fenway by a collective score of 42–9. The most talented Red Sox team since the 1940s looked utterly lost.

Somehow they righted themselves. The Red Sox miraculously won eight games in a row to end the season, tying the New York Yankees for the division lead. Just like 1948, there would be a one-game playoff to determine who went on to the American League Championship Series. Dennis Eckersley had gone 20–8 with a 2.99 ERA as the Red Sox ace. Luis Tiant and Bill Lee had both pitched very well. Zimmer passed over them both to start Mike Torrez, a steady but unspectacular pitcher who'd gone 16–13 with an ERA above the league average. The Red Sox took a quick lead on a Yastrzemski homer, only to fall behind on a cheap home run by light-hitting shortstop Bucky Dent, one of the most infamous moments in Boston history. After a furious comeback, the Red Sox found themselves with no one to use as a pinch hitter— Bernie Carbo, one of the heroes of the 1975 World Series and a consistent power threat off the bench, had been dumped for his criticism of Zimmer. Zimmer sent up .191 hitter Bob Bailey instead, and the Red Sox season was ended in their eventual 5–4 defeat.

The 1979 season was more of the same. The hitting was again excellent. The Red Sox led the league in batting average, home runs, and slugging percentage. Although Fisk went down with a predicable shoulder injury for half the season, it was offset by a breakout year from Fred Lynn, who won the batting title at .333 and hit 39 home runs to nearly double his previous high. Jim Rice hit a career-high .325, and matched Lynn's 39 homers. Bob Watson, acquired from Houston after a slow start, hit .337 in the last two-thirds of the season.

But the pitching was woefully thin. Bill Lee was dumped to the Montreal Expos for Stan Papi, a backup infielder who hit .188. (Lee won 16 games for the Expos.) Luis Tiant, an irreverent pitcher who'd also been critical of Zimmer, was allowed to go to the Yankees as a free agent. That forced the Red Sox to move Bob Stanley, their most effective reliever, into the rotation behind Dennis Eckersley and Mike Torrez, thinning out the bullpen behind Dick Drago and lefty Tom Burgmeier. The Red Sox won 91 games and were within shouting distance of the pennant race, but ended up in third place.

By 1980 the Don Zimmer era was clearly coming to a close, as everything seemed to go wrong for the Red Sox. Butch Hobson, Jerry Remy, and Fred Lynn each missed at least 50 games with injuries. Most damaging of all was Jim Rice's second broken wrist (again after being hit by a pitch), which would turn him from a great hitter into a merely good one. The team was still good offensively, but not nearly good enough to make up for its pitching, which utterly collapsed. Dennis Eckersley, troubled by alcohol problems, fell to 12–14, and he was the team's most consistent starter. The Red Sox fell to 83–77, the last four of those games (three of them losses) under interim manager Johnny Pesky, after the firing of Don Zimmer.

15. Chaos Descends: 1981–1984

The 1981 season was marred by off-field chaos, which would plague the Red Sox for years. The new ownership that had taken over since Yawkey's death was erratic, with the relationships between the team's limited partners clearly strained, and managing partner Haywood Sullivan sometimes as focused on avoiding having his position undercut as he was on beating the Yankees. In December, 1980, someone in the Red Sox front office committed an inexplicable error, mailing out the contracts for Fred Lynn and Carlton Fisk a day after the deadline had passed. The Players Association argued that Fisk and Lynn should be declared free agents (since they hadn't been tendered contracts in time), and the case went to arbitration. The Red Sox traded Lynn to the Angels in the meantime (as part of the trade he agreed to drop the appeal and sign a contract with the Angels), and hoped for the best with Fisk, who was a lifelong Red Sox fan. But in the midst of the chaos and growing bad feelings, even Fisk had had enough. Although collusion among the owners (soon to lead to another strike) kept most of them from making any offers to the All Star catcher, Chicago White Sox owner Jerry Reinsdorf finally did, and Fisk reluctantly moved on.

There was more chaos awaiting manager Ralph Houk, "the Major," a well-respected former Yankees manager who was talked out of retirement to become a stabilizing force for the Red Sox. The middle of the 1981 season was disrupted by major league baseball's second players' strike. A third of the season was wiped out, and the decision was made to play the season's second half as a separate, "split"

Key Players, 1981–1984

Luis Aponte, p
Tony Armas, of
Marty Barrett, 2b
Wade Boggs 3b-1b
Oil Can Boyd, p
Tom Burgmeier, p
Mark Clear, p
Roger Clemens, p
Dennis Eckersley, p
Dwight Evans, of
Rich Gedman, c
Ralph Houk, manager
Bruce Hurst, p
Carney Lansford, 3b
Bob Ojeda, p
Jerry Remy, 2b
Jim Rice, of
Bob Stanley, p
John Tudor, p
Carl Yastrzemski, of

season, and have the first and second half winners play each other in the playoffs. The Red Sox, expected to fall below .500, actually played reasonably well despite the talent drain. The pitching was still pretty bad, and no member of the starting rotation finished with a better than average ERA (with the exception of rookie sensation Bob Ojeda, who went 6–2 after being called up in the season's second half). The hitting, despite the loss of Lynn and Fisk, Rice's injury-related decline, and the age-related slides of 41-year-old Carl Yastrzemski and 39-year-old Tony Perez (who had helped hold the team together as a free agent pickup the previous year), was pretty good— the Sox lead the league in batting average, slugging percentage, and runs scored. Young third baseman Carney Lansford and former Sox outfielder Rick Miller were obtained (along with pitcher Mark Clear) from California in what turned out to be a terrific trade for Rick Burleson and Butch Hobson. Lansford hit .336 to win the batting title and Miller hit a surprising .291 as a fill-in for the departed Lynn in center field. Even more surprising, 29-year-old Dwight Evans suddenly went from being a decent hitter known for his defense to a terrific hitter—batting .296 and leading the league in home runs and walks.

In 1982 the Red Sox got another amazing performance from manager Ralph Houk. He guided a weak team with only two good hitters for most of the year and no reliable starting pitchers to 89 wins and a remarkable third-place finish. Dwight Evans continued his late-career transformation into a hitting star with a .292 batting average, 32 home runs, 122 runs, and 112 walks. Defending batting champ Carney Lansford went down with an injury, which opened up a lineup spot for rookie Wade Boggs, who hit .349 in 104 games. Jim Rice hit .309 with 24 homers, but was a shadow of his previous self. Somehow, Houk held the pitching together by assembling a terrific bullpen consisting of role players Bob Stanley, Mark Clear, Tom Burgmeier, and Luis Aponte, all of whom had terrific years.

By 1983 even Houk couldn't work any more magic, and the Red Sox tumbled to 78–84. The team was embroiled in chaos as Buddy Leroux attempted to take over the club from managing partner Haywood Sullivan, choosing the night of a memorial for heart attack-stricken Tony Conigliaro to announce the coup. (Eventually, Jean Yawkey would buy out Leroux and take control of the team through the Yawkey Trust, but the chaos took several years to resolve.) Carl Yastrzemski played his last season. The unsettled atmosphere was used by many to explain the Red Sox fall from the previous year, but a better explanation was that the team just wasn't very good. Carney Lansford was traded for slugging outfielder Tony Armas, a prodigious home run hitter who never walked and who was out of his league defensively in center field. Wade Boggs led the league with a .361 batting average at third, but none of the other infielders hit very well. Although the starting outfield combined for 97 home runs, no one else on the team hit very many. And the pitching wasn't good, despite Bob Stanley's 33 saves. On the positive side, the Red Sox were beginning to develop young players who could help the team rebuild. Boggs had been the first. Catcher Rich Gedman was being worked into the lineup. Outfielder Reid Nichols hit well, and looked like the fleet center fielder the team needed. (As it turned out, with Armas in center field, Nichols would never be given the chance.) The team also had five promising young starting pitchers in John Tudor, Bruce Hurst, Bob Ojeda, Oil Can Boyd, and Al Nipper.

More young players worked their way into the lineup the next year, and the Red Sox began to look like a team on the rise. Marty Barrett, a rookie second baseman, hit .303, while fellow rookie Jackie Gutierrez hit .263 at shortstop. Boston traded one of its young starting pitchers, John Tudor, for Pittsburgh's Mike Easler, who hit .313 with 27 homers as the new DH. Dennis Eckersley, the former ace fallen on hard times, was sent to the Chicago Cubs for first baseman Bill Buckner, an ex-batting champion who had lost his job in Chicago. Buckner wasn't very good, but he replaced Dave Stapleton—who had been awful—at first base. More importantly, the young pitching began to show signs of coming through. Hurst, Ojeda, Boyd, and Nipper all won 11 or more games. And a young pitching phenom drafted out of the University of Texas went 9–4 before going down with an injury: Roger Clemens.

Ralph Houk retired, leaving behind a team that had gone 86–76 and seemed to be on the way up. His replacement would be another respected baseball man, John McNamara—who would unfortunately turn out to have more in common with Don Zimmer than with Ralph Houk.

16. Almost, Again: 1985–1987

John McNamara didn't seem to have the same magic Ralph Houk did. The Red Sox played sluggishly in 1985, and did not respond well to McNamara's conservative management. Like Don Zimmer, McNamara believed in picking starters and sticking with them. Only two bench players batted more than 100 times all season, and that was as a result of an injury that took Tony Armas out of the lineup for half a season and Jackie Gutierrez's ineffectiveness at shortstop. Older players like Dwight Evans and Mike Easler saw their production drop sharply. The Red Sox hit well—leading the league in batting average and on-base percentage, and coming in second in slugging. They had solid front-line pitching, both in the rotation and the bullpen. The pitching wasn't incredibly deep, but the team had a better-than-league average ERA, despite pitching in Fenway Park. Somehow that only translated into a disappointing 81–81 record.

They would go further with a less-talented team in 1986. The Red Sox made some minor moves: they traded lefthanded starter Bob Ojeda and minor league prospects to the New York Mets for pitchers Calvin Schiraldi, Wes Gardner, and other prospects; they also traded DH Mike Easler to the Yankees for DH Don Baylor. Late in the season, with Tony Armas hurt again in center field and a gaping hole at shortstop, they made another deal, trading with Seattle for shortstop Spike Owen and outfielder Dave Henderson, neither of whom would hit .200 over the rest of the season. The team fell to eleventh in the league in home runs, and declined in batting average, slugging, and on-base percentage. Backup catcher Mark Sullivan, who happened to be the owner's son, failed to hit .200 for the second consecutive year. The first baseman didn't hit at all and couldn't play defense because of his disintegrating ankles, despite which McNamara played him in 153 games.

Somehow they made it all the way to the World Series. The offense wasn't great but it was good, with Wade Boggs hitting .357 and walking 105 times, and Dwight Evans, Marty Barrett, and Don Baylor doing a good job of getting on base (despite poor batting averages from Evans and Baylor). Even the declining Jim Rice walked 62 times—about average for his number of plate appearances, but Rice's career high. Tony Armas and Bill Buckner were gaping holes in the lineup all year, but Buckner got hot in September to finish with superficially respectable stats.

The main reason the 1986 team won 95 games was pitching. For the first time since 1979, the Red Sox had a legitimate ace. In April, Roger Clemens set a major league record by striking out 20 batters in a game. He went 24–4 that season with a 2.48 ERA and won the Cy Young award. Bruce Hurst finally developed into the top pitcher he'd been projected as, going 13–8 with a 2.99 ERA despite missing time with an injury. Oil Can Boyd was a terrific third starter (despite a midseason emotional meltdown when he wasn't selected to the All Star team, that led to him being briefly institutionalized), finishing 16–10, 3.78. When fourth starter Al Nipper faltered, the Red Sox traded Steve Lyons to the Chicago White Sox for Tom Seaver, an end-of-the-line Hall of Famer who pitched well down the stretch before getting hurt. The Red Sox needed all the starting pitching they could get; their bullpen was terrible, despite some late-season heroics from minor league callup Calvin Schiraldi (a 1.41 ERA and 9 saves in 25 games).

It didn't look like the Red Sox were going to get very far in the playoffs. They quickly fell behind in the American League Championship Series, three games to one. In Game 5, they were one strike away from elimination when Dave Henderson hit a dramatic home run against Angels' closer Donnie Moore (who went into a tailspin after the game and later killed himself). When the Red Sox bullpen blew the lead in the bottom of the ninth, Henderson came back to win the game in the eleventh with a sacrifice fly. Suddenly rejuvenated, the Red Sox went on to win the next two games of the series by a combined score of 18–5.

In the World Series, they faced a Mets team that had won 108 games, and clearly outclassed the Red Sox, at least on paper. The Mets had a terrific pitching staff, good power, and balanced hitting; they had led the National League in ERA, batting average, slugging percentage, and runs scored.

Roger Clemens was not available to pitch Game 1 (he'd pitched the last game against California), but Bruce Hurst shut the Mets down completely in their own park. Despite great pitching of their own, the Mets lost 1–0. Clemens left Game 2 early, but

Key Players, 1985–1987

Tony Armas, of
Marty Barrett, 2b
Wade Boggs 3b
Bill Buckner, 1b
Ellis Burks, of
Oil Can Boyd, p
Roger Clemens, p
Steve Crawford, p
Dwight Evans, of
Rich Gedman, c
Mike Greenwell, of
Bruce Hurst, p
John McNamara, manager
Al Nipper, p
Bob Ojeda, p
Jim Rice, of
Bob Stanley, p

the relief staff uncharacteristically shut the Mets down. The Red Sox won 9–3 and led the series two games to none, heading back to Fenway Park. After the Red Sox lost Game 3, manager McNamara made an odd decision—to start Al Nipper, who'd been ineffective all season, rather than bringing back Bruce Hurst on three days rest (as the Mets did with Ron Darling). Predictably, Nipper lost 6–2, and the series was tied. Hurst was brought back a day too late and won again, 4–2, salvaging the last of the three games at Fenway. Boston went back to New York needing to win only one of the final two games to win the World Series.

The Red Sox jumped out to an early 2–0 lead, but Clemens couldn't hold on. It didn't matter; they scored again to give Clemens a 3–2 lead going into the bottom of the eighth. They might have scored more, but McNamara let Bill Buckner (who hit .218 against lefties) hit against tough lefty Jesse Orosco with the bases loaded in the top of the eighth, instead of pinch hitting Don Baylor, who killed lefties. Buckner, who because of a bad ankle was usually removed for defensive purposes late in games when the Red Sox had the lead, was left in the game at first base. At this point, the story gets murky. Clemens had a bleeding blister, and McNamara removed him from the game. To this day McNamara claims that Clemens asked out of the game and Clemens claims he left only under protest. Calvin Schiraldi came in and promptly gave up the tying run.

In the top of the tenth inning, playoff hero Dave Henderson hit a home run to put the Red Sox ahead. They led 5–3 going into the bottom of the tenth, with Schiraldi still pitching. After getting two quick outs and coming within one strike of winning, he fell apart, giving up three singles and a run. Bob Stanley came in to pitch to Mookie Wilson, with runners at first and third in a 5–4 game. Stanley also got within one strike of the win before Wilson fouled off his next three pitches. Stanley's seventh pitch was wild (although some people feel catcher Rich Gedman could have handled it). The runner scored from third and the game was tied. On the eleventh pitch of the at bat, Wilson slapped a weak grounder to first baseman Bill Buckner. The ball went under Buckner's glove and through his legs. The winning run scored. (McNamara later said that he had left Buckner out there rather than putting in a defensive replacement because he wanted Buckner to be on the field when the team won the World Series.)

There was still a seventh game to play, but this time it was the Mets who seemed rejuvenated. The Red Sox took an early 3–0 lead as Bruce Hurst attempted to win his third game of the series. After the Mets rallied to tie, McNamara brought in Schiraldi again, only to see him give up a tie-breaking home run. The Mets, heavily favored all along, went on to win 8–5. The World Series was over.

The 1987 Red Sox went back to underachieving again. The team was loaded with talent, but McNamara didn't seem to know what to do with some of it. The Red Sox had terrific veteran hitters in Dwight Evans (.305 with 34 homers, 123 RBI, and 106 walks) and Wade Boggs (.368 with a career-high 24 homers and 105 walks). They brought up young hitters from the minors in response to injuries or ineffectiveness, and they all played well. Mike Greenwell hit .328 with 19 homers. Ellis Burks took over in center field and was far better than Armas had been, hitting .272 with 20 home runs and 27 stolen bases. Todd Benzinger hit .278 with decent power in about half a season of playing time. Sam Horn was called up and hit 14 homers in only 158 at bats. Jody Reed hit .300 in a brief infield trial. In Roger Clemens, the Red Sox had the best pitcher in the league, although after Clemens and Hurst the pitching staff wasn't very good. Still, the team wasn't as bad as it played, limping home at 78–84. One year after almost winning the World Series, a team filled with talented players looked entirely directionless.

17. Morgan Magic: 1988–1991

The Red Sox shored up one of the team's biggest weaknesses after the 1987 season, trading pitchers Al Nipper and Calvin Schiraldi to the Chicago Cubs for Lee Smith, one of the best relief pitchers in baseball. The confused ownership situation was solved with Thomas Yawkey's widow Jean Yawkey buying out Buddy Leroux's stake in the team, leaving the Jean R. Yawkey Trust as majority owner. Day-to-day control of the team passed to John Harrington, an accountant and former controller of the American League who had been a trusted associate of the Yawkeys since 1973. Nevertheless, the team continued to struggle for the first half of the season.

In June, star third baseman Wade Boggs was hit with a palimony suit by his long-time mistress, real estate agent Margo Adams, who had been traveling with the team on road trips and claimed Boggs had promised to support her. This was news to Debbie Boggs, Wade's wife. It was also unwelcome news to many of Wade's Sox teammates, who knew that their own road-trip adventures were likely to be aired in any trials. (They eventually were revealed in a notorious *Penthouse* interview, which can be read online at http://people.ne.mediaone.net/buffalohead/Margo.html.) When a shouting match erupted on the team bus between Boggs and some of his teammates, it became clear that McNamara had lost control of the team. He was fired with the team mired at 43–42, and replaced on an interim basis by longtime Pawtucket manager and loyal organization man Joe Morgan (not the same Joe Morgan who starred in Cincinnati and is now an ESPN broadcaster).

The only major change that Morgan made was to insert Jody Reed into the starting lineup at shortstop, but Morgan's folksy-but-competent style was a huge relief after the directionless McNamara. The team won 12 in a row and 19 of 20. They set a new record by winning 24 straight games at home. Morgan made the team his own, even winning a brief fistfight with fading star Jim Rice, who was offended that Morgan had pinch hit for him. Jody Reed hit .293 as the starting shortstop. Wade Boggs, despite all the acrimony, hit .366. Mike Greenwell hit .325 with 22 homers and 119 RBI, and both Dwight Evans and Ellis Burks finished the year over .290. In Roger Clemens, Bruce Hurst, and midseason pickup Mike Boddicker, the Red Sox had three frontline starters, and Lee Smith and Bob Stanley both had great years in relief. The rest of the pitching didn't amount to much, but there was enough Morgan magic to carry the team to 89 wins and victory in one of the closest division races ever—only 3½ games separated the first place Red Sox from the fifth place Yankees.

The Red Sox were swept out of the playoffs by a powerful Oakland Athletics team (they stopped using A's as a nickname) that won 104 games during the season. All four of the Oakland victories were saved by former Red Sox ace Dennis Eckersley, who had gotten control of his alcoholism and revived his career as a relief pitcher.

The Red Sox stayed competitive in 1989, although Wade Boggs and Mike Greenwell saw their hitting come back to earth a bit, and Ellis Burks, Dwight Evans and Marty Barrett missed time from injuries. (In Barrett's case, it was the beginning of the end of his career from a knee injury that had been mistreated by the club physician, right after he signed a longterm contract. Barrett would later sue the team and win.) Bruce Hurst, deeply religious and just as deeply offended by the sordid fallout of the Margo Adams scandal, left the club as a free agent, leaving Clemens, Boddicker, and newcomer John Dopson (in his single effective season with the Sox) as the only consistent starters. The relief pitching carried the team at times, led by another excellent season from Lee Smith and an equally strong one from lefthander Rob Murphy, obtained from Cincinnati for Todd Benzinger. Toward the end of the season, the Red Sox picked up 33-year-old ambidextrous reliever Greg Harris, who would be a key contributor for several years, after he was released by the Philadelphia Phillies. But the Red Sox just didn't have enough pitching to win any more than they did, with general manager Lou Gorman unable to patch the holes in the rotation that came from Hurst leaving and injuries to Oil Can Boyd. Morgan's welcome wore off a bit in 1989, and some of the players—especially Marty Barrett and fading pitcher Bob Stanley—grumbled about the roles Morgan was asking them to play. There was speculation that Morgan would never make it through the 1990 season. Morgan, for his own part, dismissed the speculations, and said that he planned to manage for three more years before retiring.

But the skeptics turned out to be wrong. Morgan still had an injury-prone lineup and a shortage of pitching in 1990, but found a way to win the division anyway. With a black hole at catcher replaced by free agent Tony Peña, a former National League superstar now reduced to a light-hitting defensive specialist, and 24-year-old longtime prospect Carlos Quintana taking over at first base for Nick Esasky, who had left as a free agent, the Red Sox still managed to lead the league in hitting and on-base percentage, although their offense was far from dominant. Dwight Evans was reduced to a designated hitter

Key Players, 1988–1991

Marty Barrett, 2b
Mike Boddicker, p
Wade Boggs 3b
Ellis Burks, of
Oil Can Boyd, p
Jack Clark, dh
Roger Clemens, p
Danny Darwin, p
Nick Esasky, 1b
Dwight Evans, of
Rich Gedman, c
Jeff Gray, p
Mike Greenwell, of
Greg Harris, p
Bruce Hurst, p
Joe Morgan, manager
Rob Murphy, p
Tony Pena, c
Carlos Quintana, of-1b
Jeff Reardon, p
Jody Reed, ss-2b-3b
Jim Rice, of
Lee Smith, p
Bob Stanley, p
Mo Vaughn, 1b
Matt Young, p

role by his bad back. In an attempt to fill the void in right field GM Lou Gorman traded Lee Smith—the team's best relief pitcher—for Tom Brunansky, a former Minnesota slugger fallen on hard times in the National League, but Brunansky turned out to be mediocre. Smith's role in the bullpen was replaced by Jeff Reardon, an aging relief star who had been lured back to his native Massachusetts as a free agent.

With no real starting pitchers besides Roger Clemens and Mike Boddicker, manager Morgan turned to castoff reliever Greg Harris, ex-UPS driver Dana Kiecker—a 29-year-old rookie—and 28-year-old career minor leaguer Tom Bolton. Somehow, the three of them combined for a 31–23 record, and the patchwork pitching staff finished fourth in the league in ERA. Together with excellent years by Clemens (21–6) and Boddicker (17–8), it was enough to give the Red Sox an 88–74 record—just enough to squeak into the playoffs in a weak division. The close race led to a terrible trade, however. Rob Murphy had inexplicably self-destructed during the season, leaving the Red Sox very thin in the bullpen behind Jeff Reardon and rookie Jeff Gray. General manager Gorman wanted to pick up Larry Andersen, a 37-year-old middle reliever who was pitching well for Houston. Houston wanted AAA third base prospect Scott Cooper, but Gorman surprised them by counter-offering AA third baseman Jeff Bagwell, who had just won the Eastern League MVP award despite playing in a terrible hitter's park. Andersen would pitch well for the last three weeks of the season and then leave as a free agent, while Bagwell went on to become a future Hall of Famer in Houston.

Once again, there was no magic in the playoffs. For the second time in three years, the Red Sox were swept by a more powerful (103–59) Oakland Athletics team. Eckersley pitched in the first three games for Oakland, picking up two saves. In the second inning of the fourth game, with the Red Sox down to their last chance at survival, Roger Clemens blew up at umpire Terry Cooney, who threw Clemens out of the game. The Red Sox went down in a 3–1 defeat.

The next year may have been Morgan's best year as a manager, and one of Lou Gorman's worst as a GM. Dwight Evans was forced to play his last season in Baltimore when the team refused to pick up his option, instead keeping Mike Marshall, who would only play 22 games in 1991. Mike Boddicker left as a free agent, signing with Kansas City. Gorman signed *three* big-money free agents to longterm contracts, only one of whom was much help in 1991. Jack Clark was a 35-year-old who had been one of the best hitters in the National League in his prime. After an awful start, he did manage 28 homers and 96 walks to go with a poor .249 batting average. Danny Darwin, a 35-year-old pitcher coming off an ERA title in a great pitcher's park in Houston, managed only 12 games before injuries ended his season. Matt Young, a 32-year-old pitcher with great stuff but astonishingly bad control, went 3–7 with an awful 5.18 ERA. After Roger Clemens and Greg Harris (only a part-time starter), the team had *no* reliable starting pitching. The bullpen was better for the season's first half, with increasingly fragile 35-year-old closer Jeff Reardon and lefty specialist Tony Fossas supported by Jeff Gray, who was having an astonishing breakout season. Then, after pitching in 50 games, Gray suffered a career-ending stroke in July. After a terrible start, Morgan started playing kids ahead of the high-priced free agents. The team went on an incredible six-week run, going 31–10 and almost catching the Blue Jays for the division title. The Red Sox managed an 84–78 record and a third place finish, remarkable under the circumstances.

18. Return to Chaos: 1992–1994

After the 1991 season, the Red Sox fired manager Joe Morgan and promoted rising star Butch Hobson from the manager's job at Pawtucket (AAA), ostensibly because they feared he would be hired by the Yankees. It was a job that Hobson wasn't ready for. He came in, replacing a popular manager, to an aging, talent-depleted team that still thought it was good. The roster was filled with players that were past their prime (Wade Boggs, Tom Brunansky, Jack Clark), weren't ready yet (Mo Vaughn) or never were any good (Bob Zupcic, Luis Rivera). Things got off on the wrong foot quickly when the best player on the team, star pitcher Roger Clemens, was late for spring training, without making so much as a courtesy call to inform his new manager. But if things were bad before Clemens showed up, they got worse when he arrived. The first real footage of Hobson to be shown in Boston in the spring of 1992 was the manager following the star pitcher around, the pitcher wearing headphones and, to all appearances, completely ignoring Hobson. Despite surprisingly good pitching, the Red Sox plummeted in the standings, finishing 73–89—their first last-place finish in 60 years. The once-powerful hitting fell apart completely. Despite playing in a good hitter's park, the Red Sox hit .246 as a team, finishing thirteenth of the league's fourteen teams in batting average and twelfth in home runs. Although the team would play better in the two years that followed, they would have losing records for three years in a row.

At the same time, other changes were going on. Owner Jean Yawkey died after a stroke at age 83. The terms of her will left her 53% of the team to the Jean R. Yawkey Trust, which was to continue to be run by John Harrington, and would also continue to disburse millions of dollars to local charities every year, particularly the Jimmy Fund. (The trust donated about $30 million to charity in 2000).

While the team continued to struggle, a transition was going on as well. Lou Gorman made two more big Free Agent signings, replacing Jack Clark with another ex-National League slugger, 38-year-old former MVP Andre Dawson, who'd had nearly

Key Players, 1992–1994

Wade Boggs 3b
Tom Brunansky, of
Ellis Burks, of
Jack Clark, DH
Roger Clemens, p
Scott Cooper, 3b
Danny Darwin, p
Dwight Evans, of
Mike Greenwell, of
Greg Harris, p
Butch Hobson, manager
Tony Pena, c
Paul Quantrill, p
Carlos Quintana, of-1b
Jeff Reardon, p
Jody Reed, ss-2b-3b
Aaron Sele, p
John Valentin, ss
Mo Vaughn, 1b
Frank Viola, p
Matt Young, p

a dozen knee operations, and bringing in 32-year-old former Cy Young Award winner Frank Viola to give the starting rotation the reliable lefthander it had lacked since Bruce Hurst's departure. Both players were troubled by injuries while in Boston. After Wade Boggs, the team's last hitting star, left as a free agent following the 1992 season, the Red Sox finally made a commitment to rebuild with young players, and the team began to improve.

First baseman Mo Vaughn, shortstop John Valentin, and third baseman Scott Cooper all moved into the lineup. Bob Zupcic was given a long audition for the center field job. The changes came too late for Lou Gorman, whose tenure began with a flurry of terrific personnel moves, but who would end up being remembered for the ones that came back to haunt him—the trade of Jeff Bagwell and the free agent signings of Matt Young, Jack Clark, Andre Dawson, and Danny Darwin. In January 1994 he was replaced by former Montreal Expos general manager Dan Duquette, a Massachusetts native, longtime Red Sox fan, and one of the youngest GMs in the major leagues.

Butch Hobson managed the team for three years, amassing a 207–232 record. This record was largely due to the lack of talent on the team. Despite that, there was never any confidence in Hobson among the fandom. He appeared to be overmatched by the job, unable or unwilling to make difficult player decisions, and not up to tac-

Jason Leader

The Red Sox tradition of lighting hope in the eyes of ailing youngsters struck a special note in 1993 for one young fan and his favorite player. On April 23 first baseman Mo Vaughn, only a few weeks into his breakout season, placed a telephone call to Jason Leader, a young patient at the Dana-Farber Cancer Institute. Jason, due to turn eleven the next day, was suffering from neuroblastoma, a cancer variant that attacks the adrenal glands and nervous system. That night the Sox were scheduled to play the California Angels at Anaheim Stadium. Jason, as a favor, asked Vaughn if he could hit a home run for him. Vaughn promised that he would try to do so. Indeed, in the seventh inning he launched a 3–1 pitch from Ken Patterson over the center field wall. Since the game was being played on the West Coast, Jason was already asleep when the homer was hit, and woke up on the morning of his birthday to the exciting news that Vaughn came through on his promise.

But the thrill for Jason didn't stop there. The fan in Anaheim who caught the home run heard about the story and sent the ball to Vaughn, who then invited Jason to meet him at Fenway Park and throw out the game's first pitch. Vaughn served as Jason's personal catcher during the ceremony and later signed the ball, "To Jason, stay strong, my friend, Mo Vaughn."

Jason Leader succumbed to cancer on August 15, 1994, at his home near Albany, New York. Since the baseball season had been suspended due to a players' strike, Vaughn was able to attend the funeral ceremonies for his young friend. Theirs was a heartwarming relationship that went beyond that of a sportsman and a fan, and truly exemplified the commitment of the Red Sox to fighting the debilitating disease and inspiring the children it affects.

tical decision making in game situations. The media called the team the "sons of Butches," at first as an affectionate tribute to Hobson, but later in a derogatory way. It was widely expected that he would be fired as soon as Lou Gorman was replaced by Dan Duquette, but Duquette left Hobson in place during the strike-shortened 1994 season. That would be Hobson's last managerial season at the major league level. After the 1994 season was officially canceled, Hobson was fired and replaced by Kevin Kennedy.

19. The Dan Duquette Era: 1995–2001

More than most general managers, Dan Duquette put his stamp on the team he ran. In seven years as the Red Sox general manager, Duquette has been both admired and reviled by fans and the media, sometimes almost simultaneously. A tremendously popular choice when he was hired by John Harrington, Duquette was hailed as a native New Englander and lifelong Red Sox fan who would understand the team and its fans in a way that no outsider could. Much of the media criticism of Duquette, however, has come because of the very New England characteristics for which he was prized—he is seen as aloof and taciturn, guarded in his conversations, keeping his own counsel and not talking to the media unless he has something concrete to say. He is criticized as a New England intellectual who takes unconventional approaches to the game of baseball, dominated by Southern and Western traditionalists. He has made a bunch of terrific player acquisitions (and a few not-so-terrific ones), rebuilt the Red Sox minor league system that he felt wasn't productive (in the process firing a number of popular media sources), mostly erased the lingering stigma of racism from the Red Sox system, and fielded strong if erratically managed teams. But he is not a great interview, and is frequently derided in the media for this lack of articulation, which is more conspicuous because Duquette followed Lou Gorman, who was comfortable with the media and sounded at ease in interviews. One of the ways that Duquette has tried to compensate for his lack of media presence is in the managers he has chosen—and this, too, has come back to haunt him at times.

A Massachusetts native, Duquette came from Dalton and attended Amherst College. In 1991, after working his way through the Milwaukee Brewers organization, Duquette became the youngest GM in baseball with the Montreal Expos. There he assembled a talented team under tight financial restrictions, relying on player development and canny trading of mature talent for prospects.

Upon joining the Sox in 1994, Duquette announced a five-year plan for rebuilding the team and its minor league system. The heart of this plan was to remain competitive without signing major free agents who would cost the team draft picks or trading away high-level prospects. The team was to be rebuilt largely through the farm system and through economical signings. In 1994, Butch Hobson's last season, Duquette went about seeing what the Red Sox farm system had to offer. Unproductive players were quickly shuttled off the roster. Minor leaguers and other players—talented castoffs from other systems who had been injured or unproductive for reasons that could be fixed—were given chances to prove themselves, in what became a hallmark of Duquette's style.

The results were mixed in 1994. While the team was still bad, fans enjoyed seeing new players who had the potential to be very good, rather than following the previous few years' strategy of signing end-of-the road veterans who still had enough left to give the team the illusion of mediocrity (to use Peter Gammons's phrase). The Red Sox used an astonishing 45 players in the strike-shortened 1994 season. (The 1995 season was also shortened before the labor problems were at least temporarily settled.) Some of those players, like catcher Damon Berryhill and center fielder Lee Tinsley, were just as mediocre as the people they replaced. Some, like catcher Rich Rowland, pitcher Scott Bankhead, and outfielders Wes Chamberlain and Andy Tomberlin, didn't justify the hype, or never regained skills that they had lost to injury. But while the first year's experiment didn't succeed, Duquette made it clear that the status quo was changing, that the team would emphasize young and under-valued players where possible, giving big-money contracts only to reward Sox players who had done well or to fill in a key missing piece, and to avoid trades of prospects for overvalued older players. That strategy would pay off in the years to come. The times when Duquette did not follow his own plan led to some of his biggest failures—such as signing Steve Avery and trading for Ed Sprague.

After the 1994 season, Butch Hobson was fired and replaced by former Texas manager Kevin Kennedy. Kennedy was polished with the media, gave a good interview, and was good at in-game strategy. His people skills would presumably allow Duquette to play a more behind-the-scenes role in rebuilding the Red Sox. Kennedy liked power hitting teams, and Duquette went out and got him one, trading center fielder Otis Nixon for former MVP Jose Canseco, signing power-hitting catcher Mike Macfarlane, and bringing in underpriced sluggers like Mark Whiten and Reggie Jefferson to complement the team's key hitters like Mo Vaughn, John Valentin, and Mike Greenwell. Once again Duquette auditioned other teams' castoffs—a record 53 players spent time on the major league roster during the season—and this time the strategy worked beautifully. Outfielder Troy O'Leary, a Milwaukee castoff, was inserted into the starting lineup and hit .308. Second baseman Luis Alicea stabilized the infield while hitting .270. Thirty-six-year-old former batting champion Willie McGee hit .285 off the bench. But most of all, Duquette found pitching. Knuckleball pitcher Tim Wakefield, released by the Pittsburgh Pirates, came up in May and carried the team for much of the year, going 16–8, 2.95 in a season when ace Roger Clemens and number two starter Aaron Sele were limited by injuries. Erik Hanson, picked up cheaply after a year of injuries in Cincinnati, went 15–5. Rheal Cormier, picked up in a trade for third baseman Scott Cooper (who had lost his job to Tim Naehring), filled in effectively as both a starter and reliever. Mike Maddux, forgotten older brother of National League superstar Greg Maddux, was very good in a middle relief role. Rule 5 draftee Vaughn Eshelman finished the year 6–3 after a surprisingly good start. Despite a lower payroll than the previous year the Red Sox went 86–58 and won the American League East before being swept out of the Division

Series (a new round of playoffs introduced along with wild card teams) by a power-house Cleveland Indians team that had gone 100–44. Boston would get its revenge a few years later.

If everything had gone right for Duquette's system in 1995, things were not so smooth in 1996. Once again, he brought in a record number of players—54 this time—and once again he found some gems. Jeff Frye replaced Luis Alicea at second base and hit .286. Catcher Mike Stanley, signed away from the Yankees, hit .270 with 24 home runs before being traded late in the season. Reggie Jefferson, hobbled by injuries the previous year, returned to health and hit .347. Tom Gordon was obtained from Kansas City and won 12 games, although he pitched inconsistently. But this year the team was never in the race. They started the season dreadfully, losing 16 of their first 20 games, before recovering to finish 85–77. There were accusations that Kevin Kennedy hadn't prepared the team properly during spring training, and whisperings about a caste system in the locker room. Kennedy was very popular among the team's star players, particularly Roger Clemens, Mike Greenwell, and Jose Canseco, but others claimed that Kennedy was quick to take credit for wins while always blaming the players for losses. Tensions grew as the season neared its end. Mike Greenwell, unhappy that the Red Sox wouldn't guarantee him a big new contract and a starting role the following season (despite his falling production), cleaned out his locker before the end of the season, even though the team was technically still in the pennant race. Clemens and Canseco both had harsh words for Duquette, and it was unclear how much Kennedy and bench coach Tim Johnson backed them.

After the season Kennedy was fired, Canseco was traded to Oakland for pitcher John Wasdin, and Clemens and Greenwell were allowed to leave as free agents. Although Greenwell never played in the major leagues again, Clemens went on to revive his career (which had been limited by injuries for several years) in Toronto, where he won two more Cy Young Awards. Although Tim Johnson was a media favorite to be hired as manager, he also was allowed to leave. (Johnson later became manager for Toronto, where he was fired after it was revealed that he had fabricated stories of wartime experiences in Vietnam—where he had never served—to inspire his players.) After reportedly being turned down in his pursuit of some high-profile managerial candidates, Dan Duquette settled on Atlanta third base coach Jimy Williams, whose folksy speaking style was slightly reminiscent of Joe Morgan. Williams was highly regarded as a coach but was a conspicuous failure in his previous managerial position with the Toronto Blue Jays. He'd managed one team that had blown a seemingly insurmountable lead by collapsing at the end of the season. And in 1989 the Blue Jays were 12–24 when he was fired—then turned their season around and won the division. Another key hire was also made, as Duquette replaced pitching coach Al Nipper with Joe Kerrigan, with whom he'd worked in Montreal (an unusual move, since managers generally select their own coaches.)

In 1997 the player movements continued, with 46 more players seeing time with the Red Sox. Duquette had said the pace of change would slow down as the Sox minor league system began to contribute more longterm members of the team. However, the minors were slow to produce the players he needed. Although shortstop Nomar Garciaparra had a tremendous rookie year and catcher Scott Hatteberg developed into a valuable contributor, there wasn't the steady flow of talent Duquette had hoped for. The lack of frontline starting pitching to replace Roger Clemens forced Duquette to lavish money on former prized Atlanta pitcher Steve Avery, who was a disaster. The team's record actually worsened in Jimy Williams's first year, when the Sox went 78–84 despite leading the league in batting average.

Reacting to the lack of productivity from the minor leagues, Duquette made changes after the season. Director of Player Development Bobby Schaefer was fired, as was Director of Minor League Operations Ed Kenney Jr., whose father had also run the minor league system for many years. Several other key minor league personnel either left as a result of the firings or were forced out. Duquette was harshly criticized for the firings, particularly by Peter Gammons, who began attacking Duquette in his weekly column in the *Boston Globe* and continued the practice when he moved on to ESPN. Gammons also attacked Duquette's emphasis on pursuing comparatively inexpensive Latin American and Asian players instead of players acquired through the amateur draft—who frequently commanded millions in signing bonuses—and others picked up the chorus.

As a manager, Jimy Williams turned out to be a mixed blessing. The press, at first hostile, and then bewildered, soon warmed to Williams's surreal quotes, which didn't always answer their questions but generally made for good copy. Unlike Kevin Kennedy, Williams never criticized his players publicly, which gave him the support of the team. But at times Williams's lineup selections would be just as surreal as his answers to interviewers' questions. And there were times when Williams and Duquette were clearly not on the same page. In the clearest example, he gave struggling pitcher Steve Avery—who was pitching dreadfully and had been pulled from the rotation—an additional start that guaranteed another year on Avery's bloated contract. Two years later he would play a declining Mike Stanley enough to guarantee an option year in Stanley's contract. These moves were popular with players, but made it more difficult for Duquette to construct a competitive team.

Williams wanted a better defensive team instead of the slugging team that Kevin Kennedy had favored, and Duquette gave it to him. Speedy center fielder Darrin Lewis, a former Gold Glove winner, was signed. Another fast outfielder, Damon Buford, was obtained as part of a trade for Aaron Sele. Mike Benjamin was signed as a utility infielder. When Jeff Frye went down with an injury, Duquette bowed to Williams's request that he sign former Atlanta second baseman Mark Lemke. Speedy rookie infielder Donnie Sadler spent time on the roster. Except for Buford, none of these players hit very well, but the team's defense did improve. The team batting average fell from first in the league to third, despite excellent seasons from first baseman Mo Vaughn and shortstop Nomar Garciaparra.

The decrease in hitting was overshadowed by the surge in pitching, however. Pitching coach Joe Kerrigan had promised great results and he delivered them. Led by new acquisition Pedro Martinez—a wiry Dominican pitcher who Duquette had traded for both in Montreal and in Boston, and who won 19 games—the team surged to second in the league in ERA in 1998. Tim Wakefield won 17 games, and

Bret Saberhagen, one of Duquette's reclamation projects who'd been picked up cheap after seriously injuring his arm, went 15–8. Tom Gordon, an inconsistent starter, was converted to the team's closer, where he was nearly invincible, setting a team record by saving 46 games. Derek Lowe (obtained along with catcher Jason Varitek in a steal of a trade from the Seattle Mariners) was erratic as a starter, but then developed into an outstanding middle reliever. Jim Corsi, repeatedly released by other teams, also pitched extremely well in relief.

The Red Sox won 92 games and a wild card spot. Once again, they faced the Cleveland Indians. After Pedro Martinez won the first game, the Red Sox lost two straight and were on the brink of elimination. There were widespread media calls for Jimy Williams to bring back Pedro Martinez on short rest for Game 4. Instead, he made the controversial decision to start erratic lefthander Pete Schourek, a late season acquisition—reasoning that the Red Sox had to win two games, and they had the best chance of winning them both if they saved Martinez for Game 5, when he would be rested. Schourek pitched extremely well, but the gamble failed anyway. Tom Gordon, who hadn't blown a save in four months, was hit hard in the eighth inning and the Red Sox lost 2–1.

The offseason revolved around a contentious negotiation with the most visible Red Sox star, slugging first baseman Mo Vaughn. Duquette and Vaughn had been conducting on-again off-again contract negotiations for some time amid an atmosphere of growing distrust. Vaughn publicly criticized the team for not supporting him after he'd wrecked a car and been arrested on suspicion of driving while intoxicated. He also criticized the team for not locking up key players to longterm contracts. When Duquette responded by signing Troy O'Leary, Darren Lewis, and John Valentin to longterm deals (all of which would come back to haunt Duquette) and signed free agent second baseman and leadoff hitter Jose Offerman to a four-year contract, Vaughn complained that signing other players first showed a lack of respect for him. Despite a series of offers from the Red Sox, Vaughn eventually signed a deal with the Anaheim Angels that briefly made him the highest-paid player in the game. Duquette drew harsh media criticism as the general manager who allowed both Roger Clemens and Mo Vaughn to walk away. There were derisive comparisons between Mo Vaughn and Jose Offerman in the media, especially when Duquette described Offerman as having replaced Vaughn's "on-base ability," which was true, but only further highlighted the loss of Vaughn's ability to hit 40 home runs a year. Heading into the 1999 season there were widespread predictions that the Red Sox would do poorly.

Key Players, 1995–2001

Jose Canseco, of
Roger Clemens, p
Brian Daubach, 1b
Carl Everett, of
Nomar Garciaparra, ss
Tom Gordon, p
Mike Greenwell, of
Reggie Jefferson, 1b-of
Kevin Kennedy, manager
Derek Lowe, p
Pedro Martinez, p
Tim Naehring, ss-2b-3b
Trot Nixon, of
Jose Offerman, 2b-1b
Troy O'Leary, of
Aaron Sele, p
John Valentin, ss
Mo Vaughn, 1b
Tim Wakefield, p
Jimy Williams, manager

Instead they won 94 games and returned to the playoffs. The hitting did fall off badly, with terrible seasons by Darrin Lewis and Damon Buford and an injury-filled year by John Valentin having as much effect as Vaughn's loss. The Red Sox finished seventh in the league in batting average and ninth in home runs—despite excellent seasons from the reviled Offerman and scrap-heap pickup Brian Daubach, and a batting title from Nomar Garciaparra (.357). But in 1999 the pitching was even stronger, finishing first in the league in ERA. Although the team had no consistent starters behind the astonishing Pedro Martinez, who went 23–4 and won the Cy Young Award, and Bret Saberhagen, who pitched brilliantly between struggles with two injuries, pitching coach Joe Kerrigan and manager Jimy Williams seemed to have an uncanny ability to get the most out of pitchers, pulling pitchers out quickly before they could get into trouble. When Tom Gordon was injured and missed most of the season, Williams plugged knuckleballer Tim Wakefield into the role, and when Wakefield began to falter Derek Lowe took over as closer. Late in the season, Duquette traded with the Chicago Cubs for reliever Rod Beck, a former closer coming off an arm injury, who pitched extremely well down the stretch. Ramon Martinez, Pedro's older brother who had been the Dodgers' ace until hurting his arm, came back from injury rehabilitation to pitch well in the season's final weeks.

In the playoffs against the Cleveland Indians once again, the Red Sox appeared to be destined for a quick exit. Pedro had to leave the first game early with a pulled muscle in his back, and appeared done for the series. The Indians won the game 3–2 with a ninth-inning run. In the second game they hammered Saberhagen, who was pitching with a shoulder that would be operated on immediately after the playoffs. Facing elimination in Game 3 and needing to win three games in a row against a powerful Indians team, the Red Sox managed to stave off defeat by scoring six runs against a weak Cleveland bullpen to break open a tie game. In Game 4 the end appeared to be in sight when Boston starter Kent Mercker was knocked out in the second inning. Instead the Red Sox erupted for 23 runs, led by 7 RBI from John Valentin, who'd had an injury-marred season up to that point. The fifth game was even more remarkable. Once again, Saberhagen was knocked out early, and this time Pedro Martinez was brought into the game in relief. Despite a back injury that made him unable to throw his fastball effectively, he held the Indians hitless with a combination of off-speed pitches and pure guile. Twice Cleveland walked Nomar Garciaparra to face the slumping Troy O'Leary, and twice he homered, driving in seven runs. The Red Sox won 12–8 and moved on to face the World Champion New York Yankees in the American League Championship Series.

The tone of the heartbreaking series was set in the first game, when Rod Beck gave up a tenth-inning home run to Bernie Williams to lose a close game. Another close loss followed before Pedro, his back improving, shut the Yankees and ex-Sox star Roger Clemens down 13–1 in Game 3. The last two games dissolved from close games into Yankees blowouts as the Red Sox seemed to self destruct amid a series of questionable umpiring calls (the most devastating one occurred when Jose Offerman was called out to end a rally, while replays show the tag missed him badly). The Yankees went on to another World Series victory, but Jimy Williams was awarded Manager of the Year.

Still, there were high hopes that the 2000 Red Sox would overtake the Yankees and challenge for the World Series. The Red Sox had the best pitching in baseball, and the single best pitcher in Pedro Martinez. A big hole in the lineup was filled over the winter when Dan Duquette traded minor league shortstop Adam Everett for Houston center fielder Carl Everett (no relation), a 28-year old coming off a season in which he hit .325 with 28 homers and 27 steals, while playing great defense. Anticipating that offensive reinforcements would be needed during the season, Duquette stocked the Pawtucket minor league club with players like Isreal Alcantara, Morgan Burkhart, and Curtis Pride, several older minor leaguers with great hitting potential. Coming into the season, optimism was high. *Sports Illustrated* even picked the Red Sox to win the World Series.

The Red Sox started the season well, and took first place in May. Although the pitching was still the best in the league—with Pedro Martinez having one of the greatest seasons ever by a pitcher and Derek Lowe taking over the closer's role full-time—the offense began to founder. Jimy Williams continued to emphasize defensive players above offense, even when the team's lack of offense reached critical levels. When John Valentin went down early with a knee injury, he was replaced by light-hitting Wilton Veras (.244 with no homers) and Manny Alexander (.211). Troy O'Leary, in the midst of a terrible divorce, didn't hit at all in the season's first half, but Williams kept playing him. Darren Lewis was awful at the plate (.241 with no power and a below-average number of walks), but Williams played him frequently, even if it meant benching a better-hitting player. Like Don Zimmer in the 1970s, Williams seemed to develop favorites and to put other players in the doghouse. When Curtis Pride, who was tearing up the International League, was called up, Williams refused to play him, preferring to stick with Darren Lewis. Eventually Williams forced Pride's release. First baseman Morgan Burkhart was called up and hit outrageously well for two weeks, but the first time he had a bad game he was sent to the bench, and barely played the rest of the year—even after first baseman Brian Daubach was injured and unable to hit effectively during the season's last month. Israel Alcantara, leading the International League in home runs, was called up and hit well. But after a terrible defensive game in Chicago in which Alcantara committed several rookie mistakes, Williams buried him on the bench, giving him only sporadic playing time the rest of the year.

Duquette's options were limited. With the team trying to negotiate a deal with the city of Boston and the state of Massachusetts for a new ballpark, and with the team likely to be sold shortly (the pending sale of the team will benefit the Yawkey Trust, which currently gives about $30 million a year to the Jimmy Fund and other charities), firing a popular manager coming off a Manager of the Year award would be difficult. At the same time, with the Yankees looking vulnerable and the rest of the division playing poorly, the Red Sox were letting a narrow window of opportunity slip away, because of his manager's reluctance to entrust playing time to unproven minor leaguers in the heat of the pennant race—no matter how badly his other players fared. In an attempt to add offensive players who Jimy Williams would actually use, Duquette began doing what he had always avoided in the past—trading young prospects for older, declining veterans with good reputations. He sent two prospects to the San Diego Padres for third baseman Ed Sprague, a former All Star who was having a good first half. He sent two more to Cincinnati for Dante Bichette, a 36-year-old slugger who had a $6 million contract. He signed veterans Bernard Gilkey and Rico Brogna, aging sluggers with good defensive reputations. The gamble failed badly. Although Williams gave playing time to most of the new acquisitions, only Bichette hit well. Although the Red Sox finished within two and a half games of the Yankees, the race wasn't really that close—a late losing streak by the Yankees closed the gap after the playoff hunt was already all-but decided. The Red Sox finished thirteenth in the league in batting average, and eleventh in home runs.

After the season, Duquette reverted to his previous style and set about addressing the team's weaknesses. Although he had a poor hitting team with a great pitching staff (including promising young pitchers such as Tomo Ohka and Paxton Crawford), there was a clamor in the media for Duquette to sign another front line starting pitcher, such as 32-year-old Baltimore free agent Mike Mussina. Duquette was criticized for his halfhearted pursuit of Mussina—although the effect of that pursuit was to cause the Yankees to pursue Mussina forcefully and sign him to a huge contract. With the Yankees having spent their free agent budget, Duquette turned to pursuing the best hitter available—Cleveland superstar Manny Ramirez, who was only 28. After signing Ramirez to an eight-year $160 million deal, Duquette signed two starting pitchers who'd been forgotten in the free agent madness, Toronto's Frank Castillo and Detroit's Hideo Nomo. Both had pitched about as well as Mussina in 2000, although Duquette signed both of them combined for about half the salary the Yankees would be paying Mussina. At that point Duquette announced that there would be no more trades of young players before the season. Having patched up the weaknesses in the lineup, the 2001 Red Sox were going to give young players like Trot Nixon, Tomo Ohka, and Paxton Crawford a chance to help their core of Nomar Garciaparra, Pedro Martinez, Carl Everett, Manny Ramirez, Derek Lowe, and company go after the World Series in 2001.

THE PLAYERS

This isn't intended to be a list of the all-time greatest Red Sox players, although you'll find those players in this section. What you'll also find here are the players who are most talked about—the heroes and villains and cult favorites and quirkiest players who have appeared with the Boston Red Sox in the last 100 years. Many of the players here were great. Some were tragic, or bizarre, or funny, or some combination of all four. Taken one at a time, they are fascinating stories, little pieces of lives that interacted with a baseball team and its fans at a particular moment. Taken together they are the fabric of Red Sox history—the people who shaped the team and were in turn shaped by the city, its ballpark, and most of all—its fans.

Don Aase—after a promising rookie season as a starting pitcher with the Red Sox, Aase was sent to the Angels in 1977 in return for second baseman Jerry Remy. After three less-than-successful seasons as a starter, Aase was converted into a reliever, and was one of the league's better relievers for the next 6 years. He saved 34 games and was an All Star in 1986, a year when bullpen failures cost the Sox the World Series.

Harry Agganis—a well-loved New England athlete, "The Golden Greek" fit the true definition of a hometown hero. Agganis was born in Lynn, Massachusetts in 1930, excelled in baseball and football at Lynn Classical High School, and continued those sports at Boston University. While his football career seemed slightly more promising (he won All-American football honors and was later drafted as the first pick of the Cleveland Browns in 1952), he chose to stick with baseball, and after just one minor league season he was promoted to the Red Sox in 1954.

Though he was a young player performing among the likes of Ted Williams and Jimmy Piersall, Agganis, because his local roots and BU success were well documented, was adoringly embraced by the New England community. With good looks, a boyish charm, and loud loyalty to his home and heritage, he was often called an Adonis. In competition for the first base job with Dick Gernert and later Norm Zauchin, Agganis finished a moderately successful rookie season with a .251 average and 11 home runs.

Shortly into the 1955 season, however, he was hospitalized with pneumonia, which resulted in the formation of a pulmonary embolism in his lung. This condition soon proved fatal. His death at the age of 26 shocked a community that had perceived Agganis as an immortal hero. Forty-five years later, however, his legend lives on, especially along the North Shore. A football award for the top senior college player in New England was named in his honor, as well as a scholarship and a road outside the BU campus.

Rick Aguilera—Boston traded prized pitching prospect Frankie Rodriguez during the 1995 season in order to bolster their bullpen with the 33-year-old Aguilera, Minnesota's relief ace and a 3-time All Star. Aguilera saved 20 games down the stretch with the Red Sox and helped them make the playoffs, but then left as a free agent at season's end in order to re-sign with the Twins. He currently pitches for the Chicago Cubs.

Israel Alcantara—one of the bizarre stories of the 2000 season, 27-year-old rookie Alcantara played well in limited duty but was scapegoated for a collapsing team's problems. Alcantara, a third baseman recently converted to the outfield, was leading the International League in home runs when he was called up to the Red Sox, who were in a tailspin and desperately needed hitting. He hit well, but in a game against the Chicago White Sox (fellow Pawtucket call-up Paxton Crawford's first major league start) Alcantara's tentative fielding turned 2 fly balls that a more experienced (or more confident) outfielder could have caught into hits. He was also thrown out on the bases. Inexplicably, Alcantara—who had spent nearly a decade of hard work trying to get to the major leagues—was widely accused by Boston media outlets of not hustling or caring about the game, all based on his single bad game. There were calls for him to be released or sent back to the minors (which would have meant losing him, since any other team could have claimed him on waivers). Manager Jimy Williams buried Alcantara on his bench, essentially going with 1 fewer offensive player even while the team languished near the bottom of the league in hitting. On the rare occasions Alcantara got playing time, he continued to hit well (slugging .578 in 21 games, one of the best figures on the team).

Ironically, during the 2000 World Series, Mets rookie outfielder Timo Perez made several questionable fielding plays and a glaring baserunning mistake that reminded many fans of Alcantara 's play in Chicago—but in a much more crucial situation. However, it was reported in the media as just a rookie misplay, the kind of mistake inexperienced major leaguers make. Alcantara was released by the Red Sox after the season, but then was re-signed to a minor league contract.

Dale Alexander—a hitting star whose career ended prematurely. Alexander had been a terrific hitter with the Detroit Tigers as a 26-year-old rookie first baseman in 1929, hitting .343 with 25 home runs and 137 runs batted in. Over the next 2 years, however, the Tigers became frustrated with Alexander's defense (he also led the league in errors his rookie year), and early in the 1932 season they traded him to the Red Sox for outfielder Earl Webb. Alexander, who'd been riding the bench in Detroit, went on a season-long hot streak as soon as he arrived in Boston, finishing the year at .367 and nosing out Jimmie Foxx (who would later play for the Sox) for the batting title. Early the next year Alexander injured his knee and was treated with hydrotherapy, then a new technique. The water was much too hot, and his leg was essentially boiled, leaving Alexander with third-degree burns. He was able to play again late in the season (hitting .281, the only time in 5 major league seasons that he hit less than .325), but not well enough to offset his defensive liability to the team. He never played in the major leagues again.

Luis Alicea—a middle infielder with good range and speed but little power, Alicea played with St. Louis before joining Boston for one year in 1995. He got a fair amount of playing time in a variety of roles, getting into 132 games, and contributed 44 RBI and 13 stolen bases. Luis is still filling this utility role today, and has played for several teams since his year in Boston. In 2000 with the Texas Rangers Alicea had the most playing time of his career (540 at bats) and his highest batting average (.294).

Gary Allenson—a weak-hitting catcher with a good defensive reputation, "Muggsy" played 6 years with the Sox at a time when the team's catching depth was poor. Because of injuries to other catchers, he often played more than his abilities warranted. Allenson was never a full-time starter, but he split time at the position in 1979 when Carlton Fisk was hurt most of the year, and 1982–83 when he competed with an up-and-coming Rich Gedman for the starting job. He hit .221 over his career.

Larry Andersen—in one of the worst trades in history, Andersen, a 37-year-old pitcher who had settled into a niche as one of the National League's best middle relievers, was obtained from Houston late in the 1990 season for third baseman Jeff Bagwell. Although Andersen pitched very well in 15 games for Boston, he was declared a free agent at the end of the season because of previous collusion by Major League owners and signed with San Diego. Bagwell, converted to first base by the Astros, turned into one of the best players in baseball and a future Hall-of-Famer. Andersen was known around the league as a practical joker and free spirit, but in Boston he is remembered only as the player the Sox received for 3 weeks in return for Jeff Bagwell.

Brady Anderson—lefthanded-hitting outfielder who debuted with the Sox to start the 1988 season. He had a gaudy minor league reputation, particularly for his speed, but found it difficult to break into an outfield that included veteran Dwight Evans and solid young players Mike Greenwell, Ellis Burks, and Todd Benzinger. He briefly covered center field while Burks was injured until July when Anderson was traded to the Baltimore Orioles along with Curt Schilling for starting pitcher (and former 20-game winner) Mike Boddicker.

The Orioles patiently kept Anderson in their outfield through four mediocre offensive seasons before he finally found his home run stroke in 1992, when he hit 21. Anderson's combination of power, defense, and speed made him an outfield fixture in Baltimore throughout the 1990s and into 2000. In 1996 Anderson took full advantage of the short right field porch in Baltimore's new Camden Yards by launching an anomalous 51 home runs. While Boddicker made a significant contribution to the Red Sox' playoff runs in 1988 and 1990, Anderson is often listed by grumbling Sox fans as one of many highly touted players who were sacrificed for veteran help during contending seasons, only to have ample success with their new teams.

Mike Andrews—solid-hitting second baseman on the Impossible Dream team of 1967. Andrews played briefly with the Sox in 1966, then took over at second base for new manager Dick Williams in 1967. He hit .263 (at a time when the league batting average was only .236), and walked frequently. His best year was 1969, when he hit .293 (tenth in the league) with 15 home runs, excellent for a second baseman at the time. His fielding was solid, if not extraordinary. Andrews was a favorite of Dick Williams, but a year after Williams was fired as manager, Andrews was traded to the White Sox for aging shortstop Luis Aparicio, a deal that helped neither team. Andrews, troubled by a chronic back injury, floundered with the White Sox before being picked up by Williams, then managing the Oakland A's, in 1973. During the 1973 World Series Andrews made 2 errors in the same game and A's owner Charlie Finley tried to circumvent baseball rules to dump Andrews in mid-series. Andrews was reinstated by baseball commissioner Bowie Kuhn, but he never played in the majors again. Williams resigned after the World Series to protest how his player was treated. Andrews's brother, Rob, was also a major league infielder.

Luis Aparicio—a shortstop who had an illustrious 18-year career that spanned parts of 3 decades. He won 9 Gold Gloves and appeared in 10 All Star games while playing for the Chicago White Sox and Baltimore Orioles, and was inducted into the Hall of Fame in 1984.

Aparicio spent the last 3 years of his career playing for the Red Sox. Never a power hitter (he hit only 83 home runs in his career), Aparicio was an excellent fielder and base stealer, and these talents were what got him to the Hall of Fame. Boston traded good-hitting second baseman Mike Andrews for Aparicio, believing the team needed more team speed and defense to succeed. Incumbent shortstop Rico Petrocelli was moved to third base to accommodate the defensive wizard. Shortly after his arrival, Aparicio went into a prolonged hitting slump, at one point going 0–54, in what became something of a lost season for the disappointing 1971 team. His bat recovered somewhat in the next 2 years, but he seldom displayed the speed that had made him a perennial stolen base leader early in his career.

Unfortunately, the main thing Aparicio is remembered for by many Boston fans is a baserunning blunder. Playing the Detroit Tigers with the pennant on the line in the last series of the 1972 season, Aparicio fell down rounding third and went back to the base, not realizing it was already occupied by Carl Yastrzemski—who was then tagged out, ending a Boston rally. The Red Sox finished the season half a game behind the Tigers, losing the pennant by the margin of that single lost game.

Luis Aponte—Venezuelan relief pitcher who didn't pitch in the major leagues until he was 27, after having been out of baseball for 3 years. After brief appearances in

1980 and 1981, Aponte made the Red Sox staff full-time in 1982, and pitched well in middle relief for the next 2 years; his unusual forkball kept hitters off balance. Aponte was traded to Cleveland for a minor leaguer and pitched decently in 1983, but he was out of baseball at age 31.

Tony Armas—a slugging outfielder who played in Boston for four years in the mid 1980s. Armas was a well-regarded 29-year-old hitter on a rebuilding Oakland team with a reputation as a fine defensive right fielder when Boston acquired him and Jeff Newman in return for former batting champion Carney Lansford and 2 others after the 1982 season. As a hitter Armas struck out a lot and seldom walked, so he was never as good as his home run numbers made him look; he also had defensive problems in center field, which worsened as his speed and throwing ability declined. In 1983 he hit a then-career-best 36 home runs and drove in 107 runs—but with a .218 batting average and a disastrous .258 on-base percentage. He was much better in 1984, leading the league with 43 home runs and 123 RBI. Armas was injured in 1985 (when he hit 23 homers in two-thirds of a season) and again in 1986, prompting GM Lou Gorman to trade for Dave Henderson from Seattle for the playoff drive. Armas got healthy and played well for the rest of the regular season, but his age and frequent injuries sapped his power; he finished 1986 with only 11 home runs, and never hit more than 13 again. He left the Sox after 1986 and finished his career with 3 more injury-plagued seasons with the California Angels.

Armas also has a connection to the Sox of the late 1990s. His son, Tony Armas Jr., was a top pitching prospect acquired from the Yankees for Mike Stanley. Armas Jr. was later traded to the Expos along with Carl Pavano for superstar pitcher Pedro Martinez.

Rolando Arrojo—Cuban pitcher who arrived late in the 2000 season from Colorado (along with infielder Mike Lansing) in exchange for Jeff Frye and Brian Rose. Arrojo was a member of the Cuban national team for many years, before defecting during the 1996 Olympics in Atlanta. There is apparently some question about his age, as Major League Baseball lists him as being born in 1968, while news reports at the time of his defection indicated that he was 32 in 1996.

Arrojo signed as a free agent with the expansion Tampa Bay Devil Rays, and was the winning pitcher in the Devil Rays' first win in 1998. He was the first rookie pitcher ever to make the All Star team while pitching for an expansion team, and the first pitcher ever to win 14 games for an expansion team. His 1999 season, however, was injury plagued, and not successful. Tampa Bay traded him to Colorado prior to the 2000 season. He was the key player, from the Red Sox point of view, in the trade that brought him from Colorado to Boston. He pitched well for Boston after arriving from the Rockies.

Steve Avery—Avery was signed as a high-priced free agent before the 1997 season, after the departure of Roger Clemens but before the arrival of Pedro Martinez. Once a phenom on the pitching-strong Atlanta Braves, the lefthanded Avery was hyped by some as Clemens's replacement in the rotation, and he was eager to settle into his new role as an ace. Skeptics, however, feared his best years were already well behind him, even though Avery was only 27 (when many players are just hitting their peak). He was coming off a 7–10, injury-marred season with the team that had won the National League pennant, and he had not won more than 8 games in 3 years, after winning 18 games twice in his first 4 years in the major leagues. Sox manager Jimy Williams, however, having seen the lefty in action while Williams was a coach in Atlanta, was enthused by Avery's arrival.

The results were disappointing all around. Avery wound up spending two subpar years with the Sox, riddled by injuries and inconsistency. His fastball had lost the velocity it had displayed early in his Atlanta career (it was down to about 80 mph, while league average is 88–90), and he had difficulty adjusting to the need to pitch more craftily as a result, especially in the powerful American League. In the middle of the 1997 season he was pulled from the starting rotation before he could make his 18th start, which would have guaranteed his contract for 1998. Sensing a calculated move by management, Avery's agent threatened to file a grievance against the team before manager Williams, reportedly against the orders of the front office, gave Avery one more start near the end of the season. He did reach 10 wins in 1998 despite a 5.02 ERA, but his most glorious moments actually came on a couple of occasions when Williams used Avery as a pinch runner in the late innings of games. In one of those games he actually scored the winning run.

Jeff Bagwell—righthanded hitter and New England native who has had a tremendous career, but not with the Red Sox. In 1990, as the Sox were struggling down the stretch, trying to hold on to the American League East division title, GM Lou Gorman made the biggest personnel mistake since Harry Frazee sold Babe Ruth to the Yankees. The Red Sox had Wade Boggs at third with highly touted prospect Scott Cooper in Pawtucket and Jeff Bagwell in New Britain. Just prior to the trading deadline, figuring that they had a surplus of third basemen, Gorman traded Bagwell to the Houston Astros for Larry Andersen. Andersen pitched 22 innings of pretty good relief during the last month of the season, as the Sox held off the Blue Jays only to be swept out of the playoffs in four games by the A's. After the season, Andersen was awarded free agency as part of the collusion settlement, and he signed with San Diego.

Meanwhile, Bagwell opened the 1991 season as Houston's first baseman and went on to win the Rookie of the Year award. He's never had an on base percentage under .368, and most seasons it has been over .400. He was the National League MVP in 1994. He's a 4-time All Star. He was one of the best hitters of the 1990s, and his numbers at New Britain had indicated the possibility that that would be the case. But they traded his career away for 22 innings of relief pitching.

Bob "Beetle" Bailey—a 35-year-old outfielder/third baseman at the end of the line by 1978, his one season in Boston. He'd had some very good years with the Montreal Expos, but hit only .191 for the Sox in 94 at-bats, mostly as a DH. Because of the trade of power-hitting reserve outfielder Bernie Carbo, who had fallen into manager Don Zimmer's doghouse, Bailey was all that was left to pinch hit in the one-game playoff in 1978, where he made a key out.

Marty Barrett—righthanded-hitting second baseman, he hit second for the Red Sox behind Wade Boggs for most of the mid-to-late 1980s, and won the American League Championship Series MVP for the 1986 AL champions. A solid defensive player, Barrett was not the most physically talented player, but was very sound fundamentally. He fooled opposing baserunners into easy outs two or three times with the hidden ball trick (where an infielder fools a baserunner into thinking he doesn't have the ball, then tags the runner out when he steps off the base). Barrett was not a great hitter, but managed to hit .280 to .300 most years and put up better than league average on-base percentage during the time when he was the everyday second baseman for the Red Sox. Barrett hurt his knee in 1989 and never played in more than 80 games again, finishing his career with 12 games in San Diego in 1991. He sued the Red Sox and then-team doctor Dr. Arthur Pappas for mistreatment of his knee injury, and eventually won in court. Barrett's brother, Tommy, was a longtime minor leaguer who also played briefly for the Sox in 1992 (while Marty was in litigation with the team).

Don Baylor—a former American League MVP (in 1979, when Fred Lynn was robbed of the award) with the California Angels, Baylor spent a single year in Boston as the designated hitter on the Sox 1986 World Series team. Baylor was always dreadful in the field (although his drop of an easy popup in Roger Clemens's 20-strikeout game gave the Rocket an extra out to set the record) and his batting average fluctuated dramatically from year to year, but he had excellent power and got on base frequently. Although he only drew an average number of walks, he had an uncanny ability to be hit by pitches (eventually setting the major league record for being hit by pitches). Boston traded Mike Easler for Baylor prior to the 1986 season in a rare swap with the Yankees. Although the 37-year-old Baylor hit only .238 for the 1986 team, he hit 31 home runs and drove in 94 runs. Perhaps most important was the appearance Baylor *didn't* make, however: In Game 6 of the World Series, with the bases loaded, 2 outs, and the Red Sox clinging to the lead in the potential deciding game of the series, manager John McNamara did not pinch hit Baylor for Bill Buckner (who hit only .218 against lefties) against lefty Jesse Orosco (who held lefthanded hitters to a .187 average)—even though the hobbling Buckner would normally have left the game for a defensive replacement anyway. Buckner was out, and the Red Sox lost the lead, the game, and eventually the series.

Rod Beck—in his prime Beck was the prototypical closer. Not only was he larger and fiercer looking than the average baseball player, he also had an above-average fastball and excellent control. Together, these factors led to him being a dominant closer for both the Giants and Cubs, amassing more than 260 saves in the 1990s. His best years were 1993, when he saved 48 games for the Giants, and 1998 when he racked up 51 for the Cubs. In 1999, Beck's fastball lost some of its zip, and it was revealed that he had bone spurs in his elbow, likely from overwork. Beck pitched poorly after the surgery, lost the closer's job with the Cubs, and was shipped to the Red Sox late that year.

Beck arrived at Fenway in the third inning of a game in which he eventually earned his first American League save. Beck helped the team to the playoffs by pitching very well down the stretch in 1999, but the image fans remember is that of Beck giving up a tenth-inning homer to Bernie Williams in game one of the ALCS. Beck spent time on the disabled list with a pinched nerve in his neck in 2000, but when able to pitch, he was an effective setup man for Red Sox closer Derek Lowe. While he no longer has the overpowering fastball that was once his bread and butter, he can still be an intimidating figure on the mound (his arm constantly swings back and forth as he prepares to throw each pitch), and he uses guile to compensate for his physical shortcomings.

Hugh Bedient—a righthanded pitcher who spent 3 years with the Red Sox from 1912–14. He went 20–9 as a 22-year-old rookie in 1912, and beat Christy Mathewson and the Giants 2–1 in the fifth game of the World Series. Mathewson and Bedient matched up again in Game 8 (Game 2 ended as a 6–6 tie), and the rookie pitched 7 strong innings in a game the Sox won in the tenth to clinch the Series. But the 1912 season was his best. After steadily declining over the next 2 years (finishing 8–12 in 1914 with a much worse than league average ERA), Bedient finished up in 1915, pitching one season for the Buffalo Blues of the Federal League.

Stan Belinda—a righthanded pitcher with an unusual sidearm motion, Belinda will probably be best remembered for giving up the home run that cost the Pittsburgh Pirates the National League Championship Series in 1992. After several mediocre seasons in Kansas City, Belinda signed with Boston in 1995, and pitched well as the setup man for closer Rick Aguilera. He was frequently injured in 1996, and the Red Sox eventually released him. Since then, Belinda has continued to be plagued with physical problems, including being diagnosed with multiple sclerosis in 1998. He once said that while the NLCS homer bothered him for years, the MS put it in perspective. He continues to battle the disease, and has signed a minor league deal with Atlanta.

Gary Bell—trade acquisition who stabilized the pitching staff in 1967, helping the Red Sox achieve their Impossible Dream. The 30-year-old Bell was in his tenth season with Cleveland, where he had several pretty good years both as a starter and a reliever. After pitching a career-high 254 innings in 1966, Bell started 1967 slowly (1–5 record), and the Indians feared that he might be washed up. In June, the Red Sox took a chance on him, trading veteran Don Demeter and prospect Tony Horton. Bell immediately proved his detractors wrong, winning 12 of his 20 decisions for Boston, with a fine 3.16 ERA. He even saved 3 games in 5 emergency relief appearances. In the World Series, he lost Game 3, but saved Game 6. Bell pitched well again in 1968, winning 11 games, with a 3.12 ERA (excellent by today's standards, but about average in that notoriously pitcher-friendly season). He made the All Star team, but his pitching tailed off in the second half. The Red Sox left Bell exposed in the 1969 expansion draft, and the Seattle Pilots (now the Milwaukee Brewers) took him. (Bell and his Pilots teammates were immortalized in Jim Bouton's classic, controversial book, *Ball Four*.) Bell struggled with his new team, and did even worse after a trade to the White Sox. After the 1969 season, he retired.

Moe Berg—a light-hitting, much-traveled backup catcher better known for his work as a spy for the United States in World War II. Berg played the last 5 of his 15 seasons with Boston (1935–39), but only appeared in 148 games. The Princeton-educated Berg spoke at least 12 languages (the running joke was "Moe Berg speaks 12 languages and can't hit in any of them"), was the star of a radio quiz show, and was dubbed "The Professor."

Dante Bichette—righthanded power-hitting outfielder/DH, Bichette was acquired late in the 2000 season in a desperate attempt to get enough offense to enable the Red Sox to squeeze into the playoffs. It didn't work, though it wasn't Bichette's fault—he performed as well as anyone could reasonably have expected him to. He hit 7 home-runs in his 30 games in a Sox uniform, with a good .518 slugging percentage. The trade was controversial, as Bichette had been one of the most overvalued (by traditional statistics) of all players in baseball for the past 8 years. Some Sox fans, looking at his home run and RBI totals, thought it was a great trade—while others, looking at his on-base percentage and the home/road splits from his time in Colorado, thought that the at-bats Bichette got could have been given more productively to similar Sox players like Israel Alcantara or Morgan Burkhart, without trading young pitching, or taking on a $7 million salary obligation for 2001.

Bichette's first 3 years were spent in California. He then went to Milwaukee for 2 more. Then, prior to the 1993 season, he was traded to the expansion Colorado Rockies. For the next 7 seasons, Bichette was a litmus test for adherents of various statistical analysis techniques. The traditionalists pointed to his (per 162 games) averages of 32 home runs and 132 RBI in declaring him a prime "run producer." The "statheads" pointed to his weak hitting outside of his home park and his inability to draw walks to proclaim him the "poster boy for Coors Field." Although Bichette hit between .298 and .340 in his 7 years playing in the thin air of Colorado (probably the most conducive environment to hitting in the history of the Major Leagues), he was never able to post an on-base percentage in the top 10 in the National League, because of his low walk totals. And Bichette benefited enormously from his home field, putting up some of the most extreme home/away splits of anyone in the game. When he signed as a free agent with Cincinnati prior to the 2000 season, many expected his numbers to drop significantly, as they did (although not as much as some predicted). His batting average (.294) and on-base percentage (.350) stayed about the same, but he hit 11 fewer home runs in 2000 than he had the year before.

So, going into the 2001 season, the Red Sox are committed to pay the 37-year-old Bichette $7 million. He does have good power and hits for a good average, and Fenway Park, while no Coors Field, may be well enough suited to his swing to enable the Sox to get decent production out of him. And unlike some big-name players who have shunned Boston, Bichette talked glowingly of the chance to play in Fenway Park (he met his wife across from Fenway), and of his admiration for Red Sox icon Ted Williams.

Max Bishop—a light-hitting second baseman with an extraordinary ability to draw walks, the lefthanded Bishop was nicknamed "camera eye." A longtime member of the Philadelphia A's before finishing his career in Boston, Bishop never played more than 130 games in any of his 12 years in the major leagues—but still drew more than 100 walks 7 times (leading the league with 128 in 1929) and scored more than 100 runs 4 times. As a 34-year-old part time player for the Sox in 1934, Bishop hit only .261, but walked 82 times—almost a quarter of his plate appearances, and more than any full-time Sox player in 2000—and had an extraordinary .442 on-base percentage. Bishop retired after the 1935 season.

Greg Blosser—lefty hitting outfielder who was the Sox first pick in the 1989 draft, ahead of Mo Vaughn, Eric Wedge, Kevin Morton, and Jeff Bagwell (among others.) At one time thought of as a top power-hitting prospect, he never developed any knowledge of the strike zone, and his swing was too long to be effective at the major league level. He finished his career with 3 hits in 39 major league at-bats in 2 short stints with the Sox during the 1993 and 1994 seasons.

Mike Boddicker—obtained in a trade that has since become controversial, Boddicker helped pitch the Red Sox to 2 division titles. Boddicker never threw very hard, although his breaking pitches were effective—he once struck out 18 in a minor league game, and had 14 strikeouts as an Orioles rookie in 1983. Boddicker was second in the Rookie-of-the-Year voting in 1983, and won 20 games in 1984, when he led the league in both wins and ERA. He followed with 3 inconsistent seasons, however, and when he started off the 1988 season 6–12, the Orioles traded Boddicker to the Red Sox for 2 young prospects, outfielder Brady Anderson and pitcher Curt Schilling.

In his new setting, Boddicker turned his career back around. He went 7–3 with a 2.63 ERA in 15 games with the Red Sox in 1988, won 15 games in 1989, and then went 17–8 in 1990 to help the Red Sox to another division title. A free agent after the 1990 season, the 33-year-old Boddicker chose to sign with Kansas City instead of returning to the Red Sox, a decision that hurt both team and player. After an average season in 1991 and a slow start in 1992, the Royals gave up on Boddicker and dropped him from the rotation. He played briefly and ineffectively for Milwaukee the next year before retiring.

The Boddicker trade has become controversial because both Anderson and Schilling went on to become stars, but it's misleading to call the trade a bad one. Both players took years to develop—and Schilling was traded repeatedly—before they became effective major leaguers, and in 1988 the Red Sox couldn't wait for pitching help. And Boddicker was everything the Sox had hoped for when they gave up 2 prospects to get him—the second best starting pitcher on the team (after ace Roger Clemens) for 3 years and 2 playoff appearances.

Wade Boggs—one of the greatest hitters to ever don the uniform of the Boston Red Sox. A third baseman, Wade got a late start to what would eventually be a Hall of Fame career, not making the majors until 1982 at the age of 24, and only then because of an injury to incumbent third baseman Carney Lansford. Boggs hit .349 that year—not an American League record for a rookie, as is commonly reported, but an impressive first season for a player who, after his fifth minor league season, was left off the 40-man roster and was available to any major league team that wanted to claim him during the Rule 5 draft (none did).

He went on to lead the American League in hitting 4 times during his years with the Red Sox, making the All Star team every year from 1985 to 1992. Drawing tons of walks and banging a gazillion doubles off Fenway's Green Monster, Boggs was one of the best hitters in the American League during the 1980s, despite his lack of speed or home run power. In fact, a good argument can be made that Wade Boggs was the best hitter in baseball at some points during the decade, particularly 1987 when he cranked 24 home runs, a career high, while leading the league in on-base percentage. Boggs's career numbers of a .328 average, 3,010 hits, and a .415 on-base percentage, accumulated over an 18-year career with the Red Sox, Yankees, and Devil Rays, place him among the best third basemen of all time—one who will enter Cooperstown as soon as he becomes eligible.

Boggs had a variety of superstitions that he followed religiously—always eating chicken on game days, for instance, and always drawing the same symbol in the dirt with his bat before hitting. His superstitions helped endear him to Sox fans in the same way Bill Lee, Luis Tiant, and Nomar Garciaparra captured Boston fans with quirky personality traits that separated them from other athletes. Boggs was also respected as a hard worker who devoted himself utterly to baseball—both in mastering the strike zone in a way few others since Ted Williams have and in countless hours spent improving his fielding at third base.

It's 1986, I'm 10 years old, and to tell the whole truth I didn't care too much for organized baseball. Like any good kid growing up on the Massachusetts border I pretended to be a Sox fan but couldn't tell you who was on the team. I remember coming home from school though, and for some reason impatiently waiting for the World Series games to start. It seemed that everyone was excited, and being 10, I loved taunting the few Mets fans that I would encounter. So for a week and a half I got to stay up late and watch my father scream at the players on the TV. I received a crash course in players like Wade Boggs and Roger Clemens. In the end I was disappointed, as we all were, but I couldn't wait for next spring to arrive; I needed to watch my new heroes correct their mistakes. That's when it started—the more I knew about the game, the more I wanted to watch.

—Paul Ryan

And yet, despite Boggs's great contributions to the successful Red Sox teams of the late 1980s, his name has become, if not anathema in Boston, at least not nearly so revered as his on-field achievements might suggest he deserves. His reputation took a hit in 1986 when he sat out the last few days of the season in order to protect his lead in the American League batting race. Boggs's reputation was further sullied in 1988 when his much-publicized extramarital affair with real estate agent Margo Adams seemed to distract a team which should have been fighting for the division lead (and yet which did not, in fact, begin to fight until after the All Star break of that year). A later incident between Boggs and an official scorer (in which Boggs asked that an error charged to himself be changed to a hit—costing teammate Roger Clemens the ERA title in 1995) helped solidify Boggs's reputation as a me-and-my-stats-first player.

Finally, Boggs did little to endear himself to Boston fans when he signed with the New York Yankees after the 1992 season. Although Boston offered him more money than anyone else following his first subpar season, it was not the longterm deal Boggs wanted, and he complained about the team's lack of respect for his accomplishments when he left. Many Boston fans have but one rule for their idols—don't play for the Yankees—and when Boggs violated that rule willingly, he lost many of his remaining fans. For many New Englanders, the sight of Wade Boggs riding a horse around Yankee Stadium in celebration of their 1996 World Series win was one that severed the emotional ties to the man who was the best third baseman in team history.

Lou Boudreau—Hall of Fame shortstop who ended his playing career with the Red Sox, after many years as one of Boston's fiercest rivals. Boudreau played for the Indians from 1938–50, combining outstanding defense and solid hitting (.295 lifetime average, with lots of doubles and walks). In 1942, at age 24, Boudreau was named Indians' player-manager, making him the youngest man ever to manage a full season in the majors. In 1946, he began employing the "Boudreau Shift" against Ted Williams, a dead-pull hitter (meaning he almost always pulled the ball to the right side when he was hitting). Boudreau put 6 fielders to the right of second base, daring Williams to bunt down the third base line or hit the ball to left field. Williams foiled the shift later that year, hitting an inside-the-park homer to clinch the American League pennant. (A similar shift would later be used against Sox star Mo Vaughn.) Two years later, Boudreau got his revenge. Not only did he win the MVP (.355, 18 homers, 106 RBI, 98 walks, and only 9 strikeouts), but he singlehandedly led Cleveland to an 8–3 win against Boston in a 1-game playoff for the American League championship. (The two teams finished the regular season tied at 96–58, forcing a playoff.) Boudreau surprised many by starting rookie Gene Bearden, and was hailed as a genius when the lefty knuckleballer won. (To be fair, Bearden won 20 games and led the league in ERA, so he was hardly unproven.) Cleveland really didn't need to worry about pitching that day anyway, since Boudreau had 4 hits, including 2 homers. And just so Boston's National League fans didn't feel left out of the carnage, Boudreau then led Cleveland to a World Series victory against the National League Boston Braves.

But 1948 was Boudreau's last hurrah. Injuries had taken their toll, and he was released after the 1950 season. The Red Sox signed him as a backup shortstop and third baseman in 1951, and he hit .267 in 82 games, with only 5 homers. Boudreau took over as manager the following year, though he retired as a player after 4 appearances. He managed the Sox for 3 seasons, never finishing above fourth place. Boudreau later managed the Kansas City A's and Chicago Cubs, and spent many years as a Cubs broadcaster. His daughter was once married to Denny McLain, prior to the former pitching star's well-publicized arrest and drug problems. Boudreau was elected to the Hall of Fame in 1970.

Oil Can Boyd—one of a trio of young starting pitchers who came up with the Sox in the early 1980s (along with Bruce Hurst and Bobby Ojeda), Dennis Boyd's unpredictable temperament sometimes overshadowed his talent as a pitcher. Boyd was never considered a great prospect the way Bruce Hurst was. Son of a Negro League player and one of 14 children, Boyd came from a small southern town and was so scrawny (only 160 pounds, although he was over 6 feet in height) that he didn't look like he could possibly be a major leaguer. As a result he had to prove himself at every minor league level before he made it to the majors.

Boyd first appeared with Boston in 1982, then made the team for good during the 1983 season, when the 23-year-old pitched well despite a 4–8 record (3.28 ERA). He was a fixture in the rotation from 1984 to 1986, with his win totals increasing to 12, 14, and 16. Boyd had good control, which allowed him to be effective even though he was sometimes hit hard. In 1986 he joined with Roger Clemens and Bruce Hurst to form a potent top 3 starter rotation on the World Series team. In July of that year, Boyd was upset at being left off the All Star team despite his 11 wins at the time. His inexplicable reaction resulted in a suspension, a disputed scuffle with police officers, a series of drug tests (all of which came up clean), and a brief hospitalization.

In 1987 Boyd developed a recurring blood clot in his shoulder, which sent him to the disabled list frequently. After 3 injury plagued seasons, he signed with the Montreal Expos as a free agent. He had a great 1990 season with the Expos, but was out of baseball after the next season, at age 31. The nickname "Oil Can" is slang for beer can.

Hugh Bradley—a part-time first baseman and utility player, Bradley hit the first home run over the Green Monster at the new Fenway Park on April 26, 1912. It was the only home run Bradley would hit that year, and one of only 2 in his 5-year career in the major leagues. When Fenway was built, some experts predicted it would be years before anyone would hit a ball over the massive left field wall. It took 6 days.

Darren Bragg—a lefthanded-hitting outfielder, Bragg is a Connecticut native who came up with Seattle in 1994. Despite a reputation as a hard worker, Bragg never consistently hit at the levels a major league outfielder needs to hit. When Seattle was gearing up for the stretch run in 1996, the Sox, who felt that they were out of things after being buried by a terrible start, traded pitcher Jamie Moyer for Bragg. Boston needed young outfielders, and Bragg was a good defensive right fielder, who approached the game in an aggressive fashion. But he still didn't hit enough, and when he hit free agency following the 1998 season, the Sox did not re-sign him. After a year in St. Louis and a serious injury, he moved on to Colorado where, in 2000, he had his worst season in the majors.

Eddie Bressoud—mediocre shortstop whose bat came alive after moving to Fenway in 1962. Bressoud had spent 6 indistinguished seasons as a utility man with the Giants, who traded him to Boston for another shortstop, Don Buddin. Bressoud got to play regularly for the first time, and he responded with a .277 average, 40 doubles, 9 triples, and 14 homers. Never known as a good fielder, Bressoud led American League shortstops with 28 errors, but his bat made up for his defensive shortcomings. As an encore, he set a career high with 20 homers in 1963, though his average fell to .260. In 1964, Bressoud had his best season, setting career highs in average (.293), on-base percentage (.374), slugging (.456), walks (72), and doubles (41). He also hit 15 homers, and was selected to the All Star team. For a shortstop in that pre-Cal Ripken Jr., pre-Nomar era, Bressoud's offensive numbers were outstanding. But in 1965, he reverted back to his pre-Boston days, batting a paltry .226 with only 8 homers. By midseason, Bressoud was benched in favor of rookie Rico Petrocelli. By late November, he was a New York Met, having been traded for Joe Christopher. Bressoud ended his career as a utility man on the 1967 World Champion St. Louis Cardinals, and he played 2 World Series games against his former team.

Ken Brett—the brother of Kansas City's Hall of Fame third baseman and hitting star George Brett, Ken Brett was a mediocre lefthanded pitcher for the Red Sox from 1967 to 1971, before drifting to 9 other teams over a 14-year career never marked by much success (he finished with an 83–85 record). He was a great what-might-have-been story, since George Brett, who once hit .390 in a season, claimed that Ken was an even better hitter who might have had a great career if he was converted from pitching to another position. Ken Brett did hit .295 with excellent power in 4 years of limited play with the Red Sox.

Tom Brewer—A starting pitcher on the dull Red Sox teams of the 1950s, Brewer had 1 excellent year and several mediocre ones. He debuted in 1954, and won 21 games in his first 2 seasons, though his ERAs were well over 4.00. In 1956, Brewer had by far his best season, posting a 19–9 record, with a very respectable 3.50 ERA (the league average was over a run higher, at 4.58). He was also named to the American League All Star team. At 25, Brewer seemed to be a rising star, but his low strikeout totals and inconsistent control indicated that 1956 was probably a fluke. Brewer was still pretty good the next three seasons, winning 38 games, with ERAs ranging from 3.72 to 3.85. But he slumped in 1960 (10–15, 4.82 ERA), and an injury ended his career after only 10 appearances in 1961.

Mike Brown—a perpetual pitching prospect who never quite made it as a major leaguer. Brown jumped from AA to the big leagues in 1982, then was decent as a rookie starter in 1983, going 6–6. He then went 1–8 with a 6.85 ERA in 1984 and spent most of 1985 pitching poorly in the minors before making the team again in 1986. After a poor start he was traded to Seattle in midseason as part of a deal for Dave Henderson and Spike Owen.

Tom Brunansky—slugging outfielder who played a pivotal role in the Red Sox pennant drive during the 1990 season. When GM Lou Gorman failed in his attempts to land a starting pitcher for unneeded reliever Lee Smith, Gorman shipped him to St. Louis for Brunansky, to fill a power hole in the lineup. Brunansky never hit for a high average, but he drew an above-average number of walks, and had been a solid power hitter in the mid-1980s with the Twins, twice topping the 30-homer mark before struggling in his 2+ years with the Cardinals. Bruno responded mightily to the new environment, including a 5-for-5, 2 homer, 7 RBI game against his former team, the Twins, during his first week at Fenway. Although he ended up hitting only .267 for the rest of the season with 15 homers, he is best known for his diving catch of an Ozzie Guillen line drive in Fenway's right field corner on the final day of the season to clinch the American League East title. Brunansky played for 2 more years as a regular with the Sox, never hitting more than 16 homers. After 2 years in Milwaukee, he returned to play briefly with the Sox again in 1994, and retired after that season with 271 career homers.

Bill Buckner—lefthanded first baseman, acquired from the Cubs early in the 1984 season for starting pitcher Dennis Eckersley (both teams were dumping ex-stars who had worn out their welcome, although Eckersley would eventually return to stardom as a reliever). Buckner played parts of 5 seasons in two different stints with the Red Sox, mostly with very bad ankles that made him look like every step was a special effort. He was a solid hitter for most of his career, but not as good as his batting average and RBI made him seem. (Although Buckner won a batting title for the Cubs, he seldom walked and had limited power.)

Buckner is best remembered for the ground ball hit by Mookie Wilson of the Mets that went through his legs in the bottom of the tenth inning of Game 6 of the 1986 World Series, the play on which the winning run scored for the Mets. This was the first time in the 1986 post-season that McNamara had not substituted Dave Stapleton for Buckner in late-inning defensive situations. Though widely derided and blamed for the loss (for instance, an old joke was revived: "Say, did you hear about Bill Buckner? He tried to commit suicide by jumping in front of a bus . . . but it went through his legs . . . ") many thought that he couldn't have made the play even if the ball had been fielded cleanly. And others think that the game was lost already, with the two run lead having been blown. He was released by the Red Sox in the middle of the 1987 season, and then signed with California.

Despite the public vilification which eventually led to him moving out of Massachusetts several years after his retirement, he signed as a free agent with the

When my grandmother came over on the boat from Latvia to Boston, she was told she had to do three things if she were to be a "real American." She had to learn English; she had to give her children American names; and she had to have a baseball team.

So, Grandma Mary, who already was fluent in Russian, German, and Yiddish, went to night school to learn English. She named her youngest child Jack. And she began a life-long love/hate relationship with the Red Sox.

Grandma did baseball stats. She did them, not in her accented English, but in Yiddish. They were a grudge match. Toward the end of her life, when she'd had several strokes and had to live in a nursing home, the doctors and nurses could be cracked up by the sight of a tiny Russian Jewish by-then-great-grandmother poised by the radio or TV and muttering Yiddish imprecations about "in der Erd" about a particularly unfair umpire or inept player.

When my mother, one of her youngest children (with the American name of Lillian and the Hebrew name of Hadassah), married my father, she moved to Ohio. The one and only time she went to a Red Sox/Indians game with my father, she stood up with the other Sox fans—and almost started a riot.

I'm a militant non-athlete who can confuse football, hockey, and basketball teams with the worst of them. Even though I've lived in New York for the past twenty years, I'm a third-generation Sox fan. My mother's and my grandmother's legacy means that, in 1986, I wailed along with the rest of the Sox fans when Bill Buckner let that ball squirt between his legs, and I mourn every season as the Sox raise my hopes toward the beginning of the year, only to crush them—again—as the season winds down. For me, as for my mother and my grandmother, being a Red Sox fan is tied up with being an American.

—Susan Shwartz

Red Sox prior to the 1990 season, and was greeted with a standing ovation from the crowd on opening day. He played 22 games, hitting badly, before being released.

Tom Burgmeier—lefthanded reliever who played a key role in the Sox bullpen in the late 1970s and early 1980s. Burgmeier was already 34 and a veteran of 10 big league seasons when the Sox obtained him from Minnesota in 1978. Although he didn't pitch particularly well that year, he was excellent for the next 4 years, including 1980 when he saved 24 games as the team's closer. He pitched 2 more strong years with Oakland before retiring at age 40.

Burgmeier was the last Red Sox pitcher to play another position in the field. He played the outfield in 1980 as part of a double switch, when Skip Lockwood was brought into the game to pitch to a righthanded hitter. Burgmeier is now a pitching coach in the Baltimore organization.

Morgan Burkhart—a switch-hitting first base/DH type, Burkhart arrived in Boston after a most unusual and winding journey. Burkhart wasn't drafted out of college, probably because (a) he went to an obscure Division II school, and (b) he's 5'10" and well over 200 pounds, so he doesn't look athletic and is short for a first baseman. Instead he ended up in the independent Frontier League, where he won the MVP award 3 years in a row. In 1998 he hit .404, had 36 homers (a league record), and drove in 98 runs in just 280 at bats—but because the league does not allow any players over 26, he was forced to move on. Burkhart signed with Boston who sent him to minor league clubs in Sarasota (where he dominated) and Trenton. He continued to get on base constantly, and finished the season with 36 homers, 108 RBI, and 96 runs scored. He played that winter in the Mexican League, leading the league in RBI, on-base percentage, slugging percentage, runs scored, home runs, and extra base hits. Not surprisingly, he was named league MVP.

Burkhart split the 2000 season between AAA Pawtucket and Boston. He made an immediate positive impression on Red Sox fans by getting a hit in his first big league at bat, and going on an extraordinary tear in his first couple of weeks in the majors. After a tough game in Baltimore in which Sidney Ponson struck him out 4 times, manager Jimy Williams seemed to lose confidence in Burkhart and he rarely played the rest of the year, even though the Sox other first basemen were either injured or playing poorly. In 25 big league games, Burkhart hit .288, with 4 homers, 18 RBI, 16 runs scored, and an extraordinary .442 on-base percentage.

Ellis Burks—came up to the Red Sox in 1987 along with fellow rookie outfielders Mike Greenwell and Todd Benzinger, all of whom put up welcome first-season performances. Burks had a rare combination of power, speed, and solid defense; his development allowed the Sox to include prized young center fielder Brady Anderson in the trade for Mike Boddicker, who helped the team win division titles in 1988 and 1990. Burks finished the 1987 season with 20 home runs and 27 stolen bases; but while his power remained relatively consistent, his supposed speed was an enigma. Often plagued by injuries, his steal totals declined to 25 in 1988, 21 in 1989, and remained in single digits for every year until 1996. In a game against the Indians in 1990, he accomplished the rare feat of hitting two home runs in the same inning. He was not re-signed after playing in just 66 games in 1992 (his relationship with Boston fans had frayed amid frustration that he'd never turned into the star many people expected), but Burks went on to enjoy great success in the National League, mainly with the Colorado Rockies in the thin air of Coors Field. His best season came in 1996, when he hit .344 with 40 home runs and 128 RBI while stealing 32 bases.

Rick Burleson—"The Rooster" was a popular shortstop on the great slugging Red Sox teams of the late 1970s. Burleson was a slick fielding shortstop with speed and a decent bat, although he didn't walk much. Although he was one of the weakest hitters in the lineup, he usually hit near the top of the order, because he *looked* like a traditional leadoff hitter—a fast guy who hit .280 but didn't have much power—and Boston managers such as Don Zimmer tended to be very conservative. In spite of batting more than 600 times a year in powerhouse lineups, he never got on base enough to score more than 93 runs in a year, and averaged about 75. Burleson was considered one of the best fielding shortstops of his day, and was an All Star from 1977–79, also winning the Gold Glove in 1979.

After 7 years in Boston, Burleson was traded to California, where he tore his rotator cuff, and reinjured it while attempting to come back. He was never able to play regularly again, and retired after a series of comeback attempts in 1987. He is currently a coach in the Cincinnati organization.

George Burns—a righthanded first baseman who spent 2 of his 16 major league seasons with the Red Sox. Burns was a decent fielder and (in the context of the era) a better than average hitter during his time with the Sox. He also has a very rare accomplishment to his credit, one that is almost always done by second basemen or shortstops. During 1923, his last season in Boston, he turned an unassisted triple play from first base, moving with a baserunner, catching a line drive, tagging the runner, and outracing the runner from second to the bag. He played for 5 different teams during his career, and had 2 stints each with Cleveland and the Philadelphia A's.

Juan Bustabad—a frequently hyped shortstop prospect who was going to be the next great star of the Red Sox in the early 1980s. He never made it to the big leagues. He is currently a minor league manager for the Los Angeles Dodgers.

Bill Campbell—the first big-name free agent signed by Boston, after going 17–5 with 20 saves and a 3.01 ERA for Minnesota in 1976. Campbell was even better for the 1977 Sox, going 13–9 with a 2.96 ERA, and temporarily setting a team record for saves (31). He hurt his arm the following season (after 2 years of ridiculous overuse by his managers), and was never the same pitcher, though he hung on with Boston until 1981. After leaving the Red Sox Campbell drifted to 5 teams in 6 years before retiring from baseball after the 1987 season.

Jose Canseco—rarely has any one player evoked such a mix of emotions from Red Sox fans as has Jose Canseco. Fans hated him as a foe, liked his power in a Sox uni-

---

When I was about six or seven, I discovered baseball. I didn't discover it in the way that leads to collecting cards, learning mounds of trivia about the players, memorizing statistics and being able to rattle them off: I just discovered baseball.

I was raised in a nonreligious household: my parents were nonpracticing Red Sox fans. Or at least I suspect so; following the Sox is said to run in the female line in the Harringtons, and my father, while largely nonpartisan, did go to college at MIT and thus was exposed to the infectious bodies of such fandom. I suspect that I was raised by non-practicing Sox fans for a specific reason, though—the only ballpark whose name I knew was Fenway. I remember peering through the sports section of *The Washington Post* as I grew up in Maryland, and deciphering the standings and the box scores. I remember the Sox second in the standings, though I do not remember which year that was, nor which month of the year, and I remember saying, "I was born in Boston. Therefore, I'm a Red Sox fan." Things are much simpler when you're seven.

For years, when asked where I was born, I have given the answer, "Fenway. The region, not the ballpark." (I was born in the Boston Lying-In, later Brigham and Women's.)

I remember sitting on the floor in my grandfather's house in Stoughton sometime

form, and despised him again when he moved on. Canseco was glamorous (at one point romantically linked with Madonna), deadly with his bat, but also outspoken, critical, and prone to reckless decisions (and sometimes reckless driving) wherever he has gone—which contributed to frequent changes of teams as soon as his skills began to decline.

Canseco started his career as one half of the "Bash Brothers" along with Mark McGwire in Oakland in 1985, where he won Rookie of the Year. In 1988 he won the American League MVP award, and became the first player ever to hit 40 home runs and steal 40 bases in the same season. By the time he was traded to Boston in 1995, injuries had reduced Canseco to a one-dimensional player, and injuries continued to plague him during his time in Boston. He still hit well when he was able to play, hitting over .300 for the first time since 1988, slugging well over .500 both years, and drawing more than his share of walks—but he batted fewer than 400 times in either season (a typical starter bats 500–600 times a year). By this point Canseco's speed was gone, and he was used in the field only as a last resort. (Before

---

before he died, watching the game, learning the rules by the process of osmosis that baseball uses to enter the minds of small children and never leave again. I remember that he gave me a baseball bat, and it was one of my most precious possessions until my father and my brother managed to lose it at one of my brother's Little League games, something which I have yet to forgive entirely.

I don't remember 1986. My grandfather died that year.

I remember 1990, though.

My kid brother also discovered baseball. And was born-again as a true, diehard, passionate Oakland fan. (He discovered baseball, I fear, while Oakland was running very high, but my respect for his loyalty has increased since he stuck with them when they weren't.)

I was twelve. He was eight. He had the baseball cards, quoted the statistics, praised the glories of Canseco and McGwire, prattled on at length. He was an Oakland fan through and through, and it was a good year to be an Oakland fan.

It was also a good year to be a Red Sox fan.

It was a bad year to watch the series for the pennant, when the two people in the house who really wanted to see it were banished to the guest bedroom and the crotchety old television that only nominally had color, and only when jiggered correctly. It was a bad year for siblings to watch the games together under such circumstances, especially with one of them a Red Sox fan, and the other rooting for the Athletics.

That was my first Red Sox heartbreak. But I did manage to avoid strangling my kid brother.

I continued as a Red Sox fan, stubborn and set in my ways: this was in my blood. I was born in the Fens.

Then I moved back to Massachusetts, and had come home, resting safe and secure in the Hub of the Red Sox universe. Here it was safe to pupate from casual fan into diehard; here I am and shall stay.

—Heather Anne Nicoll

coming to Boston Canseco was once hit in the head by a fly ball he was attempting to catch.)

One of Canseco's more bizarre injuries occurred in Fenway Park in 1993, while he was playing for the Texas Rangers. Texas (and future Boston) manager Kevin Kennedy tried to save his beleaguered pitching staff by putting Canseco in to pitch late in a game that Texas was losing badly. Canseco hurt his "pitching" arm and was lost for the rest of that year.

Boston traded for Canseco at Kevin Kennedy's request shortly after he was hired as Boston manager. The two were friends off the field, and to a certain extent Kennedy protected Canseco, who was a frequent critic of Sox general manager Dan Duquette, from management criticism. After Kennedy was fired following the 1996 season, Canseco was traded back to his first team, The Oakland A's, for promising righthanded pitcher John Wasdin. Canseco's identical twin brother, Ozzie, also played in the major leagues for 4 years without notable success. The difference in size between Ozzie and the bulked-up Jose led to speculations of steroid use by Jose.

Bernie Carbo—journeyman outfielder who spent time with 6 different teams during a 12-year major league career, including 2 stints with the Red Sox. His biggest moment of glory came in the eighth inning of the sixth game of the 1975 World Series. The lasting memories of that game are the play that Dwight Evans made in the eleventh inning, catching a deep drive off the bat of Joe Morgan and doubling Ken Griffey off of first base, and, of course, the Fisk homerun that ended the game in the twelfth. But none of the other heroics would ever have happened without Carbo pinch-hitting for Roger Moret with two outs in the bottom of the eighth and the Red Sox trailing 6–3. With two strikes, Cincinnati reliever Rawley Eastwick threw a pitch that Carbo barely got a piece of with a horrible swing, fouling it into the dirt on the third base side. Then Carbo drove the next pitch into the center field bleachers for a 3-run homer to tie the game, and set up the drama that was to follow.

Bernie was a fan favorite and frequent pinch-hitter during the 5 seasons which he spent (all or part of) in Boston. After retirement, he was an occasional presence on Boston radio, and well known for running a beauty salon in his native Detroit.

Bill "Rough" Carrigan—starting catcher on the 1912 World Champions. He was named player-manager in 1913, and piloted the Sox to back-to-back World Series titles in 1915 and 1916. He resigned after Harry Frazee bought the team, and went back to Maine to work in banking. Carrigan returned as manager for three unsuccessful seasons in the post-Ruth era (1927–29).

Frank Castillo—inconsistent starting pitcher signed by the Red Sox after the 2000 season. The 32-year-old Castillo had been 10–5 with an excellent 3.59 ERA in 2000 (league average was nearly 5.00) for Toronto, one of the Sox closest competitors in the American League East—but in only 138 innings. In 9 years in the majors as a full-time starter (mostly with bad teams) the oft-injured Castillo managed to pitch more than 200 innings only once, and won 10 or more games only 3 times.

Danny Cater—the product of one of the worst trades in Red Sox history, the 32-year-old Cater was a light-hitting utility player (he hit for a decent batting average but had no power and rarely walked) who the Red Sox gave up lefthanded relief ace Sparky Lyle to get in 1972. Lyle went on to have 8 consecutive strong seasons for the Yankees. Cater, installed at first base, hit .237 and lost his job by midseason; he played 2 more seasons as a backup for the Sox before being traded to St. Louis—his seventh team over a 12-year career.

Orlando Cepeda—the 1958 National League Rookie of the Year and 1967 National League MVP, Cepeda was a first baseman who had a borderline Hall of Fame career with the San Francisco Giants, St. Louis Cardinals, and Atlanta Braves. He was elected to the Hall by the Veterans Committee in 1999. A post-career conviction for marijuana smuggling may have had something to do with the writers not electing him to the Hall, though he missed by just 7 votes during the 1993 voting. Cepeda and Roberto Clemente are the only native Puerto Ricans in the Hall of Fame.

Cepeda (whose father was nicknamed "the Bull" and sometimes called the "Babe Ruth of Puerto Rico") was nicknamed "the Baby Bull." He hit 25 homers or more 8 times, and finished with 379. When the American League implemented the DH rule following the 1972 season the Red Sox signed Cepeda, and he was their first DH. He was just a shadow of what he had been, and not much of an asset. He hit 20 homers but that was about all, as he didn't walk much, and couldn't run well on worn out and damaged knees. He did have one moment of glory as he tied a major league record by hitting 4 doubles in a game against Kansas City in August. The Red Sox released Cepeda in March of 1974 and he signed on with Kansas City. He played badly in 33 games for the Royals before retiring.

Ben Chapman—a speedy outfielder who never hit for much power, but played well enough to play 15 seasons over 17 years in the big leagues, playing for 7 different clubs. He broke in with the Yankees in 1930 and hit at least 10 home runs in each of his first 3 years, then never hit double figures again. Tom Yawkey tried to purchase his contract from the Yankees prior to the 1936 season, when Chapman was in trouble in New York for making anti-Semitic remarks following a run-in with a Jewish fan. The Yankees didn't want him going to a competitor, and refused.

The Yankees traded him to Washington early in 1936, however, and the Red Sox acquired him from the Senators in June of 1937, along with Bobo Newsom, for the Ferrell brothers (Rick and Wes) and an outfielder named Mel Almada. Chapman spent the next year and a half in Boston, hitting well and playing a good outfield. But the Red Sox had Ted Williams coming, and after the 1938 season, Chapman was traded to Cleveland for Denny Galehouse.

His 1938 season in Boston, when he hit .340, was his last good one. He bounced around for a couple more years, coming back after the war to play ineffectively in 58 games for Brooklyn and Philadelphia. In the middle of the 1945 season he went from Brooklyn to Philadelphia, where he played and managed the Phillies through the 1948 season. He was widely known and remembered for the racial slurs he threw at

Jackie Robinson from the Phillies dugout during Robinson's rookie season in 1947. He is alleged to have repented before his death in 1966, but his playing and managing days are known as much for his bigoted and controversial behavior as for his playing ability.

Robinson Checo—a young pitching star in Japan, Checo was signed to an expensive free agent contract by Red Sox general manager Dan Duquette in the mid-1990s. When Checo failed to live up to his promise, the media ridiculed Duquette for the unconventional signing. (Checo was dubbed "The Dominican Mystery Man" by *Boston Globe* writer Gordon Edes, for instance.) Checo did pitch briefly for the Red Sox in 1997 and 1998, before moving on to the Dodgers' organization (he did not pitch in the major leagues in 2000). He is still only 29 years old.

Eddie Cicotte—righthanded pitcher who spent just over 4 year with the Sox, ending in the early 1910s. Cicotte went on to have a career that warranted Hall of Fame consideration as a member of the White Sox, leading the league by winning 28 games in 1917 and 29 in 1918. He is best known, however, for being one of the "Black Sox," the eight members of the Chicago White Sox team that intentionally threw the 1919 World Series. He was banned from baseball late in the 1920 season, after being indicted by a grand jury investigating the scandal.

Jack Clark—a veteran righthanded power hitter signed as a free agent by the Sox before the 1991 season, Clark was known for his batting eye (he'd led the league in walks 3 of the previous 4 seasons). Clark's signing was one of three big-money acquisitions made by general manager Lou Gorman at that time, along with pitchers Matt Young and Danny Darwin. He joined the Sox with 16 seasons of baseball experience behind him, the first 10 of those with the San Francisco Giants. Despite hitting a grand slam on opening day against the Toronto Blue Jays, Clark, a notorious slow starter, did not hit consistently until the second half of the season, finishing 1991 with a .249 average, 28 homers, and 87 RBI (he did walk 96 times). He retired after the 1992 season after hitting only .210 in 81 games. He also made news during his time with the Sox by filing for chapter 11 bankruptcy despite his huge contract. Clark is currently hitting coach for the Los Angeles Dodgers.

Mark Clear—an overpowering relief pitcher with a great curve who struggled with his control. Clear had a great year as the Sox closer in 1982. Clear was obtained from California along with Carney Lansford and Rick Miller in what turned out to be a great trade for Butch Hobson (who was at the end of the line) and Rick Burleson (who suffered a career-ending injury shortly afterward). Clear spent 5 years with the Red Sox, but was only effective in the first 2 years. He went 8–3 with 9 saves in 1981, and 14–9 with 14 more saves in 1982, when he also made the All Star team. Clear was always difficult to hit, but his control gradually got worse; his last year in Boston he walked nearly a batter an inning. Boston gave up on Clear and traded him to Milwaukee before the 1986 season, which turned out to be a mistake—Clear went on to have one last good year, and the pennant-winning Red Sox would fail in the World Series primarily because of the weakness of their bullpen.

Roger Clemens—nicknamed "The Rocket" for his blazing fastball, Clemens was that rarest of Red Sox commodities: a pitching prospect who lived up to his potential. In fact Clemens surpassed any reasonable expectations in his 13 seasons with the Red Sox, although his reputation has been tarnished in some fans' eyes by the bitterness that surrounded Clemens's departure from the team. Drafted out of the University of Texas, Clemens made the major leagues at age 21, less than a year after he was drafted. He pitched 18 utterly dominant games in the minor leagues for Winter Haven, New Britain, and Pawtucket, where he combined for a 1.55 earned run average and gave up only 92 hits in 128 innings (anything less than 1 hit per inning is considered good, especially for a pitcher with Clemens's excellent control).

A rookie in 1984, Clemens stepped right into the rotation with very few of the struggles most young pitchers encounter. Clemens survived early surgery on his pitching arm and went 16–9 in limited action his first 2 seasons. He blossomed into the league's best pitcher in 1986, when his 24–4 record led the Sox to the World Series. Clemens won both the Cy Young Award and MVP in 1986. He would win 2 more Cy Youngs with the Red Sox, in 1987 and 1991. Over the next 7 seasons Clemens won between 17 and 21 games every year, leading the league in earned run average 3 times over that span.

Clemens struggled from 1993 to 1996, averaging just 10 wins in an injury-plagued 4-year stretch, with losing records in 2 of those years. While he pitched well over much of that period, he no longer seemed to be the staff-carrying ace he had been while in his twenties (Clemens turned 30 in 1993). Some of this perception was based on his won-lost record with teams that had declining offensive punch. Despite his 40–39 record from 1993–96, however, Clemens was among the league leaders in ERA in 2 of those years—and would have won the ERA title in 1994 if teammate Wade Boggs hadn't convinced an official scorer to change an error charged to Boggs into a hit, adding several more earned runs to Clemens's total. (The ERA title would instead go to Steve Ontiveros, who would come out of retirement to pitch briefly for the Sox in 2000.) Clemens's relationship with the media also deteriorated during this period, and there were speculations in the media that his injuries and declining effectiveness were due to his gaining weight or otherwise being out of shape. Clemens was a great pitcher but not a great communicator, and once his superstar luster faded, some sportswriters delighted in poking fun at his sometimes-confusing statements and criticizing his perceived selfishness and his high salary. (Clemens had signed a longterm contract that made him the best-paid pitcher in the game before his performance declined.) Clemens was also criticized for failing to lead the Red Sox to the next level—although he was the ace of playoff teams in 1986, 1988, 1990, and 1995, Clemens was only 1–2 in 9 postseason starts. Clemens left the sixth (and potentially winning) game of the 1986 World Series because of a blister, only to see the bullpen blow the lead and lose the infamous "Bill Buckner" game. He also lost his temper and was thrown out of a key playoff game against Oakland.

Clemens's contract with the Sox was set to expire after the 1996 season, and attempts to extend the agreement proved fruitless. Clemens wanted another longterm deal that rewarded him as the best pitcher in the game, while Sox management was concerned about signing a 33-year-old pitcher coming off 4 good-but-not-great seasons to a big-money deal. General Manager Dan Duquette made an ill-considered remark about Clemens being in "the twilight of his career" that helped doom an increasingly contentious negotiation, although the Red Sox did eventually make a substantial offer. Clemens, for his part, made a series of seemingly contradictory statements—first he would only re-sign with the Red Sox, then only with the Red Sox or a Texas team (to be close to his Texas home), then only with a World Series contender, then only with a team that played in a different division than the Red Sox. Throughout all his statements he insisted that winning was more important than money. Instead, he ended up signing with a mediocre Toronto team (in the same division as the Sox) that offered to make him the best-paid pitcher in the game. Many Sox fans felt betrayed by Clemens's supposed about-face, coming as it did after months of media-fueled controversy and acrimony. (Circumstantial evidence of an illegal agreement between the Toronto front office and Clemens's agents while Clemens was still Sox property surfaced in 2000, but nothing was ever proven.)

In Toronto, Clemens seemed to be reborn. Whether it was a result of injuries healing or escaping the now-hostile Boston media, Clemens seemed to be more driven and in better shape in Toronto then he had been the previous years in Boston. He went 41–13 in 2 years with the Blue Jays, leading the league in earned run average both years and winning his unprecedented fourth and fifth Cy Young awards. He was then traded to the New York Yankees, where he was an important part of two World Championship teams.

Clemens is the all time Red Sox leader in victories; 192 of his 260 wins came in a Boston uniform. He leads all active pitchers in strikeouts with over 3,500, and is eighth on the all-time strikeout list. He set the record for strikeouts in an 1986 game against the Mariners in an electrifying performance and tied the record against the Detroit Tigers in 1996, confounding bitter Boston fans who thought he was playing out the string at the end of his Red Sox contract. He played in 7 All Star games, 6 of them for the Red Sox. He is certain to be a Hall of Famer as soon as he is eligible.

Boston fans' love/hate relationship with Roger Clemens continued through the 2000 season. Wildly popular in his first 8 years in Boston, and still popular in his last years in the city, when Clemens left for Toronto blame was split between Roger and Duquette, the GM who failed to re-sign him. When Clemens orchestrated a trade to the archrival Yankees, he became a player many fans loved to hate. Clemens was booed when he pitched badly against the Red Sox in the 1999 American League Championship Series. Perhaps the greatest highlight of the disappointing 2000 season was an epic pitching duel between Clemens and Sox ace Pedro Martinez. The game was won by Trot Nixon's dramatic ninth-inning home run. Clemens remains a contentious figure in Boston, sometimes booed, sometimes cheered, but always drawing huge audiences when he pitches against the Sox.

Reggie Cleveland—a righthanded starting pitcher acquired by Boston in December of 1973 from St. Louis, where he'd spent the first 5 years of his career. In 1973, Cleveland had had the best season of his career, going 14–10 in 32 starts for the Cardinals, with an ERA much better than league average. In Boston, the Red Sox got the pre-1973 version, who was worse than league average. He made 27 starts for the Sox, as well as 14 appearances out of the bullpen. He pitched slightly better in 1975, and that October, he was the first native Canadian to start a World Series game. He had another very good season in 1976, mostly out of the bullpen. In 1978, he made 1 appearance for the Sox, pitching just ⅓ inning and taking a loss, before being traded to Texas. He finished his career in 1981 with Milwaukee, pitching entirely in relief.

Michael Coleman—a former high school football star who had a great 1997 season in the minors (.305, with 21 homers and 24 steals in AA and AAA) and was anointed Boston's center fielder of the future, but alienated teammates, who derisively referred to his self-given nickname, "Prime Time." Coleman had a poor season in AAA in 1998, but hit 30 homers for Pawtucket in 1999. Expected to finally make the big club in 2000, Coleman was again sent to Pawtucket, where a wrist injury caused him to miss most of the season. Coleman was traded to Cincinnati after the 2000 season.

Jimmy Collins—Hall-of-Fame third baseman who jumped from the Boston Braves to the brand-new Red Sox in 1901 as player-manager. Collins hit .332 with 108 runs and 94 RBI for the first Red Sox team. He helped the Sox win the first World Series in 1903, as well as an American League title in 1904 (when the National League's Giants refused to play Boston in the World Series). Collins was relieved of his duties as manager during the 1906 season, and left Boston for the Philadelphia Athletics during the following season. He is often credited with being the first third baseman to position himself far off the base, enabling him to range further for balls hit to his left, and was the first third baseman to be elected to the Hall of Fame, in 1945.

Ray Collins—a lefthanded pitcher known for his ability to get Hall of Famer Ty Cobb out, Collins pitched for the Red Sox from 1909–15. During several of those years, he pitched a large number of innings, and was better than league average in ERA. He went 20–13 for the 1914 team, while throwing over 270 innings, and was limited to 104 innings in 1915, the worst season of his career, and the last.

Billy Conigliaro—weak-hitting outfielder who played 3 years for the Sox before finishing up with a year in Milwaukee and a year in Oakland. His biggest claim to fame was that he was Tony C's little brother.

Tony Conigliaro—a youthful, aggressive power-hitting outfielder with local roots whose life and career were marred by tragedy. Born in Revere in 1945 and raised in Swampscott, East Boston, and Lynn, Tony C came from a well-liked family. He signed with the Red Sox for $20,000 in 1963 and spent 1 season at Class A ball; Sox manager Johnny Pesky was so impressed by the young ballplayer that he immediately gave him a spot on the 1964 club. Conigliaro arrived in the majors with an ambitious attitude and no fears; in his major league debut at Yankee Stadium he even accused legendary pitcher Whitey Ford of throwing the spitball. A couple of weeks later, he lit up the Fenway Park opener with a home run on the first pitch he saw in his new home yard, a towering shot to left field off Joel Horlen in front of an audience of prestigious names present to honor slain president John F. Kennedy.

Despite being one of the youngest players in the league, Tony C possessed a quick swing and a brazen face, a combination that led to immediate success but also made him very unpopular among American League pitchers. He crowded the plate and challenged pitchers to throw inside, and missed many games early in his career from injuries to his right arm and left wrist after being hit by pitches. He finished his rookie season with 24 homers, and hit 32 in 1965 to lead the league at age 20. He also capitalized on his newfound popularity by signing a recording contract with RCA-Victor.

Early on, however, the Red Sox were unable to take advantage of their young star's success. Conigliaro was provided with little help in the lineup, and the pitching on the Sox teams of the mid-1960s was too mediocre to help turn his homers into wins. That changed in the Impossible Dream season of 1967, when the Sox got outstanding pitching from Jim Lonborg and consistent hitting from a lineup that featured Rico Petrocelli, George Scott, and Carl Yastrzemski. Conigliaro made his first and only All Star appearance in July of that year.

The Red Sox were in the thick of an unbelievable pennant race when the Sox met the California Angels for the opener of a weekend series at Fenway on the night of Friday, August 18. The game stayed scoreless into the fourth inning when, moments after Scott was thrown out at second trying to stretch out a single, a fan threw a smoke bomb into left field, delaying the game for 10 minutes. Fans and players in attendance were still buzzing about that surreal moment as Tony C stepped up to face Jack Hamilton with the bases empty and 2 outs. Hamilton's first pitch sailed up and caught Tony C in the face. Conigliaro barely moved when the pitch arrived; there would later be speculation that he could not see the ball against the background of white shirts in center field. The pitch broke Conigliaro's left cheekbone and damaged the retina in his eye. The Fenway crowd grew furious at Hamilton, as did Sox players who were convinced that the pitch was a spitball. A famous newspaper photo of Tony shows him sitting up in bed hours after the accident, his left eye swelled shiny like a plum.

His vision remained blurred for the rest of the season and into 1968. The rest of his career consisted of a series of comeback attempts in which he was forced to adjust to his weakened eyesight. He struggled in 1969 under manager Dick Williams, with whom he had constant disagreements, but came through with a 36-homer season under Eddie Kasko in 1970. The Red Sox helped ease Conigliaro's comeback when they acquired his younger brother Billy to join him in the outfield that year. Just as things were settling back into normalcy, however, a series of disagreements between the team and Conigliaro's father, Sal Conigliaro, led up to the Sox' decision to trade Tony C to the Angels that October, a decision that alienated the family from the team even further.

Adversity continued to follow Conigliaro after he left Boston. His vision worsened in 1971, leading to his premature retirement at age 26. An attempted return in 1975 proved unsuccessful. He finished an 8-year career with 166 home runs and a .264 batting average (a respectable average in the low-offense 1960s). In 1982 his efforts to secure a job as a commentator for Boston's WSBK-TV 38 ended after he suffered a massive heart attack. This setback debilitated Conigliaro for the rest of his life; he required chronic nursing care up until his sudden but quiet death on February 24, 1990 at the too-young age of 45. The Red Sox honored Conigliaro by wearing black armbands on their uniform sleeves that season, as they captured the eastern division title.

Gene Conley—a righthanded pitcher who started his career in Boston with the Braves, finished his career in Boston with the Red Sox, and played basketball for the Boston Celtics in between. In 1954 (the Braves' second season in Milwaukee), Conley, who hadn't pitched enough during the 1952 season to lose his rookie status, came in second in the Rookie of the Year balloting. That was probably his best season overall (14–9 with a 2.96 ERA for the Braves).

After 5 seasons in Milwaukee Conley pitched in Philadelphia for 2 years before finishing up with the Red Sox from 1961–63. He won 15 games for the Sox in 1962. He also briefly deserted the team on one bizarre occasion. In a New York city traffic jam Conley and infielder Pumpsie Green got off the team bus. Green reported to the team hotel that night, but Conley was gone for three days. For reasons that remain unclear, he had tried to fly to Israel, but was unable to because he didn't have a passport.

Conley won a World Series ring in 1957 in Milwaukee with the Braves. He also won 3 NBA championship rings as a backup center for the Boston Celtics. He blew out his arm in 1963 and was released by the Sox after the season. He had a tryout with the Indians during spring training before the 1964 season, but his days of professional athletics were over.

Billy Consolo—a very weak-hitting infielder. Many current Red Sox fans tended to think of the team as being unwilling to spend big money (at least, before the Manny Ramirez signing in late 2000), but that wasn't always the case. In fact, in November of 1952 baseball implemented a rule to discourage the large bonuses that Tom Yawkey had been paying players, requiring that any player who received a bonus of $30,000 or more remain on the major league roster for 2 years. Billy Consolo was the first victim of this rule. Whether he would ever have developed is unknowable, but it can't have helped to make the jump from high school to the majors without the option of any minor league seasoning (at the ages of 18 and 19 he was sitting on the bench and playing intermittently for the 1953–54 Red Sox). He never did learn to hit, finishing his 10-year career with 9 home runs and a paltry .315 on-base percentage. Boston finally gave up on him during 1959, and he played for 5 different teams over the next 3 years before his career ended in 1962 at the age of 27. Consolo went on to be a longtime coach. He was also a licensed barber.

Cecil Cooper—a fill-in player at first base and designated hitter for 6 seasons with the Red Sox, Cooper went on to become an offensive and defensive star with the Milwaukee Brewers. Cooper hit well in part-time play in Boston, batting between .275 and .311 with decent power in the 3 seasons he was given at least 300 at bats by the Red Sox, from 1974–76. Cooper was traded to Milwaukee for aging first baseman George Scott before the 1977 season. Scott turned out to have 1 last good season left in him, hitting .269 with 33 home runs before fading into oblivion. Cooper, installed as Milwaukee's starting first baseman, would hit over .300 for each of the next 7 years on his way to a .298 lifetime batting average, 241 career home runs, and 5 All Star Game appearances.

Scott Cooper—lefthanded-hitting third baseman during the dismal Hobson era of the early 1990s. Cooper was a highly thought of prospect who replaced Wade Boggs at third base. He once hit for the cycle in a game in Kansas City, and made two All Star teams as a member of the Red Sox (mainly because the rules state that each team *has* to have at least one All Star) but never really lived up to his promise. Cooper's main point of notoriety for Sox fans is that GM Lou Gorman wouldn't part with him in a trade for reliever Larry Andersen, so Houston had to settle for future Hall-of-Famer Jeff Bagwell instead. Red Sox fans will surely get over this trade someday, but all anecdotal evidence suggests that it won't be for a good, long time. Cooper was traded to St. Louis for Rheal Cormier after the 1994 season.

Wil Cordero—a promising young infielder acquired by the Red Sox before the 1996 season to fill their second base hole. The Sox sent pitcher Rheal Cormier to the Montreal Expos for the 25-year-old shortstop. Wilfredo Cordero was a poor defender at shortstop (he committed 33 errors in 1993), but he was fast and athletic, and had good offensive potential. The Sox hoped that moving him to second base (a slightly easier defensive position than shortstop) would help him defensively, and that he would develop into a powerful offensive threat. The plan didn't work; Cordero committed 10 errors in only 37 games at second base in 1996 before suffering a freak injury (he broke his leg after being spiked by a runner sliding into second) in May. Jeff Frye, who was brought in from Texas to fill in, played brilliantly while Cordero was out, ending Cordero's second base experiment. When Cordero came back he was a left fielder and designated hitter. The injury robbed Cordero of much of his speed, and he never developed into the star he was projected to be. His hitting was decent for a second baseman (a position that emphasizes defense, so it is hard to find good hitters who can play) but not for a left fielder (one of the easiest positions to play).

Cordero is mostly remembered for the 1997 season, in which he was arrested in a domestic abuse incident. Although his wife refused to press charges and there were conflicting accounts of what happened, many fans were outraged by the perception that Cordero didn't take the charges seriously. Cordero was eventually suspended and ordered by the team to undergo counseling. While he was suspended and supposedly dealing with the problem (and just as the furor was dying down, with many fans arguing that he should be given a second chance), Cordero appeared on an ESPN interview, relaxing at poolside in a bathing suit, and said that he and his wife didn't need counseling and didn't have any problems.

Unpopular with fans, mediocre at the plate, and a headache to the front office, Cordero was released by the Red Sox after the season. Interestingly, despite his problems in Boston, Cordero retained ties to Boston's Latino community and was reportedly instrumental in convincing superstar outfielder Manny Ramirez to sign as a free agent with the Red Sox after the 2000 season. Cordero currently plays for the Cleveland Indians.

Rheal Cormier—lefthanded pitcher who enjoyed 2 stints with the Red Sox, the first as a starter and the second as a reliever. A French-speaking native of Canada, Cormier came up with the St. Louis Cardinals as a starter and pitched decently before being traded to the Sox after the 1994 season (for third baseman Scott Cooper). Cormier went 7–5 in 48 games for the Sox in 1995, before being traded to Montreal for infielder Wilfredo Cordero (they wanted him because he was a French speaker), but only pitched one full season for the Expos. He returned to the Sox in 1999 as a free agent reclamation project following a severe injury that took almost 2 years to recover from. The Sox worked around Cormier's permanently weakened arm by converting him into a lefty bullpen specialist. He did relatively well in this role, appearing in 124 games over 2 seasons as part of an extraordinary relief corps that was one of the most effective in the league. The Red Sox declined his request for a substantial raise after the 2000 season, and Cormier signed a high-priced free agent contract with the Philadelphia Phillies.

Jim Corsi—righthanded relief pitcher, Corsi is a Newton, Massachusetts, native who bounced around the majors for 10 seasons over 12 years (including 3 separate stints with the Oakland A's) but never had a secure grip on a major league job. He was a generally effective middle reliever, without the wins of a starter or the saves of a closer. He relied on guile and control rather than an overpowering fastball. Corsi signed with Boston prior to the 1997 season, and pitched very well out of the bullpen for the Sox for 2 years. Basically, given the chance to pitch in his hometown in the twilight of his career, Corsi responded with the seasons of his life. In 1999, at age 37, he pitched very badly and was released yet again. He signed on with Baltimore but pitched only briefly for the Orioles, then retired after going to spring training with the Arizona Diamondbacks before the 2000 season.

Ted Cox—a much-heralded third baseman who had burned his way through the Sox minor league system, Cox was called up in September of 1977 and had hits in his first 6 at bats, setting a major league record. The Red Sox reluctantly agreed to include Cox in a trade to Cleveland for pitcher Dennis Eckersley the next spring. Cox never turned into the star he was projected to be, however. He made stops in Cleveland, Seattle, and Toronto but hit only .245 for his career; Cox was out of baseball at age 26.

Doc Cramer—leadoff hitter and center fielder in the 1930s and 1940s, Cramer played for 20 years in the major leagues, 5 of them with the Red Sox during the heart of his career (1936–1940). He was already a star when the Red Sox bought him and Jimmie Foxx from the cash-strapped Philadelphia A's before the 1936 season. Cramer was a 5-time All Star, 4 of his 5 appearances coming as a Red Sox player. He was remarkably consistent with the Red Sox, hitting between .292 and .311 every year and providing excellent defense. (A Philadelphia sportswriter nicknamed him Flit, after an insecticide, because Cramer was deadly against fly balls.) He rarely homered (once in his 5 years with the Sox), but was usually among the league leaders in doubles and triples, although this was more a product of how many times he came to the plate than any actual power; since Cramer led off for good offensive teams, stayed healthy, and seldom walked, he was close to the league lead in at-bats and hits every year. He holds a major league record by leading the league in at bats 7 times. He also twice tied a major league record by going 6-for-6 in a game, both times before he played for the Red Sox.

Paxton Crawford—righthanded starting pitcher called up by the Red Sox for the first time in 2000. He pitched well in limited appearances just before the All Star break, then was sent back to the minor leagues so he wouldn't get rusty during the break, with the expectation that he would be called back up 10 days later. Instead, he suffered a freak injury when he rolled out of bed and landed on a glass, cutting open his back. Crawford wasn't able to return to the Sox until September, when he again pitched well.

Steve Crawford—a hulking righthanded pitcher who spent most of the 1980s with the Red Sox, Crawford came up as a starting pitcher. Despite his imposing size and menacing appearance, Crawford was not a strikeout pitcher. He always gave up a lot of hits, and relied on good control for his success. In 1981 he lost all 5 decisions in 11 starts. He only got to start 1 more game over the rest of his 10-year career. Sent back to the minors, Crawford didn't return for good until 1984. He pitched solidly for the next 3 years as one of the only reliable relievers on teams with terrible bullpens. He filled in as closer for a while in 1985 and led the team in saves (with only 12; Bob Stanley was second with 10). He pitched well in the 1986 playoffs, winning Game 2 of the World Series in relief of Roger Clemens, but not well enough to overcome the rest of the bullpen's failings. After a poor season in 1987 he was sent to Kansas City, where he pitched for 3 more undistinguished years.

Lou Criger—Cy Young's personal catcher, Lou Criger played for 16 years, 8 of them with the Red Sox (1901–08). He played with Young in Cleveland and St. Louis as well as Boston. Criger was a terrible hitter, batting .221 for his career and hitting below .200 in 9 different seasons (league average was around .250 for most of those years.), although he did have a high walk total for the period. Not surprisingly, his career in Boston ended at the same time Young's did.

Joe Cronin—one of the greatest shortstops in baseball history, and one of 5 men to have his number retired by the Red Sox. During a remarkable 58-year career, Cronin did it all: superstar player, pennant-winning manager, general manager, American League President, and American League Chairman. He spent 24 of those years with the Red Sox, and was one of the key Tom Yawkey acquisitions (along with Lefty Grove and Jimmie Foxx) who brought the franchise back to respectability. Cronin is one of the giants of Red Sox history, though some of his decisions as an executive would haunt the team for decades.

He began his big league career with Pittsburgh in 1926, but the Pirates already had an outstanding shortstop in Glenn Wright. The Washington Senators acquired Cronin in 1928, and he became a regular a year later. In 1930, Cronin had his best season, batting .346 with 41 doubles, 13 homers, and 126 RBI, plus 72 walks and 17 steals. He won the MVP, though some sources don't consider the award official (the modern MVP award began in 1931). Cronin continued to play at a high level for Washington from 1931–34, batting over .300 three times, with over 100 RBI each year. His home park, Griffith Stadium, had the deepest left field in baseball (407 feet down the line), and it undoubtedly cost Cronin many homers, though he usually hit over 40 doubles and 10 triples a year. Reports on Cronin's defense vary. Statistical methods indicate that he was excellent in Washington, but not as good in Boston. Observers were split on his fielding, though shortstops who hit well are often assumed to be subpar defensively no matter how well they play (as is the case with Nomar Garciaparra today).

In 1933, Cronin became player-manager and piloted the Senators to their last pennant, though they lost the World Series. He also played shortstop in the first All Star Game, the first of his 7 appearances in the midsummer classic. Late in the 1934 season he married the daughter of Washington's Hall of Fame owner, Clark Griffith. During Cronin's honeymoon, new Red Sox owner Tom Yawkey offered Griffith $250,000 and shortstop Lyn Lary for his son-in-law. Griffith frantically called Cronin, who agreed that it was "an offer he couldn't refuse." The deal was finalized, and Yawkey fired Hall of Fame manager Bucky Harris to let Cronin continue doing double-duty.

But 1935 was a frustrating season for Cronin. He hit .295 with 95 RBI, but the shift to Fenway only raised his home run total from 7 to 9. As a manager, he improved Boston's record by just 2 games. Cronin's year was epitomized by a September 7 game against Cleveland at Fenway. The Sox trailed, 5–1, with the bases loaded and no outs in the bottom of the ninth. Cronin, the tying run, hit a bullet off the third baseman's forehead. The ball caromed directly into the shortstop's glove, and he started a triple play to end the game. 1936 was even worse for Cronin, as injuries limited him to 81 games (and 2 home runs).

Cronin finally figured out Fenway in 1937, and he began an outstanding 5-year stretch. During that span, he hit .307 with 99 homers and 517 RBI. In 1940 he hit a career-high 24 homers, and the Red Sox became the first big league team to have each infielder hit more than 20 (first baseman Jimmie Foxx had 36; second baseman Bobby Doerr hit 22; third baseman Jim Tabor had 21). Cronin continued to hit extremely well in 1941, his fifth standout season in a row. However, he couldn't run well anymore, and his defense was deteriorating. He played only 119 games at shortstop in 1941, while appearing in 22 at third base. The following spring, the 35-year-old Cronin decided to bench himself in favor of impressive rookie Johnny Pesky, who wound up hitting .331. For the next four years, Cronin devoted himself almost entirely to managing. (He managed the Sox to second place finishes in 1938, 1939, and 1941, and the team was clearly on the rise.) Cronin had only 355 at bats from 1942–45, and rarely played the field (54 games at first, 24 at third, and just 1 at shortstop). He was, however, a superb pinch hitter; in 1943, he hit an American League record 5 pinch-homers. He managed the Sox to another second place finish in 1942, but the team struggled in 1943–45.

After the players serving in World War II returned, Cronin felt there was no need to remain on the active roster. (His 1945 season had been ended after only 3 games by a broken leg.) He retired with a .301 average, 170 home runs, and 2,285 hits, eventually earning him election into the Hall of Fame in 1956, with a Red Sox "B" on his plaque, though his stats were slightly better in Washington. 1946 was his first year as a nonplaying manager, and everything came together—at least until the World Series. Cronin's Red Sox won 104 games, the second-most in team history (the 1912 edition had 105), and took the American League pennant by 12 games. But after an excruciating World Series loss to the Cardinals in October, the team limped to an 83–71 mark in 1947, and Cronin's managerial career came to an end. His 1,071 wins are still the most of any Red Sox skipper, though he was often criticized for overusing his pitchers and wasting his team's potent offense.

Owner Tom Yawkey kicked Cronin upstairs, and he became the Red Sox GM, serving in that capacity from 1948–58. The team went downhill in the 1950s. A commonly cited reason was the Red Sox long delay in integrating the team. While Cronin was manager, the Red Sox gave tryouts to Jackie Robinson and Sam Jethroe (later a National League Rookie of the Year with the crosstown Braves), but failed to sign either player. During Cronin's tenure as GM, they also passed on a golden chance to sign Willie Mays. The Red Sox didn't have a black player until the year Cronin left. It is unclear how much of this was the fault of Cronin, who was generally described as a kind, funny, friendly man. But the fact remains that this unfortunate period happened under his watch. Cronin had other personnel problems as well. In 1937, he instigated the trade of star pitcher Wes Ferrell, the leader of an outspoken anti-Cronin clique in the clubhouse. Also in the late 1930s, he convinced Yawkey to sell minor league shortstop Pee Wee Reese to the Dodgers, where he became a Hall of Famer. Some accounts say Cronin was jealous of the young infielder, while others indicate that he merely thought Reese wasn't good enough. Even though the Sox had another fine young shortstop in Johnny Pesky, Cronin's decision on Reese was shortsighted.

In any case, Cronin's association with the Red Sox ended in 1959, when he was elected President of the American League. He served in that role until 1973, and was nominated for Commissioner at least once in the interim. In 1974, Cronin took a largely ceremonial position as American League Chairman of the Board, a position he held for the remainder of his life. Early in the 1980s, Cronin became seriously ill, and the Red Sox decided to retire his #4 in May 1984 (at the time an honor that had been bestowed only upon Ted Williams). A Joe Cronin Night was hastily assembled, and the great shortstop watched the proceedings from a private box. Four months later, Cronin died. Nomar Garciaparra has already surpassed him as shortstop on the Red Sox all-time team, but Cronin's overall mark on the franchise is unmistakable, and will never be forgotten.

Rich Croushore—a righthanded pitcher aquired as part of the trade that also brought Rolando Arrojo and Mike Lansing from Colorado to Boston for pitchers Brian Rose and John Wasdin and infielder Jeff Frye in July 2000. Croushore had been rumored to be coming to Boston for months, so it was a slight surprise when he was assigned to AAA Pawtucket, and not called up in September when the major league rosters were expanded. He pitched fewer than 5 innings, all in middle relief.

Leon Culberson—a backup outfielder who took an injured Dom DiMaggio's place in the outfield late in the seventh game of the 1946 World Series. His weak throw to cutoff man Johnny Pesky allowed Enos Slaughter to score from first with what proved to be the deciding run of the series. Culberson was a righthanded-hitting out-fielder who had been a fill-in player while most of the stars were in the military in World War II. Although he was a decent backup (hitting .313 as a part-timer in 1946), he is mainly remembered for the throw that cost the series. He hung on in a limited role in Boston until 1947, and was out of baseball after 1948, at age 29.

Ray Culp—a righthanded starting pitcher who was a former Rookie of the Year in the National League, Culp spent the last 6 years of his career in Boston, from 1968–73. He was acquired in the winter following the "Impossible Dream" season, in hopes of providing a boost for the pitching staff and helping the team build on the success of 1967. Interestingly enough, the same offseason saw the Red Sox add Dick Ellsworth. The previous offseason, Ellsworth and Culp had been traded for each other, with Culp leaving the Phillies that he had come up with to go to the Cubs, and Ellsworth going from Chicago to Philadelphia.

Culp hadn't pitched well in either of the 2 seasons prior to coming to Boston. He had experienced arm problems the year before, but recovered and added a palm ball to his arsenal. This led to a 16–6 record and career-best 2.91 ERA in his first year in Boston. At one point during the 1968 season, he threw 4 consecutive shutouts. In 1969, Culp's 17–8 record and 3.81 ERA led to an All Star Game berth. In 1970, he tied a major league record when he struck out the first 6 men that he faced in a game in May. The 1970 season was probably his best, as he went 17–14 with a 3.04 ERA in a league where the average ERA was 3.97. Culp struggled badly in 1972 and in 1973 he only threw 50 innings before retiring.

Midre Cummings—lefthanded-hitting outfielder with tremendous talent and terrible baseball instincts. Cummings spent parts of 2 seasons with the Red Sox, primarily as a pinch hitter, in 1998 and 2000, although the Red Sox did not re-sign him at the end of either season. Although he could hit and was a fast runner, Cummings's fielding was erratic, and he ran into outs frequently on the bases. He was never able to hold onto a job at any of his many major league stops. He signed with the Arizona Diamondbacks after the 2000 season, his fifth major league team in an 8-year career.

John Curtis—A local hero from nearby Newton, Massachusetts, Curtis was considered a can't-miss prospect, but settled for a respectable 15-year career. Curtis starred at Clemson University, where he pitched 3 no-hitters. In the 1967 Pan Am games, he became the first American to defeat the Cuban National Team. The lefthander joined the Sox as a 22-year-old, pitching 1 game in 1970. After a terrific September performance in 1971 (2–2, 3.12, 19 strikeouts and 6 walks in 26 innings), Curtis was expected to be a mainstay in Boston's rotation. He had a solid rookie year in 1972 (11–8, 3.73), and an even better sophomore season (13–13, 3.58, 221 innings). But in December 1973, Curtis was traded to St. Louis in a 6-player deal (the Red Sox got Reggie Cleveland and Diego Segui). He pitched until 1984, mainly as a spot starter and long reliever, but never matched his early success.

Danny Darwin—an injury prone 35-year-old pitcher, Darwin was signed to a 4-year deal as a free agent by Sox GM Lou Gorman. Darwin was coming off a terrific year— he had won the ERA title with Houston in 1990, going 11–4 while shuttling between the starting rotation and long relief. He did pitch well for Boston while healthy, which was about half the time. He went 15–11 as a full-time starter in 1993, but it was the only year out of 4 that he was able to make more than 15 starts. Remarkably, Darwin continued to pitch for years after he left the Red Sox, playing for more than 20 years in the big leagues altogether. In some ways, Darwin was symbolic of the free agent signings Gorman made toward the end of his tenure as Sox GM—aging, expensive players signed to try to keep the club marginally competitive rather than rebuilding with young players.

Brian Daubach—minor league free agent signed by Dan Duquette shortly after the departure of Mo Vaughn. A total unknown to many Sox fans, the 27-year-old rookie first baseman suddenly attracted attention by putting up strong numbers during spring training in 1999. He continued his strong performance during the season after an injury to Reggie Jefferson opened up some playing time for him. He finished the year with a .294 average, 21 home runs, and 73 RBI as a platoon first baseman, DH, and occasional outfielder. His numbers were good enough for him to finish fourth in Rookie of the Year balloting and to become a fan favorite, with his distinctive sideburns that made him look, as one reporter put it, like a 1970s porn star.

Many fans feared that Daubach would be a 1-year wonder, like many other older rookies who experience success after finally making the major leagues, and the doubts grew when Daubach slumped horribly late in the 1999 season (his average was about .340 in August) before recovering at the end of the season and in the playoffs. However, Daubach opened the 2000 season in torrid fashion, hitting homers in his first two at-bats. Despite shaving the signature sideburns early in the 2000 season, he remained a fan favorite.

On August 16, Daubach had what many fans considered the signature at-bat of the 1999 season, the moment that most embodied the Sox refusal to quit in the face of a series of injuries to key pitchers, and overwhelming media skepticism about the team's chances following the contentious loss of Mo Vaughn to free agency. Boston had fallen behind early to an Oakland team (whom they would be dueling for a playoff spot over the next six weeks), and only great relief pitching kept them at the fringes of the game. The wind was blowing in all night, and several Boston drives that looked like sure home runs had been turned into warning-track-length fly balls. The Sox clawed back into it in the ninth inning, and Daubach came to the plate with the bases loaded, Boston down by two, and the crowd going wild. He got two quick strikes on him and then fouled off pitch after pitch before shooting a screaming line drive past the Pesky Pole—called just barely foul by the umpire amid loud booing. Despite the letdown of the foul home run call, Daubach held his focus and drove a pitch high off the Green Monster, with a streaking Jose Offerman barely beating the throw home with the winning run. Afterward Daubach (who'd had to endure clubhouse tension because of his role as a potential replacement player during the 1994 strike) looked both pleased and embarrassed—the players mobbed him, and the crowd gave him a huge standing ovation the whole time he was standing there doing a radio interview and kept on cheering until he bashfully acknowledged it. After 9 years in the minor leagues, being released by the last-place Florida Marlins, and being sent back to the minors early in the season by the Sox, Brian Daubach had made the major leagues for good.

He remained streaky with increased playing time in 2000, hitting 21 homers with 76 RBI but going through torrid hot streaks and long cold spells. After several Tampa Bay players ganged up on Daubach in an onfield brawl (and reportedly lay in wait for him after the game) and 1 stomped on his hand with cleats, he was unable to hit for the last month of the season. Manager Jimy Williams kept playing him despite the injury, leaving him with a final batting average of .248.

Andre Dawson—a righthanded-hitting outfielder, the Hawk had been a star ballplayer for years: a Gold Glove outfielder who could hit for average and power, and could steal bases. But not for the Red Sox. When GM Lou Gorman signed Dawson to a lucrative free agent contract prior to the 1993 season, he was a 38-year-old full-time DH with 17 major league seasons of wear and tear on his failing knees (he'd already had more than 10 knee operations, and would have several more while with Boston) who had already hit 399 of his 438 career home runs. He played two ineffective, injury-plagued years for Boston before finishing his career with the expansion Florida Marlins.

Rob Deer—a big righthanded outfielder, Deer came up with the San Francisco Giants but made his name as a member of the Milwaukee Brewers in the late 1980s. After 2½ years in Detroit, the Sox acquired him late in the 1993 season. At the time they made the trade, Andre Dawson was unable to play the field anymore because of the condition of his knees, and Boston was alternating Carlos Quintana, Ivan Calderon, and Bob Zupcic in right field. They were also last in the league in home runs, and hoped that Deer would address that. In his 38 games for the Sox, Deer hit 7 home runs, including one in his first Fenway Park plate appearance in a Boston uniform. But he hit .196 and only walked 20 times, and Boston finished tied with California for last in the league in home runs. The Red Sox also finished in fifth place in the AL East, and did not re-sign Deer following the season.

Deer still holds the American League record for strikeouts in a season, with his 186 whiffs in 1987. As he was going through the minor leagues, he won home run titles at 3 different minor league levels, but also led leagues in strikeouts 4 times. He was in the top 10 in the American League in strikeouts during all 8 seasons in which he played more than 100 games in the major leagues. He also walked frequently, so that his on-base percentages were not as bad as his batting averages.

He developed a cult following and fan club on the Internet, as the modern master of the so-called "Three True Outcomes," because his plate appearances so frequently ended in a strikeout, a home run, or a walk. They are the only 3 outcomes in which the pitcher-batter confrontation, which is the heart of baseball competition, is determined only by the pitcher and batter, with no help from the rest of the team. After finishing the 1993 season with Boston, Deer was out of the majors for 2 years. He finished his career hitting .180 for the San Diego Padres, with a staggering 30 strikeouts in only 64 plate appearances, in 1996.

Brian Denman—a Sox minor league phenom after going 15–3 in AA in 1981, Denman started nine games in the majors in 1982, and pitched decently—including a shutout against the Yankees in his final game. The following year in Spring Training he lashed out bitterly at manager Ralph Houk after being sent back to the minors without being given what he thought was a fair chance to make the team. Houk was not amused, and Denman was never seen in the major leagues again.

Dom DiMaggio—younger brother of Joe DiMaggio and Vince DiMaggio, Dom played his entire career for the Red Sox, mostly as starting center fielder and lead-off hitter. Dom DiMaggio wasn't a superstar like his brother Joe, but he played 10 years in the major leagues (1940–52, with the 1943–45 seasons spent in the military during World War II and 3 token appearances during 1953) without ever having a bad season. His lowest batting average was .283 (he hit as high as .328, and batted .298 for his career) and he walked frequently. As the table setter for several terrific offensive teams, DiMaggio scored more than 100 runs 6 times in his career, leading the league in runs twice and averaging over 100 runs a year for his career. He also led the league in stolen bases in 1950 with only 15 steals, at a time when stolen bases were rare.

Big Bill Dinneen—though normally overshadowed by Cy Young, this reliable #2 starter was the hero of the Red Sox first World Series victory in 1903. Dinneen pitched a 3-hit shutout against Pittsburgh in Game 2, and clinched the Sox first championship with a 4-hit shutout in Game 8. (The 1903 World Series, the first of the modern era, was a best of 9). Overall, Dinneen was 3–1 with a 2.06 ERA in the 1903 Series. Dinneen had jumped to the Red Sox from the Boston Braves in 1902. He won 21 games or more in each of his first 3 seasons with the Red Sox, but this was not as rare or prestigious a feat as it is today. Dinneen slipped a bit in 1905 and 1906, and was shipped to the St. Louis Browns early in 1907. After retiring as a player, Dinneen umpired in the American League for 29 seasons (from 1909–37).

Joe Dobson—a righthanded pitcher who spent 2 years with the Indians before being traded to the Red Sox prior to the 1941 season. With the exception of the 1942–43 seasons which he spent in the military, Dobson was one of the members of the Red Sox starting rotation through the 1950 season. He was never a great pitcher, but he was good and consistent for a long time. Dobson won 76 games for the Sox over the span of 1946–1950, a time when they went to the World Series once and just missed on a couple more occasions. He threw a 4-hitter (though 3 unearned runs scored) in Game 5 of the 1946 World Series to give the Sox a 3–2 lead in the series.

He was traded to the White Sox in December of 1950, and had what might have been his best season in 1952, going 14–10 with a 2.51 ERA. But that was close to the end of the line. In 1953 half of his appearances came out of the bullpen, then usually a home for declining pitchers. In 1954 he was back with the Red Sox, but pitched less than 3 innings in 2 games before his career ended.

Pat Dodson—a much-heralded slugging first base prospect who never quite made it. Dodson put up terrific minor league numbers, but didn't hit well in 3 brief major league appearances from 1986–1988, totalling only 99 at bats. He struck out in a third of his at bats, but also walked frequently. He didn't make it to the majors until he was 26, and was never given more than 45 at bats in a season to prove himself.

Bobby Doerr—a very good second baseman for the strong Sox teams of the 1940s. After making the team at the age of 19, Doerr became the regular second baseman in 1938 at age 20, a job he would not relinquish until 1951. An excellent fielder, Doerr showed steady improvement in his hitting through his first few years in the league, reaching highs in many major categories in 1940, when he finished seventh in the league in total bases and RBI (with 105, the first time he topped the 100 RBI mark). The next season, Doerr made the first of his 9 All Star appearances, although his overall numbers were not quite as good as the year before.

As the major league ranks began to be depleted by the war, Doerr continued to show considerable pop for a second baseman. (Since it's a key defensive position and it's hard to find players who are good both offensively and defensively, many second basemen are light hitters.) From 1942 to 1945, Doerr finished in the top 10 in doubles twice, in home runs 3 times, in RBI twice, in slugging percentage 3 times, in on-base percentage once, in hits once, and in runs once. His best wartime season was 1944, when he led the league in slugging, finished second in batting average, finished third in on base-percentage, and enjoyed top-10 status in runs, triples, home runs, and RBI. His average, on-base percentage, and slugging numbers all set career highs.

With the return of the regulars at the end of the war, Doerr was an important part of the 1946 team which blew away the competition to reach the World Series. In that World Series, while players such as Pinky Higgins, Johnny Pesky, and the injured Ted Williams had great difficulty with Cardinal pitching, Doerr was the unofficial MVP in the Sox losing effort, hitting .409, with a .458 on-base percentage, and a .591 slugging percentage. (To be fair, Doerr's hitting stats may be a little misleading. He hit .315 with 145 homers at Fenway Park, but only .261 with 78 homers on the road, so he was a great Fenway hitter, but just a good hitter away from home.)

From 1946 to the end of his career in 1951, Doerr continued to play excellent defense and hit well. In 4 of those 6 years, he had over 100 RBI (setting a career high in 1950 with 120) and twice he reached 27 home runs, putting him in the top 10 for the American League. He also led the American League in fielding percentage 4 times, in putouts 4 times, and in assists 3 times. He led the league in double plays turned 5 times, a record. He also holds the big league record with 8 double plays (fielding) in a doubleheader (in 1950). In 1948, he handled 414 consecutive chances without an error. He made 9 All Star teams.

Doerr retired young in 1951 because of major back problems. At that time, his 1,865 games played were the most in Red Sox history. After his retirement, Doerr's excellence as a fielder and slugger were belatedly recognized when he was elected to the Hall of Fame in 1986 (he used to appear frequently on "Why isn't he in the Hall of Fame" columns). His #1 was subsequently retired by the Sox, honoring the player who was the best all-time Red Sox second baseman.

Doerr made an additional contribution to the Sox as well. Dick Williams hired him as first base coach in 1967, and Carl Yastrzemski credited Doerr with helping him turn into a triple crown hitter that year. Doerr coached with Boston until 1969, and also coached for Toronto in their first 5 years (1977–81).

John Dopson—righthanded pitcher acquired from Montreal for Spike Owen after the 1988 season. Dopson first appeared in the majors briefly in 1985, but due to injuries did not resurface until 1988, when he went 3–11 with an excellent 3.04 ERA for a bad team. His first year for Boston was his best as a major leaguer; he started 28 games and went 12–8. Dopson was neither a hard thrower nor a control artist, and after more injuries (the next 2 years he appeared in a total of 5 games) he lost his ability to fool hitters. In 1992 and 1993 Dopson started 53 games and went a combined 14–22 for bad Red Sox teams. He finished his career in 1994 with the California (now Anaheim) Angels. Dopson was emblematic of the Sox second-line pitching in the late 1980s and early 1990s—a borderline major league pitcher who teased fans with flashes of brilliance and stretches of success but never developed into a consistently effective player (e.g., Tom Bolton, Eric Hetzel, Mike Rochford).

Patsy Dougherty—righthanded-hitting outfielder who spent the first 2½ seasons of his 10-season career with the Red Sox (actually the Boston Pilgrims) from 1902–04.

He hit .342 and .331 in his first 2 years with the Red Sox, but never hit higher than .285 over the rest of his career (although he led the league in stolen bases in 1908). In 1903 he hit 2 home runs in Game 2 of the first World Series. The Red Sox sent him to the New York Highlanders midway through 1904; he was later traded to the Chicago White Sox after getting into a fistfight with the New York manager.

Dick Drago—former ace starting pitcher of the expansion Kansas City Royals, Drago had begun to break down from overwork by the time Boston traded pitcher Marty Pattin for him after the 1973 season. After a mediocre 1974 season, the 30-year-old righthander moved into the bullpen in 1975, and took over as the Sox relief ace down the stretch, saving 15 games. In the playoffs he pitched well, saving 2 games and only giving up 1 run in 4 appearances—but it was a big run, costing the Sox Game 2 of the World Series. Drago was traded to California after the season and then to Baltimore the next year before returning to the Red Sox as a free agent. He pitched very well for the Sox in 1978 (saving 7 games to finish second on the team) and 1979 (when he won 10 games in relief and saved 13 more) and decently in 1980, when he was pressed into use as an emergency starter at times. The Sox traded him to Seattle during Spring Training in 1981, where Drago pitched poorly and then retired.

In 1976, while pitching for California, Drago gave up Hank Aaron's 755th and final home run.

Walt Dropo—"The Moose from Moosup" was a hulking first baseman from northeast Connecticut who was Rookie of the Year in 1950. Called up to replace the injured Billy Goodman early in the season, Dropo hit .322, with 36 homers and a league-leading 144 runs batted in. He dropped to .239 his second year, and never hit better than .281 in the major leagues again (he only hit more than 19 homers once more in 13 seasons). Boston traded him to Detroit in 1952, and he drifted from team to team for years but never recaptured the magic of his first season in the majors.

Jumpin' Joe Dugan—a righthanded third baseman who played in 85 games with the Red Sox in 1922, 21 of them at shortstop. An alumnus of Holy Cross College in Worcester, Dugan was acquired in a 3-way deal before the 1922 season. Members of the Boston press, by this time critical of every move that owner Harry Frazee made (after Frazee had sold the core of his team to the New York Yankees), claimed that the Sox had only traded for Dugan because the Yankees wanted him, and that he'd never play a game in a Boston uniform. They were wrong. He played 85 of them before being traded (along with Elmer Smith) to the Yankees on July 22 for a couple of backup players and cash. Dugan went on to become one of the key members of the Yankees' first dynasty. The trade caused some commotion in baseball since it seemed to give the Yankees—who were in the midst of a tight pennant race—an unfair advantage, and led to a June 15 trading deadline the following season.

Mike Easler—"The Hitman" was a lefthanded hitting specialist who played for the Sox in the mid-1980s and later was a controversial hitting coach. Easler had bounced up and down between the major and minor leagues for years before finally sticking with the Pittsburgh Pirates in 1980, at age 29. He was a poor outfielder, but a deadly hitter against righthanded pitching. Pittsburgh platooned Easler with a righthanded-hitting outfielder, never batting him more than 475 times in a season, but after Boston traded pitcher John Tudor for him, the 33-year-old Easler was given a shot as a full-time DH and occasional outfielder or first baseman. Easler excelled at the plate in 1984, hitting .313 with 27 home runs, but tailed off the next season (especially against lefty pitching). He was traded to the Yankees for Don Baylor, who would be the DH on the 1986 World Series team.

Ironically, Easler had been Red Sox property prior to the Tudor trade. In the late 1970s, the Sox claimed him off the Pirates roster in the Rule 5 Draft. Easler was on the Sox 40-man roster and played in spring training, but didn't make the team, and the Pirates got him back. Considering how good a hitter Easler was, he could have helped out in the late 1970s and early 1980s, and wouldn't have cost the Sox Tudor.

Easler returned to the Red Sox as hitting coach after the 1992 season, and was immediately successful. He was credited with helping Mo Vaughn's development (Vaughn continued to work with Easler after his firing). However, he fell out with the Red Sox front office, first over new GM Dan Duquette's perceived failure to back him in a dispute with Sox pitching coach Al Nipper during the 1994 winter league season (the dispute led to Easler being fired as manager of Caguas in the Puerto Rican league), then over his reluctance to coach replacement players during the 1995 strike. When bad feelings escalated into a salary dispute, Easler was replaced as Red Sox hitting coach by Jim Rice. Easler, an ordained minister, is currently hitting coach for the St. Louis Cardinals.

Dennis Eckersley—righthanded pitcher who had two stints with the Sox, in two totally disparate incarnations of his career. He came up as a fireballing starter, winning the American League Rookie pitcher of the year award in 1975 as a member of the Cleveland Indians. After 3 seasons in Cleveland, Eck was traded to Boston in March of 1978 and went on to have the best starting season of his career. He went 20–8 with a 2.99 ERA for the 1978 Red Sox team that won 99 games but lost the division title to the Yankees in a 1-game playoff. He won 4 games down the stretch as the Red Sox caught the Yankees to force that playoff. A case could be made that he pitched even better in 1979 than he had in 1978, but without the won-loss record to show it. After that he slowly spiraled downward, as the early overuse, excessive drinking, and overhanging marital problems (involving an ex-Cleveland teammate) took a toll on his fastball. Early in the 1984 season Boston traded Eckersley to the Chicago Cubs for Bill Buckner.

For a time he seemed to be rejuvenated by the change of scenery, but after a decent (though not great) 1985 season, he struggled badly in 1986, and seemed to be at the end of the road. On the eve of the 1987 season, Eckersley was traded from Chicago to Oakland in a deal involving minor leaguers. Oakland planned to use him in long relief, to shore up their bullpen. But when Jay Howell was injured, they stuck Eck into the closer's role, and he went on to record at least 33 saves in each season from 1988 to 1993, leading the league twice. He was a dominant closer, doing it with stunning control. In 1989, he pitched 57⅔ innings and walked only 3 batters. The next season, he pitched 73⅓ innings and walked 4! In 1992 he won the American League Cy Young and the American League MVP, as he saved 51 games and had a 7–1 record. Unfortunately, one of the most dramatic moments of his career was one of his few failures as the A's closer, when he gave up a 2 out, 2-run pinch hit home run to Kirk Gibson of the Dodgers to lose Game 1 of the 1988 World Series.

In 1996 at the age of 41, he rejoined former A's manager Tony LaRussa in St Louis. He saved 66 games in two years with the Cardinals, but he was no longer the same dominant factor that he had been. He lost 11 games, more than he had lost in his first 5 years as the Oakland closer.

In 1998, at the age of 43, Dan Duquette signed Eckersley as a free agent to come in as a member of the Sox bullpen. He had never moved away from the Boston area, where he had always remained popular, and was glad to pitch one more year close to home. Though he said that he still wanted to close, everyone knew that he was being brought in to support Tom Gordon, who was going through the transition from starting to closing. He provided 39⅔ innings of roughly league average relief work before retiring. He finished with 197 wins and 390 saves.

Since his retirement Eckersley has occasionally filled in as a color commentator on Red Sox radio broadcasts, where his candor, engaging style, and knowledge of the game make him an excellent analyst. In his early days as a player, Eckersley was famous for making up words, and a popular interview. Now he is as popular for having been a young hero who fell, then rebuilt his life (overcoming alcoholism and other problems) to become a hero again.

Howard Ehmke—a rare bright spot on the terrible post-Babe Ruth teams of the early 1920s, and later an unlikely World Series hero for the Athletics. Ehmke broke in with Buffalo of the Federal League, and then signed with the Detroit Tigers when the Federal League folded. He was a journeyman righthanded pitcher for Detroit from 1916–22, but blossomed after being traded to the Red Sox. He won 20 games in 1923 and 19 in 1924, with decent ERAs. In 1925, Ehmke fell to 9–20, even though his ERA was still better than average (the Red Sox were an atrocious 47–105 that season). In 1923, while pitching for the Red Sox, Ehmke pitched a no-hitter. The feat was in jeopardy in the seventh inning when A's pitcher Slim Harriss hit a ball to the wall and ended up on second, but was ruled out for missing first base. His next outing was a 1-hitter, with the only hit a disputed call on a ball that third baseman Howard Shanks, ordinarily an outfielder, failed to field cleanly.

Ehmke was traded to the Philadelphia Athletics in mid-1926. His most famous performance was probably Game 1 of the 1929 World Series, when Philadelphia A's manager Connie Mack shocked the baseball world by starting Ehmke against the Cubs. He had only pitched 11 games for the A's that year, but was secretly sent by manager Connie Mack to scout their likely World Series opponents, the Chicago Cubs. Just prior to Game 1, Mack named Ehmke his surprise starter—and the 35-year-old beat the Cubs, 3–1, setting a World Series record (since broken by Bob Gibson) with 13 strikeouts.

Nick Esasky—power-hitting first baseman acquired by the Sox from the Cincinnati Reds in December 1988 in a four-player deal involving Todd Benzinger and Rob Murphy. After six National League seasons in which he hit for good power but an inconsistent average in limited playing time, Esasky found Fenway Park—and American League pitching—to his liking in 1989. He hit .277, while leading the Sox with 30 home runs and 108 RBI. The excitement did not last for long, however, because following the season the free agent Esasky chose to sign with the Atlanta Braves. Shortly afterward his baseball career ended abruptly when he was struck by a severe case of vertigo; he played only 9 more games after leaving the Sox.

Vaughn Eshelman—lefthanded pitcher acquired by the Red Sox from Baltimore via the Rule 5 Draft prior to the 1995 season. Eshelman made an initial splash by pitching two outstanding games against the Yankees early in the year, but never lived up to the initial promise. He burned his pitching hand on a candle in his hotel room during spring training in 1997 and started the year on the disabled list. Eshelman last pitched in the majors in 1997, but he signed a minor league contract with the Mets before the 2001 season.

Dwight Evans—a tremendous defensive outfielder and one of the classiest players in baseball, who became an offensive force later in his career. "Dewey" Evans (who reportedly hated the nickname fans gave him, but tolerated it anyway) played all but one of 20 years for the Sox. After an extraordinary run through the minor leagues, Evans first appeared with the Sox in 1972, and became a starter in 1973 (when he hit only .223). He settled into the Sox lineup as a solid hitter with some power who had an extraordinary ability to field Fenway Park's difficult right field, and had perhaps the best outfield arm the team had seen since Harry Hooper. (He used to finish his warmups in the outfield with a cannon throw to the plate every game.) In the slugging Boston lineup of the mid- to late-1970s, Evans didn't have to be a great hitter, and he would eventually win 8 Gold Gloves for his fielding.

From 1972 to 1977, Evans was a .275 hitter wiho averaged about 15 home runs a year. From 1978–80, his power started to increase, but without much sign of the sudden improvement in hitting that was to come. Up to that time, Evans was best known for a great defensive play, his game-saving catch of Joe Morgan's blast in Game 6 of the 1975 series. Deep in right field Evans reached into the Sox bullpen and caught the ball. Turning, he wheeled and threw back into the infield, doubling the runner off. The runner was so amazed that the ball was caught that he was out by a mile.

Evans was a devoted disciple of Sox hitting coach Walt Hriniak, who finally got Evans to stop changing batting stances frequently and hit in a consistent manner. Evans responded by becoming a hitting star at an age when most players are starting to decline. In the strike-shortened 1981 season, Evans tied for the league lead in home runs while hitting .296 with 85 walks, easily his career high in both categories. He followed up by hitting .292 with 32 homers and 112 walks the next year, and remained a consistently deadly hitter through 1989, when he was 37. After a so-so year in 1990, the Red Sox chose not to exercise a contract option on Evans for what he'd announced would be his last season. Sadly, Evans had to finish his career in Baltimore, where he hit .270 as a part-timer.

When the tawdry Margo Adams scandal broke and it was revealed that many of the team's players were running around on their wives, Evans was one of the few players who was not caught up in the mess. It became known fairly early in his career that he was raising a severely disabled son, but Evans refused to make a big deal of it, or of any of his community involvement. He continues to live in New England, and occasionally participates in baseball clinics for children.

Evans was a 3-time All Star, who led the league in OPS twice and in walks 3 times, despite his late start as a hitter. For his career he hit 385 home runs, scored 1,470 runs, and drove in another 1,384. He also had 151 outfield assists, a total that would have been higher if runners hadn't stopped taking chances against him because of his intimidating arm. Evans was overshadowed when he first appeared on the Hall of Fame ballot, and quickly dropped from the ballot. In previous years, players like Evans have been selected to the Hall of Fame by the Veterans Committee, which was set up to look for players whose importance and talent are overlooked in the balloting. However, because of a rule change designed to weaken the Veterans Committee, Evans can never be selected to the Hall of Fame, since he failed to get at least 100 votes in the initial stage of balloting.

Carl Everett—switch hitting centerfielder, obtained from Houston by the Red Sox before the 2000 season for highly touted shortstop prospect Adam Everett (no relation) and pitching prospect Greg Miller. The trade for Everett seemed to fill two holes for the Sox going into the 2000 season. He was expected to replace some of the offensive punch the Red Sox had lost when Mo Vaughn left via free-agency before the 1999 season, and he would fill the center field position which had become a revolving door of players since the departure of Ellis Burks after the 1992 season (and by far the Sox weakest position the previous year). The trade and subsequent long-term signing of Everett were somewhat of a risk. Everett was coming off a great year

I remember it was 1983, a cloudy afternoon, and I was lying on my beanbag chair watching the Sox play. I don't remember who was playing the Sox, but they had a great outfield of Rice, Armas, and Evans. Three bangers and three very good defensive players. The rest of the team was so-so. I don't remember the game, but I remember the ending. Sox were tied in the ninth, man on third, one out. I remember holding my hands, begging, praying for a sacrifice fly. Just deep enough to score the run and get a win. I was odd; most people would root for a base hit or home run, I liked the sac fly. Dewey came up. Sac Fly . . . Sac Fly . . . I secretly chanted, twisting my body in a pretzel-like knot, trying to use all the Force I could to help the Sox.

Then came his swing . . . Fly ball to left, going back . . . damn I thought, they always disappoint . . . back, back . . . left fielder against the wall . . . back . . . back . . . into the net. Sox win. Sox *win*! Dewey's two-run home run to win the game was an epiphany and a curse. Now I live and breathe for the Red Sox and all because of a wind-aided fly to the net over the Green Monster.

—Teddy Zartler

in Houston (.325 average and 25 home runs in a hitters park, as well as 27 stolen bases and good defense) and some wondered if he could continue to produce at that level, since he had struggled before coming to the Astros 2 years previously. At age 28 he was already joining his fifth organization (having been exposed to an expansion draft by the Yankees and traded by the Marlins and Mets). He'd run into legal trouble while with the Mets (he was exonerated of charges of child neglect) and left that organization under a cloud. But after getting off to a terrific start both with the bat and his outspoken comments (Everett hated the Yankees, who had given up on him, with a passion that resonated for many Red Sox fans) Everett quickly joined Nomar Garciaparra and Pedro Martinez as one of the team's most popular players.

In his first season in Boston, Everett put up impressive numbers, hitting .300 with a career high 34 homers, and 108 RBI. He also played a spectacular and occasionally adventurous center field. The offensive numbers were in spite of a second half dropoff brought on by a hand injury, and a 10-game suspension for a confrontation with an umpire that led to accidental physical contact (which was depicted in the media as a "head bump"). Everett also clashed with manager Jimy Williams at least twice, and with teammate Darren Lewis once. The Williams incidents exposed a rift between the manager and GM Dan Duquette that persisted well past the end of the season. At the heart of this conflict was the perception that Duquette was backing his player rather than the manager, and this perception led to widespread media attacks on both Everett and Duquette. A series of trade rumors involving Everett soon followed, though they mostly seemed to be media-inspired wishful thinking. The furor gradually blew over as other off-season news competed for space in the papers. Everett and Williams eventually met at the winter meetings, purportedly to clear the air, and Everett agreed to suggestions that he work on anger management. Media anger at Duquette vanished in the wake of his signing Cleveland superstar Manny Ramirez to a free agent contract.

Jeff Fassero—lefthanded pitcher who started his career in, and was a very effective starting pitcher for, Montreal during the early 1990s. Fassero went to Seattle prior to the 1997 season, and pitched well for 2 years. He had elbow surgery after the 1998 season, and pitched horribly in 1999. Seattle traded him to Texas, where he attempted to regain his form working out of the bullpen. Prior to the 2000 season, Dan Duquette, who had been the general manager in Montreal when Fassero came up, signed him and reunited him with his Montreal pitching coach, Joe Kerrigan. Fassero started 23 games for the 2000 Sox, and made 15 appearances out of the bullpen. He was inconsistent, occasionally very effective and occasionally shelled. He made a stir later in the season when he vocally complained about being pulled out of a game instead of being allowed to work out of trouble. He signed with the Chicago Cubs after the 2000 season.

Rick Ferrell—One of the most controversial and least-qualified Hall of Famers ever, Ferrell played very well for the Red Sox in parts of 5 seasons (the last 4 of them with his younger, more famous brother Wes). An outstanding defensive catcher, Ferrell hit for solid averages, drew a good number of walks, and rarely struck out (never more than 20 times in a season for Boston), but had little power. He began his career with the St. Louis Browns in 1929, and was traded to Boston early in the 1933 season. With the Sox that year, Ferrell batted .297 with 72 RBI, and caught all 9 innings in baseball's first All Star Game. (Ferrell was named to the first 6 American League All Star Teams.) He hit .297 again in 1934, .301 in 1935, and .312 with a career-high 8 homers in 1936.

Early in 1937, the Ferrell brothers were traded to Washington for Bobo Newsom and Ben Chapman. Rick got some nice press with the Senators in 1945, when he caught a staff of 4 knuckleballers (a notoriously hard pitch for a catcher to handle). He retired in 1947 with a .281 average and 28 homers (Wes, a pitcher, hit .280 with 38 home runs!), and little expectation of ever making the Hall of Fame. Ferrell only earned a grand total of 3 votes from the baseball writers, but was a surprise selection by the Veterans Committee in 1984, when he was 79 years old. Many writers blasted the Veterans Committee for picking elderly ex-teammates instead of more qualified candidates from other eras. Some writers wondered if the Veterans Committee had meant to select Wes instead, and others called for the abolishment of the Committee altogether. But the unassuming Ferrell handled the controversy gracefully, and lived his last 11 years with the satisfaction of having a plaque in Cooperstown, deserved or not.

Wes Ferrell—temperamental but talented pitcher who starred (along with his older brother and catcher Rick) on the Red Sox teams of the mid-1930s. Ferrell began his career with Cleveland, winning 21 or more games in each of his first 4 full seasons (1929–32). Known for his blazing fastball, occasional control problems, and power-hitting (he hit 9 homers in 1931, and his 38 career home runs are the most of any pitcher), Ferrell was one of the game's best young pitchers. But a sore arm limited his effectiveness in 1933, and new Red Sox owner Tom Yawkey took a chance on him the following season, trading 2 bit players and $25,000 to Cleveland for Ferrell. Ferrell responded with a 14–5 record and a deceptively good 3.63 ERA (the American League ERA that year was 4.50, common for that high-offense era). In 1935 Ferrell tied a career high with 25 wins, leading the league, while batting .347 with 7 homers. He had his sixth 20-win season in 1936, leading the league with 301 innings pitched and 28 complete games.

After a disastrous 3–6, 7.61 start in 1937, Wes and his brother Rick were traded to Washington. Ferrell had some success with the Senators, but arm problems forced him to retire at age 33 with only 193 career wins. His 4.04 lifetime ERA seemed high to Hall of Fame voters, but was actually excellent for an American League pitcher of the 1930s. Ferrell has sometimes been mentioned as a possible Hall of Fame candidate, especially in light of his brother's surprise selection, but remains a longshot.

Boo Ferriss—a shooting star of a pitcher, the righthanded Dave "Boo" Ferriss won 21 games as a 23-year-old rookie newly discharged from the military in 1945. He followed it up by going 25–6 to lead the league in winning percentage and made the All

Star Game the next year. Ferriss threw almost 540 innings those 2 years for the pitching-starved Sox, and hurt his arm from the overwork. He managed to win 12 games in 1947, but was only able to start 9 games in 1948. He never won another major league game after 1948. He later coached for the Red Sox before becoming baseball coach at Mississippi State.

Mark Fidrych—eccentric righthanded pitcher who was the American League Rookie of the Year in 1976 while pitching for Detroit. Nicknamed "The Bird," Fidrych was known for exaggerated motions on the mound and for talking to the baseball before throwing it. He won 19 games in 1976 while leading the league in ERA, but after throwing 250 innings and 24 complete games at age 21, he never threw more than 81 innings in a season in the majors again. Fidrych, a Worcester, Massachusetts native, is of note to Red Sox fans because he finished his pro career with 2 seasons in Pawtucket, retiring in June 1983 with a 9.68 ERA.

In 1975, for no apparent reason, Dutch TV decided to show some pictures of a game called baseball. A team called the Reds was playing a team called the Red Sox. Nobody in my part of Holland knew what *that* was all about, but those people on TV in America seemed pretty excited about it. They all went berserk when this guy used a big stick to hit this ball over a large green wall. The guy who hit that ball over the wall then started jumping up and down, his teammates ran towards him and started hugging him, and the crowd just kept cheering for like forever. It was 1975. Carlton Fisk won game 6 of the World Series for the Red Sox. I was nine years old, and I got hooked on the Red Sox right then and there.

Now, in Holland (or The Netherlands if you will), baseball is a small sport. It's hardly ever on TV. Sure, the Dutch National Team always ends up playing the Italians for the European Baseball Championship and those teams take turns winning the title, but who cares? Baseball wasn't even introduced to the South of Holland until (about) '80. That's 1980, not 1880.

In Holland, if you want to talk sports you better talk about soccer, speed skating, or cycling. Anyone in Holland who knows more about Joe DiMaggio than the fact that Simon and Garfunkel mentioned him in a song and the fact that he was once married to Marilyn Monroe is considered to be either a possibly dangerous freak or someone with way too much time on his hands!

So, who are you going to talk to about this game called baseball and that team called the Red Sox in 1975 in the south of Holland?

Answer: Everyone.

Who cares?

No one.

Where are you going to learn more about those Red Sox?

Nowhere; you can't learn more about them.

Still, I never forgot the pictures on TV in 1975.

Fast forward to 1990: I'm 24. I played some high school softball (baseball is considered too difficult to learn and too dangerous to play in Holland high schools), and I'm

Lou Finney—a key reserve for the Red Sox in the early 1940s, Finney was a left-handed-hitting outfielder/first baseman who hit for a good average but without much power or ability to draw walks. Boston picked Finney up from the Philadelphia A's early in the 1939 season, and he hit .325 the rest of the way, leading the league with 13 pinch hits. He hit .320 the following year—playing almost every day because of injuries to other players—and made his only All Star appearance. Finney hit in the .280s his remaining 3 years in Boston (interrupted for a year by wartime military service). His brother, Hal Finney, also played in the major leagues.

Carlton Fisk—Pudge (a nickname he acquired as a child, because well, apparently he was) is arguably the definitive Red Sox player—not just because he is a native New Englander (born in Vermont, raised in New Hampshire), but also because of his strange relationship with the organization. Though he played high school and American Legion baseball, his sport of choice was basketball, and his dream was to

learning to play baseball the hard way, at the expense of some teeth lost on a bad hop (I think at age 24 and up, it's inevitable to learn baseball the hard way) and I'm at this tournament in the west of Holland. They have this small fan shop. They sell baseball cards. They sell *Red Sox* baseball cards! Suddenly I'm learning about this guy called Clemens, who seems to be a pretty good pitcher. It turns out in the old days a guy called Williams played there for just about forever. Then a guy called Yastrzemski took the job of playing there forever. There's this guy called Jody Reed, an outfielder called Plantier, a guy called Brunanski, another one called Boggs. Wow! I just increased my knowledge of the Boston Red Sox by like 10,000%!

After that, things speeded up a lot. In 1994 or so CNBC or some station like that started showing live MLB games for a year or two on Friday night. That is, up until the World Series started; then those Friday night games magically disappeared. But anyway, I'd be up from 2 AM until 5 AM watching Pettitte and the Yankees dominate the Red Sox the night after Mo Vaughn hit 3 dingers vs the Yankees (which, of course, wasn't on TV).

Next we got CNN and CNN text: after reading those daily 3 line game reports for a whole season, I was actually able to puzzle together a Red Sox line-up from those bits of information: Clemens, Wakefield, Sele, Vaughn, Valentin, Naehring, Greenwell, etc . . .

Then, August 1996. Two games in Fenway: Red Sox vs the Angels and Red Sox vs. the A's and I was there. In person! Clemens won the game vs the Angels while striking out 15 or so and Wakefield beat the A's while giving me a heart attack every time Big Mac came to the plate. I wouldn't have left Fenway for the duration of my holiday, but my girlfriend kept telling me she wanted to stay in a hotel, not in a ballpark.

Nowadays, thanks to the Internet, all the Red Sox info I need is only a click of a mouse button away. OK, so we still don't get Major League Baseball or any other baseball for that matter on TV in Holland. But since you can watch live camel racing from Egypt, brought to us by Iraqi television, I guess some smart TV guy will think about bringing us MLB next. . . .

—Toine Otten

one day play for the Celtics. Fortunately for baseball, as Fisk himself put it, "I didn't grow into a power forward." In 1967 he was drafted as the fourth pick in the first round of the amateur draft by the Red Sox. Reportedly, the only reason he lasted that long was that the 3 teams drafting ahead of Boston knew Fisk would never sign with any team except the Red Sox.

In 1969 Fisk made his big league debut, appearing in 2 games without reaching base. He appeared in 14 games in 1971, getting his first 2 home runs and 6 RBI. Fisk became a regular in 1972, appearing in 131 games and hitting .293, with 22 home runs and 61 RBI. He was named Rookie of the Year, the first to win that award unanimously. He also won his only Gold Glove in that year.

In 1975 Pudge hit a walk-off home run in the tenth inning of Game 6 of the World Series, which many consider to be one of baseball's greatest moments. It is remembered because it won what was already a great game, and for the visual of Fisk frantically waving the ball fair. This one hit is among the most replayed moments ever. It is considered by some to have reignited interest in the game of baseball.

In 1980, in a situation that is to this day shrouded in some mystery, the Red Sox mailed Fisk's new contract to him 2 days late, making him a free agent. So after more than a decade in the Red Sox organization, Carlton Fisk signed a contract with the Chicago White Sox, for whom he played until he retired in 1993.

By the time that retirement came about Fisk's name riddled the record books. Major League records include: 2,226 games as a catcher, 72 home runs after age 40, and 351 home runs as a catcher. He also holds the American League record for most home runs by a catcher in a single season, 37 in 1985. He was named to 11 All Star teams. As a Red Sox player Fisk hit 162 home runs and had 568 RBI. His highest batting average was .331 in 1975.

Fisk was inducted into baseball's Hall of Fame on July 23, 2000, in his second year of eligibility (a seeming victim of a glut of talented first year eligibles the previous year, including Nolan Ryan, George Brett, and Robin Yount). On August 4, 2000, his number 27 became only the fifth uniform number to be retired by the Red Sox. (The number 72 that he wore in Chicago was also retired by that team.) There are likely few long time Red Sox fans who would not include Carlton Fisk on a list of their favorite Red Sox players, or the 1975 home run as their favorite baseball memory.

Bryce Florie—a decent righthanded reliever who started his career in San Diego, then moved to Detroit. He came to Boston to support the Sox bullpen in the middle of 1999. In August of 1999, when Jimy Williams refused to start Pedro Martinez because he arrived late to the ballpark, Florie started and pitched well for 4⅔ innings. Pedro relieved and ended up getting the win, though there was every indication that Jimy tried to get Florie through the fifth for the win, and he was just out of gas.

On September 8, 2000, in the eighth inning of a game against the Yankees, Florie took a line drive to the face off the bat of Ryan Thompson, in an incident eerily reminiscent of Dick Pole's injury in 1975. Florie never lost consciousness, but it was a bloody, gruesome event that shattered his eye socket and ended his season. There was concern for a time that he would lose the sight in his right eye as a result of the hit. It is unclear when—or if—he will be able to resume a baseball career.

Mike Fornieles—a righthanded relief pitcher, the Cuban-born Fornieles spent all or part of 7 seasons with the Red Sox. He was generally an average, or slightly below average, pitcher during his career. In 1960, however, he led the American League in appearances with 70, and in saves with 14. He made the All Star team in 1961, when he had 15 saves, though his ERA skyrocketed to 4.68. Relief pitching star Dick Radatz (the Monster), who came up with Boston in 1962, later credited Fornieles with teaching him the batters in the American League, and how to close out games effectively.

Tony Fossas—Cuban-born, Boston-raised reliever who practically defined the term "lefty specialist." In 1991, after spending most of his career in the minors, Fossas achieved his boyhood dream of pitching for the Red Sox. Since Fossas was very tough against lefty hitters, but struggled mightily against righties, Boston gave him as narrow a role as possible. Whenever a tough lefthanded hitter came up in a key situation, Fossas entered the game. Very often, he'd depart after facing just the one batter. During Fossas's 4 years in Boston, he appeared in 239 games, yet only pitched 161 innings. Because of his limited role, it's hard to judge Fossas by traditional statistics, but he was generally effective against lefties (though righty pinch-hitters murdered him). The Red Sox had mixed feelings about Fossas, and continually searched for a more complete pitcher to replace him. He was taken off the 40-man roster in 1993 and 1994, but the Sox couldn't find anyone better, and re-signed him both years. Fossas finally left in 1995, had 3 good years with St. Louis, and retired after the 1999 season.

George "Rube" Foster—a little righty who pitched exceptionally from 1913–17, before retiring with arm problems. Foster only appeared in 19 games as a rookie, but came into his own in 1914, going 14–8 with an amazing 1.70 ERA (second in the league to teammate Dutch Leonard's incredible 0.96). In 1915 the Sox had perhaps their best pitching staff ever; Foster and Ernie Shore led the way with identical 19–8 records. (Rookie Babe Ruth was 18–8, while Leonard and Smokey Joe Wood each won 15). The Sox easily beat the Phillies in the World Series, and Foster won both his starts, including the clinching game. Boston defended its title in 1916, but injuries limited Foster to 14 wins (including a no-hitter against the Yankees on June 21). He planned to retire after the World Series, but was talked into returning. Foster, in constant pain, struggled through 17 games in 1917, going 8–7. Unable to continue pitching, he went back home to his ranch in Oklahoma, leaving the game at age 29 with a 58–33 record and a 2.36 ERA.

Another Rube Foster—born Andrew Foster—was a star pitcher who helped create the Negro League, and is in the Hall of Fame.

Pete Fox—though never a great hitter, this righthanded outfielder did hit for a good average several times. Fox spent the first 8 years of his 13 year career in Detroit, before coming to Boston in 1941, and finishing in 1945. He had a reputation as a solid outfielder, and was considered a key part of the successful Tiger teams of the mid-1930s. He started the season in left field in 1941 in place of Ted Williams, who had a bone chip in his ankle and couldn't run or field to start the year. He was an All Star during the war-depleted 1944 season.

Jimmie Foxx—unquestionably one of the greatest hitters ever to play the game, "Double X" was the heart of the Philadelphia A's lineup that dominated baseball from 1929 through 1931. Red Sox owner Thomas Yawkey acquired Foxx in 1936 as A's owner/manager Connie Mack sold off his best players in a Great Depression-related firesale. Acquisitions like Foxx and pitcher Lefty Grove led to the 1930s Red Sox being nicknamed "the Gold Sox," a monicker meant to mock Yawkey's attempts to use his vast financial resources to transform one of the worst teams of the 1920s into a contender overnight.

A catcher when he debuted in the majors in 1925 at the age of 17, Jimmie Foxx spent his first three years in the majors enjoying limited playing time at several positions (catcher, third base, first base, and the outfield) before Connie Mack decided to give him a more regular role. Finally given the chance to establish himself at first base in 1929, Foxx responded by leading the league in on-base percentage, finishing third in slugging percentage, and placing in the top 10 in a number of other major statistics while leading the A's to the World Championship. Knowing a good thing when he saw it, Mack left Foxx at first base. Foxx continued to hit as well as anyone in the league, and the A's proceeded to win the World Series in 1930 and 1931, the first team ever to win 3 consecutive World Series.

Jimmie Foxx's batting accomplishments are too many to list here. He hit for average and power, walked constantly, and was durable. He spent all or part of 20 seasons in the majors, and hit over .300 in 14 of those seasons (winning 2 batting titles along the way). He hit 30 or more homers in a season 12 times, leading the league in homers 4 times and in slugging percentage 5 times. He had 7 seasons with more than 100 walks (and another with 99), and led the league in walks twice. He scored more than 100 runs 11 times and drove in more than 100 runs 13 times, leading the league 3 times in RBI (with astonishing totals of 169, 163, and 175 those years). Some highlights include Foxx's 58 homeruns in 1932 (two away from Ruth's single-season record) which led to a .749 slugging percentage and the first of his 3 MVP awards; his winning the triple crown in 1933 which earned him his second MVP; his selection to the American League All Star team every year from its inception in 1933 through 1941; his nearly winning his second triple crown in 1938 when he led the league in average, RBI, on-base percentage, slugging percentage, total bases, and walks—although he hit 50 home runs that year, he finished second to Hank Greenberg (who had 58) in that triple crown category; and his third MVP in 1938 for leading the Red Sox to a second-place finish behind the Yankees.

It is said that when Ted Williams joined the Red Sox to start the 1939 season, a teammate, struck by his brashness, told the young Williams to be more humble with the line, "Wait till you see Foxx hit." Williams's response was "Wait till he sees me hit!" His one-liner is even more daring when one keeps in mind that Foxx had won his third MVP in the previous season.

As it happened, Foxx's career was almost over at this point. He continued to hit quite well in 1939 (his .360 average and .694 slugging percentage), but his heavy drinking was about to derail his career. In 1940, his average fell below .300 and his slugging below .600 (still good numbers, but a subpar season for Double-X). In 1941, his slugging percentage fell to .505 (his lowest mark since he was 18). In 1942, after 30 games (with a slugging percentage in the mid-.400s), Boston put Foxx on waivers. He was picked up by the Cubs, but his numbers continued to plummet. The Cubs gave Foxx another 15 games (in 1944) to see if he could straighten out his life enough in order to hit as he once did, but he had nothing left. Foxx retired.

World War II was still being waged, however, and he was able-bodied enough to fill major league ranks, so the last-place Phillies asked Foxx to come back, perhaps hoping he could recover his stroke, and if not, he could at least draw fans from his old Philadelphia A's past to come to the ballpark to watch him in his swansong. The prodigious power was no longer there, but his arm was still live enough that the Phils tried him as a pitcher—Foxx compiled a 1.59 ERA in 22 innings of pitching.

Foxx retired for good following the 1945 season (after which the major league regulars returned from their wartime duty). His 534 home runs were second only to Ruth (and that was despite hitting only 42 home runs after the age of 32). He was elected to the Hall of Fame in 1951, a great player whose final numbers could have been even greater had his addiction to the bottle not caused his career to go south at age 33. (Fans of the movie *A League of Their Own* will recognize that Tom Hanks's character, the manager of the Rockford Peaches, was based on Jimmie Foxx, who really did manage in the All-American Girl's Professional Baseball League).

Joe Foy—a righthanded-hitting third baseman and minor league phenom, Joe Foy spent the first 3 years of his career with the Sox and played decently. He was the starting third baseman on the 1967 Impossible Dream team, and led the league in both double plays and errors twice while with the Sox. His batting averages are unimpressive today, but he played at a time when pitching was king. He had some power, could steal bases (fifth in the league in 1968), and walked frequently (among the league leaders in 2 of his 3 years with the Sox). Foy developed a weight problem and when he failed to deal with it Red Sox management shipped him to Kansas City.

Foy is mostly remembered for being part of a terrible trade a year after he left the Red Sox. After stealing 37 bases and having a good hitting year for Kansas City in 1969, Foy was traded to the New York Mets for Amos Otis and Bob Foster. Foy, troubled by substance abuse problems, never played full-time again and was out of baseball at age 28, while Otis went on to an illustrious 17-year career. Foy's drug problem may have contributed to his early death in 1989, at age 46.

Buck Freeman—had he been born 30 years later, the now-forgotten John "Buck" Freeman might have been regarded as one of the game's greatest sluggers. But at the turn of the twentieth century home runs were rare, and Freeman was seen as more of a curiosity than a star. The 5'9" lefty swinger became a regular outfielder with the National League's Washington team in 1899, hitting .318 with 25 triples, a league-leading 25 homers, and 122 RBI. No other National Leaguer hit more than 12 home runs that year, and Freeman's 25 were tied for the second-most in a nineteenth-century season. Freeman moved to the National League's Boston Braves in 1900, and jumped to the Red Sox in their inaugural 1901 season.

Freeman's first 3 seasons with the Red Sox were excellent. He hit a career-high .339 as the team's first baseman in 1901, with 15 triples, 12 homers, 114 RBI, a .400 on-base percentage, and a .520 slugging percentage (outstanding in the dead ball era). Freeman moved back to right field in 1902, and led the American League with 121 RBI, while hitting .309 with 19 triples and 11 homers. His average slipped to .287 in 1903, but Freeman's league-leading 13 homers and 104 RBI helped the Sox win the first modern World Series. During the 8-game Series, Freeman hit 3 triples and batted .281. Freeman led the American League in triples in 1904, with 19, but his other numbers began to slip. He played regularly in 1905 and 1906, and briefly in 1907, but only hit 5 more major league home runs.

Modern historians have had difficulty judging Freeman. His power numbers were among the best of his era, but his era was marked by pitching, defense, bunting, and daring baserunning—"inside baseball," rather than the station-to-station style of today's game. Never much of a fielder or baserunner, Freeman was often criticized by his peers, yet may have helped pave the way for Babe Ruth and the home run revolution. If nothing else, Freeman began the Red Sox tradition of high-power, low-defense outfielders.

Jeff Frye—righthanded-hitting second baseman, signed as a free agent by the Red Sox off of Texas's Oklahoma City team early in the 1996 season. The injury-prone Frye, who had hit very well in Texas before being buried in the minors after one of many knee injuries (he was picked up by the Red Sox on the recommendation of manager Kevin Kennedy, his former manager on the Rangers) hit very well for the Sox and ended up as the team's starting second baseman. Frye had little power, but always hit for a good average and did a decent job of getting on base, while playing an acceptable second base. The Red Sox rewarded Frye for his performance with the first multiyear contract of his career following the 1997 season, but he blew out his knee in the first baserunning drill of the spring in 1998, and was lost for the season. He came back to play intermittently in the 1999 and 2000 seasons before being traded to Colorado in the Rolando Arrojo deal.

Denny Galehouse—righthanded pitcher who was a surprise starter in one of the biggest games in Red Sox history. Galehouse was a 36-year-old veteran pitching on fumes at the end of the 1948 season, which he had spent as a decent fill-in behind 5 other starting pitchers. He had a 109–117 career record, and had won more games than he lost in only 3 of his 14 big-league seasons. With the Red Sox and Cleveland Indians tied for the league lead on the last day of the season, manager Joe McCarthy inexplicably chose Galehouse to start the 1-game playoff that would decide who went to the World Series. To no one's surprise, the Red Sox lost the game, and the pennant, 8–3. Galehouse played in only 2 more major league games.

Rich Garces—hefty relief pitcher from Venezuela. Garces, a converted center fielder despite his oversized appearance, spent most of the early 1990s pitching in the Minnesota farm system. He split time in 1995 between the Cubs and Florida Marlins before joining the Sox for the 1996 season. In 1996 and 1997 he continued to be an unimpressive and injury-prone middle reliever for the Sox, spending a good portion of 1997 in AAA Pawtucket. Garces fared better in 1998, and became an excellent setup man (with an extraordinary 1.55 ERA) in 1999. By the 2000 season he was a fan favorite, affectionately called "El Guapo" (the beautiful one) in response to his roly-poly body and unkempt appearance on the mound. Garces was one of many workhorses in a heavily worked bullpen in 2000; he appeared in 64 games, posting an 8–1 record with a 3.25 ERA.

Nomar Garciaparra—considered the cornerstone of the current Red Sox team, Garciaparra—known simply as "Nomar" to most Boston fans—is a quiet leader who sets an example with his brilliant on-field play as opposed to being a vocal leader. One of 3 extraordinary shortstops who all came to the major leagues around the same time (the others are Alex Rodriguez and Derek Jeter), Garciaparra is a so-called "five tool" player; he hits for power, average, has good speed, a strong arm, and is a good defensive player. Although he has a reputation as a free swinger—like Mike Greenwell before him, Garciaparra frequently swings at the first pitch he sees—Garciaparra's walk rates have gone up every year and he seldom strikes out. In the field his great range and strong throwing arm lead to frequent spectacular plays and the occasional wild throwing error (particularly since he has thrown to poor defensive first basemen for most of his career).

Anthony Nomar Garciaparra ("Nomar" is his father's name spelled backward) was selected in the first round of the 1994 draft, the first pick by new Red Sox GM Dan Duquette. Garciaparra had been a member of the 1992 US Olympic Baseball Team, and had starred on a Georgia Tech team alongside catcher (and current team-mate) Jason Varitek and outfielder Jay Payton (now with the New York Mets). The Milwaukee Brewers had tried to sign Nomar as a teenager, but Garciaparra had insisted on going to college for 3 years—where he studied business management—in case something went wrong in his baseball career. As a youth, baseball was not even his best sport—Garciaparra was a southern California soccer standout.

Despite an early season injury, Garciaparra was called up to the majors at the end of the 1996 season after posting impressive numbers at AAA Pawtucket. Garciaparra was immediately thrust into the starting lineup, replacing shortstop John Valentin, one of the team's most valuable players, who was slowed by nagging injuries. (Later rumors claimed that manager Kevin Kennedy told Valentin that GM Duquette was forcing him to play Nomar over Valentin). Garciaparra played in 24 games for the Sox that year, driving in 16 runs and hitting four home runs (the first off future teammate John "Way Back" Wasdin.)

The controversy continued into the spring of 1997. New manager Jimy Williams first said that the shortstop job was Valentin's to lose, then said that Valentin and Garciaparra would openly compete for the job, but then handed the job outright to Garciaparra after only a few spring training games had been played. Valentin was moved to second base (displacing Jeff Frye) and then to third base after an injury to incumbent Tim Naehring. This shuffling created a disruption in the clubhouse and angered Valentin, who briefly left the team before settling down to play well at both second and third.

The clubhouse rumblings quieted when it became evident that Nomar was the Sox shortstop of the future. Batting first on a team without a natural leadoff hitter, Garciaparra hit .306 with 30 home runs (a rookie shortstop record), led the league in total bases (a single is 1 base, a double is 2 bases, etc.), and set a record for a leadoff hitter (since broken by Anaheim's Darin Erstad) with 98 RBI. He shattered the record for extra base hits by a rookie shortstop, which had stood since 1924, as well as the records for runs, doubles, total bases, and slugging percentage by a rookie shortstop. Garciaparra also hit in 30 straight games, a rookie record and the second-longest streak ever by a Red Sox player, on his way to being a unanimous selection for American League Rookie of the Year.

In the years that followed, Garciaparra continued to put up exceptional numbers. His 24-game hitting streak in 1998 was the longest in the majors that year. After Mo Vaughn left as a free agent following the 1998 season, it was widely speculated that pitchers would be able to pitch around Garciaparra in the weakened Sox lineup and his production would decline. Instead, he won the batting title in 1999, hitting .357, and won it again in 2000 by hitting .372—the first righthanded batter in 60 years to win back-to-back batting titles. He was an All Star in 3 of his 4 full seasons in the major leagues, winning the rookie home run derby in 1997.

Garciaparra hit two grand slams in one game against the Seattle Mariners on May 10, 1999. While his home run totals diminished from a career-high of 35 in 1998 to 21 in 2000, he continues to be a dangerous power hitter, among the league leaders in extra base hits.

Garciaparra is known as one of the most superstitious ballplayers in baseball, with an array of rituals he follows every game that rivals those of former Sox star Wade Boggs. He climbs the steps out of the dugout almost sideways, steps with both feet on each step, kisses his bat, and crosses himself repeatedly. While in the batter's box he continually tugs at his batting gloves and taps his toes with his bat (both holdovers from his youth, when he had to adjust his older brother's hand-me-down equipment). He still wears a decaying warmup jersey from Georgia Tech under his uniform, and he reportedly plays the same cassette on the way to the park every game.

After his outstanding rookie season, the Red Sox signed Garciaparra to a multi-year contract, a bold and risky move considering the team could have kept him at a much lower price for several years and would have been liable if Garciaparra became hurt or ineffective. The gamble paid off, however; when Garciaparra became a superstar he was already signed through the 2003 season at far less then his potential market value.

Garciaparra is a rare Red Sox star who is as popular with the media as he is with fans. He combines an all-out playing style and vigorous work ethic (which may also contribute to frequent nagging injuries) with a self-deprecating manner and boyishly enthusiastic speaking style. While Derek Jeter receives more national attention, Nomar has made appearances on *Saturday Night Live* and the sitcom *Two Guys and a Girl*, attends and sometimes interacts with wrestlers during WWF shows, is friends with female soccer star Mia Hamm (and remains a soccer fan), and has been romantically linked at various times with actress Lauren Holly and hockey player Cammi Granato in tabloid stories.

Larry Gardner—one of the best third basemen of the 1910s and early 1920s, Gardner was a key member of 3 World Series winners for Boston. The lefty-swinging Vermont native joined the Red Sox in 1908, a year after Hall of Fame third baseman Jimmy Collins departed. Gardner became the team's regular second baseman in 1910, and moved to third midway through the following season. A .289 lifetime hitter with little power and average speed, Gardner's statistics aren't overwhelming by today's standards. But in the dead ball era, third base was much more of a defense-oriented position, thanks to the greater emphasis on bunting and baserunning. Hitting was considered a bonus, making a player like Gardner extremely valuable. Gardner had his best Red Sox season in 1912, batting .315 with 86 RBI and 25 steals for the World Champions. He also played for the 1915 and 1916 champs, hitting .308 in the latter season. In 1918 Gardner and Tilly Walker were traded to the Philadelphia Athletics for star first baseman Stuffy McInnis. (Walker went on to tie Babe Ruth for the league lead in homers, with 11.) A year later, Gardner joined his ex-Sox teammate Tris Speaker in Cleveland. In 1920, Gardner won his fourth World Series ring, driving in 118 runs and batting .310 for the Indians. The advent of the lively ball certainly helped Gardner's numbers, and he put up nearly identical stats in 1921. He ended his 17-year career in 1924.

Wes Gardner—righthanded pitcher acquired with Calvin Schiraldi from the Mets in the Bobby Ojeda trade. He had a great arm (the Mets had hoped he'd turn into the next Dwight Gooden before they gave up on him), but never lived up to what people expected from his physical skills. After teasing Red Sox fan with glimpses of potential for 5 years, Gardner finished his career in 1991, splitting 26 innings between Kansas City and San Diego. In 5 years in Boston, he recorded 20 wins and 12 saves.

Rich Gedman—a rare lefthanded-hitting catcher, Gedman worked hard to turn himself from an undrafted, overweight first baseman into one of the league's premier catchers before abruptly flaming out. Gedman debuted in September 1980 (as a pinch hitter for Carl Yastrzemski) and spent most of the next 3 years platooning with light-hitting Gary Allenson. Although Gedman hit for a good average, he wasn't productive as a hitter, since he drew a below-average number of walks and hit only 11 home runs combined in those 3 years. In 1984 Gedman blossomed as a hitter under the tutelage of unorthodox Sox hitting coach Walt Hriniak, playing in 133 games and hitting 24 home runs. The next year he hit a career-best .295 with 18 homers. He began to struggle at the plate in 1986 but was still productive, hitting 16 homers while batting .258.

That year, however, was the year the Sox made the World Series and Gedman was the catcher behind the plate for Bob Stanley's wild pitch that allowed the Mets to tie Game 6. Gedman had developed a fine throwing arm, but he was at best an average defensive catcher; many other catchers could have prevented Stanley's pitch from getting away—and if Stanley had gotten out of the inning without the wild pitch, the Sox would have won the World Series. In 1987 Gedman appeared in only 52 games because of injuries and ineffectiveness. His hitting deteriorated to the point where he looked helpless at the plate, a caricature of the odd swing that Hriniak advocated. The Sox finally gave up and released Gedman in 1990. He played sparingly for Houston and St. Louis until 1992, but never recovered his batting ability.

Billy Goodman—versatile singles hitter who played for the Red Sox in the late 1940s and 1950s. A lifetime .300 hitter (.306 with Boston), Goodman also drew a fair number of walks, but had only 19 homers in a 16-year career. He debuted in 1947, and became the team's regular first baseman in 1948. Goodman made the All Star team in 1949 (hitting a rather empty .298), but he lacked the power of his predecessor, Rudy York. After an injury to Goodman early in 1950, slugger Walt Dropo took over at first base and went on a seasonlong tear.

Although Goodman no longer had a regular position when he returned to the team, he got into 110 games at 5 different positions and won the batting title (.354). He was a backup at first and third base, and took over in left field after Ted Williams got hurt in the All Star Game. When Williams returned, Goodman resumed his utility role, until another Hall of Famer got hurt. Bobby Doerr had a career-ending back injury in 1951, and Goodman replaced him at second base. He continued to hit near or above .300 each year, though his defense didn't remind anyone of the great Doerr. He made the All Star team again in 1953, when he hit .313 and only struck out 11 times in 514 at bats. Early in 1957, the Red Sox traded Goodman to Baltimore for young reliever Mike Fornieles. Goodman played until 1962, mainly as a backup. He didn't have enough power for a first baseman or left fielder, or enough defense to be a top second baseman, but the easygoing Goodman was certainly good to have around.

> At 46 years of age I suffered a devastating stroke that partialy paralyzed the left side of my body. As I recovered some use in my affected areas (eyes, arm, and leg) one of the things that seemed to be in my favor is a never-give-up never-get-depressed attitude. I attribute this at least in part to my being a Red Sox fan. I figure the horrors the Sox put us through year after year make life's horrors a little easier to take. Many of the people I've told this to don't seem to see the correlation, or think it's a bit silly, but to me it's real and true. The real correlation boils down to the old adage, "that which doesn't kill you makes you stronger." In many ways the stroke has made me stronger; in many ways being a Red Sox fan continues to make me stronger.
>
> —Don Violette

Tom Gordon—righthanded reliever who had an extraordinary transition from starter to reliever, only to see his career sidetracked by injury. Gordon made a splash as a 21-year-old rookie with the Kansas City Royals in 1989, going 17–9 with a good 3.64 ERA. He never developed into the star they hoped however; Gordon pitched consistently but won 12 games or fewer in each of the next 6 seasons. Although he had one of the best curves in baseball and a good fastball, Gordon didn't have control of any additional pitches that would allow him to fool hitters consistently. Traded to the Red Sox in 1996, he won 12 games again but pitched inconsistently. Sox pitching coach Joe Kerrigan suggested that Gordon might be more successful as a relief pitcher—where he would only face each batter once and his curve would be most effective.

Gordon began pitching in relief late in the 1997 season, and recorded 11 saves. The next season Gordon became the full-time closer, with fading relief pitcher extraordinaire Dennis Eckersley signed to the pitching staff to help tutor Gordon in the role. Gordon's contract was restructured as well, essentially giving him a new 3-year deal with lucrative incentives if he was successful in his new role. Gordon responded with an extraordinary 1998 season, saving a league-leading 46 games and going months without blowing a save—until his luck ran out with a heartbreaking loss in the playoffs against the Cleveland Indians. Gordon won the Rolaids Relief award, and achieved another kind of immortality when Stephen King's short novel, *The Girl Who Loved Tom Gordon*, came out the following spring.

Unfortunately, Gordon's good fortune didn't last. An injured elbow cost him most of the 1999 season. He feuded with the team's management and medical staff over his course of treatment (the team wanted him to try resting rather than season-ending surgery), pitched poorly on his return, and then was forced to have surgery after all—which meant he would miss the entire 2000 season as well. Although his relationship with the team was mended somewhat, the Red Sox did not pick up Gordon's $4.5 million contract option for the 2001 season, and he signed as a free agent with the Chicago Cubs.

Jeff Gray—promising, often-dominating reliever whose career abruptly ended after suffering a stroke. Gray, a college teammate of Jody Reed at Florida State, put up excellent minor league numbers in the Reds' system. However, he wasn't regarded as a prospect, and only appeared in 5 big league games (in 1988). The Reds traded Gray to the Phillies in 1990, but he was released after spring training. Gray signed a minor league deal with the Red Sox, and pitched well in Pawtucket, earning a promotion to the majors. Though Gray's stats weren't great (2–4, 4.44 ERA), he was an unsung hero for the Sox, earning 9 saves while closer Jeff Reardon recovered from a serious back injury. He entered 1991 as Reardon's set-up man, and was superb, allowing only 39 hits and 10 walks in 61 innings, while posting an outstanding 2.34 ERA. Gray did the dirty work, stifling seventh and eighth inning rallies, while Reardon got the glory, setting a team record (since broken by Tom Gordon) with 40 saves.

Then tragedy struck. Sitting in the clubhouse before a July 30 game against Texas, Gray felt dizzy, with numbness on his right side, and his speech became slurred. He collapsed, and doctors later revealed that Gray had suffered a stroke. The news was shocking, since Gray was only 28 years old, and had appeared to be in perfect health. The tough reliever promised to come back, and he spent months rehabilitating. Gray had to re-learn many motor functions, and could only get his fastball back to the 80 MPH range. He pushed himself as far as he could, and tried to pitch in the minors in 1992, but it became sadly evident that Gray would never regain his old form. The Red Sox hired Gray as a minor league pitching coach, and he remained in the organization until 1999, when he moved to the Reds' system. Gray also operates the highly successful Beef O'Brady's restaurant in Sarasota, Florida.

Pumpsie Green—the first black player to play for the Red Sox, who were the last team in the major leagues to integrate. Although the Red Sox had tried out Willie Mays and Jackie Robinson in the 1940s (and then chosen not to sign them) it wasn't until 1959 that a black player was signed. Elijah "Pumpsie" Green spent 4 years with the Sox as a utility infielder and pinch hitter, never batting more than 260 times in a season or hitting higher than .260. Although Green ended the Sox white-only policy, tinges of racism toward black and Hispanic players persisted for many years, and the last vestiges were only rooted out in the 1990s under general manager Dan Duquette. (In a welcome sign, when superstar free agent Manny Ramirez chose to sign with the Red Sox in December 2000, he did so partially because of the team's diversity and welcoming climate toward players of all races.)

Mike Greenwell—"Gator" was a Red Sox outfielder from 1985–1996. Called up as a pinch hitter for the stretch drive in 1986, the lefthanded-hitting Greenwell replaced a fading Jim Rice in the lineup in 1987 and seemed to be the next great Red Sox left fielder. At the time there was a great deal of media attention focused on the nearly unbroken succession from Ted Williams to Carl Yastrzemski to Jim Rice to Mike Greenwell, although the talk gradually died down when it became clear that Greenwell would not be a Hall of Famer. In 1987 Greenwell hit .328 with 19 home runs in limited playing time, and he followed with a .325, 22 home run season as a full-time starter in 1988 (when he finished second in MVP voting to Jose Canseco); Greenwell was an All Star in 1988 and 1989. Although he continued to hit for average (a .303 lifetime batting average), his power gradually decreased (only 130 home runs over 12 seasons, despite his strong start), and the lack of production made it harder to overlook his weak defense. Although he started out as a fan favorite and remained popular in Boston even as he declined as a player, Greenwell left under acrimonious circumstances, cleaning out his locker before the end of the 1996 season when he was told he would only be brought back as a reserve, not a starter. As an injury-plagued free agent with little power and poor defense, he drew little interest from other teams, and finished his career in Japan in 1997. Greenwell now works as a hitting coach for the Cincinnati organization.

Doug "Dude" Griffin—a light-hitting second baseman with big sideburns, Griffin came to Boston from California after the 1970 season, along with pitcher Ken Tatum and outfielder Jarvis Tatum, for Tony Conigliaro. Ironically, the 1974 team lost

Griffin when he was hit in the head by a pitch from Nolan Ryan. (Conigliaro had also been the victim of a famous beaning.) Griffin spent the last 7 years of his career in Boston,. never hitting higher than .266 in a season.

Lefty Grove—an utterly remarkable pitcher who some analysts, including Bill James, consider the best ever. Like Pedro Martinez, Grove posted mind-boggling numbers in an offense-dominated era. He pitched from 1925–41 and had a career ERA of 3.06; during that time the average American League ERA ranged from 4.02 to 5.04. Grove won 300 games—with 9 seasons of 20 or more wins—and led the league in ERA a record 9 times. He only lost 141 games, and his .680 winning percentage is fourth all time among retired pitchers. Early in his career, just to pass the time between starts, Grove was one of baseball's first "closers," saving 55 games. He had his greatest years with the Philadelphia Athletics, but had plenty left after joining Boston in 1934. In 8 seasons with the Red Sox, Grove had an excellent 105–62 record and 3.34 ERA. He still ranks among the team's all-time leaders in several pitching categories.

Born Robert Moses Grove (the family name was originally Groves, and many writers used the pluralized version), Lefty joined the minor league Baltimore Orioles in 1920—6 years after they sold a lefthander named Babe Ruth to the Red Sox. Grove was outstanding with Baltimore, winning 108 games in 5 years, but owner Jack Dunn refused to sell the overqualified pitcher to the majors until he was 25 years old. (As great as Grove was, he might have had upwards of 350 major league wins had Dunn been less stubborn.) Connie Mack of the Athletics bought Grove for a then-record $100,600, but was mocked when the young pitcher struggled as a rookie. He led the American League in strikeouts (as he did in each of his first 7 seasons), but went 10–12 with a 4.75 ERA. Grove also led the league in walks, and developed a reputation for immaturity. His temper tantrums angered teammates, especially after he blamed them for making errors—Lefty always made sure to use his right hand, though, when he punched walls or lockers.

Grove's control improved in 1926, and he won his first ERA title. He followed that with three 20-win seasons. But in 1930, Grove took his game to a new level, winning pitching's Triple Crown (league leading 28–5 record, 2.54 ERA, and 209 strikeouts—not to mention an American League-best 9 saves), and leading the A's to their second consecutive World Championship. Believe it or not, Grove was even better in 1931. He repeated his Triple Crown, going 31–4 with a 2.06 ERA and 175 strikeouts, while completing 27 of his 30 starts (and saving 5 games in 11 relief appearances). Only one pitcher has won 30 or more games since (Detroit's Denny McLain, 31–6 in 1968), and Grove was rewarded with the MVP Award. At one point in 1931, he tied an American League-record by winning 16 games in a row—though he forever blamed Hall of Fame teammate Al Simmons for ending the streak. Simmons was injured, and his replacement misjudged a fly ball, leading to a 1–0 loss.

Grove won 25 and 24 games in 1932 and 1933, but the Great Depression put the Athletics in dire financial straits. Manager/owner Connie Mack had broken up a great team in 1915, and he was forced to do the same in the 1930s. New Red Sox owner Tom Yawkey, eager to spend big money on the biggest stars he could get, gladly gave Mack $125,000 for Grove. (Yawkey would later acquire another Hall of Famer from Mack: first baseman Jimmie Foxx.)

Red Sox fans were eager to see their new star, but there was one problem: Grove's workload, which typically included 10–15 emergency relief appearances, had taken a toll. With the Athletics, he had relied almost exclusively on his blazing fastball, but he was now 34 years old. Grove's velocity was down, and his arm was bothering him for the first time. Expectations were high, but Grove couldn't get on track in the spring of 1934. Doctors first thought his sore arm was caused by dental problems, but it still hurt even after 3 abscessed teeth were removed. The stubborn Grove decided to pitch through his pain, while teaching himself a now-needed curve ball, but he had a disastrous season (8–8, 6.50 in only 109 innings).

Thought to be washed up, Grove rebounded in 1935, winning 20 games and leading the league in ERA for the sixth time (2.70). He repeated the ERA title in 1936 (his 2.81 was over 2 runs better than the American League's 5.04) and won 17 games. Grove won 17 games again in 1937, the last season in which he pitched more than 200 innings. By this time, Grove almost never pitched in relief, and he needed more days off between starts. But while his workload was diminished, Grove was still a very valuable spot starter, winning 29 games (and his eighth and ninth ERA titles) in 1938–39. His performance declined as a 40 year old (7–6, 3.99), leaving him 7 wins shy of 300.

For some reason a myth has persisted that Grove was horrendous in 1941, and that the Sox kept sending him out there, even if he was bombed, until he won 300. This isn't entirely true, as his 4.37 ERA was near the league average. Grove started the season well enough, going 6–2, but lost his next two starts. Finally, on July 25, 1941, Grove beat Cleveland for number 300, but it wasn't pretty: a complete-game 12-hitter in a 10–6 slugfest. His longtime teammate Jimmie Foxx had the game-winning triple. Though overshadowed by Ted Williams's quest for .400 and Joe DiMaggio's 56-game hitting streak, Grove's achievement was duly celebrated. He was the twelfth pitcher, and the first modern lefthander, to win 300 games. Uncharacteristically, he even threw a big champagne party for his teammates at a luxury hotel.

Unfortunately, that was Grove's final victory. He lost 2 more games before injuring his ribcage. Though urged to retire, Grove came back to pitch the season's final game (Game 2 of the famous doubleheader in which his good friend Ted Williams went 6-for-8 to finish at .406). He lost, though few noticed or cared, and finished the year at 7–7.

Grove contemplated coming back for another season, but Yawkey gently talked him out of it, since Grove had already achieved so much. He officially retired in December 1941, though he contemplated a comeback in 1942, when World War II thinned out the Red Sox pitching staff. Yawkey offered Grove a job as pitching coach, but he decided to return to his Maryland hometown, where had several business interests (and later coached youth baseball). Grove was elected to the Hall of Fame in 1947, and he died in 1975.

Jackie Gutierrez—flashy, Colombian-born shortstop, best known for his habit of loudly whistling during games. Gutierrez joined the Red Sox in late 1983, and replaced Glenn Hoffman as the regular shortstop the following year. He had spectacular defensive tools, including speed and a fine arm, but often botched routine plays. The rookie hit .263 and stole 12 bases, but had only 17 extra base hits and 15 walks. Still, the Sox had high hopes for Gutierrez, and fans loved his enthusiasm. But while his defense was more consistent in 1985, his average sank to an unacceptable .218. Hoffman regained the starting job in the second half, and Gutierrez was traded to Baltimore after the season for reliever Sammy Stewart. The Orioles had Cal Ripken Jr. at shortstop, so Gutierrez barely played—and never learned how to hit. By 1988, his once-promising big league career was over.

Erik Hanson—a righthanded pitcher, Hanson started 6 games with Seattle in 1988, then went 27–14 over the next 2 years—including an18–9 mark in 1990, establishing himself as one of the American League's best starters. Injuries and inconsistency plagued him after that season, and he lost 17 games for Seattle in 1992. After the 1993 season, he signed with Cincinnati, where despite continuing arm problems he pitched for the Reds until the 1994 strike hit.

When the labor dispute was settled in the spring of 1995 Hanson, along with many other players who had been without contracts, went through a free agent spring training session in Homestead, Florida. Dan Duquette signed Hanson out of the Homestead camp, and he went 15–5 for the 1995 American League East–champion Boston Red Sox. Noted for a biting curveball and a nasty forkball, chronic elbow problems made throwing the curve nearly impossible in Hanson's year with the Red Sox. He fought constant elbow problems to strike out 139 batters, and his record greatly benefited from excellent run support. (His gaudy won-loss record helped him to the All Star team.) In the playoffs, he started Game 2 at Jacobs Field in Cleveland, and pitched fairly well, giving up 4 runs over 8 innings to the powerhouse Indians, who had managed to win 100 games even in the strike-shortened season, but the Red Sox were shut out by Cleveland righty Orel Hershiser and Hanson took the loss.

In the offseason, Hanson's salary demands were more than Boston was willing to pay, and he signed as a free agent with the Toronto Blue Jays. After a 1996 season in which he was basically a league average starter for the Blue Jays, injury problems struck again. He pitched only 15 innings in the 1997 season, and finished his career with 41 innings in 1998.

Carroll Hardy—a righthanded journeyman outfielder who began his major league baseball career in 1958 in Cleveland, Hardy was never a good hitter, though he did have a couple of memorable pinch-hitting at-bats. He had played defensive back for the San Francisco 49ers during the 1955 National Football League season before the Red Sox acquired him in 1960, and he became the answer to a couple of trivia questions. In September of 1960 Hardy became the only man to ever pinch-hit for Ted Williams, who had fouled a ball off his ankle and had to leave the game in the middle of his at bat. Hardy bunted into a double play. Six days later, Williams hit a home run in his last major league at-bat at Fenway. After Williams went out to left field in the top of the ninth, Hardy replaced him, and Williams left the field to a standing ovation. In his career, Hardy also pinch-hit for a young Roger Maris (hitting a 3-run homer) and Carl Yastrzemski. He also played for the Twins and Padres in an 8 season career that spanned 10 years.

Tommy Harper—speedy outfielder who holds the Red Sox record for steals in a season. Harper played 3 seasons for the Sox toward the end of his career. In 1973 he stole 54 bases while hitting .281 with 17 home runs and an above-average number of walks (league average was .259). He was an average hitter for most of his career, though (career batting average of .254), and slumped to .237 with 28 steals the following year. After his playing career ended, Harper coached for the Red Sox, but left the team bitterly after making accusations of racism at the Red Sox spring training facility in Florida. He returned as Red Sox first base coach for the 2000 season, and as a de facto hitting coach for many players who preferred Harper to batting coach Jim Rice.

Ken Harrelson—Nicknamed "Hawk" by catcher Duke Sims, for his large, hooked nose (Harrelson even took to wearing "Hawk" on the back of his uniform, instead of the customary last name) the always-flamboyant Ken could easily have been baseball's poster child for 1960s fashion and style.

Harrelson began his big league career in 1965 with the A's. In 1967 Harrelson publicly called A's owner Charlie Finley a menace to baseball. This so enraged Finley that he released Harrelson, who was then courted by 7 teams. The contract he eventually signed with Boston included a then-nearly unheard of $73,000 bonus. The Red Sox were in the thick of a pennant race, and Harrelson helped some, appearing in 23 games and hitting 4 homers, with 16 runs batted in. In 1968 Harrelson hit 35 home runs and drove in a league-leading 109 runs. He was extremely popular with the fans, and when he was traded to Cleveland in early 1969 fans picketed Fenway Park. (Harrelson was also unhappy with the trade, and threatened to retire instead of accepting it.)

George Will's book *Bunts* tells a possibly legendary story that on the day of a night game in which he didn't expect to play, Harrelson played 36 holes of golf. Finding himself in the lineup, Harrelson wore his golf gloves to protect his blistered hands when he came to bat. Thus the origin of the batting glove, a staple for today's players.

Harrelson broke his leg in 1970, missed most of that season, and remained unhappy playing in Cleveland. He quit baseball in 1971 to become a pro golfer, something he had threatened to do repeatedly. This attempt ultimately failed, and since then "Hawk" has spent time as an outspoken (as always) but popular (as always) broadcaster for the Chicago White Sox, and even served a short, rocky stint as the White Sox general manager in the mid-1980s. While his playing star shone for a short period of time, it was never boring.

Greg Harris—ambidextrous pitcher who revived his career with the Red Sox in the early 1990s. Harris was a much-traveled player who'd been a failure as a starter but a very successful middle reliever throughout the 1980s. Boston picked the 33-year-old up on waivers in August 1989, after the Phillies (his sixth team) decided they didn't need him. Over the next 5 years Harris pitched well in a variety of roles for the Sox, playing the same kind of swingman role on the pitching staff that Bob Stanley had before him and Tim Wakefield would after him. He spent most of 1990–91 in the starting rotation, then as a reliever was among the league leaders in appearances in 1992–93. The workload seemed to catch up with him in 1984, when he pitched terribly at age 38, and the Red Sox released him. He went on to pitch for 2 more teams, including an excellent 1995 season, after which he retired.

Harris threw righthanded with the Red Sox, but was truly ambidextrous, and claimed he could pitch equally well from either side. He had a special 6-fingered glove made that could be used with either hand, to allow him to switch hands during games. Red Sox GM Lou Gorman, however, refused to allow Harris to throw lefthanded during a game, feeling it would make a mockery of the game.

Mickey Harris—a righthanded pitcher who came up with Boston in 1940 and pitched poorly in limited innings. In 1941, even though the Red Sox were the top scoring team in the league, he managed to go 8–14, despite having an ERA significantly better than league average. He was one of the first Red Sox players to be drafted into the military in World War II, and was gone from 1942–45. When he came back in 1946, he went 17–9 for the first Red Sox pennant winners in 28 years. He was the losing pitcher in 2 games of the 1946 World Series, though he didn't pitch particularly badly.

But that was the only season of his career in which he won as many as 10 games. He pitched extremely well in 1947, but arm injuries limited him to only 51⅔ innings pitched. In 1949 he was traded to Washington, and was eventually moved to the bullpen full time. In 1950 he led the American League in both saves (with 15) and games appeared in (with 53). He pitched two more years, for Washington and Cleveland, pitching entirely out of the bullpen, and not particularly well. His career ended with Cleveland in 1952.

Billy Hatcher—an outfielder with an inconsistent bat and a reputation as a base stealer with Cincinnati and Houston, he was traded to Boston in 1992, where his speed and hitting both deserted him. His one great moment in Boston was a scintillating straight steal of home, one of the highlights of the dreary 1993 season.

Scott Hatteberg—after short visits in 1995 and 1996, the lefthanded-hitting Hatteberg came to the Red Sox to stay in 1997. A top catching prospect valued for his defense, Hatteberg had not hit particularly well in the minors, and only made the team because he was out of options, and the Red Sox could not return him to the minors without the risk of losing him. To everyone's surprise, he hit .273 through the 2000 season, with decent power and the ability to walk frequently. He has been used primarily as a platoon player (recently with Jason Varitek) most of his career, though in 2000 he was used as a DH in several games. Ironically, because he has hit very well for a catcher, many people assume that Hatteberg's defense is poor and he is in the major leagues just for his bat—even though it was his defense that got him to the majors in the first place.

Dave "Hendu" Henderson—very few players made such an impact in a short period of time in a Sox uniform. He arrived in May 1986, coming (along with Spike Owen) from the Seattle Mariners in exchange for Mike Brown, Mike Trujillo, and Rey Quinones. Henderson played only 111 games for Boston (and 12 more in the post-season) before being traded to the San Francisco Giants early in the 1987 season. He had already become part of Boston history, even before joining the team, as he was the victim of 3 of Roger Clemens's 20 history-making strikeouts against the Mariners in April.

But his moment to shine came in Game 5 of the 1985 American League Championship Series in Anaheim against the California Angels. Though he managed only 1 hit in 9 at bats during the American League Championship Series, that hit was a doozy. In the ninth inning of Game 5, with the Red Sox 1 strike away from losing the game and the series, Hendu hit a 2-out, 2-run homer off Angels' relief ace Donnie Moore to vault the Sox into the lead. Then in the eleventh inning he drove in the winning run with a sacrifice fly. The home run in the ninth was probably one of the 3 most dramatic home runs in Red Sox history (along with Carbo's and Fisk's in Game 6 of the 1975 World Series). Henderson followed with another huge home run that was overshadowed: His homer in Game 6 of the World Series would have been the game winner if the Red Sox relievers hadn't failed to hold the lead.

In the late 1980s Hendu played several years as a key component of the power-house Oakland A's before finishing with 1 year in Kansas City. Tragically, Donnie Moore went into a tailspin after giving up Henderson's home run. In July 1989, Moore shot his estranged wife and himself, in front of their 10-year-old son. Moore died, but the wife eventually recovered.

Joe Hesketh—lefthanded pitcher who joined Boston for the pennant drive in 1990 and stayed for 4 more mostly undistinguished years. He did pitch well in 1991, when he went 12–4, splitting time between starting and relief. He once got so distracted arguing with an umpire that he allowed a baserunner to steal second, third, and home.

Pinky Higgins—Higgins was a hard hitting and steady fielding third baseman, who in his 12-year career twice drove in 106 runs. Today he is better remembered for his unfortunate racial views than for his baseball skills. After starting his career with the A's (where he hit for the cycle in 1933), Higgins was traded to Boston for the 1937 season. In 1938 Higgins had 12 consecutive hits (the last 8 in a doubleheader) to break Tris Speaker's 18-year-old major league record of 11. In a 1940 World Series game he set a record by handling 10 chances at third base.

Higgins retired as a player after playing in all 7 games of the 1946 World Series for the Red Sox.

Higgins returned to Boston to manage the Red Sox from 1955 to 1959, was kicked upstairs, then managed again from 1960 to 1962. His low key manner and patience with young players made him popular with some, although his teams never finished higher than third place. Higgins also served for a while as the Red Sox Vice President and GM. He was fired as GM on September 16, 1965, the day Dave Morehead threw the last no hitter by a Red Sox pitcher.

As a manager and administrator Higgins was closely tied with the Red Sox reluctance to integrate. Author Al Hirshberg interviewed Higgins in the 1950s and claimed that Higgins said, "There'll be no niggers on this ballclub as long as I have anything to say about it." Earl Wilson, Boston's first black pitcher, was particularly vocal about Higgins's treatment of black players—and was traded after speaking out.

In 1969 Higgins was convicted of negligent homicide and jailed in Louisiana after killing someone in a DUI incident. He ran over 4 highway workers, one of whom died. Higgins served only 2 months of a 4-year sentence. Two days after he got out of prison he died of a heart attack.

Butch Hobson—former Alabama quarterback who played third base for the Red Sox during the late seventies. One of the reasons that the Red Sox lineup looked so strong during the 1978 season was that Clell Lavern "Buch" Hobson, hitting ninth, had hit 30 home runs in 1977. He was never good, however, at actually getting on base, finishing his career in 1982 with a career .297 on-base percentage. He was a fan favorite for the way he played the game (with reckless abandon), several times falling down dugout steps to go after foul ball pop-ups. This led to severe problems during the 1978 meltdown, however, as he played the season constantly re-adjusting loose bone chips in his throwing elbow. During that 1978 season he hit only 17 home runs and committed an astounding 43 errors at third base—mostly poor throws—before he was finally benched in late September.

Hobson later managed the team for 3 unsuccessful years, amassing a 207–232 record. He had 1 more significant event that related to the Red Sox. He was serving as the manager of the Phillies AAA team, the Scranton Wilkes-Barre Red Barons, when he received a package from someone in his hometown. The police arrested him that night for cocaine possession. He claimed that he must have received the package by mistake, and many fans were extremely surprised, but the word from the beat writers who covered the team was that no one was surprised by the arrest. The Red Sox connection to the cocaine story? When he received the package and was arrested his team was playing in Pawtucket against the Pawtucket Red Sox. Hobson currently managies an independent team in New Hampshire.

Glenn Hoffman—strong-armed, weak-hitting shortstop who replaced Rick Burleson in the early 1980s. A highly touted minor league prospect, Hoffman made the team as a backup infielder in 1980. Because of Butch Hobson's injuries and ineffectiveness, Hoffman got significant playing time at third base. He fielded well and hit an encour-

Two and a half years ago I suffered a stroke that partially paralyzed my left side. It severely limited my ability to walk, especially in crowded, uncertain conditions. At one time, something like a ball game at Fenway Park was out of the question.

On Sunday September 25, 2000, the last day of the home season for the Boston Red Sox, I attended my first post-stroke game.

We got lucky in the parking, getting a spot 50 yards or so from the main gates. I bought a traditional Sox cap before even entering the park and had pictures taken in front of the park by my brother, who apparently understood the significance of the event. Once through the turnstiles, I had to get a program and a yearbook. We went to our seats through the twisting, rising ramp. When I got my first sight of the field, tears came to my eyes. I hadn't expected this degree of emotion. We found our seats, which was tough, as going down steps is my biggest challenge. Got seated about 15 minutes before game time. Though it's work for me to stand, I did my duty and stood for the National Anthem (part of the whole experience).

The game got under way under threatening skies. It rained some early, but we stayed dry because we were in box seats just to the first base side of home plate. Ohka was very impressive for 7–plus innings, but Mussina was a little better. Baltimore scored its only run in the 8th. The Sox had a couple of good scoring chances late, but failed to score while having the game-tying run thrown out at the plate in the ninth. A disappointment, but it did not spoil the specialness of the day for this disabled fan from Vermont.

I've seen many games at Fenway, some very memorable for many reasons, but while I don't remember my first game, I'm never likely to forget this one. We already are planning a trip next spring. I ain't done with Ye Olde Towne Team yet.

—Don Violette

aging .285, though he lacked the power associated with that position. After Burleson and Hobson were traded for third baseman Carney Lansford, Hoffman moved back to his natural shortstop spot. But while Hoffman was a very capable fielder, his bat regressed (.231 and .209 in 1981–82). He improved to .260 in 1983, but his on-base and slugging percentages remained well below average. Hoffman lost his starting job to Jackie Gutierrez in 1984, but regained it the following year, when he hit a surprising .276, with more power than usual. An irregular heartbeat cost Hoffman most of the 1986 season, and he was traded to the Dodgers early the next year. Hoffman managed the Dodgers in the second half of 1998, and his younger brother Trevor is a star reliever on the San Diego Padres.

Harry Hooper—part of an extraordinary outfield on the great Sox teams of the 1910s (along with Duffy Lewis and Tris Speaker), Hooper was known for his excellent throwing arm. Hooper would later draw comparisons to another outstanding Sox right fielder, Dwight Evans, who also had a great arm and was a similar offensive player in many ways. Hooper was one of the Sox few good hitters on the pitching-dominated teams of the teens (he played for the Red Sox from 1909 to 1920). Although he was inconsistent from year to year, he hit .281 over a 17-year career with a little power (usually 10–15 triples and 3–4 home runs a year, pretty good in the dead ball era when the league leader in homers usually hit 9 or 10 and the league batting average was in the .240s), drew a lot of walks, seldom struck out, and was a prolific base stealer. Hooper is still the Red Sox career leader with 300 stolen bases. Hooper was selected to the Hall of Fame, but there was some criticism of his selection, since he was seen as a very good—but not necessarily great player. This perception may come from his spending many years playing in the shadow of center fielder and fellow Hall of Famer Tris Speaker, a career .344 hitter who outshone Hooper in nearly every facet of the game.

Sam Horn—slugging first baseman who was dumped in the Red Sox housecleaning of the late 1980s. Horn was slow and a poor fielder, but he had a ton of power. When he was called up as a 23-year-old in 1987, he hit 14 home runs in only 158 at bats (a pace of about 50 for a full season) and looked like the next great Boston power hitter. He walked frequently, but he also struck out at an astonishing pace—almost a third of hit plate appearances ended in strikeouts. He hit poorly in very brief appearances over the next 2 years, and was released without ever being given a chance to earn more playing time. Horn played well as a part-timer for 2 seasons in Baltimore, and then appeared sporadically in the major leagues until 1995.

Dwayne Hosey—a 28-year-old career minor leaguer, Dwayne Hosey hit .338 with 12 extra base hits and 3 steals late in 1995, although his defense in center field was adventurous. He was given a shot as the starting center fielder the next year, but when he failed to hit in the first 28 games of the 1996 season, Sox management gave up on him and gave the job back to incumbent center fielder Lee Tinsley and Milt Cuyler. Curiously, all 3 center fielders that played regularly for the Sox that year were switch hitters. Hosey was eventually sold to the Yakult Swallows in the Japanese League. He played in the independent Northern League in 2000, and was signed by the Anaheim Angels following the season.

Tom House—a lefty reliever, House's biggest moment in baseball was as a footnote. On April 8, 1975 he was in the bullpen in Atlanta and caught Hank Aaron's 715th home run. This home run set a new career home run record. House was unimpressive in 1976 and part of 1977 with the Red Sox, winning 2 games and losing 3.

Elston Howard—a righthanded-hitting catcher, Howard spent the vast majority of his 13-year career with the Yankees, making the All Star team 9 times and winning the American League MVP award in 1963. He was still playing for the Yankees when the 1967 season started and broke up Billy Rohr's no-hit bid in Yankee Stadium in April. Traded to the Sox during that season, he was a backup on the 1967 pennant winners. He finished out his career by playing in 71 games for the Sox in 1968.

Waite Hoyt—Hall of Fame pitcher, best known as the ace of the powerful 1927 "Murderer's Row" Yankees, who pitched for the Red Sox in 1919 and 1920. The Brooklyn-born Hoyt was signed by New York Giants manager John McGraw as a 15-

year-old, but pitched only 1 game for the Giants before being sent to Boston. Still a teenager, Hoyt went 4–6 as a spot starter with the Sox in 1919, and was 6–6 in the same role the following year. After the 1920 season, he and catcher Wally Schang were traded to the Yankees for second baseman Del Pratt. Along with ex-Sox like Babe Ruth and Herb Pennock, Hoyt helped the Yankees begin their long string of championships. He won 237 games during his 21-year career, and was elected to the Hall of Fame by the Veterans Committee in 1969. Hoyt is often cited as one of the least-deserving Hall of Famers, but his 45 wins in 1927–28, along with his engaging personality, inflated his reputation. A gifted storyteller and part-time vaudeville singer, Hoyt was one of the first ex-jocks to go into broadcasting, doing Cincinnati Reds games on the radio for 24 years.

Long Tom Hughes—a righthanded pitcher, Hughes spent 1½ of his 13 seasons with the Red Sox. At the age of 24, Hughes went 20–7 for the 1903 Red Sox team that won the first World Series. He only threw 2 innings in the World Series, giving up 2 runs and taking the loss in Game 3. He was called "Long Tom" because of his height.

Tex Hughson—one of a number of good pitchers for the Red Sox in the 1940s whose career ended prematurely due to arm trouble. Debuting in 1941, Hughson led the league in wins (22) and innings (281) the next year at age 26. For this, Hughson earned his first trip to the All Star Game, an honor he earned each of the next 3 years. Over this 3-year period, Hughson pitched 750 innings, with ERAs of 2.59, 2.64, and 2.26. Missing the next season because of World War II, Hughson did not pitch again until 1946, when he won 20 games (fifth in the league) while pitching 278 innings (third in the league) with a 2.75 ERA. With Hughson and Boo Ferriss (25 wins) leading the staff, the Red Sox easily won the American League pennant, but lost to the Cardinals in the World Series.

Unfortunately, what looked like a potential juggernaut was damaged when both Hughson and Ferriss developed arm trouble. Hughson declined to a 3.33 ERA in 189 innings in 1947, and then only threw 96 more innings over the next 2 years before retiring at age 33. Those fans who believe that managers should be wary of having their pitchers throw too many innings point to Hughson to support their argument. Red Sox fans, meanwhile, can only wonder at what Red Sox history might have been had the foursome of Hughson, Ferriss, Ellis Kinder, and Mel Parnell been able to stay healthy throughout the latter half of the 1940s and early 1950s. Certainly, it seems likely that the Sox would at least have won pennants in 1948 and 1949 (in both seasons they finished second by a single game). Ah, what might have been!

Bruce Hurst—one of a group of young starting pitchers the Red Sox developed in the early 1980s, along with John Tudor, Bob Ojeda, Al Nipper, Oil Can Boyd, and Roger Clemens. He debuted in 1980, but did not make the majors full-time until 1982. Although he was considered a better prospect than Boyd or Ojeda (who came up about the same time), Hurst struggled badly at first. (He was 3–7 in 1982 with a 5.77 ERA.) But Hurst gradually blossomed into a good pitcher (if not a star), and started 30 or more games in 8 of the next 9 seasons. In 1986 (when Hurst started only 25 games because of injury) he went 13–8 with a 2.99 ERA and was a huge factor in helping the Sox get to the World Series. Hurst pitched well in the Series as well, starting Game 1 against the Mets (staff ace Roger Clemens had started Game 7 of the American League Championship Series against the Angels and was unavailable) and winning the game 1–0 for the Sox in the Mets' home stadium.

Hurst continued to pitch well for the Sox for the next 2 years, and had his finest year (18–6) in 1988, when the Sox once again made the playoffs. However, Hurst, a devoutly religious man, was deeply offended by a number of sordid scandals involving Red Sox players (including the very public allegations made by Wade Boggs's mistress, Margo Adams) and left the team as a free agent following the season.

Reggie Jefferson—lefthanded-hitting first baseman who spent 5 seasons with the Red Sox. Jefferson spent time with Cincinnati, Cleveland, and Seattle before signing with the Red Sox prior to the 1995 season. Never a good defender, he spent most of his time in Boston as a platoon DH. He hit righthanded pitching well, but was never able to hit lefties. (Jefferson actually started his major league career as a switch hitter, but eventually abandoned righthanded hitting entirely.) During the later parts of the 1997 season he complained in the media that he wasn't going to get a chance to win the batting title, even though he was leading the league in hitting, because he wasn't getting enough at-bats. That changed after his platoon partner Mike Stanley was traded to the Yankees, but Jefferson slumped badly down the stretch, and finished up eighth in the league in batting. After that season, his playing time was limited by recurring back problems.

Jefferson was left off of the postseason roster in 1999 (with third baseman John Valentin questionable because of injury, the Sox opted to carry a second third baseman instead of Jefferson), and after complaining loudly in the press, he left the team. He might have been added prior to the Yankee series had that not happened, and he might have made a difference. Jefferson signed a one-year contract with the Seibu Lions of the Pacific League in Japan prior to the 2000 season.

Ferguson Jenkins—Hall of Fame pitcher who won 284 games in 19 major league seasons, but only 22 in his 2 years with the Red Sox. Fergie Jenkins became a star with the Cubs, winning 20 or more games every season from 1967–72. In 1971 he won the National League Cy Young Award, with a 24–13 record and a 2.77 ERA (excellent for a pitcher in Wrigley Field, a hitter's park). He was traded to Texas in 1974 and promptly won a career-high 25 games. After a disappointing 17–18 season in 1975, Jenkins was traded to Boston for promising outfielder Juan Beniquez.

He appeared to be a perfect addition to a team that nearly won the World Series, yet needed another starter. But Jenkins, who had pitched over 300 innings 5 times in his career, wasn't as durable or dominating with Boston. He pitched 209 innings in 1976, going a mediocre 12–11 though his ERA was a very solid 3.27. In 1977 Jenkins was 10–10 with a 3.68 ERA (good in a particularly high-offense season). But he only pitched 193 innings and only struck out 105 hitters (he had 7 prior 200-strikeout seasons). More importantly, he never got along with Red Sox manager Don Zimmer, a conservative, old-school, often uptight man. Jenkins was a member of The Loyal Order of Buffalo Heads, a faction of anti-Zimmer players led by Bill Lee, Bernie Carbo, Jim Willoughby, and Rick Wise. The name was initiated by Jenkins, who said that the buffalo was the dumbest animal, and thus reminded him of Zimmer. The manager barely pitched Jenkins down the stretch in 1977, despite the close pennant race, and the veteran was sent back to Texas after the season for pitcher John Poloni, who never appeared in a game with Boston. Jenkins, who would surely have come in handy for the Red Sox in 1978, spent the season with the Rangers, going 18–8 with a 3.04 ERA—exactly the kind of year he usually had before joining Boston.

In 1980, while still with Texas, Jenkins was arrested for drug possession at a Canadian airport. He denied the charges, saying he was set up, and the judge dismissed the case citing the pitcher's strong record of community service and status as a Canadian sports hero (he was born in Chatham, Ontario, and was arguably the best Canadian-born player in baseball history). Jenkins rejoined the Cubs for his final two seasons, and retired in 1983 as the only pitcher ever to have over 3000 strikeouts, yet under 1000 walks.

In 1991, he became the first (and so far, only) Canadian to make the Hall of Fame. He was first eligible in 1989, but suffered because Yaz, Johnny Bench, and Gaylord Perry were also on the ballot for the first time. Also, since he was so consistent, yet never played for a pennant-winner, Jenkins was underrated for most of his career—especially compared to peers like Bob Gibson, Tom Seaver, and Steve Carlton.

Shortly after his making the Hall of Fame, Jenkins's wife died of injuries from a car accident. Two years later, his live-in girlfriend killed herself and Jenkins's young daughter at their ranch. A deeply religious man, Jenkins has done his best to persevere after these tragedies. He has since remarried, and has returned to baseball as a coach and minor league instructor.

Jackie Jensen—a righthanded hitter who excelled at both football and baseball at the University of California-Berkeley. A gifted athlete with numerous talents, the "Golden Boy" earned several honors in both sports at Berkeley. As a freshman fullback he played in the East-West Shrine All Star game, and he went to the Rose Bowl as a junior, finishing fourth in voting for the Heisman trophy that year.

Jensen's baseball talents were diverse as well. He excelled as both a hitter and a pitcher for the Golden Bears, and even played against Yale first baseman and future US president George Bush in the first NCAA World Series. He is in fact the only man in history ever to play in an East-West football game, a Rose Bowl, a baseball All Star game, and a major league World Series.

In 1949 Jensen decided to forgo his senior year to play professional baseball. He made his major league debut with the New York Yankees the following year, on the brink of Joe DiMaggio's retirement. He hit .249 in parts of three seasons with New York (including a promising .298 with 8 homers in limited action in 1951) before the Yanks sent Jensen to the Washington Senators, opting to go with future legend Mickey Mantle instead.

In Washington Jensen enjoyed playing time and production, averaging 82 RBI in his 2 seasons there. The Red Sox were impressed by his play and traded Marty McDermott and Tom Umphlett to get him before the 1954 season. Jensen's offensive numbers exploded with the Sox, as he launched over 20 homers in each of his first 6 seasons in Boston (including 35 in 1958), and topped 100 RBI 5 times. More impressively, his contact hitting was terrific for a power hitter. In an 11-year career, Jensen's season high for strikeouts was just 69, and he walked frequently. Despite this ability he hit over .300 just once, in 1956. He was a player of many tools, including speed (he reached double digits in stolen bases 7 times, including a league-leading 22 in 1954 at a time when stolen bases were uncommon). His 35 homers, along with a .286 average and 122 RBI, earned Jensen American League Most Valuable Player honors in 1958. The following year he won his only Gold Glove award.

As Jensen flourished through the 1950s, so did postwar baseball. The game expanded to the West, eventually taking teams such as the Dodgers and Giants to California. With this expansion came the more frequent use of airplanes to transport teams around the country. This presented an emotional problem for Jensen, who could not overcome his fear of flying. Based on this fear, Jensen surprised the baseball world by choosing to retire at age 32, despite a successful 1959 season (he'd led the league in RBI for the second straight year). He attempted a brief comeback with the Red Sox in 1961 but retired again after a disappointing performance. He finished his short career with a .279 average and 199 home runs.

"Indian Bob" Johnson—one of the most underrated players in major league history, Johnson never seemed to be on the right team at the right time. In his 13-year career, Johnson made 8 All Star teams and drove in 100 or more runs 8 times, while playing consistently good defense in left field. But despite his fine stats and colorful (if politically incorrect) nickname, Johnson is largely forgotten today.

Johnson, a half-Cherokee, joined the Philadelphia Athletics in 1933, replacing Hall of Famer Al Simmons. Connie Mack would soon dump 3 more all-time greats (Lefty Grove, Mickey Cochrane, and Jimmie Foxx), and the A's began a 4-decade tailspin. But Johnson continued to play extremely well, hitting around .300 with 25–30 homers and 85–90 walks a season. He was traded to the Washington Senators in 1943 for Bobby Estalella (the grandfather of the current Giants catcher), but had a subpar season.

Tom Yawkey bought Johnson from Washington in 1944, and Indian Bob filled in ably for Ted Williams, who was in the military. Johnson led the American League with a .431 on-base percentage and batted .324, with 40 doubles, 17 homers, and 106 RBI. To be fair, the quality of baseball during World War II was weak, as stars like Williams were in the service. But Johnson was still one of the league's best hitters, and he started in the All Star game. Johnson didn't do as well in 1945, when he slipped to .280, with only 12 homers, though he made the All Star team again. After the season, the 39-year-old Johnson retired. As usual, his timing was horrible. Just as he joined the A's too late to play on their great teams, he left the Red Sox too soon to enjoy their great 1946 season. Several statisticians have lobbied for Johnson's inclusion in the Hall of Fame, and he was clearly better than several outfielders who are in in the Hall. However, he has never been mentioned as a serious Veterans Committee candidate, and he'll likely remain on "best players not in the Hall" lists.

Johnson's brother Roy, who also had a .296 lifetime average, played outfield for the Red Sox from 1932–35.

Earl Johnson—a lefthanded pitcher who went 40–32 with Boston over the course of 7 seasons, from 1940–50. Johnson was one of the first Red Sox players lost to military service (in the fall of 1941), and when he came back, he was the war hero in the Boston clubhouse. In the Battle of the Bulge, his actions earned both Bronze and Silver Stars, and at one point he received a battlefield promotion to lieutenant.

Over ¾ of his appearances were out of the bullpen. He was the winning pitcher, in relief, of Game 1 of the 1946 World Series. Johnson had his best season in 1947, throwing 142⅓ strong innings and winning 12 games. In 1951, he finished his career pitching 5⅔ weak innings for Detroit.

Sad Sam Jones—righthanded pitcher who is a footnote to the worst moment in Red Sox history. Jones was the last player sold to the Yankees in 1921. In 1918, Jones went 16–5 with a 2.25 ERA for the World Series winning Red Sox. He followed that up in 1919 by going 12–20, and 13–16 for the now-Ruth-less Sox in 1920. In 1921 he went 23–16 before being sold to the Yankees. Jones pitched 14 more seasons in the majors, but his best was in a Sox uniform.

Eddie Joost—played but 1 season for the Red Sox, the rather forgettable 1955 season in which, at the age of 39, he played in 55 games, batting a lowly .193. As had been a trademark throughout his 17-year career, his good batting eye allowed him to draw walks even when his ability to hit the ball was in question. Thus, though he hit only .193, he got on base at a .299 clip (which is not actually all that good in and of itself, but is amazing considering the man could not really hit the ball anymore). Thus the man who walked over 100 times in 6 consecutive seasons in the heart of his career, despite never hitting well enough to really warrant pitchers' actually pitching around him, left the game the same way he entered it—walking.

Ed Jurak—a utility infielder who spent four years with the Red Sox from 1982 to 1985. His big moment of glory came when he caught, in his glove, a rat which was running around on the field during a game at Fenway.

George Kell—Hall of Fame third baseman who played in 15 major league seasons, all in the American League. Kell, a contact hitter with consistently low strikeout numbers (his high total for a full season was 37), spent the prime of his career with the Detroit Tigers before joining the Red Sox in 1952. In parts of three seasons with the Sox he hit .305, and his season high of 12 home runs came in 1953. He was traded to the White Sox in 1954. He retired in 1957 with a .306 career average, and was inducted into the Hall by the Veterans Committee in 1983.

Dana Kiecker—an ex-UPS driver who came out of nowhere to win a spot as a 29-year-old rookie and folk hero on the 1990 Red Sox. He pitched reasonably well for a thin pitching staff, and was a surprise starter in the playoffs against Oakland (where he pitched well in a losing cause). He didn't have overpowering stuff, and the next year he wasn't fooling anybody anymore. Kiecker's ERA nearly doubled in 1991, and he was out of baseball at age 30.

Ellis Kinder—one of many young men whose careers were abbreviated because of contributions to his country during World War II, Ellis Kinder did not begin his major league career in baseball until 1946, by which time he was already 31. Kinder began his career with the St Louis Browns, for whom he toiled for 2 seasons before being acquired by the Red Sox in a trade.

Kinder's arrival, along with the emergence of young lefthander Mel Parnell, helped spark the dormant Red Sox who, after winning the pennant in 1946, languished at a distant third in 1947. The 1948 team finished tied for first with the Cleveland Indians. To start the all-important 1-game playoff to determine the pennant, manager Joe McCarthy passed over Kinder and Parnell, as well as Joe Dobson (who led the team in innings pitched) and Jack Kramer (who led the team in wins) in order to pitch journeyman Denny Galehouse. The Indians went on to win the game handily (and thus the pennant), depriving Boston of its best chance for a subway series (since the Boston Braves were the National League pennant winner). As it happens, Cleveland has not won a World Series since beating the Braves 4–2 in 1948.

Kinder had an even better season in 1949, going 23–6 with a 3.36 ERA in 252 innings, providing a 1–2 punch along with the 25–7 Mel Parnell that gave the Red Sox a chance to clinch the pennant on the final weekend of the season. Unfortunately, needing only 1 win to make it to the World Series, the Red Sox were swept in a 2-game series by the hated New York Yankees.

Perhaps influenced by the Yankees' use of reliever Joe Page, the Red Sox moved Kinder to a prominent role in the bullpen, where he continued to pitch well and blaze trails for the emerging role of bullpen ace. In 1951 he was 11–2 with a 2.55 ERA and a league-leading 14 saves. In 1953 Kinder was even better, going 10–6 with a 1.85 ERA and again leading the league in saves (with 27).

Two subpar seasons followed, after which Kinder was waived. His career was nearly over: he pitched briefly (though reasonably effectively) for the Chicago White Sox and St Louis Cardinals before retiring in 1957. Fondly remembered by the parents of the baby boomers, Ellis Kinder was a very good pitcher for Red Sox teams that twice finished within a game of making the World Series. He also helped usher in the new era of the bullpen ace with some excellent years in the pen. An all-time Red Sox staff might well include the versatile Kinder, if not as a starter, then at least in the pen.

Jack Kramer—righthanded pitcher who began his career with the St. Louis Browns in 1939. In the early part of his career, Kramer struggled badly with his control, and only made it to the majors for good in 1944 during the player shortage. In 1948 he came to Boston in the same trade that brought Vern Stephens and Ellis Kinder. He was a 3-time All Star in St. Louis, but never made it to the All Star Game again. In 1948, his first season in Boston, he went 18–6 and led the league in winning percentage. He managed to do this despite having an ERA that was virtually league average because he played for a powerhouse offensive team. He pitched badly in 1949, 1950, and 1951, finishing up his career pitching mostly out of the bullpen for the New York Giants and then the New York Yankees. In his final season he actually pitched for each of the pennant winners, the Giants and the Yankees, but didn't last long enough on either roster to make it to the postseason.

Roger LaFrançois—a New England native, LaFrançois was a catcher who spent the entire 1982 season with the Boston Red Sox, but got only 10 at bats in 8 games—one of the reasons that few teams carry 3 catchers any more. That was his only time in the major leagues.

Carney Lansford—third baseman who played 2 strong seasons for the Red Sox before losing his job. Lansford (along with Mark Clear and Rick Miller in his second tour of duty) was obtained from California for Rick Burleson (who was about to blow out his arm) and an end-of-the-line Butch Hobson after the 1980 season. As the starting third baseman in 1981, the 24-year-old Lansford hit .336 and won the batting title in a strike-shortened season. He hit .301 the following season, but Wade Boggs's development into a star hitter left him without a position (since the Sox wanted to play Boggs at third, rather than first base, where he spent most of his rookie year). Lansford was traded to Oakland as part of a deal for Tony Armas after the 1982 season, and went on to have a long career with the Athletics.

Lansford was a very good player, but he was never a star with the Red Sox—he didn't have much power (although he hit 19 home runs 3 times for other teams) and drew a below-average number of walks. He had excellent speed for a third baseman but the Sox rarely stole bases as a team (he stole as many as 37 for the A's, though). As a fielder his reputation was better than his actual skills—he was notorious for acrobatically diving to stop balls that fielders with more range would field standing up.

Mike Lansing—a second baseman acquired along with Rolando Arrojo from the Colorado Rockies in the 2000 season. This trade was viewed negatively by many Red Sox fans, as Lansing has not hit well since undergoing back surgery in 1999, and the Red Sox are obligated to pay him a $7 million salary in 2001. In a minor footnote to Red Sox history, Lansing—who looked like he was going to be an offensive star early in his career—was the reason that Montreal was able to trade Delino DeShields for Pedro Martinez in 1994. Had Martinez remained in Los Angeles and blossomed the way that he did in Montreal, he would never have been available when the Red Sox acquired him (since the Expos could not afford to pay a superstar like Martinez, while the Dodgers could). The Montreal general manager who traded DeShields for Martinez? Current Red Sox GM Dan Duquette.

Bill Lee—there is an adage in baseball that two factors contribute to being a "flake," being a lefty pitcher, and being from California. Lee was both, in addition to being highly intelligent and frequently misunderstood. Upon seeing the Green Monster for the first time, Lee asked, "Do they leave it there during games?" This comment is said to have earned him his nickname of "Spaceman," which stuck. Lee was also responsible for nicknaming onetime Red Sox manager (and Lee nemesis) Don Zimmer "the gerbil," which also stuck.

Never an overpowering pitcher, Lee relied on the excellent control he had of his average fastball and above-average curveball. He also occasionally threw a pitch that was dubbed the "Leephus" pitch, basically a slow-pitch softball pitch, that batters often found impossible to time. Lee never had what would be called a great season, but had several very good years, including a 9–2 season as a reliever in 1971, 3 straight 17-win years as a starter with the Red Sox (1973–75) and a 16-win season with Montreal in 1979, his first year there after being traded.

Lee's ongoing feud with Don Zimmer—an old-school manager who wanted nothing to do with the free-spirited Lee—escalated badly, and Zimmer's inability to handle Lee arguably cost the Red Sox a pennant in 1978. Lee was seen as the leader of a group of independent-minded players called the Buffalo Heads (among them Jim Willoughby and Bernie Carbo) who were embraced by fans. Zimmer, unable to cope with the Buffalo Heads, refused to play them—even when his talented team began breaking down from injuries and overwork. When Bernie Carbo's reliable bat was dumped at midseason, Lee left the team briefly in protest, which further infuriated Zimmer. Lee was the only lefthanded starter on the team, but Zimmer left him in the bullpen and used terrified rookie Bobby Sprowl in a key series against the Yankees, to disastrous results. After the season, Lee was given away to the Montreal Expos for infielder Stan Papi, who hit .188 in his only full season with the Red Sox. Lee continued to be a controversial free-thinker in Montreal. He retired early in the 1982 season, at least in part as a protest to the Expos for releasing his friend Rodney Scott.

Lee's history of being controversial has showed up in many areas, and he still occasionally expresses these opinions. He has publicly expressed a dislike for several of baseball's innovations over the years, including domed stadiums and the designated hitter. He once told journalists that he used marijuana "sprinkled on cereal," then later claimed he was putting them on. Lee now lives in rural central Vermont, where he played semi-pro baseball for years after retiring.

Mark Lemke—a light-hitting second baseman who manager Jimy Williams insisted on having for his 1998 Red Sox team—the first of a bunch of light-hitting middle infielders who would crowd the Red Sox roster over the next several years. Lemke had briefly been a starter for the Atlanta Braves while Williams coached there, and had built a reputation based on hot streaks in the 1991 and 1996 playoffs. By 1998, Lemke was unemployed—mainly because he didn't hit much (he'd only hit above .255 once in 10 seasons) but wanted a substantial salary. When Red Sox starting second baseman Jeff Frye suffered a season-ending knee injury, GM Dan Duquette finally gave into Williams's public campaign and signed Lemke to a $1 million contract. Lemke hit .187 in 31 games before a concussion ended his season. Unable to find a major league job after his contract with the Red Sox expired, Lemke went on to become a knuckleball pitcher for the New Jersey Jackals, an independent league team.

Dutch Leonard—though Bob Gibson's 1.12 ERA in 1968 is commonly cited as the single-season record, the modern mark actually belongs to Hubert "Dutch" Leonard, an overlooked star from the dead ball era. (The all-time ERA record belongs to Hall of Famer Tim Keefe, with a 0.86 in the 85-game 1880 season, but conditions were very different.) The lefthanded Leonard joined the Red Sox in 1913, going 14–17, despite a 2.39 ERA. But it's fair to say he improved in his sophomore season. Leonard had a 19–5 record, including 7 shutouts, and his ERA was an incomprehensible 0.96. The American League had a very low 2.73 ERA in 1914, but Leonard's numbers are still remarkable. He allowed only 139 hits and 60 walks in 225 innings (anything less than 1 hit an inning is good), while fanning 176.

Leonard never approached his landmark 1914 season, but he was a valuable member of the 1915–16 championship staffs, winning 33 games, plus another in each World Series. His ERA jumped to a more human 2.36 in 1915, and remained the same in 1916. On August 30, 1916, Leonard pitched a no-hitter against the St. Louis Browns. He won 16 games in 1917, and 8 more in an injury-shortened 1918 season (including a no-hitter against Detroit on June 3). Leonard didn't pitch in the 1918 World Series, and the Sox traded him to the Yankees afterward, along with Duffy Lewis and Ernie Shore. The Yanks promptly sold Leonard to Detroit, where he spent 5 mediocre seasons. He retired with 139 wins and a 2.76 ERA.

In 1926 Leonard found himself at the center of one of baseball's biggest scandals. He gave American League President Ban Johnson copies of two letters he got in 1919. One was from his then-teammate Ty Cobb; the other was from ex-Red Sox star Joe Wood, then with Cleveland. The letters allegedly proved that Cobb and Cleveland's Tris Speaker (both were player-managers) fixed a meaningless late-season game, though Speaker's name wasn't directly mentioned. But when Johnson asked Leonard to testify at a hearing, the ex-pitcher refused. He recanted his story, supposedly because he feared Cobb's wrath. Commissioner Landis refused to suspend anyone, due to lack of evidence. Angry and embarrassed, Johnson decided to ban Cobb and Speaker from managing, but allowed them to sign with the Philadelphia Athletics as free agent players (as opposed to player/managers).

In 1933, another Dutch Leonard began a successful 20-year pitching career. Emil "Dutch" Leonard was a righty knuckleballer, and was no relation to Hubert, though the two are often confused for one another.

Darren Lewis—a light-hitting center fielder who joined the Red Sox in 1998. Lewis typified the change in team philosophy which occurred in the late 1990s. Signed to a short-money contract almost as an afterthought, the 30-year-old former Gold Glover brought defense and speed to the Sox. He won the starting center field position when he had a hot first half. Receiving the most playing time of his career (585 at bats in

155 games), Lewis cooled off in the second half of the season but still put up his best offensive numbers (.352 on-base percentage and .362 slugging percentage, still mediocre for a center fielder). After the season, Lewis was signed to a surprising longterm contract (given his age and his poor offense in previous seasons); there were suggestions that GM Dan Duquette gave Lewis a contract as part of a campaign to re-sign Mo Vaughn, who was close with Lewis.

Lewis struggled offensively in 1999 and became a role player when the Sox traded for Carl Everett before the 2000 season. Manager Jimy Williams liked Lewis's defense and attitude, however, and used him as a platoon right fielder (despite his weak throwing arm), to rest starters, and as a late-inning defensive replacement. Lewis still saw plenty of playing time in 2000—some would argue that he received too much playing time, given the continuing decline of his hitting skills. His notable 2000 moment was a loud clubhouse confrontation with Everett—the outspoken star center fielder who took Lewis's job—during Everett's problems with Jimy Williams.

Duffy Lewis—left fielder who joined Tris Speaker and Harry Hooper in one of baseball's most famous outfields. Lewis played 8 seasons with Boston, winning 3 World Series. He hit over .300 twice, with a high of 109 RBI on the 1912 World Champs, but is best remembered for his defensive skills. The original Fenway Park had a small hill in left (where the Green Monster is now) nicknamed "Duffy's Cliff" because of Lewis's deftness in playing it. He went to the Yankees in 1919, a year before Babe Ruth.

Tim Lollar—a lefthanded relief pitcher who, during the 1986 season, accomplished the rare feat of finishing the year with a 1.000 Winning Percentage and a 1.000 batting average. He was 2–0 out of the bullpen, despite pitching very badly. Then during a game in Kansas City lineup moves forced him to pinch-hit, and he singled up the middle in his only at-bat. He spent only 2 years in Boston, and 1986 was his last year in the majors.

Jim Lonborg—though many players contributed to the miracle, when Red Sox fans think of the Impossible Dream year of 1967, they usually think of 3 men: pitcher Jim Lonborg, slugger Carl Yasztremski, and manager Dick Williams. Lonborg tied for the league lead in wins that season with 22, was second in the league in innings pitched with 273, and won the American League Cy Young for his efforts. He won 2 games in the World Series (including the amazing Game 2 effort in which he nearly recorded the second no-hit game in World Series history). Pitching Game 7 on only 2 days rest, Lonborg had nothing left, and Bob Gibson and the Cardinals won the game and thus the Series. Still, the future seemed bright for the Sox that winter—the team had come out of nowhere, a half game out of last place in 1966, to win the pennant in 1967 with a young, talented team. Unfortunately, over the winter Lonborg broke his leg in a skiing accident and it took a number of years for him to regain the fine form which he enjoyed in that 1967 season (by which time he was no longer pitching for the Sox). He pitched for Milwaukee in 1972, then spent 7 years with the Philadelphia Phillies, during which he finally regained his effectiveness, winning 17 games in 1974 and 18 in 1976.

Derek Lowe—tall, lanky righthanded pitcher acquired by general manager Dan Duquette in one of the great heists of all time. As the Red Sox fell out of contention before the trading deadline in 1997, he managed to turn shell-shocked reliever Heathcliff Slocumb, who everybody wanted him to just release, into Derek Lowe and Jason Varitek from the Mariners, who were desperate to upgrade their bullpen. (Why they thought that Slocumb would accomplish that remains unclear.)

Lowe had struggled as a starter in Seattle and also struggled initially as a starter in Boston. But he pitched well in short and medium relief, and clearly had great stuff. His big strength is a sinking fastball, and he throws a lot of ground balls. In 1999 he was one of the most valuable pitchers in baseball, setting up first Tom Gordon, and then Tim Wakefield after Gordon was injured. He then settled into the closer's role himself, and finished the season with 15 saves. In 2000 he started as the team's full-time closer, and saved 42 games over the course of the season. Despite his terrific success as a reliever, Lowe has expressed a desire to return to a starting role, and there has been intermittent talk of converting him back into a starter.

I got my curse from my Dad. He grew up a Brooklyn Dodger fan. He entered the Navy upon graduating college and upon coming home found an empty Ebbets Field. As a Dodger fan he had a natural animosity towards the Yanks. In the sixties his baseball interest waned as a result of the move of his team and a lack of national coverage. In the seventies his interest picked up again and while he never lost his venom toward the Skanks he found it hard to root for a team on the other coast. Since the Sox already had a natural rivalry with the Yanks he began to follow them and as an impressionable youngster I did too. My brother is also afflicted and me, my Dad, and my brother will do our best to teach my young (two-year-old and nine-month-old) nephews about the horrors of King George. My first Sox game at Fenway was in 1981 and Ojeda was a rookie. It was versus the Yanks in August or September and Ojeda brought a no-hitter into the ninth with the Sox up 2–0. At this point Oscar Gamble or someone doubled off the wall. The no-hitter was gone but the Sox held on.

—Jim Tiberio

Sparky Lyle—a lefthanded reliever whom the Red Sox gave away in a truly awful trade. Lyle pitched 27 games for the 1967 Impossible Dream team as a 23-year-old rookie, and gradually developed into the team's top reliever, saving an average of 18 games from 1969 to 1971 with an ERA below 3.00 in 4 of his 5 years with the Sox. After the 1971 season he was deemed expendable (fellow lefty Bill Lee had gone 9–2 in relief that year) and was traded to the Yankees for Danny Cater, a journeyman infielder who would hit .237 as a replacement for the also-traded George Scott at first base. Lyle, 27 years old when he was traded, was just entering his prime, and would have 8 good-to-great years in a row before losing his effectiveness. He saved a league-leading 35 games for the Yankees in 1972; Bill Lee and Bobby Bolin tied for the Sox team lead with 5 each.

Fred Lynn—in 1975, lefthanded centerfielder Lynn and fellow "Gold Dust Twin" Jim Rice proved to be possibly the best tandem of rookies that a team ever put together. Lynn, in addition to winning the first of his 4 Gold Gloves, became the first (and only) major leaguer to win the Rookie of the Year award and the Most Valuable Player award in the same season. He was second in the league in batting average, fifth in on-base percentage, first in slugging, and first in OPS. On one memorable June night in Tiger Stadium he hit 3 home runs and drove in 10 runs. Those accomplishments—at the age of 23—heralded the advent of an outstanding career. Lynn was an excellent fielder, almost to the point of being reckless in the outfield. Lynn's collision with the outfield wall at Fenway during the sixth game of the 1975 World Series led to the padding that now covers those walls.

Lynn played well for the Red Sox for 6 years, including a 1979 season that was even better than his rookie campaign. After starting to use then-obscure Nautilus weight training machines, Lynn led the league in batting average, on-base percentage, and slugging. He was fourth in RBI and in runs scored. He hit 39 home runs (his previous season high was 22) and drove in 122 runs, while winning another Gold Glove for his defense in center field—but somehow he lost the MVP award to Don Baylor of California.

Following the 1980 season, the Red Sox made one of the great unexplained baseball screwups. They mailed out the contracts of Lynn and catcher Carlton Fisk a day after the deadline for offering player contracts. Knowing that Lynn would almost certainly be declared a free agent, the Sox were forced to trade him at a fire sale price to the California Angels, with whom Southern California native Lynn signed a longterm contract. The trade helped neither Lynn—the ultimate Fenway Park hitter—nor the Sox. Lynn played well, but never again had a great season after 1979. He did win one more Gold Glove in 1982. He won the All Star game MVP in 1983, hitting the first grand slam in All Star game history (a homer that essentially ruined the career of pitcher Atlee Hammaker, who never got over throwing the bad pitch in front of millions of fans). But Lynn was frequently hampered by injuries. He tore up knees and bruised ribs with his reckless style of defense, but he also lost time to muscle pulls and strains that led people in some quarters to question his toughness.

After 4 years in California he signed a free agent contract with the Orioles following the 1984 season. Still a good player but no longer a star, Lynn spent 3 full years in Baltimore, during which he hit 23 home runs in each season. He was traded to Detroit late in the 1987 season, and eventually finished up by playing 90 games for the San Diego Padres in 1990. He was not anywhere near the player that he had been, finishing with 6 home runs and 23 RBI before retiring.

His career never fulfilled the promise it had shown in the beginning. He finished his 16-year career with 306 home runs and 1,111 RBI. He never made it to the Hall of Fame, though, interestingly enough, his college roommate did. His roommate at USC was Pittsburgh Steeler Hall of Fame wide receiver Lynn Swann.

Steve Lyons—"Psycho" was a highly-thought-of third base prospect who never really panned out for the Red Sox (career average of .253). He came up in 1985 and was used mostly in the outfield, then was traded to the White Sox for Tom Seaver in 1986, and returned as a utility player in 1991. He had a third tour of duty with the Red Sox from late 1992 to early 1993. His most famous moment in the major leagues came in 1990 when he slid into first base safely in a cloud of dust and unthinkingly got up, called time, and dropped his pants in front of 30,000 spectators to shed the dust and grit. He is now a Fox sportscaster.

Mike Macfarlane—a longtime Kansas City catcher with a good bat, Macfarlane came to Boston amid great fanfare in 1995. Things never really worked out for him in Boston, and he ended up as a part time catcher, hitting 15 home runs while driving in 51 runs. A steady if unspectacular performer, Macfarlane had one memorable moment as a member of the Red Sox. In a 2–2 game he hit a ninth-inning walk-off home run to near dead center field against the Yankees on a Sunday afternoon. In Game 1 of the 1995 playoffs, he dropped a throw to home plate, costing the Red Sox at least one run. (He wasn't charged with an error, but it was a catchable ball, and helped cost Boston the game.) After the 1995 season Macfarlane returned to Kansas City and went back to being a productive player. He retired after the 1999 season.

Mike Maddux—a righthanded relief pitcher who came up with the Phillies in 1986. In his 15-year career in the majors, he pitched mostly out of the bullpen (he came up as a starter, but got only spot starts after 1988). Despite his long career, he was only the second best pitcher in the Maddux family, overshadowed by his younger brother Greg, a 4-time National League Cy Young award winner and future Hall of Famer. When Mike and Greg faced each other for the Phillies and Cubs in September of 1986, it marked the first time in baseball history that rookie brother pitchers had faced each other. Mike carved out a career as a useful relief pitcher with several different clubs.

He signed with Pittsburgh prior to the 1995 season, but was released when he refused to accept a minor league assignment. The Red Sox picked him up (becoming his sixth team and his first in the American League), and he pitched very effectively for the team. He was 4–1 in 89 innings for the Sox, as that 1995 team won the American League East by 7 games over second place New York. He pitched in 2 games against the Indians in the Division series, allowing no runs. He was also effective in 1996, though not as effective, and for fewer innings. The Red Sox did not re-sign him following 1996, and he pitched for 4 more teams over the next 4 years. He threw 27 innings for the Houston Astros during the 2000 season.

Tom Maggard—the Red Sox top draft pick in 1968, Maggard was a promising catching prospect. He was playing in AAA Pawtucket in September, 1973 when his arm swelled up after being bitten by an insect. After treatment attempts didn't improve the injury, he was sent home to California, where he died 2 weeks later. Maggard was 21 years old.

Ron Mahay—because he had agreed under pressure to participate as a replacement player during the 1994 strike, young center fielder Mahay was ostracized in his brief time with the Red Sox as an emergency callup in 1995, particularly by pitchers Roger Clemens and Tim Wakefield. After being sent back to the minor leagues, the Red Sox converted the light-hitting Mahay into a pitcher—a conversion he took to surprisingly quickly. By 1997 he was back with the team as a 26-year-old lefthanded relief pitcher, and pitched very well in limited duty. Mahay shuttled between Pawtucket and the Red Sox the following year, then failed to win a job in 1999. He was out of minor league options and so could not be sent back to Pawtucket without giving other teams a chance to claim him. He was picked up by Oakland, where he pitched only briefly. He pitched for both Oakland and Florida (after Oakland released him) in 2000.

Frank Malzone—one of the best third basemen in Red Sox history, Malzone's steady hitting and excellent defense endeared him to Fenway fans for 11 seasons. From 1957–64, Malzone made 8 All Star teams and averaged 84 RBI a season, making him one of the few bright spots on an otherwise dreary ballclub.

Though he was born near Yankee Stadium, Malzone signed a contract with the Red Sox in 1948. He struggled for a while in the minors, and then missed two seasons while serving in the Korean War. Malzone didn't make his big league debut until late 1955, at age 25. He won the third base job in 1956, but was sent back to the minors after batting only .165. During the previous offseason, Malzone and his wife had lost an infant daughter, and the grief may have contributed to his poor play.

In 1957, Malzone reclaimed his spot as the starting third baseman. He responded with arguably his best season (.292 average, 15 homers, a career-high 103 RBI). His defense won raves, and he set a record for third basemen (since broken) with 10 assists in a game against Washington. Malzone also became the first player to lead his position in games played, putouts, assists, errors, fielding percentage, and double plays in the same season. (Despite the errors, he made enough plays to lead in fielding percentage.) He earned the brand-new Gold Glove Award, a trophy honoring the best defensive players at each position. (Malzone won the first 3 Gold Gloves for American League third basemen, until Brooks Robinson came along in 1960. Robinson then won the award an amazing 16 straight years.) Though he'd have been considered a rookie under today's rules, Malzone was ineligible for the Rookie of the Year award, based upon his limited experience in 1955–56. Several Boston writers filed a petition to make him eligible, but the Baseball Writers Association of America rejected the protest. As a result, Yankee shortstop Tony Kubek, whose numbers were inferior to Malzone's, won the award. (One writer voted for Malzone anyway, to protest the BBWAA's ruling.)

Malzone continued to be among the best American League third basemen for the next few years. His 1958 and 1959 numbers were nearly identical to his "rookie" stats. He slumped a bit in 1960 and 1961, hitting .271 and .266, with 14 homers each year. Malzone rebounded in 1962, hitting a career-high 21 homers, and hit .291 the following season. Looking beyond the solid batting averages and RBI totals, Malzone was somewhat overrated as a hitter. His home run totals weren't that impressive for a third baseman, not to mention a righty hitter in Fenway Park, and he didn't walk a whole lot. But Malzone was extremely consistent and durable, and his defense was a major asset.

However, he showed signs of slipping in 1964. Malzone hit a weak .264, with only 13 homers and 56 RBI, and a poor .372 slugging percentage. He slumped to .239 in 1965, with only 3 homers, and ended the year platooning with young Dalton Jones. At 35, and clearly on the decline, Malzone was no longer in the team's plans, and the Red Sox released him after the season. He played one more year as a backup with the California Angels, but retired after batting .206.

After his playing career ended, Malzone rejoined the Red Sox organization, serving in several roles, most notably as a scout. Still active at age 70, Malzone now scouts other major league teams, filing reports on opponents and possible trade targets. He was inducted into the Red Sox Hall of Fame in 1995 for his contributions to the franchise, on and off the field.

Felix Mantilla—used mostly as a reserve in his 11 seasons with the Milwaukee Braves (1956–61), the Mets (1962), the Red Sox (1963–65), and the Astros (1966), Felix Mantilla hit only 89 career home runs, and had a .261 lifetime batting average. In the conventional wisdom he was a utility infielder, a useful guy to have as a back-up in the field, but not someone who should bat very often. Yet in his 3 years with Boston he would shatter that image.

Mantilla was primarily a shortstop with the Braves, but he was versatile. He played second, third, the outfield, and even some first base in the majors. In six seasons with Milwaukee he was regarded as a "good field, no hit" player. From 1957–61 he hit between .215 and .257 while averaging only 180 at bats a season. He totaled 18 home runs in those years. Then in 466 at bats with the Mets in 1962 he hit .275 with 11 home runs. That winter he was traded to Boston for 2 noteworthy, if not illustrious players, Tracy Stallard and Pumpsie Green.

When Mantilla got to Boston perspectives changed quickly. First, he was a good hitter. Second, he wasn't a good shortstop. In 1963 he played only 27 games at short, 11 in the outfield, and 5 at second. He hit .315 with 6 home runs in 178 at bats, walked 20 times, struck out only 14, and made no errors at second or in the outfield. His career years were to come in 1964–65 when the Red Sox realized they needed to get his bat in the lineup.

Mantilla hammered an amazing 30 home runs in 1964. He played in 133 games, had 425 at bats and hit .289, with a .553 slugging percentage. He also was close to flawless in the field, making only 1 error in 48 games in the outfield, 1 error in 45 games at second base, and none in 6 games at shortstop. (He did make 3 errors in 7 games at third.) In 1965 he had a career high 534 at bats and his power dropped, although he still hit .275 with 18 home runs and 92 RBI—very respectable for a second baseman, where he played 123 games that season. On the eve of the 1967 season he was traded to Houston for future Red Sox manager Eddie Kasko. After Mantilla some people began to question the accuracy of conventional brandings of players.

Josias Manzanillo—a great Red Sox pitching prospect in the late 1980s, Manzanillo blew out his elbow from pitching too much at age 18. After missing 2 years recovering from the injury, he was never the same pitcher, although he eventually made it to the big leagues for 1 game with the Red Sox as a 23-year-old in 1991. He drifted in and out of the major leagues for 6 different teams, including 3 separate stints with the Mets, but never won more than 3 games in a season. Manzanillo's injury woes also continued. While pitching for Seattle in 1997, he was hit by a line drive off the bat of Manny Ramirez, and had to have surgery to remove a testicle. He appeared in 43 games for Pittsburgh in 2000, the most in his career.

Juan Marichal—known as "The Dominican Dandy," this Hall of Famer pitched 11 games with Boston in 1974, his next-to-last season. Marichal, who had won 20 games 6 times with the Giants, went 5–1 with a 4.87 ERA (a poor ERA at a time when the league average was about 3.60). Although he was near the end of the line when the Red Sox picked him up to help fill out a thin pitching staff, Marichal finished his career at 243–142 with a 2.89 ERA, and became the first Dominican to make the Hall of Fame.

Mike Marshall—outfielder/first baseman who played most of his career with the Los Angeles Dodgers. Although Marshall had been a much-heralded prospect, he never became a great hitter (or even a very good one) but he did have some "pop in his bat," hitting 20 or more home runs 3 times. The Red Sox picked Marshall up late in the 1990 season to strengthen the bench for the stretch run and the playoffs. It didn't help much. Marshall contributed very little, hitting just 4 homers in 112 at bats. He had only 1 hit in 3 games in the 1990 playoffs as the Red Sox were swept in 4 games by the Oakland A's.

He started the 1991 season in Boston but played badly and was released early in the year. There's a sad irony to this, since the Red Sox kept Marshall on the roster instead of longtime star Dwight Evans, who was forced to finish his career in Baltimore. Marshall was picked up briefly by the California Angels, but he appeared in only 2 more games before retiring.

Marshall was an odd hitter , because he had a rare "reverse platoon," meaning that he hit righthanded pitchers better than lefties, even though he was righthanded.

Pedro Martinez—born in the Dominican Republic, Martinez is the middle of 3 pitching brothers, all of whom have pitched in the Red Sox organization. Martinez made his major league debut for the Los Angeles Dodgers (for whom he had signed when he was 16) and was immediately tagged as not having what it takes to start in the majors by then-Dodger manager Tommy Lasorda, a normally astute judge of baseball talent. This led to him pitching mostly in middle relief during his stay with the Dodgers—although as a 21-year-old he pitched extremely well in that role.

Traded to the Montreal Expos for highly thought of second baseman Delino DeShields in 1994, Martinez blossomed as a starter; at one point that season he pitched 9 perfect innings before giving up a hit in the tenth inning of a scoreless game. In 1997 Martinez won the National League Cy Young award with 18 wins, finishing the season with more than 300 strikeouts and an ERA under 2.00 (a combination that had not been done since 1912). He also received the third-lowest run support of all National League starters, a problem that continues to plague Martinez. (Ironically, Montreal traded DeShields to make room for Mike Lansing, currently a backup infielder with the Sox, who they thought would be a bigger star.)

After the 1997 season, Montreal was forced to dump salary and traded Martinez to the Red Sox for top pitching prospects Carl Pavano and Tony Armas Jr. There was a short period where it appeared that Martinez—who was a year away from free agency—might not sign a contract with the Red Sox. But within days GM Dan Duquette convinced Martinez to sign a contract that would make him a Red Sox player for at least 7 years—and, at that time, the highest paid player in the game.

Martinez's reception in Boston was slightly mixed in 1998. Enthusiastic fans,

---

If I give you a brief run through my background perhaps you'll understand why I was destined to follow the Red Sox. I am from England and the football (soccer) team I support is called Sunderland. Pre-war they were one of the top teams in the country, known at various times as "The Bank of England Club" and the "Team of All Talents", and they won the League Championship six times and finished runners up five times. After the war things became decidedly mediocre with successes being on a small scale with failure invariably following soon after. Until recently they played at Roker Park which had been their home for 99 years, and while affectionately viewed by the team's supporters, was considered a relic from a previous era by others.

Anyway I was given the opportunity to visit Boston and in September 1999 I arrived. To me I always associated Boston with the Red Sox and along with the Harlem Globetrotters and the Dallas Cowboys they were the only teams I knew of that played American sports. The Dallas Cowboys were the top team when they started to show coverage over here, the Harlem Globetrotters toured over here, but the Red Sox?

During my stay the Red Sox came to my attention while watching a sports broadcast. I saw Pedro on the mound while a cheering crowd stuck "KKK" up on the wall. After a bit of research I discovered that it meant nothing more sinister than one inning's work for the maestro but the first seeds of interest had been sowed. I wanted to see this baseball team while I could. However, with perhaps the worse timing of all time, my visit coincided with the Red Sox's longest road trip of the season so there was no way of seeing them play! Never mind, perhaps I could check out the ballpark while I was in the area. With a little bit of investigation I found out that guided tours were given so off I went.

There is something magical about a sports arena before the competition starts. Lying dormant in the middle of a brick and concrete jungle, it doesn't need much to awaken it. Before the first pitch is thrown, the first ball kicked, or the lights turn green all things are possible. Once the game starts those options rapidly disappear. When the place is empty this feeling is magnified and becomes a lot more intimate. Hence as I walked up the ramp and looked down on the playing surface of Fenway Park for the first time no longer could I hear the traffic or the sounds of the road works going on happy to have a new ace after Roger Clemens's departure following the 1996 season, were eager to show their support. A midseason stretch of less than stellar performances (later blamed on illness), made fans uneasy as it reminded them of the failed Steve Avery experiment of the year before. The criticism of Martinez by some fans and media weighed heavily on him, to the point that during off-season negotiations between the Red Sox and Ramon Martinez (Pedro's older brother), Pedro cautioned Ramon about the unforgiving Boston media. Martinez went on to post very good numbers in 1998, going 19–7 with a 2.89 era and 251 strikeouts—excellent numbers but not quite the dominance he showed in 1997 or would show in the next 2 years. On the strength of Martinez's year the Red Sox made the playoffs as the wild card. Playing against the Cleveland Indians, the team that had dismissed them from the 1995 playoffs, the Red Sox could only manage to win 1 of 4 games—the game Martinez started.

---

outside. I imagined myself about to deliver the game winning blast over the wall or pitching the perfect game.

It was an oasis away from the real world outside! The whole stadium seemed steeped in history and tradition. It was as familiar to me as Roker Park was in so much that here was a ballpark that had developed over time as opposed to being a modern "development." Even the large manual scoreboard had its equivalent in Sunderland! It was possible to imagine baseball being played here for generations.

It's a cliché I have read many times since then but I remember being struck by how green the grass was. Every nook and cranny held a tale that modern highly designed space-conscious stadiums could never know. While I was taking in all this the guide was recounting the quirks and history of Fenway. As I have previously mentioned I knew nothing about baseball. To me bleachers were people that changed the color of their hair, bullpens contained livestock, and I assumed the Green Monster was kept caged behind that big wall with the scoreboard on it!

I returned to England to discover a late night baseball game. I saw the postseason games against the Indians, saw Darren Lewis hit 3–5 and thought he was a superstar (Give me a chance—I was still learning!) and started reading up on the history. The more I read the more I was convinced. Now I am desperately saving so I can return to Fenway this time at the same time as the Red Sox! I must be one of the few people ever to be converted to the cause by not seeing the team play.

In closing the more astute of you may have noticed that I said that Sunderland had played at Roker Park until recently. What has happened since then? Well they now have moved to a brand spanking new stadium and, while we have sacrificed the intimacy and history of Roker, we now have the third highest level of support in the country, the leading striker in Europe playing for us, and have enjoyed our most successful season for over fifty years. A fair trade? Despite my initial reservations I think so. I only hope that should Fenway Park pass into history that, like Roker Park, it will not have been in vain. Just please don't let it be before I return!

—Colin Smith

During the off-season the Red Sox would sign Pedro's brothers, Ramon and Jesus, both pitchers. Ramon, the older brother, had been the Dodgers' ace before a serious injury. (There was some debate over whether Ramon was signed for his pitching skills or for his potentially stabilizing effect on the often-emotional Pedro.) Ramon would pitch little during the regular season, but pitched well for the Sox into the playoffs before a disappointing 2000. Jesus, the youngest of the 3, pitched poorly in Sarasota (A) and since has bounced around several organizations.

Martinez's 1999 season was incredible. By the All Star break some people thought that he might win 30 games, a milestone for pitchers equivalent to a hitter having a .400 batting average. A few nagging injuries and poor run support would keep his wins down for the second half of the season, however. Starting the All Star Game in Boston, Martinez struck out 5 of the first 6 opposing hitters and was named the All Star Game MVP. He would continue to pitch masterfully throughout the season, winning the Triple Crown for pitchers with a 23–4 record, a 2.07 ERA, and 313 strikeouts (making him the only pitcher to strike out 300+ in both leagues). His 313 strikeouts in 213.1 innings meant that an incredible 48.9% of his outs came by way of the strikeout. He issued only 37 walks in over 213 innings, giving him a strikeout to walk ratio of 13.2, an all-time single-season record. He won 4 Pitcher of the Month awards, the first player to accomplish that feat. Along with this came a unanimous American League Cy Young Award.

In 17 postseason innings Martinez allowed no runs, struck out 17, and had a 2–0 record—despite battling injury. The highlight of that postseason was a near-perfect appearance in which Martinez shut down a potent Cleveland offense on guile alone. Obviously in pain (and unable to lift his arm above his head) Martinez used his pin-point accuracy and kept the Indians' lineup off guard by changing speeds and arm angles. In a performance that will go down in Red Sox lore, Martinez pitched 6 perfect innings, defeating the Indians and sending the Sox to meet the Yankees in the American League Championship Series. The Red Sox lost the series, plagued by poor fielding, poor relief pitching, and bad calls by the umpires—the only win being a much-hyped matchup between Martinez and Roger Clemens at Fenway Park. Martinez was the unanimous Cy Young winner, and would have won the league MVP, but he was entirely left off the ballots of two writers (who believed that pitchers shouldn't be MVPs, despite explicit rules from the BBWAA that pitchers must be considered.).

In 2000 Martinez was even better, posting an 18–6 record with a 1.74 ERA. He was again victimized by poor run support, or his won-lost record would have been much better.

Several things set Martinez apart from other pitchers. Martinez has near-total mastery of 3 pitches. His best pitch is a fastball that sometimes hits 96 on the speed gun. He backs this up with a sharp curve and a devastating changeup. This triple mastery leads to pinpoint control—the reason for the high strikeout and low walk totals. Martinez's long slender fingers allow him to be creative with his pitches, changing his grips to get more movement on his fastball, or to change his curve from a sharp break to a more looping "lollipop curve." He mixes in occasional sliders and changes his arm angle, altering the action of the pitch and forcing the batter to change his line of sight.

Martinez has also displayed the ability to compensate when one or more of his pitches isn't working. Martinez is also willing to pitch inside, seemingly a lost art. Early in his career Martinez gained a reputation as a "head hunter," a rep that has followed him his entire career, with good and bad consequences. (Ironically, he got the reputation as a *batter* in the National League when he went after a pitcher who hit him.) Pedro has never actually hit anyone in the head. While he uses his reputation to intimidate batters, because his control is so good when Martinez hits a batter it is often perceived to be on purpose even if it is not. This led to a much-publicized squabble with the Cleveland Indians in 2000. (He threw inside at catcher Einar Diaz, who thought Pedro had tried to hit him. Cleveland pitcher Chuck Finley retaliated by hitting a Boston player, after which Martinez hit Indians second baseman Roberto Alomar in the posterior—so as not to hurt him—for which Martinez was ejected. After he admitted to purposely hitting Alomar, Martinez was fined and suspended for 5 games.)

In May, Martinez would again be matched against Roger Clemens, winning 2–0 on national TV in the season's best pitching duel. In the beginning of September Martinez's reputations for dominance and headhunting would collide. In a game against the Tampa Bay Devil Rays Martinez hit the first Tampa Bay batter of the game, Gerald Williams. Williams rushed the mound, touching off a brawl. After the fight was ended, 4 different Devil Ray pitchers tried to hit Red Sox batters. After another bench-clearing skirmish, attention turned to the fact that while Martinez was not retaliating (Tampa Bay seemed to be trying to get him thrown out of the game) he *was* pitching a no hitter. The no hitter would be broken up in the ninth inning—immediately following Martinez placing his crucifix in his back pocket because the chain had broken on the previous pitch.

Martinez—known simply as Pedro in Boston—is the only player to rival Nomar Garciaparra's popularity among fans, his teammates, and the press. His popularity with the Dominican community in Boston is such that the Boston Globe reports on his games in Spanish as well as English. Fans post K signs to record his strikeouts—not just at Fenway, but in other parks as well. (This used to be true of Roger Clemens as well.) During games when Pedro is not on the mound he is an enthusiastic cheerleader, and a boisterous prankster (one game to such an extent that his teammates taped him to a dugout pole and gagged him; Nomar of course stood guard so that no foul balls would hit his ace). In another favorite moment Martinez wore a Yoda mask with his uniform.

Martinez also shares Nomar's tendency to speak his mind, such as in 2000, when he was one of the few players to publicly support center fielder Carl Everett after the media turned on him. (Like Everett, Martinez has feuded in the past with manager Jimy Williams, particularly after Williams bumped him from an August 1999 start for being late to the ballpark.)

Martinez has also played a role in breaking down Boston's reputation as an unwelcoming city for minorities. The city has welcomed Martinez, and his popularity has given exposure to the area's thriving and vibrant Latin community. His popularity also yielded another unexpected bonus for the team: One of the reason's superstar free agent Manny Ramirez signed with the Red Sox was that his mother urged him to go to Boston because Martinez was there—even though she doesn't know anything about baseball.

Besides being the best pitcher currently in baseball, Pedro Martinez compares favorably with baseball's most legendary pitchers—especially given the proliferation of hitting in today's game. And much of the Pedro Martinez story is yet to occur.

Ramon Martinez—tall, lanky righthanded pitcher, now known as Pedro Martinez's big brother. When Pedro started, he was known as Ramon's little brother. In 1990 at the age of 22, Ramon had a tremendous season for the Dodgers, going 20–6 while leading the National League in complete games, and making the top 10 in numerous other pitching categories. He looked like the next great pitcher in the National League, but never quite lived up to the standards that he set that season. He has never had another 20-win season, or another year with an ERA under 3.00.

He was hurt in the middle of the 1998 season and had to have shoulder reconstruction surgery. Sox GM Dan Duquette signed him as a free agent in the offseason, and he joined the Red Sox prior to the 1999 season, though he wasn't healthy enough to pitch until late in the year. He made 4 effective starts in September of 1999, helping the Red Sox wrap up the wild card. In the playoffs, he pitched well in one start against the Indians and one against the Yankees. Many Sox fans were encouraged and felt that he would be back in form for the 2000 season, but that did not turn out to be the case. His first start of 2000, in Seattle, turned out to be a precursor of the season to come, when he gave up five runs in the first inning, capped by a Jay Buhner 3-run homer. He occasionally pitched well but frequently got into serious trouble early in the game. He finished the season averaging fewer than 5 innings per start , with an ERA over 6.00. The Red Sox declined to pick up his $8 million contract option for the 2001 season. Martinez drew little interest as a free agent, and wound up returning to his original team, the Dodgers.

John Marzano—a light-hitting catcher who debuted with the Sox in 1987. Marzano had been heavily publicized as a college star at Temple University and as a member of the US Olympic team, but in the majors he was a perpetual free swinger who displayed only occasional power. He shuttled back and forth between Boston and Pawtucket for six seasons, serving as backups to such players as Rich Gedman, Rick Cerone, and Tony Peña. After his release from Boston following the 1992 season, he was out of the major leagues until he resurfaced with the Texas Rangers in 1995. He spent parts of the next three seasons with the Seattle Mariners.

Marzano's most memorable moment came in a 1991 game against the Tigers, in which he may have saved the career of ace pitcher Roger Clemens. After being hit by a Clemens fastball, Tigers outfielder John Shelby charged the mound—with the bat still in his hand. With his pitcher a sitting duck, Marzano sprung from his catching position and, loaded with gear, caught up to Shelby and tackled him from behind.

With that move Marzano earned a great amount of respect from fans, coaches, and his fellow players.

Carl Mays—a starting pitcher who played for 3 World Series winners in his 4-plus years in Boston (winning 18, 22, and 21 games as a full-time starter from 1916–18). In 1919, he left the club under mysterious circumstances. Two weeks later, new team owner Harry Frazee sold him to the Yankees for $40,000, in a portent of things to come (Frazee would soon sell Babe Ruth and most of the other Red Sox stars to the Yankees).

Mays is best known for killing a man during a baseball game. Mays threw underhanded, but had a devastating fastball. On August 16, 1920, he hit Cleveland shortstop Ray Chapman with a pitch; Chapman died 12 hours later without ever recovering consciousness (batters did not wear protective helmets at the time, or for many years afterward). Mays played 9 more years in the big leagues after the incident, 3 times winning 19 games or more.

Mickey McDermott—a lefthanded pitcher who looked like he was going to become a star, Maury "Mickey" McDermott first played for the Red Sox at age 19. He was an average pitcher for several years, before breaking out with an 18–10 season as a 24-year-old in 1953. When McDermott was traded that offseason for Jackie Jensen, many fans were outraged: McDermott was a rising star, extremely popular in Boston's Irish community, and known for singing in Boston nightclubs. The trade turned out to be a good one, however—Jensen became a star for the Red Sox and McDermott never won more than 10 games in a season again.

Willie McGee—a singles-hitting outfielder with a good arm, range, and speed, McGee is as famous for the year he didn't join the Red Sox as the year he did. In 1990, when the Red Sox were fighting for a playoff berth and McGee (hitting .335) was available in a trade, Red Sox GM Lou Gorman famously said "What would we do with Willie McGee?" McGee went to the Oakland A's instead—a team that would go on to beat the Red Sox in the playoffs.

McGee had a long career with the St. Louis Cardinals (where he hit .353, the highest average ever for a switch hitter, in 1985) and the San Francisco Giants before joining the Red Sox in 1995. By this time the 36-year-old McGee was well past his prime due to age and injuries. In 67 games as a pinch hitter, late inning defensive replacement, and occasional starter, McGee hit .285, but walked just 9 times. He stole only 5 bases (he averaged 25 a year over his career, and once stole 56 in a season) and was caught stealing 9 times. It was his only year in Boston. After 1995 he returned to St. Louis, where he was a part-time player until age 40, retiring in 1999.

Stuffy McInnis—a Gloucester native, Jack "Stuffy" McInnis joined the Philadelphia Athletics as a teenage shortstop in 1909, but became a star after moving to first base 2 years later. Though the nickname seems ridiculous in the Manny Ramirez/Alex Rodriguez era, McInnis was part of the Athletics' great "$100,000 Infield" (with Hall of Famers Eddie Collins and Home Run Baker, and shortstop Jack Barry). McInnis hit for high averages in Philly (over .300 in 6 of his 7 full seasons) and virtually never struck out, though he had little power (20 lifetime homers) and rarely walked. He was a legendary defensive player, and the first first baseman to go into a split when stretching for throws.

In 1918, the rebuilding Athletics traded McInnis to his hometown team for long-time third baseman Larry Gardner and outfielder Tilly Walker. McInnis wasn't as effective with Boston, where he slumped to .272, but he earned his third World Series ring. He hit .305 in 1919 and .297 in 1920, though his lack of power became a liability with the advent of the lively ball. In 1921 McInnis hit .307 and set 2 notable records. He had 584 at bats, but only struck out 9 times—the fewest ever of any Red Sox player with over 500 at bats. McInnis only made 1 error, and his .999 fielding percentage set a big league record for first basemen that stood for 63 years (Steve Garvey was a perfect 1.000 in 1984). Despite the records, McInnis was traded to Cleveland after the season for George Burns, a first baseman with more power. He retired after the 1927 season with 2,405 hits and a .307 lifetime average.

Jeff McNeely—a once highly thought of prospect, Jeff McNeely was an outfielder who played a total of 21 innings in the majors, all during the 1993 season. He was one of the fastest players that the Sox have had, stealing 6 bases without being caught during his brief stint in the majors.

Sam Mele—outfielder/first baseman who came up with the Red Sox in 1947 then bounced around baseball for the next 10 years. He spent time with 6 separate teams, not counting 2 stints with the Red Sox. (He was traded in midseason 4 different times.) He was never a great hitter for average or for power, with a career high of 16 homers in 1952 (though his 36 doubles did lead the American League in 1951, while he was playing for Washington). He once drove in 6 runs in the fourth inning of a game against Boston while playing for the White Sox, hitting a 3-run homer and a 3-run triple. After his playing career ended, he managed the Minnesota Twins for 7 seasons, leading them to the World Series in 1965. Mele was also a longtime scout for the Red Sox (serving the Boston area), and is currently a scouting consultant for the team.

Kent Mercker—a 32-year-old lefthanded pitcher attempting to make a second stint with the Red Sox in 2001. Mercker pitched briefly for Atlanta in 1989, and spent the 6 following years in a Braves uniform, pitching mostly out of the bullpen until being moved to the starting rotation in 1994. Mercker signed with Baltimore as a free agent but after 12 dreadful starts in 1996 he was traded to Cleveland, where he moved back to the bullpen.

He signed with Cincinnati for the 1997 season, and pitched effectively, starting 25 games for the Reds with a good ERA (but an 8–11 record, mostly due to bad luck and poor run support), but Cincinnati didn't exercise their option for 1998. He signed with St. Louis and went 11–11, despite not pitching as well as he had the year before.

After starting poorly with the Cardinals in 1999, he was traded to Boston where he pitched extremely well in 5 starts down the stretch, including winning the game in which the Red Sox clinched the American League Wild Card berth in September. He was ineffective in the playoffs, getting shelled in only 1⅓ innings in Game 4 of the Division Series (though Boston ended up winning the game 23–7). After the season Mercker once again found himself a free agent.

Mercker spent the 2000 season with the Anaheim Angels. On May 11 he suffered a cerebral hemorrhage while pitching against Texas. He spent 12 days in the hospital, including 4 days in intensive care. Remarkably, he was pitching again in only 3 months, starting against the Yankees on August 12. On August 22, he beat the Red Sox in Fenway Park, his first win since he had clinched the Wild Card for the Sox the previous September. A free agent once again after the 2000 season, Mercker signed a minor league contract with Boston in January, with a spring training invite to try to earn a spot on the staff. Also in January, he was honored at the Boston Baseball Writers' annual dinner as a co-winner of the eleventh annual Tony Conigliaro award, given annually to "the player who best overcomes an obstacle and continues to thrive through the adversity."

Lou Merloni—a native of Framingham, Massachusetts, and Nomar Garciaparra's close friend and former AAA roommate, it's really too soon to call Merloni a "local kid made good," but in limited play he has become a local kid made popular, attested to by the chants of "Lou, Lou, Lou" that accompany him to the plate. Though his skills are average for a major leaguer, Lou has a hard-nosed, not afraid to get his uniform dirty attitude that is appreciated by Red Sox fans. Merloni saw action at several infield positions in both the 1998 and 1999 seasons, hitting .281 after a hot start in 1998 (including a homer in his first Fenway Park at bat), but slumping to .254 in 1999. With his chances of making the major leagues slim in 2000, the Red Sox sold the 29-year-old Merloni's contract to a Japanese team, where he could make more money than he would as a fringe player in the United States. Merloni met with little success in Japan (not unusual for an American player) and after being released he returned midway through the season to sign to a minor league contract with the Red Sox. It was good timing for both Merloni and the team, due to an early season-ending injury to third baseman John Valentin, and the failure of everyone else who had tried to replace him. Though not flashy, Merloni provided stability at that position with steady defense and hit .320 down the stretch. He is currently a backup infielder with the Red Sox.

Catfish Metkovich—center fielder for the Red Sox during World War II, when most of the team's regular players were in the military. George Michael Metkovich was an undistinguished hitter with some speed as a baserunner; he was good enough to remain a part-time player in the major leagues after the war ended. He played as a part timer in 1946 after Dom DiMaggio returned to reclaim his job in center field, then drifted to 5 other teams in the next 6 years

Rick Miller—lefthanded-hitting outfielder who served two stints with the Red Sox, Miller had a long career as a platoon and backup player without ever being a full time starter. He batted more than 400 times only twice in 12 years with the Red Sox. (Most full-time players bat 500–600 times in a season.) Miller was a fine center fielder (he won a Gold Glove for the Angels in 1978), fast runner (although only an average base stealer), and a decent hitter who drew more than his share of walks but didn't have much power (his career high in home runs was 6). Despite his lack of power, Miller tied a major league record by hitting 4 doubles in a game. (Three other Sox players, Billy Werber, Al Zarilla, and Orlando Cepeda have also tied the record.) Miller played for the Sox from 1971–1977, and during this time married the sister of teammate Carlton Fisk. Miller signed with the Angels as a free agent, then was traded back to the Sox in the ill-fated Fred Lynn trade before the 1981 season. He played until 1985, the last few years mostly as a pinch hitter.

Bill Monbouquette—"Monbo" was a native of Medford, Massachusetts, who was the ace for very weak Red Sox teams from 1958 to 1965. Without an overpowering fastball, Monbouquette relied on changing speeds and on pinpoint control. Monbouquette had at least 13 wins each year from 1960 to 1964, including a 20–10 record in 1963—quite an accomplishment on a team that finished 76–85. He had tied for the league lead in losses on a dreadful (62–100) team in 1965, but with a decent 3.70 ERA.

A 4-time All Star, Monbouquette's career highlights include striking out 17 Senators in 1961 (at the time the second-best ever in the American League), and a 1–0 no-hitter against Early Wynn of the Chicago White Sox on August 1, 1962.

After the 1965 season Monbouquette was traded to Detroit. After a brief stay he moved on to the Yankees in 1967 (where he pitched well), and the Giants in 1968 (where he retired after going 1–7). Monbo was inducted into the Red Sox Hall of Fame in 2000.

Bob Montgomery—a 10-year career backup catcher with the Sox, from 1970–1979, never batting more than 254 times in a season. "Monty" was a weak-hitting backup to Pudge Fisk and Jim Rice's golfing partner. Like many career backups, he was a favorite of underdog-rooting fans. After his playing career ended he spent several years as an English-butchering color analyst on Red Sox television broadcasts.

Dave Morehead—righthanded pitcher who threw the last Red Sox no-hitter in 1965 (a year in which he led the league in losses with 18). Only 1,247 fans attended the game. As a promising 19-year-old rookie Morehead threw a shutout in his first game in 1963, but he would have only 1 winning season in his 8-year career; he went 5–4 as a part time player on the 1967 Impossible Dream team. His overall record in 6 years with the Sox was 35–56.

Rogelio Moret—better known as Roger to Boston fans, the biggest concern with Moret early in his career was whether his slender frame could hold up under the rigors of pitching in the big leagues. It was a legitimate concern, for while he at times pitched brilliantly (he was 13–2 in 1973 and 14–3 in 1975, leading the league in winning percentage both years), he was often hurt. In 7 other injury-plagued seasons he managed only a 20–22 record, splitting his time between the starting rotation and the bullpen.

Moret appeared in relief in Game 2 of the 1975 American League Championship Series, and was credited with the win while pitching a scoreless sixth inning. He also gave up the game winning hit in Game 3 of that year's World Series, but was not credited with the loss. He spent the last 3 years of his career with Atlanta and Texas, where he was less than effective.

Ed Morris—top pitcher on terrible Sox teams in the 1930s who suffered a macabre death. Morris had played briefly with the Cubs in 1922 but didn't resurface in the major leagues until 1928, when he went 19–15 as a 28-year-old rookie on a team that lost 96 games. He led an equally bad team in wins again the next year. He was stabbed to death by a jealous husband at a fish fry in the spring training of 1932.

Jamie Moyer—a lefthanded starting pitcher and the son-in-law of ex-Notre Dame University Head Basketball Coach Digger Phelps, Moyer came up with the Cubs in 1986. He had his first better-than-average pitching season in 1988, but with poor run support, and he finished the season at 9-15. The Cubs traded Moyer to Texas following the year, and he spent 2 years there, moved on to St. Louis for a year before signing with Baltimore prior to the 1993 season. In Baltimore, he pitched well for 2 years, before struggling in short innings in 1995. The Red Sox signed him as a free agent prior to the 1996 season.

The 1996 Red Sox, defending American League East champions, started the season at 6–19, and were never realistically in the race. Moyer pitched well for Boston, and took advantage of strong run support in his games to go 7–1 for Boston, before being traded to Seattle for Darren Bragg. Since the trade to Seattle, Moyer has continued the blossoming process, pitching well for Seattle in 1996, and being one of the best starters in the American League from 1997–99. In 2000 he spent time on the disabled list, and was not particularly effective when he was pitching. He'll be 38 years old in 2001, and what he's got left, if anything, remains to be seen.

Rob Murphy—a lefthanded reliever obtained from Cincinnati as part of the Nick Esasky trade, Murphy had a terrific season in 1989. Murphy was 29 and coming off 3 good seasons, but was still not well known as a player (not unusual for a middle reliever). Murphy and Lee Smith held together a bad relief corps in 1989, with Murphy appearing in 74 games and posting a 2.74 ERA. In 1990, with talk of Murphy being moved into a closer's role, everything fell apart. His ERA more than doubled (opposing hitters hit over .400 against him), and he was ineffective all year. The Red Sox traded him to Seattle during Spring Training the next year for pitcher Mike Gardiner. Although Murphy would recover some of his effectiveness and pitch decently again, he never had another dominant year like 1989.

Buddy Myer—lefthanded-hitting infielder who played third base for the Red Sox in 1928. They Red Sox acquired Myer from Washington late in the 1927 season, and in 1928, he led the American League with 30 stolen bases while playing for the Red Sox. The Senators were so convinced that they'd made a mistake, that they traded 5 players to the Sox after the 1928 season in order to get Myer back. He did eventually play on 2 All Star teams in 1935 and 1937. In 1935 he won the American League batting title by going 4 for 5 in the season's final game, while Cleveland's Joe Vosmik was sitting out the game to protect his average. With the exception of the 1 season in Boston, he spent his entire 17-season career in Washington, retiring after the 1941 season.

Tim Naehring—righthanded-hitting infielder whose 8-year career with the Sox was riddled by injuries. The 23-year-old Naehring came up to the Sox in 1990 touted as a guy who could hit for good power, a rare commodity at that time for middle infielders, and played well in his initial tour of duty. Handed the starting shortstop's job the next spring, Naehring hit a ghastly .109 in 20 games, including an 0 for 39 slump, before the Red Sox shut him down to see what was wrong. Back and leg trouble kept stifling his development (he hit .231 the following year) until it was discovered that one of his legs was actually shorter than the other. To curb this problem he was fitted with a platform to wear in his shoe, to readjust the discrepancy and take the pressure off his lower back. The adjustment helped, and Naehring hit .331 in 1993. By this time, however, John Valentin was already established at shortstop, so Naehring moved to the less laterally demanding third base (where he was terrific defensively), allowing the Sox to trade Scott Cooper. Finally given the chance to play regularly, Naehring put up solid numbers for the Sox, hitting over .300 in 1995 (he led the league in hitting going into June) and launching a career-high 17 homers in 1996.

An elbow injury in 1997 effectively ended Naehring's Red Sox career, shortly after he had turned down more money from the Cleveland Indians to re-sign with the Red Sox as a free agent. Because of a quirk in the free agent rules it would have cost the Red Sox more than $4 million to keep him. Although the Red Sox offered him other jobs in the system, Naehring did not want to retire, and reluctantly signed with his hometown Cincinnati Reds. After attempting a comeback with the Reds, he took a position in that organization's front office, and is considered a rising front-office star. He finished his career with a .282 average.

Naehring was an active community leader during his time with the Sox, involving himself in numerous local charity events, and even leading the construction of a Little League field shaped as a miniature Fenway Park in Cincinnati (for a picture, see www.redsoxdiehard.com/players/naehring.html).

Mike Nagy—a righthanded pitcher, Nagy came up with Boston in 1969 as a 21-year-old phenom, and went 12–2 for the Sox with a very good ERA. However, as with many pitchers that are successful at an early age, arm injuries resulted, probably because of the excessive workload for his age. He pitched 128⅔ innings in 1970, and never threw more than 41 in any season after that. After 4 years in Boston, he spent a year in St. Louis and another year in Houston. He was done at the age of 26 after the 1974 season.

Jeff Newman—one of many poorly thought out acquisitions in the early 1980s, Newman was a 34-year-old righthanded-hitting catcher with some power (he'd hit 22 home runs in a terrible hitter's park in 1979, in his only year as a full-time starter). He was heralded by the Sox front office as a natural Fenway hitter who would shower doubles off the Green Monster. He hit .189 with 3 home runs, and quickly lost his job to light-hitting Gary Allenson. In a way, this was a blessing in disguise; if Newman had been adequate as a starting catcher, Rich Gedman, then a 23-year-old part-time player, would probably never have been given the chance to develop into the key starter he would be from 1984 to 1986.

Reid Nichols—a fast center fielder who looked like a rising star in the mid-1980s. Nichols had a reputation as the fastest player in the Red Sox system, and had call-ups with the team in 1980 and 1981 without hitting much. In 1982, as a 23-year-old, he was finally given real playing time in the outfield and blossomed, hitting .302 with mid-range power for a team with light-hitting Rick Miller in center and beginning-to-fade Jim Rice in left. Instead of increasing Nichols's playing time in 1983, the Sox traded for one-dimensional power hitter Tony Armas, who hit .218 with 36 home runs but only 29 walks in over 600 plate appearances and was overmatched in center field. Nichols again hit well as a fourth outfielder, batting .285, drawing walks about twice as often as Armas, and increasing his power slightly. The next year his playing time was cut in half and he was ineffective. Traded to the White Sox in 1985, Nichols never batted more than 150 times in a season again and was out of baseball before his thirtieth birthday. He remains a what-might-have been—a player who performed well in the only times he was given regular work (on mediocre teams that could have used an infusion of speed and youth), but who was never given a shot to develop into a full-time player.

Al Nipper—righthanded pitcher who came through the Red Sox farm system and debuted in the majors in 1983. He outpitched fellow rookie and close friend Roger Clemens during their rookie seasons in 1984. Never overpowering, he was a middle-of-the-rotation starter for the Red Sox from 1984–87, although he never had another winning season after 1984. John McNamara was heavily criticized for starting Nipper in Game 4 of the 1986 World Series, despite Nipper's 10–12 record and 5.38 ERA (league average was 4.18), a game that Nipper predictably lost. Nipper threw a beanball at Darryl Strawberry in the first Red Sox–Mets game after the 1986 World Series, during 1987 Spring Training. Apparently, Nipper had vowed to get back at Strawberry for the Series, and his attempt to keep his word was popular with some fans.

After 1987, Nipper and Calvin Schiraldi were traded to the Cubs for Lee Smith (one of the Red Sox great trades), but he never pitched regularly in the major leagues again. Nipper later worked as a pitching coach in the Sox system, including a stint as the major league pitching coach during the musical-pitching-coaches phase of the Butch Hobson era in the early 1990s. He was supposed to be the next great pitching coach, but instead left the Red Sox organization under acrimonious circumstances, after several disagreements with general manager Dan Duquette.

Otis Nixon—speedy, switch-hitting outfielder signed as a free agent by the Sox prior to the strike-shortened season of 1994. The veteran Nixon was the long-desired lead-off hitter with speed sought by a club dragged down by an unproductive, singles-hitting offense. The sight of speed on the basepaths was a refreshing one for Sox fans, and Nixon gained an early popularity with the Fenway crowd. In his only season with Boston he hit .274 (while stealing 42 bases in 52 attempts, in just 103 games). Despite the strong numbers, the 35-year-old Nixon was part of the trade that brought Jose Canseco to Boston after Kevin Kennedy (who wanted a team of sluggers) was signed on as manager. Nixon, who didn't hit above .263 until his ninth year in the majors, continued to play well for years after most of his contemporaries were forced to retire. He spent 17 years in the majors with 9 different teams, during which he hit .270 with 620 career steals.

Trot Nixon—lefthanded outfielder drafted by the Sox in the first round in 1993 (Lou Gorman's last draft). Christopher Trotman Nixon was a highly touted, five tool prospect, a great high school quarterback as well as a baseball star (as well as a neighbor to Hall-of-Famer Catfish Hunter). Back problems plagued Nixon's minor league career, however, and it was uncertain if he would ever live up to his expectations. After showing great strides in improving his offense at AAA Pawtucket in 1997 and 1998, Nixon won a platoon right field job with Boston in 1999. Replacing Darren Bragg, a good fielder and gritty player but only a so-so hitter, Nixon showed that he also went all out on every play. This approach to the game put him in good graces with manager Jimy Williams, who stuck with Nixon despite his .105 batting average in April. (Nixon was out of options and couldn't be sent back to the minors unless the Sox wanted to risk losing him to another team). Nixon turned things around and hit well the rest of the year, bringing his average up to .270 with 15 home runs (12 of them in the season's second half).

As was the case with several Sox hitters in 2000, Nixon had an up and down season with the bat, finishing at .276 with 12 homers—similar to his first season rather than the dramatic improvement many people projected. His playing time was sometimes inconsistent, which seemed to affect Nixon's timing; although there was talk of making him the full-time right fielder, he continued to be platooned with light-hitting Darren Lewis, even against lefthanders who were better against righthanded hitters. When he did get to face lefty pitching, he was much improved from his 1999 struggles.

Nixon's 2000 highlight came in the top of the ninth inning of a nationally televised pitching duel between Pedro Martinez and Roger Clemens at Yankee Stadium. With the score 0–0, Trot belted a Clemens pitch for a 2-run homer that was the eventual game winning hit. Although trade rumors hovered around Nixon in the 2000 off-season, GM Dan Duquette reportedly refused to part with Nixon in several deals, considering him a potential cornerstone of the club's future.

Hideo Nomo—a righthanded pitcher, this former Japanese league star was the National League Rookie of the Year while pitching for the Dodgers in 1995. Known for his long, twisting delivery (in which he frequently turns his back to the hitter, much as El Tiante did), Nomo has always been a strikeout pitcher. In 1997, after only pitching in 444⅔ innings, Nomo reached the 500 strikeout mark faster than any other pitcher in major league history.

After 3½ years in LA, with ERAs rising each year, he was traded to New York in 1998, where he pitched poorly in 16 starts for the Mets. Following offseason elbow surgery he was released by the Mets toward the end of spring training. He signed a minor league contract with the Cubs that called for him to be brought to the majors or released after 3 starts, and the Cubs opted to release him. Shortly thereafter, the Brewers signed him, and he came up to Milwaukee in May. He pitched well for Milwaukee and signed a 1-year contract to pitch for Detroit during the 2000 season. He pitched inconsistently, however, and Detroit chose not to pick up his option for the 2001 season. The Red Sox signed him to a 1-year contract in December of 2000, as one more potential piece of their 2001 rotation.

Buck O'Brien—righthanded pitcher, O'Brien came up for 5 starts with Boston in 1911. A native of Brockton, Massachusetts, O'Brien's specialty was a spitball, still legal at the time. In 1912 he went 20–13 for the World Series champion Red Sox, throwing over 275 innings. However, O'Brien went 0–2 in the 1912 Series that the Sox won in 8 games.

The most controversial loss came in Game 6. With the Sox leading the Series 3–1–1 (Game 2 had ended in an 11-inning 6–6 tie), Smoky Joe Wood was expected to start in the Polo Grounds. But the owner of the team, James McAleer, approached manager Jake Stahl and convinced him to hold Wood back. Had Wood won, the series would have been over that day, but a Sox loss meant that Wood would pitch in Fenway, to a tremendous gate, the next day. Stahl relented, and O'Brien got the start. He may have been out drinking late the previous night, not expecting to play, certainly not to start. Everyone on the team expected Wood to start. But whatever the cause, O'Brien gave up 5 runs in the first inning and the Sox lost 5–2. On the train back to Boston, Joe Wood's brother Paul, who had lost $100 by betting on a game he expected his brother to start, got into a fight with O'Brien and gave him a black eye. The whole sequence of events also exacerbated tensions that had been present on the team all year between the Catholic players, including O'Brien, and the Protestants, including Wood. The newspapers had even referred to the groups as "knights" and "masons."

After the season, Buck spent the winter touring with Hugh Bradley and two former teammates as a vaudeville act called the "Red Sox Quartette." They toured all of New England, featuring novelty tunes such as "Buck O'Brien, The Spit-ball artist," and O'Brien came to camp out of shape in 1913. After 12 starts and 3 relief appearances, in which he went 4–9, he was traded to the White Sox, where he went 0–2 to finish the season, and his career.

Jose Offerman—switch-hitting second baseman acquired as a free agent following the 1998 season. Although Offerman was one of the best-hitting second basemen in baseball, the Red Sox were widely ridiculed for signing him to a 4-year contract for $6 million a year—mainly because Offerman has never quite lived down the reputation he built early in his career for being an overhyped and underachieving player. (The joke was picked up by the national media, and actor Samuel Jackson made fun of the signing during the Espy Awards ceremony.) Offerman was signed around the same time the Red Sox lost powerful first baseman and local icon Mo Vaughn to free agency. Although the 2 players were very different, many fans saw the Offerman signing as a feeble attempt to replace Vaughn. General manager Dan Duquette didn't help matters when he said that Offerman would replace Vaughn's "on-base ability," which was true, but only highlighted the fact that Offerman lacked both Vaughn's power and his charisma. Offerman converted many of his critics when he started the 1999 season with a blazing hot streak, although the first 2 years of his contract yielded mixed results overall.

Offerman started his career as a shortstop with the Dodgers in 1990. He quickly gained a reputation as a poor fielder (and the nickname "Awfulman"), committing 42 errors in his first full year, and following with other 35+ error seasons. Throughout most of his years in L.A. Offerman was a poor offensive player as well. He reached double digits in steals only twice in 6 years (although he did steal 30 bases in 1993). In 1995 he showed flashes of what he could do offensively, posting respectable numbers for a shortstop, including an on-base percentage of .389.

Moving on to the Kansas City Royals, he had a fine offensive year in 1996, posting an on-base percentage of .384 and stealing 24 bases. That season also marked the beginning of his move away from shortstop. He would get about 30 starts each at both short and second base, and 80 starts at first base. (While his offensive numbers were good for a middle infielder, they were below-average for a first baseman.) He committed 10 errors at shortstop while committing only 1 at second base. In 1997 Offerman was strictly a second baseman, committing only 9 errors in 101 games. He continued to hit as well, and in 1998 he established himself as a great leadoff hitter, scoring 102 runs, stealing 45 bases, and posting a .403 on-base percentage—as well as effectively pricing him out of small-market Kansas City's budget.

Offerman started the 1999 season under intense media pressure. Early reports out of spring training had manager Jimy Williams thinking of using Offerman at first base and designated hitter while letting Jeff Frye play second. An injury to Frye and the emergence of first baseman Brian Daubach put an end to the unfortunate experiment (paying a good offensive second baseman $6 million is one thing, while paying that same player to be a poor offensive first baseman is altogether different). Offerman eventually posted a .391 on-base percentage and scored 107 runs (although his steals dropped to 18 with manager Williams reluctant to let Offerman run). A knee injury drastically reduced Offerman's effectiveness in 2000—dropping his on-base percentage by almost 40 points and his stolen bases to 0 (he was caught 8 times), while limiting his ability to play second base.

Ben Oglivie—an outfield prospect who seemingly wasn't going to pan out, the lefty-hitting Oglivie was inconsistent and not very good in parts of 3 seasons for the Red

Sox, who gave him to Detroit for a washed-up Dick McAuliffe after the 1973 season. With Detroit and Milwaukee, Oglivie blossomed as a hitter, although he always remained inconsistent. In 1980, when the powerhouse Red Sox of the late 1970s began to fade, Oglivie had his best season, hitting .304 with 41 home runs for Milwaukee.

Tomo Ohka—the first Japanese player in Red Sox history came to the club as an afterthought. Dan Duquette had been sending older minor leaguers to Japanese teams for several years, and the Yokohama BayStars gave him the obscure Tomokazu Ohka, a righthanded pitcher, to return the favor. Little was expected from Ohka, but he surprised everyone with a perfect 15–0 record (2.31 ERA) at Trenton and Pawtucket. He pitched briefly in the majors in 1999, but returned to Pawtucket the following year, making headlines with an astounding 76-pitch perfect game. This led to another big league audition, and the 24-year-old Ohka was the team's second-best pitcher down the stretch (3–6 because of the team's poor hitting, but with an excellent 3.12 ERA). Ohka is expected to be a mainstay in the rotation for years to come.

Bob Ojeda—one of a group of pitchers developed by the Sox in the early 1980s who went on to long but not great careers. Ojeda was a soft thrower who never overpowered hitters but got them out with smarts and location. After a brief stay with the Sox in 1980, Ojeda was called up from the minors at the end of the strike in 1981, and had a terrific second half, leading to tremendous expectations. He had a terrible year in 1982, but established himself as a solid, consistent starter over the next 3 years (with nearly identical ERAs around 4.00 each year). Ojeda's best year for the Sox was in 1984, when he went 12–12 in 216.1 innings. His 137 strikeouts that year were the second highest in his career.

Ojeda was traded to the Mets in 1986 for four minor leaguers, including prospects Calvin Schiraldi and Wes Gardner (Red Sox GM Lou Gorman was a former Mets GM and knew the organization that the Sox would face in the World Series later that year very well). Ojeda went on to brief stardom in New York, going 18–5 with a 2.57 ERA in 217.1 innings for the World Champions (all career bests for Ojeda) and starting 2 games against his old team in the World Series.

He spent 4 more years with the Mets, never winning more than 13 games. In 1993, after two years with the Dodgers, he joined the Indians. During spring training he was injured in a boating accident in which teammates Steve Olin and Tim Crews died. He appeared in only 9 games in 1993, 2 more for the Yankees in 1994 and then was out of baseball at the age of 36.

Troy O'Leary—an outfielder with a good bat, the 25-year-old O'Leary was snatched off waivers from the Milwaukee Brewers in 1995. O'Leary quickly took over in right field for the outfielder-poor Red Sox, but his difficulties with Fenway's enormous right field caused him to be moved to left, where he eventually developed into an excellent fielder. O'Leary's quiet manner and strong work ethic made him a key supporting player in the late 1990s teams, built around a few star hitters like Nomar

The Red Sox Fan Handbook

Garciaparra and Mo Vaughn. O'Leary is a solid player, but not a star; he has a life-time batting average of .280 (and has hit over .300 twice with the Sox), but has below-average power for a left fielder (averaging 17 homers a year, at a time when the league is offense-oriented) and doesn't walk much. In 1999 O'Leary hit a career-best 28 home runs and seemed on the verge of stardom, but he got off to a terrible start in 2000 amid a difficult divorce (it was rumored that a Sox minor leaguer was involved). After a trip to the disabled list to get his head together O'Leary did come back to play well the second half of the season.

O'Leary played an extraordinary role in Boston's 1999 American League Division Series victory against the Cleveland Indians. Boston was on the verge of elimination in Game 5, especially when starter Bret Saberhagen was knocked out of the game in the second inning. Twice that night Nomar Garciaparra was intentionally walked with men on base to pitch to O'Leary (who had a career playoff average of .094 at the time). Both times O'Leary followed with a home run, driving in a series-record 7 runs (tying teammate John Valentin, who did it the game before). Later in the game with Garciaparra at bat, a man on base, first base open, and O'Leary waiting on-deck, players from the Red Sox dugout could be heard saying, "Go ahead, walk him again!"

Steve Ontiveros—a righthanded pitcher, Ontiveros edged out Red Sox Roger Clemens for the American League ERA crown in strike-shortened 1994. Pitching mostly out of the bullpen for the Oakland A's, Ontiveros barely qualified with his 115⅓ innings. After being out of the majors for over 4 years, he signed with the Red Sox in August of 2000, and in a critical September start in Detroit, he started instead of hot rookie Paxton Crawford. Ontiveros got only 3 outs while giving up 6 runs, and the Red Sox lost badly. Less than a week later, however, he earned a measure of redemption when he pitched 2⅓ scoreless innings against Cleveland in a vital game when starter Rolando Arrojo was knocked out early. Ontiveros was awarded with the win when the Red Sox came back for a 9–8 win. Ontiveros signed a minor league contract with the New York Mets before the 2001 season.

Spike Owen—shortstop acquired along with Dave Henderson in the stretch run of 1986 from the Seattle Mariners for 4 players. Owen had been a teammate of Roger Clemens at the University of Texas, and earlier in 1986 he had been Clemens's nineteenth strikeout victim in the game in which Clemens set the record with 20 whiffs. Known more for his glove than his bat, Owen would hit just .183 for the Sox for the remainder of the season, before churning out a .429 in the playoffs against the Angels and .300 against the Mets in the World Series. In August he tied an American League record by scoring six runs in a nine-inning game, during a 24–5 Sox rout of the Cleveland Indians. Owen played 2½ years with the Sox before being traded to the Expos in December 1988. He also played with the Yankees and Angels before retiring after the 1995 season.

Stan Papi—utility infielder whom the Sox traded pitcher Bill Lee (who manager Don Zimmer was determined to dump) to Montreal for after the 1978 season. Papi was not considered a prospect; at age 28 he was coming off a .230 season, and not yet an established major leaguer. He went on to hit .188 in his only full season with the Red Sox, while the banished Lee won 16 games for Montreal.

Mel Parnell—a dominant lefty, Mel Parnell was the best pitcher for the Red Sox from 1948 through 1953. A rookie in 1947 (not 1948 as David Halberstam's *Summer of '49* might have you believe), Parnell led the 1948 team in ERA. His emergence as a dominant pitcher, along with the acquisition of Ellis Kinder over the winter, helped transform the third-place 1947 team into the excellent 1948 team which finished tied atop the standings with the Cleveland Indians. Because of the tie, a one-game win-ner-take-all playoff was played between the two teams. Instead of Parnell, who had led the team with a 3.14 ERA (good for fourth in the league) and who had finished second on the team in innings pitched, manager Joe McCarthy opted to start jour-neyman Denny Galehouse, who promptly lost the game, allowing the Indians to advance to the World Series and depriving the Sox the chance to play their crosstown rival, the Boston Braves.

Parnell followed up his excellent 1948 performance with an even better one in 1949. He led the league in wins (25), innings pitched (295), and complete games (27). He was second in the league in ERA (2.77), second in winning percentage (his .781 was only bettered by teammate Ellis Kinder), and fourth in shutouts (4). It was like-ly the best performance by a Sox pitcher since Lefty Grove in 1936, and the best any would see from a Sox pitcher (give or take Frank Sullivan in 1955) until Roger Clemens in 1986. And yet, despite Parnell's heroics, despite Kinder chipping in 23 wins, and despite Ted Williams's winning the triple crown, the Sox finished second to the hated New York Yankees by a single game. With a chance to win the pennant by winning 1 of its final 2 games, the Sox lost both games to the Yankees, and with them the pennant.

Though he never had another season to match 1949, Parnell continued to be the ace of the Red Sox staff into the 1950s. He finished in the top ten in the league in ERA, wins, and innings pitched in 1950, 1951, and 1953. An All Star in 1949, Parnell made the All Star team again in 1951. Unfortunately, injuries to fellow pitchers, losing Ted Williams to injury and the Korean War, and other factors combined to waste Parnell's excellence—the team finished third in the league in 1950 and 1951, sixth in 1952, and fourth in 1953. By 1954 Parnell's run of dominance was over as his arm gave out. After winning 21 games and pitching 241 innings in 1953, Parnell would win only 12 more games over the next three years while pitching only 269 innings. His 10-year career ended after the 1956 season. Red Sox fans would not see a pitcher as good for as sustained a period until Roger Clemens's emergence in the late 1980s.

Marty Pattin—a righthanded pitcher, "Bulldog" spent 13 seasons in the major leagues, coming up with California in 1968. He was taken by the Seattle Pilots in the Expansion Draft after the 1968 season, and went with Seattle to Milwaukee when they became the Brewers in 1970. After the 1971 season, Pattin was traded to Boston with Tommy Harper in a 10-player trade that sent Jim Lonborg, Ken Brett, and

George Scott to Milwaukee. Pattin won 17 and 15 games in his two seasons with Boston, with an ERA at about league average levels. His 17 wins in 1972 led the staff for the Sox team that finished just half a game behind Detroit. Pattin was traded to Kansas City following the 1973 season, and he finished his career there, retiring after the 1980 season.

Rudy Pemberton—a former Detroit prospect who had signed with the Red Sox as a minor league free agent, the 26-year-old Pemberton was called up late in 1996 and went on an extraordinary tear, hitting .512 with 9 extra-base hits and 3 steals in 13 games. He won a job as a platoon right fielder the following spring, but after a slow start at bat and an erratic time in the field, manager Jimy Williams grew disenchanted with Pemberton. He was sold to a Japanese team and has not resurfaced in the major leagues.

Jesus Peña—not to be confused with Red Sox prospect Juan Peña, Jesus is a lefty pitcher who was picked up from the White Sox very late in the 2000 season. The Red Sox bullpen had been terrific all year but had suddenly self-destructed due to injuries (notably to Hipolito Pichardo and Rod Beck), and the team desperately needed to shore up their pitching staff. Peña appeared in only 2 games, giving up 1 run.

Tony Peña—an all-star catcher with Pittsburgh and St. Louis, Peña came to the Red Sox as a 32-year-old in 1990, and was credited with helping stabilize the Sox pitching staff. Peña was popular for his distinctive catching stance—he stuck one leg out, instead of the squat most catchers use—and for his unpredictable snap throws to first base. Peña had been a good hitter and great fielder early in his career, winning Gold Gloves from 1983 to 1985, and going to the All Star Game 5 times between 1982 and 1989. He still fielded well with the Red Sox, but his once-lethal throwing arm was less deadly than it had been, and he no longer hit well. Peña hit .261 in 1990, but faded to .181 in 1993, his last year in Boston. After losing his starting job in Boston (Peña's batting average dropped to .181 in 1993), he continued playing as a backup catcher for Cleveland (for whom he hit a game-winning home run against the Red Sox in the 1995 playoffs) and Houston until 1997, when he retired at age 40.

Herb Pennock—Hall of Fame lefthanded pitcher who, like so many other young Red Sox stars, was sold to the hated Yankees during Harry Frazee's Reign of Error. Known as "The Knight of Kennett Square" (his Pennsylvania hometown), Pennock began his career as a teenager with the Philadelphia Athletics. Ironically, Pennock came to the Red Sox in the same way he left. Connie Mack was losing money during World War I, and he sold many of his best players, giving Boston the promising Pennock in 1915. The lefty pitched sparingly from 1915–17, and served in the war in 1918. In 1919 Pennock blossomed, going 16–8 with a 2.71 ERA. He won 16 more games in 1920, but the Sox had already begun their descent into 2 decades of futility. Pennock pitched valiantly for 2 more years, winning 23 games total, with ERAs near the league average (low 4.00s).

Prior to the 1923 season, Boston gave Pennock to the Yankees (as if Ruth hadn't been enough), where he rattled off win totals of 19, 21, 15, 23, 19, and 17. Pennock pitched for 3 Yankee World Champions, and was 5–0, with 3 saves and a 1.95 ERA, in World Series play). He rejoined the Red Sox for his final year, 1934, going 2–0 with a 3.05 ERA as a long reliever. Pennock finished his 22-year career with 241 wins, and he made the Hall of Fame in 1948, earning more votes than anyone on the ballot that year, including such greats as Al Simmons, Jimmie Foxx, and Dizzy Dean.

Tony Perez—longtime Cincinnati Reds star first baseman (and Hall of Famer) who helped hold together a collapsing Red Sox team in 1980. Considered washed up at age 38, Perez played a surprising 151 games in 1980 and led the team in home runs as the last Don Zimmer-managed Sox team fell apart amid injuries and internal discord. Perez played 2 less-than-successful years as a part-timer with Boston before moving on to Philadelphia at age 41.

Johnny Pesky—playing on Red Sox teams with Ted Williams, Johnny Pesky tended to be somewhat overshadowed, but made many marks on the team's history as a slick-fielding shortstop and a fine contact hitter. John Paveskovich (who eventually changed his legal name to his nickname of Johnny Pesky) only hit 17 homers in his 13-year career. Several of those hit in Boston curled around the foul pole down the very short right field line in Fenway Park, which would eventually become known affectionately as "The Pesky Pole." Perhaps the most amazing Pesky stat is that he struck out only 218 times in his entire career.

As a rookie in 1942 Pesky amassed a then-Red Sox rookie record 205 hits and a .331 batting average, finishing second in the batting race to Williams. He then left for service in the armed forces. World War II would cost him the next 3 seasons, from 1943 to 1945. Upon his return in 1946, Pesky picked up right where he had left off, helping to lead the Red Sox to the 1946 pennant by again leading the league in hits and batting .335. In one stretch, he had 11 hits in a row, and once scored 6 times in a game, an American League record at the time.

In 1947 (marriage and a 30-pound weight gain didn't seem to cause him to miss a beat) he led the league in hits for the third straight year. He also had a 27-game hitting streak that year.

Pesky was moved to third base in 1948, and while his average dropped to .281, he adapted well in the field, leading the league in double plays. He returned to shortstop in 1951, but was traded during the 1952 season.

In an example of how history can sometimes be unfair, despite a very good career, Pesky is perhaps best remembered for 2 plays he didn't make. In Game 7 of the 1946 World Series with the game tied, Enos Slaughter was on first when a bloop double was hit to center. Slaughter ran on the pitch, Pesky took the relay from weak-armed Leon Culberson with his back to the plate, checked the runner at first, and threw late to the plate, allowing Slaughter to score. The rest, as they say, is history. The debate rages to this day over whether or not a quicker throw would have caught Slaughter, but the broadcaster's often replayed agonized cry of "Pesky holds the ball" became accepted as a misplay that cost the game.

In 1952, while playing in Detroit, Pesky had trouble getting a ground ball out of his glove in the third inning of Virgil Trucks's attempt at a second straight no-hitter. Originally called a hit, Pesky admitted to misplaying the ball, and the play was changed to an error, preserving Trucks's no-no.

After his playing days were over, and after spending some time elsewhere, Pesky returned to the Boston organization in 1961 as a minor league manager, and managed the parent club for the 1963 season and most of the 1964 season. He was interim manager after Don Zimmer was fired late in the 1980 season. From 1969 to 1974, Pesky was color man for Red Sox TV and radio broadcasts.

An organization employee in different roles for many years, in recent years his on-field duties ended (which brought about no small amount of public outrage from fans used to seeing Pesky in uniform), but the lasting image more recent fans attending games will always hold of Johnny Pesky is that of him hitting fungos to players. Pesky is now in his eighties, and remains a Red Sox employee as well as a respected part of Red Sox history.

Rico Petrocelli—regardless of what effect future players named Rico may have on Red Sox history, the name "Rico" will likely always refer to one man to longtime Red Sox fans . . . Rico Petrocelli. (And despite the pronunciation of the Judd Hirsch TV detective show, *we* know how it's really said.) An infield mainstay for the Red Sox for over a decade, Petrocelli was a rarity of the day, an infielder who combined a very good glove and a bat loaded with power. This was best displayed in 1969 when Rico hit 40 homers, a record for a shortstop at the time, while making only 14 errors, tying another shortstop record at the time.

The lasting image that most fans likely hold of Petrocelli is of him catching what appears to be a routine popup. The reason it is frequently played as a part of highlight shows is that it was also the final out of the final game of the regular season of the 1967 "Impossible Dream" pennant drive. Along with Yaz and Reggie Smith, Petrocelli was part of a first in the 1967 World Series: 3 home runs in 1 inning. Petrocelli hit 2 homers that game, the only 2 he would hit in his 14 World Series games.

In 1971 Petrocelli uncomplainingly moved to third base when the Sox acquired slick fielding Luis Aparicio. The move didn't faze Petrocelli, who led the league in fielding at third base that year.

A series of injuries began to slow Petrocelli down in the mid-1970s. Elbow problems in 1974, and a leg injury and beaning in 1975 all limited his playing time (though he appeared in all 7 games of the 1975 World Series, hitting .308). Inner ear problems led to his retirement in 1976. Petrocelli was a 2-time All Star during his career, which was spent entirely in a Red Sox uniform (another rare feat, both then and now). In the years since his retirement, Rico has played several roles in the Red Sox organization, including managing and announcing for minor league teams.

Hipolito Pichardo—a slender righthanded pitcher from the Dominican Republic, Pichardo came up with the Kansas City Royals, pitching well out of the starting rotation in 1992–93, his first two seasons in the majors. In each of the next 4 years he pitched entirely out of the bullpen, before starting 18 games for the Royals in 1998. For a time, he was the Royals' closer, saving 11 games in 1997. Generally he was around league average or slightly better. He had elbow surgery following the 1998 season and missed all of 1999. Red Sox general manager Dan Duquette signed Pichardo to a minor league free agent contract in February of 2000 as a reclamation project, and called him up to Boston in May. Pichardo pitched extremely well for the Red Sox out of the bullpen, throwing 65 innings in 38 games, with 1 save and a 6–3 record and, relative to the league, the best ERA of his career.

Jimmy Piersall—righthanded-hitting outfielder who enjoyed a productive but somewhat inconsistent 17-year career, mostly in the American League. Piersall came up to the Red Sox in 1950 and spent his first 9 seasons in Boston, hitting about .275 (at a time when the league average was about .255) with decent power numbers. He never hit more than 19 homers in a season, but did lead the league in doubles in 1956. A solid defender and above-average baserunner, he reached double figures in steals 3 times while with the Sox, and 5 times in his career.

Piersall possessed a dynamic personality and was known for some bizarre habits, including one episode of talking aloud to Babe Ruth's monument while playing outfield at Yankee Stadium. Often he would attempt to loudly distract opposing players, a tactic that led to his frequent ejection from games. On one occasion late in his career he tried to defend Ted Williams by roaming wildly in his outfield position, a trick he called "The Williams Shift." Both Piersall and his manager protested vehemently after Piersall was ejected.

Piersall was plagued by well-publicized emotional troubles at the beginning of his career that culminated when he suffered a nervous breakdown during the 1952 season. He spent part of that year in a sanitarium, and made a successful comeback the year following. Rather than shy away from his ordeals, Piersall was not afraid to speak openly about them, and did so with a brave sense of humor. He went on to document his experiences in the book *Fear Strikes Out*, which was later made into a motion picture starring Anthony Perkins. Piersall was actually disappointed with the lead actor's portrayal of him, claiming that Perkins "threw a baseball like a girl."

Piersall went on to become a 2-time All Star with the Sox, and later enjoyed success with the Cleveland Indians before winding down his career with the Washington Senators and the Los Angeles/California Angels. He hit a career-high .322 for Cleveland in 1961.

A bizarre moment of baseball history occurred on June 23, 1963, during his brief stint with the New York Mets. After hitting the one-hundredth home run of his career into the right field stands at the Polo Grounds, Piersall took his trot around the bases—backward. This quirkiness didn't impress manager Casey Stengel, who cut Piersall 2 days later. Piersall remained in baseball after his retirement in 1967, working as a coach, in the front office, and in the broadcast booth. He later enjoyed some small acting roles, including a television appearance on *The Lucy Show*.

Phil Plantier—power-hitting lefthanded outfielder who came to the big leagues with the Red Sox at a time when the minor leagues were bare. Plantier tore up the minor leagues, but team officials were skeptical that he could hit major league pitching with his crouched hitting stance (once described as looking like he was sitting on a toilet). Plantier could generate a lot of power and a lot of air, striking out about a quarter of the time. Called up in 1991, Plantier appeared in 53 games and hit .331 in only 148 at bats, with excellent power. Plantier seemed poised for big things at the major league level. (He was often linked with Yankee slugger Kevin Maas, who came up about the same time and had similar early success, although neither turned into stars.)

The next year Plantier struggled in 108 games, hitting only .246 in 349 at bats, with an awful .361 slugging percentage. The Red Sox, not convinced he could hit, shipped Plantier to San Diego for promising reliever Jose Melendez (who was only able to pitch 32 innings over the next 2 years). Plantier went on to hit 34 home runs and drive in 100 runs for the Padres. Injuries and lack of confidence in his unorthodox batting stance soon undermined Plantier's career, however. Over the next few years he played with Houston, San Diego (two different times), Oakland, and ended his career in 1997 with St Louis.

Dick Pole—a promising righthanded pitcher in the mid-1970s, Pole was International League MVP while playing for AAA Pawtucket in 1973, leading the league in ERA and strikeouts. Pole pitched briefly with the Sox in 1973 and 1974, then joined the rotation full time in 1975. On June 30 Tony Muser hit a line drive that shattered Pole's face, and cost him most of his vision in one eye. (A scarily similar accident happened to Sox reliever Bryce Florie in 2000.) Although Pole came back to pitch again (even appearing briefly in the 1975 World Series) he never regained his effectiveness, and retired at age 27 with a 25–37 career record. Pole went on to a long coaching career, including stints in the Red Sox organization as bullpen coach and Pawtucket pitching coach. He is now pitching coach for the Cleveland Indians.

Curtis Pride—a deaf center fielder who was signed three times by Sox GM Dan Duquette (twice for the Red Sox and once for the Expos where he made his major league debut in 1993). Pride was a serviceable outfielder and lefthanded hitter who played well when given starting roles, but did not play well coming off the bench over the course of his career. Pride was called up from AAA Pawtucket in 2000 during a stretch when the Sox outfield was riddled by injury and ineffectiveness (Pride was tearing up the International League at the time), but Sox manager Jimy Williams barely played him, preferring to go with light-hitting Darren Lewis and slumping Troy O'Leary. After getting into only 9 games in the 2000 season, Pride was released to make room for returning players. He signed a minor league contract with the Montreal Expos for 2001.

Carlos Quintana—righthanded-hitting first baseman and outfielder who put up promising numbers for his first two full seasons before fate sadly intervened. Upon the loss of power-hitting Nick Esasky to free agency following the 1989 season, rookie outfielder Quintana competed with journeymen Bill Buckner and Billy Jo Robidoux for the first base job in 1990 before taking over the position full time in May. Chubby and likable in a quiet way, Q could not replicate Esasky's power numbers, though he proved to be a solid run producer throughout 1990 and 1991, and had a terrific defensive reputation. That offseason, however, Quintana was involved in a hideous car accident in his home country of Venezuela while racing his brothers to the hospital after a shooting, and he missed the entire 1992 season. Ironically, manager Butch Hobson had just announced that Quintana would be the starting first baseman that season, rather than talented prospect Mo Vaughn. Quintana unsuccessfully attempted to return in 1993, paving the way for Vaughn to become a star.

Dick Radatz—an intimidating relief pitcher who dominated the league for 3 years before breaking down from overuse, "The Monster" helped define the modern closer's role. As a 25-year-old rookie in 1962, the 6'6" Radatz led the league in appearances, saves, and wins in relief. The next two years his workload increased; Radatz went 31–15 with 54 saves those two seasons, leading the league in relief wins both years and saves in 1964. He made the All Star team both years; in the 1963 game he struck out Willie Mays, Duke Snider, Willie McCovey, and two others in two innings of work. Radatz's *worst* ERA in those first 3 years was 2.29 (league average was about 3.60). He was almost unhittable, with a blazing sidearm fastball that helped him post astonishing strikeout totals. By 1965, after three years of pitching 2 or 3 innings at a time several games in a row, he was much less effective, finishing with a losing record (9–11) and a 3.91 ERA. He never recovered his effectiveness, drifting from the Red Sox to 4 other teams over the next four seasons with a 3–11 record. He is now a Boston-area radio show host. Ironically, he is one of the leading opponents of pitch counts and other measures thought to protect pitchers from overuse.

Manny Ramirez—one of the best and most feared righthanded power hitters in baseball for the last half of the 1990s while playing for the Cleveland Indians. Following the 2000 season, the Red Sox made him the second-highest paid player in baseball as the first big-time free agent signing for the team since they signed reliever Bill Campbell in 1977. Ramirez was one of the most desired free agents in baseball, as he is a complete hitter, and still only 28 years old. In each his last 2 seasons in Cleveland, he has led the league in both slugging percentage and OPS. In short, he is exactly what the Red Sox needed following their offensively anemic 2000 season.

And they paid big money to get him. The Red Sox typical free agent pursuit has ended up with the big players going elsewhere, and the Sox signing out of the bargain bin. That didn't happen this time. Interestingly, the 8 year, $160 million contract that they signed didn't seem as outrageous as it did when the information leaked out. Between the time that they made the offer, which would have made Ramirez the highest-paid player in baseball, and the first $20-million-a-year player in history, the

Texas Rangers signed Alex Rodriguez to a 10-year, $252 million contract that makes Ramirez's deal seem almost reasonable.

Ramirez played right field in Cleveland, but probably will DH or play left in Boston, since Fenway Park has one of the most difficult right fields in baseball. He has never been a great defender, and early in his career earned a reputation as a careless baserunner—but his on-base percentage has been over .400 in 4 of the last 6 years, and he's hit at least 38 home runs in each of the last 3.

Jeff Reardon—righthanded relief pitcher who was one of several different pitchers to break the all-time saves record during the early 1990s, when the roles of relief pitchers were changing and save totals skyrocketed. A native of Massachusetts, Reardon had already had a long and productive career, mostly for the Expos and Twins, when the Red Sox signed him as a free agent prior to the 1990 season. The Red Sox already had Lee Smith as a closer, but GM Lou Gorman thought that the team could be upgraded by trading Smith for an outfielder and signing Reardon. Shortly into the season Smith was traded to St. Louis for the soon-to-be-disappointing Tom Brunansky.

Reardon pitched for the Red Sox for 2½ years, recording 88 saves. His high for the Sox was 40 saves in 1991. With his seventh save of 1992 he passed Rollie Fingers to become the all-time MLB leader in career saves (though he has since been passed by Lee Smith, Dennis Eckersley, and John Franco.) But despite the gaudy save numbers, Reardon was not dominating, and before the trading deadline in 1992, the Sox traded him to Atlanta. He pitched for 3 teams over the next 3 years, retiring after the 1994 season.

Jody Reed—a heralded shortstop prospect who was a key part of the 1988 "Morgan Magic." Reed had played briefly for the Sox in 1987 and was a reserve early in 1988. When Joe Morgan replaced John McNamara as manager, he moved the 25-year-old Reed into the starting lineup, replacing Spike Owen at shortstop (Reed played a few games at second as well). Reed hit .293, walked frequently, and hit a lot of doubles to help key a Sox resurgence that led to the Eastern Division title. Reed finished third in the Rookie of the Year voting that year.

Because of Marty Barrett's declining knees, Reed was moved to second base midway through the following season. He remained remarkably consistent for the next 3 seasons, hitting better than .280 with 40 or more doubles each year. After an off year in 1992 (.247 with only 27 doubles), Reed was left unprotected in the 1992 Expansion Draft. Colorado drafted Reed and immediately traded him to the Dodgers, where his batting average returned but his power did not. Reed rejected a lucrative free agent contract from the Dodgers only to find that no one else was willing to make a long-term commitment to him. He drifted between 3 teams over the next 4 years, playing decently until his bat failed him in 1997 and he was released. He now runs a baseball school in Tampa, Florida.

Pee Wee Reese—Hall of Fame shortstop for the Brooklyn Dodgers in the 1940s; Reese came up through the Red Sox system but never played for the team.

Supposedly, player-manager Joe Cronin (also a shortstop) was jealous of Reese, and he was sold to Brooklyn for next to nothing.

Jerry Remy—a lefthanded-hitting second baseman, Remy hit leadoff for the great slugging Red Sox teams of the late 1970s and the weaker early 1980s teams. Obtained as a 25-year-old veteran from California before the 1978 season to shore up the Sox weakness at second base, Remy was a good but not great hitter (especially against righthanded pitching) and a solid defensive player. He batted .280 to .300 every year, but with little power and a below-average number of walks for a leadoff hitter. In his 3 years with the Angels Remy stole from 34 to 41 bases a year, but he was never a great base stealer (he had above-average, but not great, speed and was caught stealing a lot). He stole 30 bases his first year with the Red Sox, but persistent knee injuries and the team's lack of emphasis on base-stealing limited him to 16 steals a year or fewer for the rest of his career.

Remy had a reputation as a great bunter, and frequently bunted for base hits. He would attempt to bunt for a hit at least once a game, and experimented with different bunting techniques throughout his career. His combination of speed (on a lead-footed team) and scrappiness (as a hustling but undersized infielder who played well even though he didn't look like a major league hitter) made Remy a fan favorite, and he remains popular in New England. Although injuries cut his playing career short (4 of his 7 Boston seasons were shortened by injuries) he continues to be involved with the Red Sox as a television color commentator.

Jim Rice—star left fielder who had the unenviable task of replacing Hall-of-Famer Carl Yastrzemski (who had replaced Ted Williams). Jim Ed Rice was a high school star from South Carolina drafted in the first round by Boston in 1971. Reportedly he was such a good athlete in his mostly segregated hometown that the school board redrew the school zones so that Rice could attend the mostly white high school (the line passed through his bedroom) and compete in several sports—but not his little sister. Rice was noted for great strength; on at least one occasion a bat snapped in half when he checked his swing, as if it had been smashed into a wall.

Rice debuted with the Sox in 1975 as one half of "The Gold Dust Twins," with fellow rookie sensation Fred Lynn. Rice helped lead the Red Sox to the postseason in 1975, but late in the season was hit by a pitch which broke his arm, causing him to miss the American League Championship Series and the World Series. (Oh what might have been?) Rice hit .309 with 22 homers and 102 RBI that year (at a time when hitters were not as dominant as today), and finished second to Lynn in the Rookie of the Year balloting. (Lynn also won the league's Most Valuable Player award.)

Rice continued to blossom as a hitter, and from 1977 to 1979 was arguably the best hitter in baseball, averaging about .320 (league average was about .265) with at least 39 home runs each year. In 1978 Rice was named league MVP, and was the first player in 37 years to amass 400 total bases in a season. In 1980 Rice was hit by a pitch that broke his wrist. Although he came back to play well, he was never the league's dominant hitter again; although Rice played 10 more years in the majors, he only reached

30 home runs once more (after doing it the previous 3 years) and reached .300 in only 3 of those years. Since Rice didn't walk much, hit into a lot of double plays, and was never a great defensive player (he worked hard to go from being terrible early in his career to decent as the years went on), he needed to hit for both power and average to be effective. Late in his career Rice started experiencing vision problems and became a singles hitter for his last few years in the majors (he had only 31 homers in his last 3 years combined), before retiring after the 1989 season. He finished his career with a .298 lifetime batting average and 382 home runs, just short of the .300 average and 400 homers that would have made him a near-certain Hall of Famer.

When we went to Fenway regularly in the 1970s, the group consisted of myself, my brother (about 15 years old), my uncle, and his son (same age as my brother). My cousin didn't like hot dogs, and so partway through the game asked his dad if he'd get him a cheeseburger. My ultra-careful uncle wouldn't let him go to the concession stand alone. So my uncle went down to a concession stand right near the closest exit (an important point to the eventual humor of this tale) and waited in the long line to order the requested food. While he did so, the Sox loaded the bases, and Jim Rice strode to the plate. You can see it coming, can't you? Rice of course hits a granny, which my uncle, who likely paid for the lion's share of this trip, and drove the whole 350+ miles, misses. But wait, it gets better (worse?). My cousin, in his natural excitement, jumps out of his seat, runs to where his dad is waiting in line and announces "Hey dad, Jim Rice just hit a grand slam." Nothing like rubbing it in, eh? But wait, the good (bad?) isn't over quite yet. My uncle finally gets to order the burger and is told "Sorry sir, we're out of hamburgers."

My uncle laughs about it with us today (25 or so years after the fact most anything can look funny), but on that day, there was little joy from one quarter of that particular Vermont contingent in Fenway Park.

—Don Violette

Rice was uncomfortable in interview situations (he sometimes came off as being surly or unapproachable), and like many Boston stars was not particularly popular with the press. Although he is eligible for the Hall of Fame and a fairly strong candidate (though not a shoo-in), Rice has not done especially well in voting—which some people have blamed on his poor relationship with the media (since the voting is done by longtime baseball writers). He was generally very popular with the fans, however, mostly because he produced on the field regularly for many years.

Rice remained a Red Sox employee after his 16-year career (all played with the Sox) ended. He served as hitting coach from 1997 to 2000, but after a huge initial improvement in hitting, the team's batting average declined for 3 straight years, and many players seemed to prefer being coached by first base coach (and ex-Expos hitting coach) Tommy Harper rather than the aloof Rice. Rice is now a roving instructor for the Red Sox.

Frankie Rodriguez—a onetime top prospect of the Red Sox (although when they drafted him, they were unsure whether he was a pitcher or a shortstop). Rodriguez and the team finally decided to bring him along as a pitcher, and he was in the majors in 1995 at age 22. He pitched badly for Boston before being traded to Minnesota for ace reliever Rick Aguilera, on the night of the trading deadline. The deal had been much talked about, and many fans knew about it before it was announced (the Sox were playing in Minnesota that night, and during the game Rodriguez and Aguilera both were called in from their respective bullpens, and disappeared into the clubhouses).

Rodriguez pitched 3 years for the Twins before moving on to Seattle in 1999. He has never lived up to his expectations, but is still only 28 years old.

Billy Rohr—lefthanded pitcher who made one of the most memorable debuts in major league history. In April of the Red Sox magical "Impossible Dream" season of 1967, Rohr made his first major league start at Yankee Stadium and took a no-hitter into the bottom of the ninth. Yastrzemski kept the no-hitter alive in the 7th with a "tremendous catch" of a ball off the bat of Tom Tresh. Elston Howard singled with two outs in the ninth and Rohr had to settle for a 3–0 shutout win. He beat the Yankees again in his next start, and then never won another game in a Sox uniform. He won one game for Cleveland in 1968 and retired with a 3–3 major league record.

Brian Rose—much-heralded starting pitcher from New Bedford, Massachusetts, drafted by the Sox in 1994. In the minors he was often compared with Carl Pavano, another great Red Sox pitching prospect, and the Montreal Expos were given their choice of Rose or Pavano (they picked Pavano) in the Pedro Martinez trade. A control pitcher, Rose had excellent minor league numbers, but struggled with inconsistency at the major league level. Called upon to fill in for an injured Juan Peña in May 1999, Rose pitched brilliant games against the Yankees and Indians, two of the best teams in the American League (he allowed only 1 earned run in his first 3 starts). But after 2 months of solid pitching he became ineffective (he went 5 straight starts without lasting more than 4 innings) before going on the disabled list with a "tired arm." He continued to struggle in 2000, pitching brilliantly at times but ineffectively at others—and pitching especially badly with runners on base. He was sent back to the minor leagues in June to regain his form then traded to Colorado as part of a deal for pitcher Rolando Arrojo in July.

Rich Rowland—a power-hitting catcher, the Sox acquired Rowland from the Detroit Tigers in April of 1994, trading John Flaherty in an exchange of catching prospects who were to become free agents following the season. Both were players that had bounced up and down in their organizations, spending time in the majors but not figuring in their teams' plans. Rowland was reputed to be a lumberjack in the off-season. At the time of the trade, Rowland's age was listed as 27, but a month later Globe reporter Nick Cafardo discovered that he was actually 30. Rowland appeared in 46 games for the Sox in 1994, hitting the only 9 home runs of his career. After appearing in 14 more games for Boston in 1995, his major league career ended.

Joe Rudi—a good-glove, decent-hit outfielder, Rudi made his name as a key member of the Oakland A's teams that won 3 straight World Series in the mid-1970s. He won

3 Gold Gloves while in Oakland, and led the American League in both doubles and total bases in 1974. When A's owner Charlie Finley began dismantling the team because he didn't want to meet the players' salary demands, the Red Sox acquired Rudi and relief pitcher Rollie Fingers for $2 million. But commissioner Bowie Kuhn stepped in and halted the sale, on the grounds that it was not in the best interest of the game. Rudi signed with the California Angels as a free agent following the 1976 season.

When the Red Sox were faced with losing Fred Lynn in 1980 because they hadn't mailed out his contract in time, Lynn agreed to accept a trade to California. Joe Rudi finally became a member of the Red Sox in this trade. But he was basically done as a player. He hit dreadfully for the Sox, and re-signed with the Oakland A's after only one season in Boston. He only played one more year for Oakland before retiring at the age of 35.

Red Ruffing—Hall of Fame pitcher who began his career on a horrid Red Sox team, but became a star with the Yankees. Charles "Red" Ruffing pitched for Boston from 1924–30, pitching about as badly as his team played (39–96, with ERAs around the league average). He lost a staggering 25 games in 1928, though his 3.89 ERA was respectable, and he lost 22 more decisions in 1929. After an 0–3 start, the Sox sent him to the Bronx for Cedric Durst and $50,000. Going from a last place team to a nascent dynasty did Ruffing good; as a Yankee he was a fabulous 231–124 (adding 7 World Series wins as well). From 1936–39 the Yanks won 4 straight championships— and Ruffing won 20 or more games each season. He was also one of the best hitting pitchers in history, finishing with a .269 average and 36 homers. Had he not lost 4 toes on his left foot as a child, costing him his speed, Ruffing might have achieved his dream of being a big league outfielder. Instead, he had to settle for a 273-win career, earning him election to the Hall of Fame in 1967.

Pete Runnels—one of the most unlikely batting champions ever, Runnels was a 30-year-old middle infielder (an age at which most players are declining) with the Washington Senators when he was traded to Boston for Albie Pearson and Norm Zauchin after the 1957 season. Runnels had only hit over .300 once in 7 years with Washington, and was coming off a .230 season. In Fenway Park—a lefthanded line-drive hitter's paradise—Runnels found an ideal home; in 5 years with the Red Sox Runnels never hit below .314, and he won batting titles in 1960 and 1962. Although he didn't have much power, Runnels walked quite a bit, and was one of a few bright spots on mediocre Red Sox teams in the twilight of the Ted Williams era. Runnels played all over the infield for the Red Sox, splitting his time between second and first base, as well as filling in at shortstop and third base. He was traded to Houston for Roman Mejias after the 1962 season. After leaving Fenway, his batting average dropped 70 points, and he was out of baseball the following year. (The trade was bad for both players; Mejias was also gone after the 1964 season, his average dropping nearly 60 points on coming to Fenway.)

Jeff Russell—talented but inconsistent closer who saved 33 games in his only full season with the Red Sox. Russell signed with Boston as a free agent in 1993, after an up-and-down 10-year career. He began as a promising starter with Cincinnati, was traded to Texas, and eventually became a pretty good reliever. Russell saved 38 games in 1989, with a 1.98 ERA. He posted similar numbers in 1992, but was part of a block-buster August 31 trade to Oakland for Jose Canseco. The A's used Russell as a setup man for Dennis Eckersley, and he held opponents scoreless in his 8 appearances. But Toronto beat Oakland in the American League Championship Series, and the A's decided that Russell was too expensive to re-sign. Boston, after trading Jeff Reardon the previous year, needed a closer, and Russell fit the bill. He had a terrific 1993 season (33 saves, 2.70 ERA), though an ankle sprain caused him to miss most of September. Coincidentally or not, Russell was never the same pitcher after the injury. He saved 12 games for the Red Sox in 1994, but his 0–5 record and 5.14 ERA didn't sit well with Dan Duquette. In July, Russell was traded to Cleveland for two pitchers: reclamation project Chris Nabholz, and washed up Steve Farr (who had once been a good closer). Neither player contributed to the Red Sox, and Russell retired after two more seasons.

Babe Ruth—lefthanded pitcher, lefthanded-hitting outfielder. The two best hitters in baseball history have played for the Red Sox. The second best, Ted Williams, spent his entire career in a Boston uniform. The best hitter in baseball history spent the majority of his 6 years in Boston in the pitching rotation, winning 89 games and helping to lead the Red Sox to World Series victories in 1915, 1916, and 1918.

The 21-year-old George Herman "Babe" Ruth started 41 games for the Red Sox in 1916 and pitched 323 innings while leading the league with a 1.75 ERA. He was on a career path that may well have led to the Hall of Fame as a pitcher if he hadn't converted to the outfield. His .671 won-lost percentage is still the ninth highest in baseball history. His career ERA of 2.28 is 14th all-time. His shutout in the opening game of the 1918 series extended his World Series scoreless inning streak to 29 innings, a record that stood fo 43 years (it was broken in 1961 by Whitey Ford).

Over the 1918–19 seasons he made the transition from pitcher and occasional outfielder to pretty much full-time outfielder. Some anecdotes indicate that the impetus for this was Hall-of-Famer Harry Hooper, the Red Sox captain at the time, suggesting to manager Ed Barrow in 1918 that Ruth play the outfield on days when he wasn't pitching. Hooper had apparently noticed an increase in attendance on days when Ruth was pitching. In 1919 the left-field position opened up for Ruth to play full time when Broadway producer and Red Sox owner Harry Frazee traded Duffy Lewis, along with Ernie Shore and Dutch Leonard, to the Yankees for players and cash.

Following the 1919 season Frazee sold the contract rights to Babe Ruth to the New York Yankees in order to pay off debts which threatened to end his theater production business. The Yankees owner, Colonel Jacob Ruppert, in return for Ruth, paid Frazee $125,000 ($100,000 according to some sources,) and lent him $300,000 more, with Fenway, and the land it was sitting on, as collateral. (Yes, the New York Yankees held a mortgage on the Boston Red Sox's stadium until Tom Yawkey paid it off in 1933.)

He went on, of course, to become the greatest slugger in the history of the game. When he retired he held the records for highest career slugging percentage, highest career on-base percentage, most home runs in a season, most home runs in a career, and numerous others. He literally changed the way the game was played. In 1919 Ruth hit 29 home runs. There were three players tied for second in the league, with 10 apiece. The Red Sox had only 4 that were not hit by Ruth. Four out of the 8 teams in the league had fewer than Ruth's 29 home runs. In 1920 George Sisler of the Browns hit 19 home runs to finish second behind Ruth. Ruth hit 54. No other *team* hit 54 home runs. The fact that his name has become almost a cliché sometimes takes away from what he actually accomplished.

Babe put up most of these numbers while playing for the New York Yankees. If Red Sox fans actually have a complex with regards to the Yankees, this is the source. The best player in baseball, playing in the age of the reserve clause, had no power to leave. His entire career could have been played in Boston. But Boston's owner considered the Red Sox a secondary concern to his Broadway shows, and sold off the Red Sox assets to finance his stage productions.

In fact, the first Yankees World Series winners in 1923 had *11 players* on the roster who had been acquired from Boston between 1919 and 1922. Sixty-four of their 98 wins went to pitchers who had pitched for the Red Sox during their last World Series win in 1918, and 17 more went to Waite Hoyt, who joined the Red Sox in 1919 and was sent to the Yankees in 1921. The Yankees' dynasty was basically founded as Red Sox South because Harry Frazee was more interested in financing musicals than fielding a baseball team. Of the 8 position regulars for the World Series champion 1918 Red Sox, all were gone from Boston by 1922, including Hall of Famers Harry Hooper and Babe Ruth. Two of them, Ruth and Everett Scott, went directly to New York. The 4 members of the starting rotation were all gone by 1922, all 4 of them directly to New York. (Dutch Leonard never actually pitched for the Yankees, though, being immediately traded to Detroit.)

Babe Ruth is still the all-time major league leader in slugging percentage (.690) and OPS (1.162) , and his career .474 on-base percentage is second only to Ted Williams. (To put Ruth's career on-base percentage in perspective, in high offense 1999, the highest American League on-base percentage was Edgar Martinez's .447. The highest National League on-base percentage was Larry Walker's Coors Field-aided .458.) Ruth's numbers are staggering. But the bottom line is this: Babe Ruth was a great pitcher who developed into the greatest hitter in the history of the game. The Red Sox had him and sold him. And Red Sox fans have to lament what could have been.

Ken Ryan—a hard-throwing righthanded relief prospect who never turned into the star many fans expected. Ryan pitched briefly with the Sox as a 23-year-old in 1992, then pitched well but inconsistently in limited action in 1993, going 7–2. In 1994 he took over the closer's role for half a season, saving 13 games with a 2.44 ERA. But the following year he pitched inconsistently again, struggling badly with his control. The Sox, in need of a closer and unsure how long it would take Ryan to develop into one, packaged him with outfielder Lee Tinsley in a trade to the Philadelphia Phillies for reliever Heathcliff Slocumb. With the Phillies, Ryan followed the same pattern before injuries derailed his career—one great year followed by two inconsistent seasons.

Gene Rye—lefty-hitting outfielder who played for the Sox in 17 games during the 1931 season, his only stint in the majors. He's worth mentioning because of a feat he accomplished in the Texas League during the 1930 season, while playing for Waco. He hit 3 home runs and drove in 7 runs during 1 inning in a game against Beaumont, the first time that any professional baseball player had accomplished that feat.

Bret Saberhagen—an extraordinarily effective but injury-prone starting pitcher. Saberhagen had a long and impressive career before joining the Red Sox as a free agent in 1997. In 1985 he became the youngest pitcher to win the American League Cy Young award (at age 21), and in 1989 he won the award again. After 7 years with the Kansas City Royals and 4 with the New York Mets, Saberhagen was traded to the Colorado Rockies during the 1995 season. He suffered a shoulder injury and had surgery in May 1996, missing the entire season. Red Sox GM Dan Duquette signed the still-injured Saberhagen as a reclamation project, and Saberhagen spent most of 1997 rehabbing with several of the organization's minor league teams before joining the parent club late in the season. Saberhagen started 6 games for the Sox that year, but except for occasional flashes pitched ineffectively, finishing 0–1 with a 6.98 ERA. Most un-Saberhagen like were the 10 walks issued in just 26 innings (Saberhagen always had pinpoint control). Things turned around in 1998 and 1999, however. In 1998 Saberhagen had a 15–7 record with a good 3.92 ERA, and in 1999 he was 10–6, with an excellent 2.95 ERA. He issued only 11 walks in 119 innings pitched in 1999. This was very much like the Bret Saberhagen of old—who holds the major league record for fewest walks per 9 innings at 1.66.

Unfortunately he continued to be plagued by injury, first missing time after cutting his foot on a broken glass at a party he threw for his teammates, then pitching through shoulder pain in the 1999 playoffs, where he was not effective. The shoulder injury turned out to be serious, and Saberhagen's 2000 season was lost to surgery and rehabilitation. Saberhagen remains with the Red Sox, although it's uncertain how much he will be able to pitch again.

Donnie Sadler—a diminutive infielder drafted by the Red Sox in 1994, some scouts considered Sadler a better shortstop prospect than Nomar Garciaparra. Gifted with extraordinary speed, defensive range, and a strong throwing arm, Sadler was heavily hyped in the media as "the most exciting player in the Red Sox organization." With Garciaparra blocking him as a shortstop, the Sox experimented with Sadler in center field and second base in an attempt to find him a position. Sadler, a favorite of manager Jimy Williams, would end up playing defensively at second base, shortstop, all 3 outfield positions, and occasionally third base. Sadler's lack of offensive production kept him from earning a permanent job with the Red Sox. Despite his small size Sadler seldom walked, and was unable to hit the ball on the ground to utilize his great speed. Sadler spent the 1998 through 2000 seasons shuttling between Boston and Pawtucket, hitting .242 over 156 games (with an awful .283 on-base percentage). After the 2000 season, with Sadler out of options that would allow the Red Sox to send him back to the minor leagues without the risk of losing him to another team, Boston traded Sadler to the Cincinnati Reds as part of a deal for infielder Chris Stynes.

Joe Sambito—an elite relief pitcher with Houston for 5 years, from 1977 to 1981, Sambito was a 33-year-old coming off 3 injury-filled years when he joined the Red Sox for the 1986 season. He was expected to reinforce the Red Sox weakness in left-handed relief pitching, possibly to assume the closer's role, and at least to stabilize the team's weak bullpen and take some of the pressure off the overworked Bob Stanley. Sambito never fully regained his effectiveness, however; he had 12 saves in 1986, but was frequently hit hard and was unable to pitch consistently. Stanley made a career-high 66 appearances in his worst season to that point, and by the end of the year Calvin Schiraldi was the closer. The pennant-winning Sox went into the 1986 postseason with their bullpen still a problem.

Jose Santiago—righthanded pitcher who played a key role on the 1967 Impossible Dream team. Santiago came to the Red Sox in 1966, after 3 years as a part-timer in Kansas City. Inserted into the rotation that year, the 26-year-old Santiago was mediocre on a mediocre team, winning 12 games and losing 13. He spent most of the next season in the bullpen, bailing out a pennant-winning team that had only 1 reliable starter. He finished with a 12–4 record, tied for second on the team in wins. The next year he was inserted back into the rotation and started the season brilliantly (9–4 with a 2.25 ERA) before hurting his arm. He pitched briefly in each of the next 2 years, but would never win another game in the majors.

Wally Schang—underrated catcher who played semi-regularly with the 1918 World Champions. Schang hit .306 and .305 the next two years, before joining Babe Ruth and many other ex-Sox on the Yankees. He played in a total of 6 World Series with the Athletics, Red Sox, and Yankees, retiring with a .284 average in 19 seasons.

Curt Schilling—a minor league pitching prospect traded to Baltimore as part of the Mike Boddicker deal in 1988. Traded twice more, Schilling took years to establish himself as a major leaguer, but now is one of the best starting pitchers in the game. He is sometimes cited by fans as a future star that the Red Sox allowed to get away, but the criticism is unfair; Boston knew they were trading 2 good prospects to Baltimore for Boddicker, but they needed help in the pennant race that year and were willing to give up future talent to have a chance at winning in 1988.

Calvin Schiraldi—righthanded pitcher who came to the Sox in the winter of 1985 from the Mets in the Bobby Ojeda deal. Big, strong, and from Texas, Schiraldi was a much-hyped prospect who was envisioned as the Sox closer of the future. He appeared in 25 games down the stretch in 1986, earning 9 saves and helping to bolster a collapsing bullpen. His terrific half-season was a crucial reason the Sox won their division, but the magic wore off in the playoffs. The still-inexperienced Schiraldi pitched poorly and couldn't hold the Mets in the World Series. The inability of Schiraldi and Bob Stanley to hold the lead against the Mets in Game 6 was perhaps the biggest factor in the Sox failure to win a World Series that they had all but wrapped up—and paved the way for Bill Buckner's infamous misplay that finally lost the game. Schiraldi was an average pitcher for the Sox the next year and was shipped off to Chicago (along with Al Nipper) for Lee Smith—one of the Sox great trades.

Pete Schourek—a lefthanded pitcher who spent 2 stints with the Red Sox. Schourek won 18 games for Cincinnati in 1995, but never won more than 8 games in any of his other 9 seasons in the major leagues. Schourek was obtained in a trade from Cincinnati for the 1998 stretch run, and pitched decently for the Red Sox. His biggest moment with the Red Sox came during the 1998 American League Division Series against Cleveland, when he was named by manager Jimy Williams to start the deciding Game 4 (ahead of ace Pedro Martinez, who would have been working on short rest). The decision was widely criticized, but Schourek pitched well in a losing cause, throwing 5⅓ innings of scoreless ball against a potent Indians lineup.

Allowed to move on that off season, Schourek signed a 2-year free agent contract with the Pittsburgh Pirates, who released him during spring training in 2000, after which he re-signed with the Red Sox (although because of the contract, the Pirates were still paying most of his salary). His 2000 record of 3–10 was somewhat deceptive; early in the year he pitched very well but received poor run support, and he had arm problems in the season's second half. In a valiant but ultimately vain move, Schourek put off surgery to try to help the team down the stretch, but was unable to pitch effectively. He had surgery after the season ended, and signed a minor league contract with the Red Sox for 2001.

Don Schwall—a young pitching star who never matched his rookie promise, Schwall first made the big leagues in 1961, along with fellow rookie Carl Yastrzemski. Schwall had been a basketball star at the University of Oklahoma, and seemed to be on his way to baseball stardom as well; he went 15–7 as a 25-year-old rookie on a bad team, pitched in the All Star game (there were actually 2 All Star games that year), and was the second Boston player to win the Rookie of the Year award. (Walt Dropo was the first.) Schwall struggled with his control in his 2 seasons with Boston, and in 1962 his wildness caused him to fall to 9–15 for an equally bad Red Sox team. Still seen as a valuable pitcher, Schwall was traded to Pittsburgh for slugger Dick Stuart after the 1962 season. After an unsuccessful career as a starter Schwall was used mostly in relief, but while his control improved he never returned to the consistently dominant form of his rookie season. He was out of baseball at age 31.

Everett "Deacon" Scott—the prototypical good-field/no-hit shortstop, Scott is best-known for holding the consecutive game record broken by Lou Gehrig (and then Cal Ripken Jr.). Scott debuted in 1914, and his batting averages ranged from .201 to .241

in his first 5 years. He had no power, almost never walked, and didn't run well, but his glove enabled him to play regularly for 3 World Champions. In 1916 Scott began 2 streaks. He led American League shortstops in fielding percentage for the first of 8 straight seasons, and, on June 30, played in the first of 1,307 consecutive games. Scott improved to a career-high .278 in 1919, and his average stayed in the .260s the next 2 years. But, like many of his teammates, Scott wound up on the Yankees, going to the Bronx with Joe Bush and Sad Sam Jones after the 1921 season. The Deacon was the shortstop on the first Yankee championship team (1923), but by 1925 his defense had begun to slip. On May 5, Scott was replaced by Pee-Wee Wanniger, ending his record streak. Ironically, less than a month later, teammate Lou Gehrig began his 2,130 game streak by pinch-hitting for Wanninger. Scott retired a year later, and his streak is currently third on the all-time list.

George Scott—"Boomer" was a slugging first baseman and excellent defensive player who spent 9 years with the Red Sox in 2 tours of duty, but had most of his best years elsewhere. Scott had a good rookie year in Boston as a 22-year-old in 1966, hitting 27 home runs and driving in 90 runs (as well as leading the league in strikeouts). He was a key player in the Impossible Dream year of 1967, when he hit .303 (fourth in the league), although his power dropped off a bit. The next year his offense mysteriously fell apart. In a year when pitchers dominated, Scott hit only .171 with 3 homers. He recovered somewhat over the next 3 years, when he split time between first base and third base, but never came close to matching the promise of his first 2 seasons. Traded to Milwaukee after the 1971 season, Scott finally became the consistent .280 hitter with the power the Sox had hoped for; Scott would lead the league in homers and RBI in 1975. The Red Sox tried to make up for their mistake by trading Cecil Cooper to Milwaukee to get Scott back in 1976, but that move backfired. Scott had only 1 good year left, while Cooper went on to become a star.

Although Scott is remembered as a slugger, he was a terrific defensive player at a position usually reserved for offense-first players. During his career he won 8 Gold Gloves at first base, a record at the time.

Tom Seaver—a Hall-of-Fame pitcher who was great with the Mets in the 1970s and good with the Reds in the early 1980s. He was traded to the Red Sox by the Chicago White Sox for the 1986 stretch drive. He pitched in 16 games, going 5–7, but was injured and unable to play in the playoffs, which pushed the ineffective Al Nipper back into the World Series rotation. Seaver retired after the end of the 1986 season.

Diego Segui—a journeyman pitcher who played for 8 teams in a 15-year career, Segui was a reliever for the Red Sox in 1974–75, when he was near the end of the line. He led a 1974 team in transition with 10 saves and 108 innings of relief, and had 6 more saves on the 1975 American League pennant winners, where he was mostly a long reliever. Segui finished up his career with the expansion Seattle Mariners in 1977, which made him the only person to play for both the Seattle Pilots and the Seattle Mariners. Segui's son, David, is currently a major league first baseman.

Aaron Sele—a starting pitcher drafted by the Red Sox in the first round in 1991 (he and Sox catcher Scott Hatteberg were college teammates at Washington State), Sele was heralded as the best starting pitcher to come out of the Red Sox system since Roger Clemens. He made the majors in 1993, posting a 7–2 record with a 2.74 ERA in 18 starts in his rookie year, and displaying one of the best curveballs in baseball. After missing most of the 1995 season due to injury, Sele struggled in 1996 and 1997, posting ERAs above 5.00 in both seasons. Sele became a focus of controversy on the team; he failed to regain the consistent form he'd shown as a rookie and was accused of being "gutless" by Roger Clemens and others. The Red Sox had hoped that Sele would be able to succeed Clemens as the ace of the rotation, but he never reached the next level with Boston. He was traded to Texas in an offseason deal that brought role players Jim Leyritz and Damon Buford to the Sox before the 1998 season. Sele would go on to revive his career in Texas, winning 19 games in 1998 and 18 more in 1999 (although his ERA remained high, he played for a terrific offensive team), before going to Seattle as a free agent for the 2000 season.

Jeff Sellers—a righthanded pitching prospect who never fulfilled his promise. He made 4 starts for the Sox as a 21-year-old in 1985, going 2–0 and looking like the future star he was supposed to become. It was the only winning record he would have in the major leagues. Sellers played for parts of 3 seasons but was never able to crack the starting rotation full-time despite many opportunities, given the lack of depth on the Sox pitching staff (he had ERAs around 5.00 each year, at a time when league average was about 4.20). After he went 1–7 in 1988 the Red Sox gave up on him and his career was over at age 24.

Ernie Shore—a righthanded pitcher who pitched well for the Sox from 1914–1917 (65–42 and a 2.45 ERA over his 7-year career, at a time when the league average was about 2.70). His great moment came as a relief pitcher in 1917 (one of only 2 relief appearances that year) when he replaced Babe Ruth, who had been thrown out for arguing the umpire's ball four call on the first batter. Shore picked off the runner Ruth had walked, then retired the next 26 batters in order—a perfect game. (Major League Baseball retroactively decided this didn't count as a perfect game in the early 1990s, when they also took away Red Sox pitcher Matt Young's no hitter). After World War I, Shore followed Babe Ruth to New York, where he pitched badly for 2 years. He was done as a major leaguer at age 29.

Sonny Siebert—curveball specialist whom the Red Sox acquired in the controversial Ken Harrelson trade. Siebert, whose real name was Wilfred, had several good years for the mediocre Cleveland Indians in the mid-to-late 1960s. (He chose baseball over basketball, having been drafted by the NBA's St. Louis Hawks.) In 1966, he pitched a no-hitter against Washington. Early in the 1969 season, the Red Sox sent Harrelson to Cleveland (though the slugger initially failed to report) in a 6-player deal. The key player for Boston was Siebert and he pitched well, going 14–10 with a 3.80 ERA and 5 saves, while splitting his time between the rotation and bullpen. In 1970, Siebert focused exclusively on starting, and he won 15 games, with a fine 3.44 ERA. Part of the reason for his success was better control: in 45 more innings, he walked 16 fewer hitters than he had in 1969. He was even better in 1971 (16–10, 2.91 ERA, only 220 hits and 60 walks in 235 innings), and earned a spot on the American League All Star team. Siebert slipped into mediocrity the following season, however, as his record fell to 12–12, and his ERA went up nearly a run, to 3.80. After 2 ineffective relief appearances in 1972, Siebert was sold to Texas. He finished his career in 1975, retiring with a 140–114 lifetime record.

Al Simmons—a Hall of Fame outfielder who played 40 games with the Red Sox in 1943, at the age of 37. Simmons had driven in more than 100 runs in his first 11 seasons with the Athletics and White Sox, but hit only .203 for the Red Sox. He had 2,897 hits when he joined Boston, but only mustered 27 with the Sox and 3 more in his final season, finishing 73 hits shy of the 3,000-hit milestone. He was known as "Bucketfoot Al" for his peculiar batting stance.

Ted Sizemore—light-hitting second baseman who was the 1969 National League Rookie of the Year for the Los Angeles Dodgers. He spent his entire career in the National League, with 4 different teams, before the Red Sox traded catcher Mike O'Berry (and cash) to the Cubs for Sizemore in August of 1979. Sizemore actually caught 2 games for the Red Sox that season. He finished his career with 5 hits in 29 at-bats for the 1980 Red Sox before being released.

Heathcliff Slocumb—intimidating relief pitcher acquired prior to the 1996 season from the Philadelphia Phillies in a 6-player deal which sent young relief pitcher Ken Ryan and journeyman center fielder Lee Tinsley to the Phillies. The 6'3" 220-pound Slocumb was a menacing figure on the mound, with a good fastball and a nasty slider. Though he was effective as the Sox closer in 1996, posting a 3.02 ERA with 31 saves, Slocumb constantly seemed to be in trouble because of his wildness on the mound. Although he allowed only 68 hits in 83 innings of work, he also walked 55 batters, allowing a dangerously high number of baserunners. The next year, his wildness caught up with him, leading to 5 losses and a 5.79 ERA—losing the support of fans, who were terrified whenever he took the mound in a close game. Fans were glad to see him traded to Seattle by General manager Dan Duquette, and were even happier when the two prospects the Sox received in return—catcher Jason Varitek and pitcher Derek Lowe—both turned into solid major leaguers.

Lee Smith—burly righthanded relief pitcher who spent 3 years with the Sox en route to becoming one of baseball's most accomplished closers. Smith came up in 1980 and spent the first eight seasons of his career with the Chicago Cubs, for whom he notched 180 saves. The Red Sox, desperately in need of bullpen stability, traded pitchers Al Nipper and Calvin Schiraldi to get Smith after the 1987 season—in what turned out to be a terrific trade.

Although Smith's debut with the Sox was tarnished when he surrendered a game-winning home run to Alan Trammell of Detroit on Opening Day 1988, he gave the Red Sox everything their bullpen had been lacking. In his 2 seasons with the Sox he saved 29 and 25 games (he was among the league leaders both years; no one on the 1986 team had more than 16) with extraordinary strikeout numbers and almost unhittable power, although his sometimes erratic control led to some less-than-pretty performances. He was a major factor in 1988 as the Sox won their division, and he pitched nearly as well in 1989.

The signing of Massachusetts native Jeff Reardon before the 1990 season created a surplus of closers on the team. Early in the season the 32-year-old Smith was traded to the St. Louis Cardinals for disappointing right fielder Tom Brunansky. Smith continued his success with St. Louis and a string of other teams before retiring in 1997 with 478 saves, first on baseball's all-time list. He was a 7-time All Star (5 times after the Sox traded him), led the league in saves 4 times, and was a 3-time winner of the Rolaids Relief Man of the Year Award.

Reggie Smith—switch-hitting outfielder, Smith spent the first 8 years of his career with the Red Sox, coming up in 1966 at the age of 21. He had been a shortstop in the Minnesota Twins minor league system but the Sox put him in the outfield (first in center, then in right). He hit over .300 three times, won a Gold Glove, and made the All Star team twice as a member of the Red Sox. He was traded (with Ken Tatum), to the Cardinals for Rick Wise and Bernie Carbo following the 1973 season. He was an All Star during his first two seasons in St Louis, then was traded to the Dodgers in June of 1976.

During the 1977 season Smith combined with Steve Garvey, Ron Cey, and Dusty Baker to become the first set of four teammates to hit 30 or more home runs in the same season. Knee, ankle, neck, and shoulder injuries hampered the last 5 years of his career; Smith finished in 1982 at age 37, playing 99 games at first base for the Giants in his one season in San Francisco. At the time of his retirement, his 314 career home runs were second only to Mickey Mantle among switch hitters, he was the only switch-hitter with 100 home runs in each league, and he was the only switch-hitter to homer from each side of the plate twice in each league. He was also, with Frank Robinson, one of only 2 players to appear in World Series and All Star games in each league.

Tris Speaker—"The Grey Eagle" was a spectacular center fielder for the dominant Red Sox teams of the early twentieth century. First coming to the bigs in 1907, Speaker didn't play full-time until 1909, when he hit .309. He would hit .322 or over for the next 9 years, and he finished with a .345 career average in 22 years of major league play. He was a brilliant defensive center fielder—possibly the best of his era and considered one of the all-time greats at the position. After the 1915 season the 28-year-old Speaker was shipped to Cleveland after refusing to accept a pay cut, where he won the batting title with a .386 average and hit better than .340 eight more times.

Bobby Sprowl—lefthanded pitcher thought to be a strong prospect, who was brought to the majors during the Red Sox swoon in September 1978. Pawtucket manager Joe Morgan thought that Sprowl wasn't ready, but lefty Bill Lee was buried in manager Don Zimmer's doghouse (for, among other things, calling the manager a "gerbil" in the press, an appellation that stuck in many corners of Red Sox Nation) and the Sox needed a pitcher. Sprowl made 3 starts for the Sox, going 0–2. His last appearance in a Red Sox uniform was the fourth and last game of the "Boston Massacre," when he never made it out of the first inning.

Chick Stahl—a player/manager who killed himself under controversial circumstances. Charles Sylvester "Chick" Stahl was a good-hitting center fielder who became the club's manager late in 1906, replacing Jimmy Collins as player/manager of a truly dreadful team (the Red Sox lost 20 games in a row at one point, and 19 in a row at home). The following spring, Stahl reportedly told Collins that he couldn't take the strain of managing, before drinking carbolic acid. There's also been a persistent rumor, though never proven, that Stahl killed himself over romantic entanglements. Stahl had recently gotten married but supposedly learned that he had gotten another woman pregnant. He was 34.

Jake Stahl—a righthanded-hitting outfielder who came up with Boston in 1903 and played 28 games for the team that won the first World Series. He spent the next 3 seasons in Washington, managing the team in 2 of those seasons. Stahl was independently wealthy, and played only for the love of the game. After being out of baseball in 1907, he signed with the Yankees in 1908, and then was traded back to Boston in midseason. He played first base for the Sox in 1909 and 1910 before retiring. In 1912, Boston owner James McAleer hired him as player-manager, and Stahl came out of retirement. He played in 95 games for the 1912 team, and managed them to the World Series title. After being replaced in the middle of the 1913 season by Bill Carrigan, Stahl was out of baseball for good. Jake Stahl was not related to Chick Stahl, although some accounts mistakenly claim the two men were brothers.

Matt Stairs—once a top prospect with the Expos, Stairs had stalled in the Montreal system by the mid-1990s. Dan Duquette, who had signed Stairs while he was GM in Montreal, brought the lefthanded-hitting outfielder to Boston as a minor league free agent in 1995. Stairs was sent down to AA (the Sox AAA affiliate at Pawtucket had too many outfielders), where he thoroughly dominated the league. Stairs wasn't much of a fielder, and didn't look athletic, so he had trouble getting a chance to play in the major leagues, no matter how well he hit. He finally made the Red Sox as a pinch hitter late in the 1995 season, before moving on to Oakland as a minor league free agent. In Oakland he showed what all the hype had been about, hitting .298 with 27 home runs in 1997 and following with 2 more excellent seasons before an off year in 2000.

Tracy Stallard—a mediocre righthanded starting pitcher who came up with the Sox in 1960. Stallard is best remembered for giving up Roger Maris's 61st home run on

October 1, 1961, at Yankee Stadium. After 3 years in Boston Stallard joined the woeful expansion Mets. He lost 37 games in 2 years before finishing his career with 2 years in St. Louis.

Lee Stange—Stange had a tough luck season for the Red Sox in the pennant-winning season of 1967, finishing with only an 8–10 record despite a fine 2.77 ERA. He was scheduled to start a pennant-deciding 1-game playoff game that year, had the season ended in a tie. Instead he worked out of the bullpen during the World Series. He continued to relieve in 1968 and saved a staff-high 12 games. Stange's best major league year was in 1963 when he had a 12–5 record with the Senators. While with Cleveland in 1964 Stange performed the statistical oddity of striking out 4 men in one inning. (Tim Wakefield did the same thing for the Red Sox in 1999, after one of the batters he struck out reached on a wild pitch.) After retiring, Stange served as pitching coach for several teams, including the Red Sox.

Bob Stanley—while notorious for his wild pitch/passed ball in Game 6 of the 1986 World Series, Stanley was a valuable pitcher for many years. Stanley first pitched for the Sox in 1977, appearing in 41 games and starting 13. This swing man role would be his most effective with the Sox for the next 12 years, but he was used in many other roles as well. In 1978 Stanley went 15–2 with 10 saves and a 2.60 ERA. (He only started 3 games that year.) In 1979, Stanley was moved into the rotation, starting 30 games and going 16–12 with 1 save and a 3.99 ERA. After pitching poorly as a starter in 1980, he was moved into a relief and spot-starting role, where he thrived, setting a record by pitching 168.1 innings in relief in 1982 (and finishing second in the league in ERA). In 1983 he was made the closer for a bad Red Sox team. That year Stanley appeared in 64 games and saved 33. He followed that up in 1984 with 22 more saves before moving back to being a middle reliever and part-time closer. In 1987 Stanley went back to starting most of the time and had his worst year (4–15 with a 5.01 ERA in 20 starts). After pitching in 1988 and 1989 exclusively as a reliever, the 34-year-old Stanley retired to care for a son who had cancer. He later became a pitching coach in the Mets system.

Stanley was known for his palm ball, which he threw almost every pitch; it was slow and looked very hittable, but its crazy action would make people think of darting butterflies. He never struck out very many batters, but he had good control and threw a lot of double play balls. Stanley is also one of 2 pitchers to have both 100 saves and 100 career wins.

During the Margo Adams scandal, it was alleged that Wade Boggs and Steve Crawford arranged for Stanley to be seduced by a stripper while the team was on the road. Boggs supposedly came into the hotel room in mid-seduction and took pictures of Stanley and the stripper, so Stanley—who had a reputation for gossiping—could be blackmailed into not talking about his teammates' extramarital escapades.

Never really a fan favorite, Stanley had a habit of capturing beach balls thrown around by fans and killing the balls with a rake in the bullpen. He also counts as a local kid done good; he was born in Portland, Maine.

Mike Stanley—Stanley started out as a catcher for the Texas Rangers before moving to the Yankees prior to the 1992 season. After 4 very good years in New York he signed as a free agent with the Red Sox, and was their catcher for most of 1996. Stanley had been considered a light-hitting backup catcher with the Rangers, but blossomed into a good hitter for the Yankees at age 30, when he hit .305 with 26 homers. He continued to hit well in Boston, posting solid but not great batting averages with good power and high walk totals. Stanley played 97 games at DH for the Red Sox in 1997 before being traded back to the Yankees. At the time it seemed a relatively minor matter. The Red Sox, out of the postseason picture, acquired minor league pitchers in exchange for a major league bat, as the Yankees prepared for the postseason. It turned out to be a very big deal on a couple of fronts, however. First, one of the pitchers obtained, Jim Mecir, never pitched for the Red Sox, but was selected in the expansion draft by Tampa Bay, enabling the Red Sox to avoid losing outfielder Trot Nixon (who would probably have been selected otherwise). The other big aspect was the acquisition of Tony Armas Jr. This minor league pitcher, son of former Red Sox outfielder Tony Armas, was a key reason why the Red Sox were able to put together a better trade for superstar pitcher Pedro Martinez than the Yankees were.

Stanley finished the 1997 season with New York and signed with Toronto in the offseason. The Red Sox re-acquired him in the middle of the1998 season, trading minor league pitchers Peter Munro and Jay Yennaco, as they prepared to go to the playoffs after winning the Wild Card. He remained with Boston, playing first base and DHing (injuries prevented him from catching any longer), until midway through the 2000 season. In a move that caused some consternation among his teammates (Jeff Frye was particularly outspoken) and the media, the Red Sox released Stanley, believing that his bat had slowed significantly. He signed on with Oakland, and finished the season better than he had started it, though not well.

At his best, Stanley was a disciplined hitter with decent power. He was always reputed to be an excellent teammate and a good clubhouse presence.

Mike Stanton—the Red Sox acquired Stanton, a lefthanded reliever, from the Atlanta Braves in a trading deadline deal in 1995, and he threw 21 solid innings for Boston, helping them to win the American League East. At times during his stay in Atlanta, Stanton had been the Braves' closer, including 1993, when he saved 27 games. During 1996, Boston traded Stanton to Texas, and following the 1996 season he signed with the New York Yankees. He has been a significant part of the Yankees' strong bullpen since then.

Dave Stapleton—pressed into emergency service in 1980 when Jerry Remy was injured, 26-year-old rookie Stapleton had the season of his life, hitting .321 in 449 at bats (although without many walks or much power). He had a solid second season as a utility player in 1981, hitting .285 in limited playing time (with more walks and home runs), and was inexplicably given the first base job for the next 2 years, where his limitations as a hitter were magnified. He stuck around as a rarely used defensive replacement for 3 more years, and is best remembered for a game when he was *not* on the field—in the sixth game of the 1986 World Series, when Stapleton was not substituted defensively for Bill Buckner, who let a ground ball go between his legs to allow the winning run to score. Stapleton accomplished the bizarre statistical feat of having his batting average go down every single year of his career—from .321 to .285 to .264 to .247 to .231 to .227 to .128.

Gene Stephens—an obscure backup outfielder who had one of the best innings in baseball history. On June 28, 1953, the Red Sox exploded for an American League-record 17 runs in the seventh inning against the Tigers. The Sox drew 6 walks and had 14 hits—3 of them by Stephens, a 20-year-old rookie. Stephens is the only player ever to get 3 hits in an inning, earning him a place in the record books. He only hit .204 in 1953, however, and spent the following season in the minors. Stephens returned in 1955 and played for Boston until 1960, almost exclusively as a pinch-hitter or defensive caddy for Ted Williams. Stephens's only other claim to fame: he was later traded even-up for Marv Throneberry, a cult legend for his blunders on the 1962 Mets.

Vern Stephens—a power-hitting shortstop known as "Junior" or "Buster" by most writers and fans, Stephens was already a 4-time All Star when the Red Sox acquired him prior to the 1948 season. He went on to make the All Star team 4 more times during his 5 years in Boston. Before Ernie Banks came along, Vern Stephens was the best power-hitting shortstop in the history of the game. In 1945 (admittedly a war year, with many top players in the service), his 24 homers for the St. Louis Browns led the American League. During his first 3 years in Boston he hit 29, 39, and 30 home runs. In addition, he led the league in RBI during both 1949 and 1950, helped in large part by having Ted Williams on base in front of him most of the time. His 159 RBI in 1949 is still the most by any big league shortstop. His 39 homers that year were a record at the time for a shortstop. (Ernie Banks broke it in the National League, but it stood in the American League until Sox player Rico Petrocelli hit 40 in 1969.)

Helped out by the manpower shortage, Stephens was a regular in 1942 at the age of 21. He came up with the St. Louis Browns and spent the first 6 years of his career with them.—7 if you count the 3 games he got into in 1941. In 1946 he briefly jumped to the outlaw Mexican League, but came back after 3 games when his father and one of the Browns' scouts went down to get him. Commissioner Chandler suspended the players that remained in Mexico for up to 5 years.

In November of 1947 the Red Sox traded 10 players and $375,000 to the Browns to get Stephens, along with pitchers Jack Kramer and Ellis Kinder and infielder Billy Hitchcock. Stephens was dropped into the lineup at shortstop, incumbent Johnny Pesky moved to third, and the Sox went on to win at least 94 games in each of the next 3 years—twice losing the pennant on the last day of the season.

There was some controversy when Stephens joined the Red Sox about who would play shortstop. Since Pesky was smaller and had no power, everyone assumed Stephens would play third base. Stephens was actually a solid defensive shortstop, but was perceived as poor—since he didn't fit the speedy, singles-hitting image of shortstops at the time. This perception led many people to think that Stephens typified the Red Sox lack of concern for the subtleties of the game. Phil Rizzuto wasn't in Stephens's league as a hitter, but was widely regarded as the top American League shortstop of the time, on the strength of his fielding, baserunning, and bunting. So Stephens, who would have been a big star today, was viewed in his era as a selfish, one-dimensional player.

The 1950 Red Sox were the last team to hit .300, and it was Stephens's last really good year, at the age of 29. By 1951 he was starting to show the results of injuries to his legs, and he played only 109 games, a number he wouldn't match again. His stats were still good, but he was on the way down. 1951 was the last season he ever slugged over .500 (.501) and it was the last time that his on-base percentage was over .350 (.364). The Red Sox released him after 1952, and he spent the next 3 years bouncing between the White Sox and the St. Louis Browns/Baltimore Orioles, playing some shortstop but mostly third base. In his 5 years in Boston he hit 122 home runs and drove in 562 runs, and was a key component of several Red Sox teams that were very good, though not quite good enough.

Stephens, who was said to be a heavy drinker, died in 1968 at age 48.

Jerry Stephenson—a minor league pitching phenom in the early 1960s, Stephenson wrecked his arm in AAA pitching off a wet mound and was never the same. He pitched 1 game for the Sox at age 19 and would pitch in parts of 5 seasons for the team without ever regaining the promise he showed before his injury. He later pitched for 2 other teams without any greater effectiveness, and was out of baseball at 26.

Stephenson's father, Joe, also played in the major leagues, and his son is a minor league pitching prospect who has also been set back by injuries. Stephenson is currently vice president of scouting for the Red Sox, after scouting for the Dodgers for many years.

Jeff Stone—a speedy outfielder who came up with the Phillies in 1983 but never developed as expected. After a stint with the Orioles he came over to the Sox during 1989, and was mainly used as a pinch-runner and late-inning defensive replacement, getting only 15 at-bats in 18 games. He is mainly remembered for his only hit of the 1990 season, a late-inning pinch single that drove in the winning run of a game at Fenway against the Blue Jays, as the 2 flawed teams were battling for the American League East title. Stone's moment of glory came in the last week of the season, as the Red Sox held off Toronto to win the East by 2 games.

Dick Stuart—nicknamed "Stonefingers" for his poor fielding, Stuart was a slugging first baseman who spent two contentious years with Red Sox teams in the early 1960s. Obtained from Pittsburgh after the 1962 season as part of a deal for pitcher Don Schwall and catcher Jim Pagliaroni, Stuart hit 42 home runs and led the league in both RBI and errors. By the next year he was feuding constantly with manager Johnny Pesky (whom Stuart called "Needlenose"), and although he continued to hit well (.279 with 33 homers at a time when the league average was less than .250), many people saw the clubhouse discontent as the source of the team's problems (the Sox lost 85 games in 1963 and 90 in 1964). After the 1964 season Pesky was fired as manager and Stuart was given away to the Philadelphia Phillies for pitcher Dennis Bennett, who would win only 12 games for the Sox over the next 3 years. The strategy failed; despite a happier clubhouse, the Sox hit 21 fewer home runs as a team and lost 100 games in 1965.

Chris Stynes—27-year-old righthanded-hitting infielder-outfielder acquired from the Cincinnati Reds in November 2000 for infielder Donnie Sadler and outfielder Michael Coleman, two perennial prospects who did not figure into the Red Sox 2001 plans. A 6-year major league veteran, Stynes played 2 years (1995 and 1996) in Kansas City, and the last four in Cincinnati. Over his career he has hit very well at times and inconsistently in others, and has been used mostly as a reserve. Only twice has Stynes appeared in more than 100 games, which includes last season, when he filled in for injured Reds' starters by hitting .334 with 12 homers in 380 at bats.

Frank Sullivan—a very good pitcher for the Red Sox during the 1950s. From 1955 through 1957, Sullivan pitched 742 innings, with ERAs of 2.91, 3.42, and 2.73 (league average was around 4.00). In all 3 years he appeared in the top 10 in innings pitched and ERA, and he was selected to the All Star team in 1955 and 1956. Unfortunately, after throwing over 240 innings for three straight years, Sullivan dipped to 199 innings in 1958, 177 innings in 1959, and 153 innings in 1960. His ERA similarly worsened, to 3.53, 3.95, and finally 5.10 in 1960. Having used up most of Sullivan's arm, the Red Sox traded him to the Phillies for pitcher Gene Conley. Sullivan would pitch 226 more innings for the Phillies and Twins over the final 3 years of his career, retiring after the 1963 season at age 33. Pitching his best years while the Red Sox were mediocre, Sullivan's name has rarely received the same recognition as players like Hughson, Ferris, Kinder, or Lonborg—who did not pitch nearly as well as Sullivan, but were lucky enough to pitch for contending teams, helping them maintain better-remembered places in Sox lore than the superior but forgotten Frank Sullivan.

Marc Sullivan—a backup catcher during the mid-1980s, the suspicion was that Sullivan made the team only because his father was part-owner Haywood Sullivan, who had also been a backup catcher with the Sox. Marc struggled to hit .200 in the minor leagues, much less in the majors. His on-field highlight may have been a game in May 1986 when he provided the game-winning run by being hit in the rump with the bases loaded in the bottom of the ninth. He played in 137 games over a 5-year career with the Red Sox, hitting .193 in his best season (his father hit .161 in 1960, his only complete season with the Sox).

Jeff Suppan—a righthanded pitcher who was a top prospect, Suppan made his major league debut during the 1995 season. In 1997 he made 22 starts for the Sox, pitched badly, and was not protected during the expansion draft that stocked the Tampa Bay Devil Rays and the Arizona Diamondbacks. General manager Dan Duquette was widely criticized for not protecting him, in a situation that was reminiscent of previous GM Lou Gorman's loss of popular Eric Wedge. By leaving him out, however, the Sox were able to pull back both Trot Nixon and minor league pitcher Tony Armas Jr., who was later the key to the Pedro Martinez deal. Suppan pitched badly for Arizona before being traded to Kansas City during the 1998 season. He has developed into a slightly better-than-average starting pitcher, and may still get better, but at this point it does not appear that the Red Sox made a mistake in not protecting him.

Jim Tabor—a third baseman with the Sox from 1938–1944, Tabor had a reputation for hard drinking. He once stretched out to field a ball hit down the third base line and failed to get up. Everyone rushed over, thinking he had been hurt. He was drunk—he'd just passed out.

Tabor wasn't much of a power hitter (he hit more than 16 home runs in a season only once in his 9-year career), but in a July Fourth doubleheader in 1939 he put on one of the most extraordinary power displays by a Sox player. After homering in the first game, Tabor hit 3 home runs (2 of them grand slams, one of those an inside the park home run) in game 2. Tabor was out of baseball at age 33, and died before he was 40.

Frank Tanana—a star pitcher with the California Angels before he hurt his arm, Tanana was a 28-year-old struggling to regain his effectiveness when the Sox obtained him as part of the desperation Fred Lynn trade before the 1981 season. He went 4–10 in his only season with the Sox. Although his fastball never did come back, Tanana eventually became an effective junkballer, and was able to pitch in the major leagues for more than 20 years.

Jesse Tannehill—a lefthanded pitcher whose career began in 1894 with Cincinnati in the National League. After 2 years out of the majors, he resurfaced with Pittsburgh in 1897. From 1898–1902, he won 18 to 25 games every year, while pitching very well for the Pirates. After commissioner Ban Johnson of the upstart American League helped the Yankees sign the established pitcher away from the National League, Tannehill went 15–15 for New York in 1903. The Sox traded Long Tom Hughes to the Yankees for Tannehill after they won the World Series in 1903. He won 21 games for Boston in 1904, and 22 the next year, despite not pitching quite as well. It was all downhill after that, however. After 4½ years in Boston, he was traded to Washington. In 1911, he finished his career at the age of 36 in Cincinnati, the same place where he'd started at the age of 18.

Jose Tartabull—a weak-hitting (even for the pitching-dominated 1960s) outfielder, Tartabull spent parts of 3 seasons with the Sox, including the 1967 Impossible Dream team. Jose ran for Tony C. the night that Conigliaro was beaned, but is best remembered for a throw he made against the Chicago White Sox, when he threw out Ken

Berry who tried to score on a short line drive to right. Tartabull, who had a weak arm, made what might have been the best throw of his career. Elston Howard blocked the plate; the Red Sox won and moved into first place. Jose's son Danny was a power-hitting outfielder who later played in the major leagues for 6 teams, including the Yankees.

Birdie Tebbetts—a popular, talented catcher on the "near-miss" Red Sox teams of the late 1940s, George "Birdie" Tebbetts spent over 60 years in Major League Baseball. He began his playing career in 1936 with the Tigers and quickly gained a reputation as a standout defensive catcher, though he was below-average offensively. Early in 1947 the Red Sox traded catcher Hal Wagner for Tebbetts, whose hitting improved after moving to Fenway. Catching had been a problem for Boston since Hall of Famer Rick Ferrell was traded 10 years earlier, but Tebbetts filled the void. Ironically, he was very similar to Ferrell: he was strong defensively, had solid batting averages, not much power, good walk totals, and few strikeouts. Tebbetts hit .299 during the remainder of 1947, and made the All Star team in each of the next two seasons, batting .280 and .270 while driving in 126 runs (league average was about .260). Tebbetts set career highs with a .310 average and 8 homers in 1950, but he only played in 79 games. That December the Sox sold him to Cleveland, where he played his last 2 seasons. Tebbetts later spent 11 years as a big league manager (Reds, Braves, and Indians), and many more as a scout. In 1979, the Hall of Fame named Tebbetts to its Veterans Committee, which votes on old-time players, managers, executives, and umpires. He served on the Veterans Committee until his death in March 1999.

To celebrate baseball's centennial in 1969, each team held fan voting to select an all-time all star team. Red Sox fans elected Tebbetts as the team's best catcher. Another voting was held in 1982, and Tebbetts made the second team, behind Carlton Fisk. Rick Ferrell might have been a better selection, but Tebbetts was certainly one of the best catchers in Red Sox history.

Lee Thomas—an outfielder/first baseman who played for 6 teams in 8 years. The lefthanded-hitting Thomas had looked like a future star in his first 2 years in the league, when he averaged .287 with 25 homers, but he never matched those numbers again. He had a good year for a bad Boston team in 1965, hitting .271 with 22 homers. After retiring at age 32 he went into management, eventually becoming the general manager of the Philadelphia Phillies. Thomas is currently a key aide to Red Sox GM Dan Duquette.

Luis Tiant—ask any Red Sox fan to compile a list of their 10 most beloved Red Sox players, and Looie (the spelling is a Tiant nickname) Tiant's name would appear on the vast majority of them. Tiant, the son of one of Cuba's greatest pitchers (Luis Tiant Sr., who pitched in the Negro Leagues), started his big league career with the Cleveland Indians in 1964. He had a breakthrough season in 1968, when he developed his trademark pitching motion, in which he turned his back, showed the batter his uniform number, and hesitated before spinning to deliver the pitch to the plate.

This motion was the antithesis of the way a pitcher should pitch, and could be used by any coach as an example of how *not* to pitch. (Current Sox starter Hideo Nomo has a pitching motion reminiscent of Tiant's.) The awkward windup worked nicely for Tiant, however. In 1968 Tiant had a 21–9 record with 9 shutouts and a league leading 1.60 ERA (albeit in a great year for pitchers). In a 2-game stretch (one vs. the Red Sox), Looie struck out a then record 32 batters.

The Indians wanted to protect their new superstar, and insisted that he skip his usual Winter League pitching. This proved to be disastrous as Tiant had a dreadful 1969 season. He was traded after that season, and a short but good turn with the Minnesota Twins ended with a hairline fracture shoulder injury and his release. Tiant signed a minor league deal with the Atlanta Braves, but was cut there and ended up with the Red Sox Louisville team. He made it to Boston that year but had an unimpressive 1–7 record. For all intents and purposes, he looked washed up.

Tiant started to put it back together in Boston, and in 1972 was 15–6 and won his second ERA title at 1.91 (again in a great pitching year, but still quite an accomplishment). He was 20–13 in 1973, and 22–13 in 1974, while also racking up a league-leading 7 shutouts (today, 7 complete games of *any* type is a rarity). He was the ace of the 1975 pennant winning team, going 18–14 and leading the team in innings pitched. In postseason play that year Tiant's Red Sox legend grew. He beat the 3-time world champion Oakland A's in the first game of the American League Championship Series with a 3-hitter. He followed this with 2 vastly different wins against the Cincinnati Reds in the World Series. In the first game he was dominant in a 5-hit 6–0 shutout. He followed this up in Game 4 with a 5–4 win in which he struggled, relying on guile and bullheadedness to prevail. After batting only once in the regular season (in only the third year of the DH), Tiant also had a hit in each of these games and provided some comic relief while trying to run the bases, something he was clearly unfamiliar with. He also pitched Game 6, which was delayed repeatedly, but was long gone before the twelfth-inning heroics that made that game among the greatest Series games ever.

Years ago I had two cats. One I named El T after Luis Tiant. Nothing about this cat reminded me of Mr. Tiant, but the kittens' mother was named Mozambique after the country (my father was enamored with the sound of the word), and at the time Cuba had invaded there and we were calling the unborn kittens Cubans because they were in Mozambique, get it (hey, we were kids). So I guess it was a short leap of logic (?) for this Red Sox fan to name one of these kittens after our Cuban superstar of the day.

Yesterday I acquired my second parakeet. The first one is female so it didn't seem right to name her after a Sox player (she became B.B. for Bird Brain, because she is), but the new one is a male and is now known as Pedro (proper pronunciation for *this* Pedro is with a roll of the "R.") It was either that or Nomar, but for some reason Pedro sounds better for a bird. It appears to fit, because my initial observations indicate that he is fun-loving and easygoing. Of course if he displays an occasional temper I may have to rename him Carl (Everett).

—Don Violette

Tiant was 21–12 in 1976, but declined somewhat after that, though he still had 12 wins in 1977 and another 13 in 1978. In 1979 Tiant was a free agent, but amid the confused Red Sox ownership situation he was barely pursued, and ended up signing with the New York Yankees (an act that has earned other ex-Sox players a quick trip to the dirty rotten traitor list, but did little to tarnish Looie's legend—perhaps because it was seen as ownership's fault rather than Tiant's). He had 1 effective season with the Yankees, but faded fast after that.

Beyond his unorthodox motion, Looie also hardly looked the part of an athlete—he was balding, overweight, and no one quite knew how old he was. (As with many Cuban players, Tiant was rumored to be years older than his listed age.) He spoke with a heavy Cuban accent and a high squeaky voice that had no business coming from a man of his age and size. He was also well known for smoking oversized cigars almost anywhere, including during interviews and while receiving whirlpool treatments. All of these quirks only furthered his popularity with the fans, his fellow players, and the press. In his heyday, Tiant was one of the game's great pressure pitchers—a guy you'd want to pitch a must-win game. Fenway crowds would break out with a "Looie, Looie, Looie" refrain when he climbed the hill to pitch. Tiant was recently inducted into the Red Sox Hall of Fame, and in a nice turnabout, at the game where his longtime catcher Carlton Fisk's number was retired, Tiant caught the ceremonial first pitch thrown by Fisk. Fisk also gave Looie the ultimate compliment, by saying Tiant that was the best pitcher he ever caught. (Fisk also caught Tom Seaver, who was selected to the Hall of Fame with the highest vote percentage ever.)

Tiant played for years in the Mexican League after his career in the majors was over. He also served as pitching coach for Venezuela in the 2000 Olympics, and is currently baseball coach at Savannah College of Art and Design.

Mike Torrez—a starting pitcher who will always be associated with the Sox failure to win in 1978. Torrez was an average starting pitcher, a workhorse who won a lot of games because he played for good teams and was seldom injured. He had poor control (he led the league 3 times in walks allowed) but in his best seasons did not give up a lot of hits. Torrez had his best season in 1975, winning 20 games for the Orioles, before being traded first to Oakland and then to the Yankees. Signed as a free agent by the Red Sox after the 1977 season, Torrez was trumpeted by Sox management as a pitcher who was going to help the team—with a great offense but thin starting pitching—close the gap between themselves and the Yankees. Torrez pitched solidly but unspectacularly in 1978, going 16–13 despite an ERA that was 20 points worse than league average. With the Red Sox and Yankees tied for first place on the last day of the season, manager Don Zimmer chose Torrez to start the 1-game playoff which would decide who went to the league championship series and who went home (there was no wild-card team at this point). Torrez pitched well for 6 innings, but then gave up a 3-run home run to light-hitting shortstop Bucky Dent (forever afterward known as "Bucky Bleeping Dent" by Boston fans), and walked another batter who scored as well in the Sox eventual 5–4 loss.

Torrez pitched 3 more years with Boston. He won 16 games again in 1979, but then was less effective as the Red Sox offense began to decline in the early 1980s (although he went 10–3 in an injury-filled 1981 season). After being traded to the New York Mets for a minor leaguer, Torrez's lack of control led to a scary moment in 1984, when he beaned Houston's shortstop Dickie Thon, nearly killing him. (Thon made it back to the major leagues but was never the same player again.)

John Tudor—one of a group of young Red Sox pitchers developed in the early 1980s. Although he actually made his debut in 1979, he didn't make the Red Sox full-time until 1982, when he went 13–10 with a 3.63 ERA. The next year (Tudor's last with the Sox) he won 13 games again for a poor ballclub. The following winter Tudor was traded to Pittsburgh for hitting specialist Mike Easler (who was later traded for Don Baylor, an essential cog on the 1986 World Series Team).

Tudor flowered in Pittsburgh (12–11 with a 3.27 ERA for a bad team) but was traded to the St. Louis Cardinals, where he spun two beautiful seasons. In 1985 he went 21–8 with a 1.93 ERA in 275 innings pitched (he outpitched Mets rookie Dwight Gooden down the stretch to help the Cardinals make the World Series that year). From 1987 on, Tudor was almost constantly injured, but pitched well when he was healthy. He continued to pitch for 5 more years with St. Louis and LA, still a quality pitcher, but was never able to pitch more than 150 innings in any of those seasons.

Julio Valdez—a marginal infielder who shuttled between Pawtucket and the Red Sox from 1980 to 1983, playing a total of 65 games. In 1983 he was arrested in mid-game on a statutory rape charge involving a 14-year-old girl, and never resurfaced in the major leagues.

John Valentin—"Val" has never been a superstar, but the former ninth-place hitter on his college team has had a quietly remarkable career, marred by injury and a playing-related controversy, but featuring some wonderful highlights. Valentin came up in 1992 to replace the injured Tim Naehring, and quickly settled in at shortstop. He hit well for a shortstop his first 2 years, then broke through with a .316 average and .505 slugging percentage in the strike-shortened 1994 season—good numbers for any position. He was even better the next year, hitting .298 with career highs in home runs (27), runs (108), RBI (102), walks (81), stolen bases (20), and slugging percentage (.533), all while playing very well at the most demanding defensive position on the field. After hitting .306 in 1997, a season in which he was moved first to second base and then to third base, Valentin has struggled with injuries since, and his offensive numbers have declined as well.

Brief controversy erupted in Spring Training 1997 when Valentin was asked to move to second base to make way for shortstop phenom Nomar Garciaparra. This happened just a few days after being assured that he'd have a chance to compete to keep his job. Valentin left camp temporarily (with the club's permission) and threatened to quit. Eventually he accepted the move, as well as a subsequent move to third base to replace the injured Tim Naehring—and he played well defensively at both positions. The controversy fizzled out when it became clear just how extraordinary a player Garciaparra was.

Valentin has had a career filled with highlights. His first home run in his rookie year of 1992 was a grand slam. In 1994 Valentin turned only the tenth unassisted triple play in major league history by catching a line drive for the first out, stepping on second for the second out, and tagging the runner heading for second for out number 3. In 1995, Val and Mo Vaughn (his Seton Hall college teammate) each hit grand slams in an 8–0 win over the Yankees, the only time 2 grand slams were responsible for all the runs scored in a game. In another game that year, Val was 5–5, with 3 homers and 4 runs scored. He became the first shortstop to have 15 total bases in a game.

Valentin hit .467 in a losing cause in the 1998 American League Division Series. In the 1999 ALDS he was instrumental in the Red Sox coming back after falling behind 2 games to 0 to Cleveland, starting with a home run in Game 3. The next day, in a game in which the Red Sox scored a major league postseason-record 23 runs on 24 hits, Valentin had 4 of those hits, 2 of them home runs, while driving in 7 runs. In Game 3 of the American League Championship Series, in which Pedro Martinez dominated the Yankees, Val contributed a home run and 5 RBI, hitting .348 overall in the series.

Early in 2000, after 2 injury-marred years, Valentin was making a routine play on a ground ball when his knee blew out and he went down in a heap. The injury required extensive reconstructive surgery and caused Valentin to miss the rest of the season. He is attempting to come back with the Red Sox in the 2001 season.

Jason Varitek—a switch-hitting catcher acquired along with pitcher Derek Lowe from the Seattle Mariners in 1997 for closer Heathcliff Slocumb. Varitek was arguably the best catcher in NCAA history. (He was a teammate of Nomar Garciaparra at Georgia Tech). He was a first-round pick of Minnesota, but refused to sign for the amount of money they offered. Seattle took him in the first round a year later, but he waited nearly a year to sign, on the advice of agent Scott Boras. This greatly damaged Varitek's career, and he never put up good numbers in the minors. By the time the Red Sox got Varitek he was considered a major bust. A strong spring performance in 1998 won him the right to platoon with lefthanded-hitting catcher Scott Hatteberg instead of catcher/DH Jim Leyritz, who had been acquired during the off-season for that purpose. In 1999 Varitek was handed the starting catcher job when Hatteberg missed most of the season with an injury. Making the most of his opportunity, Varitek impressed many by hitting 20 home runs and playing well defensively, restoring his reputation as one of the game's top young catchers. In 2000 his power dropped due to a series of nagging injuries, but he retained his reputation for handling a pitching staff well.

Mo Vaughn—a hulking first baseman nicknamed "The Hit Dog," Maurice Vaughn played college ball for 3 years at Seton Hall alongside future Red Sox teammate John

Valentin before being drafted by the Boston Red Sox in the twenty-third round in 1989. Vaughn was heavily hyped based on his minor league numbers and made it to the majors quickly. He did not hit well at first, however, and split 1991 and 1992 shuttling between AAA and the big leagues (and hitting .243 in the majors). Although the jury was still out on whether Vaughn would become the star he was projected to be, he was thrust into the starting role by a freakish injury that eventually ended fellow first baseman Carlos Quintana's career. Given a third chance at success, Vaughn played very well, hitting .297 with 29 home runs and 101 RBI. This would be the last year Vaughn would hit less than .300 for the Red Sox. In 1994 his batting average rose to .310. Vaughn was the bright spot in a rather impotent batting order in the final year of the mostly forgettable Hobson era.

In 1995 Vaughn's 39 home runs, 126 RBI, and .300 batting average earned him the American League Most Valuable Player award in one of the closest votes ever. (Some fans argue that teammate John Valentin should have won the award instead.) Vaughn followed with 44 homers, 143 RBI, and a .326 batting average in 1996, and 35 homers, 96 RBI and a .315 batting average in 1997. In 1998 Mo hit 40 home runs, drove in 115 runs, and batted a career high .337, losing the batting title to the Yankees' Bernie Williams on the final day of the season. Vaughn was a 3-time All Star with the Red Sox.

As Vaughn matured as a player, his offensive numbers continued to improve, but he became prone to defensive lapses. Mo was also known on occasion not to run out ground ball outs, and looked heavier every year. These events brought some criticism from the press and fans, although Vaughn remained tremendously popular in Boston, as much for his larger than life personality and community involvement as for his hitting.

Vaughn exhibited a flair for the dramatic, both on and off the field. A couple of representative examples are Game 1 of the 1998 American League Division Series, when Vaughn blasted 2 home runs and drove in 7 runs, and the home opener in that same year, when he hit a walk off grand slam home run to beat the Seattle Mariners. Outside of the park he was also in the news, most notoriously when he was arrested for driving while intoxicated after hitting a disabled car on the shoulder of a highway, while on his way home from a Providence strip club. Vaughn publicly criticized the team for failing to support his side of the story and fought the charges in court— with his lawyer arguing that Vaughn failed field sobriety tests because he had gained so much weight in the offseason that it had affected his coordination. Vaughn won the case, but from that point on his relationship with the team—and with many fans—was strained. (The strip club—the Foxy Lady—took advantage of the publicity after Vaughn left the team, hiring a plane to tow a "Welcome Back" banner over Fenway when he returned with the Angels.)

As Vaughn approached free agency, several attempts to sign him to a longterm contract broke down acrimoniously, and communications went from strained to surreal. Vaughn first said that he would sign if the Red Sox locked the core of the team into longterm deals, but after GM Dan Duquette signed several players to lucrative deals, Vaughn accused him of lacking respect by signing other players before him. Vaughn also accused the team of hiring private investigators to follow him. Later

Vaughn would accuse the Red Sox of causing his father's urinary infection—claiming it was brought on by his father being upset at his increasingly strained relationship with the team's management and fans.

After the 1998 season Vaughn signed a lucrative multiyear contract with the Anaheim Angels, making him one of the game's best-paid players. Because of a lingering ankle injury in 1999, and because the Anaheim ballpark is less suited to his hitting style than Fenway Park is, Vaughn's numbers declined somewhat in California, although he remains a good hitter (even in the current era of great offenses). Ironically, time has healed some of the bitterness between Vaughn and the Sox, and some of his comments have hinted at a desire to return to the volatile Boston environment—where the passion for the game matches Vaughn's own intensity, unlike California, where he and the Angels are little fish in a big pond.

Wilton Veras—a much-hyped third base prospect for the Red Sox who fell out of view after a terrible 2000 season. Veras was called up as a 21-year-old in 1999 and given significant playing time because of an injury to third baseman John Valentin. Veras fielded well and hit for a good average (.288) in 188 at bats, but with little power and virtually no walks. Still, his performance was seen as an important stepping stone to a permanent major league position. When Valentin was hurt again in 2000, Veras again was called up, but this time looked lost in the major leagues, rarely getting on base and making 13 errors in only 49 games before being returned to the minors (where he also played badly). Veras is still only 23 years old.

Mickey Vernon—a solid first baseman for 20 big league seasons, primarily with the Washington Senators, Vernon played for the Red Sox in 1956–57. The line-drive hitter won 2 batting titles and played in 7 All Star Games, though chronic back problems limited his power. In the winter of 1955 Vernon was sent to Boston in a 9-player deal. The 38-year-old had a fine first season with the Red Sox, hitting .310 with a career-high .405 on base percentage. In only 403 at bats, Vernon hit 15 homers and drove in 84 runs. But he struggled in 1957, hitting .241 with 7 homers in limited playing time. Vernon was released after the season. After drifting to 3 teams over the next 3 seasons Vernon retired in 1960. He finished his career with a .286 lifetime batting average and 2,495 hits.

Frank Viola—star lefthanded pitcher who was a member of the Sox from 1992–94. "Sweet Music" Viola began his career with the Minnesota Twins, pitching badly for a couple of years before he blossomed in 1984 as a 24-year-old. He was the ace of the 1987 World Series champions, and won the World Series MVP award. In 1988 he pitched even better, going 24–7 and winning the American League Cy Young. After his agent made a "pay-me-or-trade-me" demand public, Viola was publicly criticized for his contract demands by teammates Gary Gaetti and Kent Hrbek, and Minnesota traded him to the Mets in 1989 on the July trading deadline. It was a huge deal at the time, the defending Cy Young winner traded for a large package of young pitchers (including future stars Rick Aguilera and Kevin Tapani).

In New York he became a teammate of Ron Darling—his opponent, and the losing pitcher, in one of the greatest games in NCAA playoff history. (Darling, pitching for Yale, had no-hit Viola's St John's team through 11 innings, but Viola shut Yale out as St. John's won 1–0 in 12 innings.) Viola, a native Long Islander, pitched very well for the Mets in 1990, winning 20 games while leading the league in innings pitched and finishing fourth in ERA. But the fickle New York fans turned on him as he faltered down the stretch in 1991, struggling with various nagging injuries. In the offseason he signed with the Red Sox as a free agent.

He pitched well for Boston in 1992–93, though these were among the weakest offensive teams in Sox history, so he didn't have very impressive won-lost records. He wasn't pitching at his previous Cy Young level, but he was a better-than-average American League starter. Then, in May of 1994 at Fenway, he threw a pitch to the backstop, clutched his pitching elbow awkwardly, and headed toward the dugout with the ball still in play. The injury required extensive reconstructive surgery, and he never pitched again for the Sox. In a long attempt to come back from the injury, Viola made 3 ineffective starts for the Cincinnati Reds in 1995, and 6 ineffective starts for the Toronto Blue Jays in 1996—winning only 1—before retiring.

Clyde Vollmer—journeyman outfielder who came up with the Cincinnati Reds and played with the Red Sox from 1950–53. In a 10-year career that included Cincinnati, Boston, and 2 stints in Washington, he hit 69 home runs. 13 of them came during about a 1-month stretch during July 1951, many of them winning games. One was a sixteenth-inning grand slam against Cleveland, the latest in a game that any major league grand slam had ever been hit. The power disappeared as quickly as it came, however, and "Dutch the Clutch" finished up his career at the age of 32 in 1954.

Hal Wagner—a light-hitting part time player before World War II, Wagner spent part of the war working in a defense plant during the days and catching for the Philadelphia A's on weekends. Boston acquired him and made him the starting catcher in 1944. The lefthanded-hitting Wagner was batting .332 and the Sox were in contention for a pennant until he, pitcher Tex Hughson, and second baseman Bobby Doerr were all drafted within 2 weeks of each other. After the war Wagner held on to the Red Sox catching job for a year, hitting .230 for the 1946 pennant winners, before spending the rest of his career as a part-time player.

Tim Wakefield—an entertaining but frequently disgruntled knuckleball pitcher who has pitched for the Sox in a variety of roles since 1995. Wakefield had been a first baseman (he couldn't hit well enough to be a major leaguer) who began pitching in the minor leagues. His only effective pitch was the hard-to-control knuckleball, which would dance around the strike zone unpredictably (he did occasionally mix in not-very-fastballs or curves). Called up by Pittsburgh late in the 1992 season, the 26-year-old Wakefield went on an astonishing tear, going 8–1 and holding opposing hitters to a .232 average. The next season the magic was gone; Wakefield couldn't throw strikes with his knuckleball and hitters hammered his other pitches whenever he threw them. Pittsburgh sent him down to the minors, hoping he would regain his effectiveness, but by the next season he couldn't get anyone out in the minors either. The Pirates released Wakefield after a miserable year in AA ball, and Red Sox GM Dan Duquette signed him early in the 1995 season as a reclamation project.

Called up in May, Wakefield went on another extraordinary roll. With Sox ace Roger Clemens injured for long stretches, Wakefield was the team's best starting pitcher. He went 16–8 with a 2.95 ERA and, despite a late-season slump, finished second in the league in ERA. He was never as good again, but did pitch solidly for the next 3 years, winning 17 games in 1998. In 1999 he began the season poorly and lost his starting spot, but then pitched well in relief. Tom Gordon was injured, so manager Jimy Williams used Wakefield as his closer for the middle of the season. He was effective in that role, saving 15 games, although he frequently terrified fans by giving up walks and long fly balls in the late innings of close games. In 2000, he was shuttled between starting and relief, but never pitched consistently.

Like most knuckleball pitchers, he could be unhittable for long stretches and then would be completely ineffective. When the ball failed to break sharply enough or when he was forced to throw other pitches, Wakefield gave up enormous home runs. Although he pitched well at times, Wakefield never had a firm spot in the pitching rotation because of his inconsistency, and he sometimes complained when he felt he wasn't being used appropriately. As the Sox player representative he spoke up on other issues as well, and he talked freely and indiscreetly to the press when players he considered important to the team were traded or not re-signed. As a result, he seemed to always be complaining. The Sox had given him a longterm contract through the 2000 season, but when they declined to guarantee his option year for 2001, Wakefield began complaining further. He did not like the way he was being switched between starting and relief, and told the media that he didn't consider it fair that the Red Sox took advantage of his flexibility by using him in so many different situations (his versatility was one of his greatest assets to the team). After Wakefield declined to start in the last game of the 2000 season (he considered it a meaningless game) his Red Sox career appeared to be over, but after testing the free agent market briefly he signed a 2-year contract to remain with the Red Sox.

Bill Wambsganss—a second baseman who spent the 1924 and 1925 seasons with the Red Sox after 10 years in Cleveland. Best known for being the only man to ever complete an unassisted triple play in the World Series, he accomplished the feat for Cleveland against the Brooklyn Dodgers in Game 5 of the 1920 Series.

Bob Watson—a good (but not great) hitting first baseman/outfielder for many years with the Houston Astros, Watson was traded to the Red Sox a third of the way through the 1979 season to replace the end-of-the-line George Scott. The 33-year-old Watson had started the season hitting .239 and the Astros dumped him, thinking he was in decline. Instead, Watson went on an incredible tear for the rest of the season, hitting .337 for a great-hitting Red Sox team that would fall short of the pennant because of its thin pitching. After the season he went on to the Yankees as a free agent and played reasonably well for a year, then not so well for a couple of years afterward, but he is remembered for his great 1979 effort.

Watson was briefly a celebrity in 1975, when he scored baseball's millionth run. He went into the front office after finishing as a player and was general manager of the 1996 Yankees World Series winners.

Earl Webb—outfielder who set a flukish major league record for doubles in 1931 that still stands. Webb only played 2 full seasons with the Red Sox, as the starting right fielder on dreadful teams, and played for 5 teams in 7 years in the majors. He was a perfect fit for Fenway Park, a lefthanded line drive hitter who could take full advantage of the park's dimensions. He hit .323 and .333 in his 2 seasons with the Sox, but never hit above .301 elsewhere. Webb hit 67 doubles in his extraordinary 1931 season, but not more than 30 in any other year.

Eric Wedge—as a 24-year-old rookie catcher called up in 1992, Wedge excited Sox fans by hitting 5 homers in just 68 at bats for a team without much else to cheer for. Wedge needed surgery for an elbow injury in the off-season, and Boston left him off its protected list for the Expansion Draft, figuring no one would risk taking an injured player. There were howls from Boston fans when Colorado selected Wedge, but the Sox gamble turned out to be correct. Wedge was able to play in only 9 games for Colorado because of his injury. He briefly returned to the Red Sox in 1994, but was out of baseball at age 26. He is now managing a minor league team in the Cleveland organization.

Billy Werber—one of the first good players the Sox bought from the Yankees after Tom Yawkey put an end to 15 years of Harry Frazee's fire sales and Bob Quinn's penuriousness, Werber was as important as a symbol of how things had changed as he was as a player. Werber was a speedy 24-year-old rookie infielder who'd had 2 brief stints with the Yankees when the Sox got him in 1933. After spending the rest of that season splitting time between third base and shortstop, Werber took over at third in 1934, and had an extraordinary season—hitting .321 with 62 extra base hits, scoring 129 runs, and leading the league with 40 stolen bases. He would lead the league in steals again in 2 of the next 3 years. But he never had a season like 1934 again, although he remained a decent hitter (Werber didn't have more than so-so power, but he walked a lot and usually hit around the league average at a time of good offenses). He was sent to the Philadelphia A's in 1937, and played for 2 more teams before retiring in 1942.

Sammy White—the regular Red Sox catcher from 1952 through 1959. He averaged 120 games per year behind the plate during that stretch. His most notable career achievement came in June of 1953 when he became the first twentieth century player to score 3 runs in a single inning, as the Red Sox scored 17 in the seventh inning of a game against the Tigers. He wasn't a good hitter, but was considered to be a fine game-caller and framer of pitches.

White was traded to Cleveland with Jim Marshall for Russ Nixon in March 1960. White retired rather than go to Cleveland, and the trade was canceled. During the 1960 season, the Sox ended up getting Nixon and Carroll Hardy in another deal. White's rights were traded to the Milwaukee Braves in June 1961, and he came out of retirement. He spent the season backing up Joe Torre in Milwaukee, and the 1962 season in Philadelphia also as a backup, before retiring.

During his brief 1960–61 retirement, White operated a bowling alley called Brighton Bowling Alleys, which became famous as the site of a mass murder during the 1970s.

Ted Williams—Teddy Ballgame, The Splendid Splinter, The Kid. If there is any question that Babe Ruth was the greatest hitter in the history of baseball, it is raised by the performances of number 9, Theodore Samuel Williams. There might be some debate over the order of the best 2 hitters in baseball history, but not the composition of the pair. The raw numbers are impressive enough. Williams was the last man to hit .400, hitting .406 in 1941, just his third season in the majors. (While the .406 batting average gets the bulk of the press, the most astounding thing that Williams accomplished in 1941 was his .551 on-base percentage, the best in major league history, including the 1800s.) Williams's 521 career home runs placed him third (behind Ruth and Jimmie Foxx) when he retired after the 1961 season. His .344 lifetime batting average is still ninth on the all-time list, and the highest of any player whose career started after 1920. He won the triple crown twice (leading the league in batting average, home runs, and RBI in the same season). He also won the MVP twice, and deserved it several more times.

Looking beyond the traditional triple crown statistics, Williams was the best hitter in history at the most important offensive baseball skill—getting safely to first base. He is the all-time major league baseball leader in on-base percentage at .481. He made outs in fewer than 52% of his plate appearances, the only player in baseball history to accomplish that. It is actually difficult to put Williams's career on-base percentage into proper perspective. The singlemost important skill that an offensive player has is the skill of not making outs. Williams did it better than anyone else ever did. There have only been 38 single season on-base percentages in Major League history that were higher than Williams's *career* .481, and they were compiled by only 18 players, including Ruth 9 times and Williams 7. And 8 of the other players played predominantly in the nineteenth century. He's still second to Ruth on the all-time lists for both slugging and OPS.

Williams played right field as a rookie in 1939 and then, with the exception of about 5 seasons lost to military service, he was as much a fixture in left field at Fenway as the Green Monster until 1960. He was an indifferent fielder, but a passionate hitter. All evidence suggests that he was always ready, willing, and able to talk hitting with anyone, anywhere. In 1971 he co-authored, with journalist John Underwood, possibly the best book about hitting ever written, *The Science Of Hitting*.

Beyond baseball, Williams lived life on a large scale. He was, in many ways, the American that John Wayne played in the movies—the Hemingway hero exemplifying grace under pressure. He was the greatest baseball player of his day, and spent nearly 5 years of what should have been the prime of his baseball career flying fighter jets in two different wars. He never made it overseas for World War II, but flew 39 combat missions over Korea from 1952–53 as wingman to future astronaut John Glenn, who once called Williams "the best jet pilot I ever saw." He was a skilled hunter and sportsman (who got in trouble for taking a shotgun to Fenway Park's pigeon population). He retired from baseball and went on to acclaim as a master fly fisherman.

Williams always had a flair for the dramatic. In 1952, expecting to be called up for active duty in Korea, he hit a home run in his last at bat at Fenway. In September 1960, heading into retirement, he hit another home run in his last at bat at Fenway.

Williams's relationship with the Boston media, the "knights of the keyboard," was very rough for many years, particularly with famed *Boston Daily Record* columnist "Colonel" Dave Egan. Reporters' dislike for Williams cost him several MVP awards, since some writers refused to vote for him altogether, no matter how well he played. Indeed, Williams's feelings toward the fans and the city were mixed during his career, and those mixed feelings were mutual. Williams received far more than his share of boos from the Fenway faithful. In return, he occasionally aimed foul balls at fans who were particularly vocal in their criticism.

My family immigrated to Canada from Italy in March of 1955, near the end of the NHL season. By the time I could (barely) make myself understood in English, I was watching playoff hockey games at the home of the kid across the hall. His family had come to Ajax from Windsor (across the river from Detroit), so he was a Detroit Red Wing fan. So I became a Detroit Red Wing fan. Following his lead, Ted Lindsay was my favorite player.

When summer came I was astonished at how everybody was trying to hit a ball with a strange-looking stick, and when someone managed that, everyone tried to catch and throw it while others ran all over the place. In about ten minutes one afternoon I was introduced to the concept of baseball. Perhaps it was its somewhat anarchic appearance, but as far as playing it, I was hooked. This sandlot variety was the only baseball I knew. The only time baseball was on television was on Saturday afternoons, and we were too busy playing to watch.

The following year (by this time I actually knew the rules!), I was learning the intricacies of playing second base (pretty good), hitting (lousy), and the English language. Another boy, John Brewer, with whom I made friends, was a Yankee fan. I had very little idea of who the Yankees were. I'm eight years old at this time, one year of English under my belt, quite bright and learning quick but I had a bit of difficulty reading newspapers, much less the sports pages. But I had, by absorption, learned most of the team names.

When John Brewer (pity he was a Yankee fan) asked me which was my favourite team, I considered ingratiating myself by saying the Yankees, but I couldn't bring myself to do it (I had *no* knowledge of baseball history at this time). Thinking furiously, I ran down the names of the teams I knew and linked the Detroit *Red Wings* with the Boston

Following a booing early in his career, Williams resolved never to tip his cap to the fans again. Not even the standing ovation following the home run that marked his last career at bat altered that. But in the years following his retirement, the frictions that remained between city, fans, and superstar gradually softened. Early in the 90s, the street that runs behind the Green Monster was renamed from Lansdowne Street to Ted Williams Way. In 1995, the third harbor tunnel of the massive Boston Big Dig was named after Williams.

One of the lasting memories of the 1999 All Star Game, held at Fenway Park 38 years after Williams's retirement, will always be the appearance of Ted Williams on the Fenway Park infield. Major League Baseball chose the top 50 players of the twentieth century and the living members were introduced to the crowd on the Fenway infield prior to the All Star Game. The greats of the game were gathered, but when Williams came out in a golf cart, that was the feature attraction. All of the greats of baseball clustered around Williams, wanting to shake hands, or even to touch his arm. The All Stars of 1999, accustomed to being surrounded by smiling kids, were a group of smiling kids themselves around Williams. And in the broadcast booth Tim McCarver said "You find yourself asking, 'Can't this go on forever?' to nobody in particular." There's no doubt that the sight of Ted Williams being surrounded by the great players of not only the 1999 season, but the entire twentieth

---

Red Sox. Boston, I told him. The Red Sox.

Hmph, he replied. You only like them because they have Ted Williams. Well, I thought. Since the *Red Wings* had Ted Lindsay and the *Red Sox* had Ted Williams, my choice seemed obviously fated. No, I told him, I like them because they're my favourite team. The Yankee fan was disgusted and regaled me with tales of Babe Ruth, Lou Gehrig, Joe DiMaggio, Mickey Mantle, et al. I had no easy rejoinder, so I went to the library and pored through volumes of sports history for three evenings. When next we met I could hold up my end of the argument, having committed to memory pages of statistics and historical data. He knew a lot more about baseball than I did, so in order to continue arguing intelligently, I had to keep learning, with the accent on the Red Sox.

When Ted Williams retired I had saved my pennies to take a bus to Boston (I ran away from home, technically) to see him play for the only time in my life. I saw his last game. I was apprehended and returned to Canada four hours after the game.

In '67 I attended all four games at Fenway and two in St. Louis. In '75 I saw both games against Oakland at Fenway. I saw the first two games of the Series and two games in Cincinnati. I saw all three games in Boston, and almost went broke. Due to the rain, I ran out of money (but had tickets) and spent a night in the park under three days worth of newspapers until someone took me in for the rest of the week.

In '86 I had pretty well given up hope, but ended up in Fenway for the final game of the American League Championship Series. I saw the second game in New York against the Mets and two of the three games at Fenway. I went to New York but could not acquire tickets for the final two games. I cried, though.

—Mario Martinelli

century, will be the lingering memory from the 1999 All Star Game, for anyone that was watching.

Williams has been troubled by a series of minor strokes and by heart problems in recent years (he had bypass surgery in 2000), limiting his activities severely. He remains involved, however, at least peripherally, with Boston baseball, and in retirement has gained the love of Boston fans and the adulation of the Boston media.

Jim Willoughby—reliever whose removal from Game 7 of the 1975 World Series remains one of the most controversial decisions in Red Sox history. Willoughby was acquired from the Cardinals in 1975, in exchange for promising infielder Mario Guerrero. He began the season in the minors, but pitched well down the stretch for Boston (5–2, 8 saves, 3.54 ERA in 24 games). In the World Series, Willoughby was dominant. He didn't allow any earned runs in his 3 appearances covering 6⅓ innings. In Game 7, he cut off a Reds rally in the seventh inning, keeping the score tied at 3, and pitched a perfect eighth. In the bottom of the eighth, manager Darrell Johnson pinch-hit for Willoughby, even though there were two outs and nobody on. Willoughby's replacement, Cecil Cooper, was an excellent hitter mired in a horrible 1-for-18 slump. Cooper fouled out to third baseman Pete Rose and rookie Jim Burton took over on the mound. The Reds scored off Burton in the top of the ninth, and the Sox came up empty in the bottom half, losing the game and the World Series. Fans continue to debate Johnson's decision to this day, especially since the obscure Burton had to be used in such a crucial spot.

Willoughby had a good year in 1976, despite a 3–12 record. He pitched 99 innings in relief, saving 10 games and posting an excellent 2.82 ERA. But, like his fellow Buffalo Heads, Willoughby didn't see eye-to-eye with Don Zimmer, who became manager in mid-1976. He wasn't used much in 1977 (31 games), and wasn't particularly effective (6–2, 4.94 ERA, only 2 saves). Right before Opening Day of 1978, the Red Sox sold Willoughby to the White Sox, where he pitched fairly well before injuries prematurely ended his career.

Earl Wilson—a righthanded pitcher, Wilson was the first black pitcher in Red Sox history. Drafted in 1953 as a catcher, he made his major league debut in 1959 against the Tigers. He allowed no hits but walked 9 in his 3⅔ innings, leaving with a 4–0 lead. That lack of control led him to bounce up and down between Boston and the minors before sticking for good in 1962. In 1961, he didn't pitch at all in the majors.

In June of 1962 Wilson became the first black pitcher to throw a no-hitter in the American League. He beat the Angels 2–0, and drove in the winning run with a third-inning home run off of California starter Bo Belinsky. Owner Tom Yawkey rewarded the feat with a $1,000 bonus.

The control difficulties were not behind Wilson, however. In 1963 he walked a league-high 105 batters, and tied the American League record with 21 wild pitches. In 1966, after complaining about unequal treatment with the Sox, he was traded to the Detroit Tigers, where he made the *Sporting News* all star team. He pitched 4 more seasons for the Tigers before finishing as a member of the San Diego Padres in 1970.

He finished his career with a 121–109 won-loss record, and an ERA that was basically league average for his career. He wasn't a good hitter, but had excellent power for a pitcher, finishing his career with 35 home runs in only 740 career at-bats.

Rick Wise—workhorse who won 19 games for the 1975 Red Sox, and had a solid but unspectacular 18-year career. Wise pitched for the Phillies and Cardinals from 1964–73, giving his teams lots of innings, ERAs around the league average, and about 13–17 wins a year (with nearly as many losses). He remains best-known for one of baseball's greatest single-game performances on June 23, 1971. In addition to no-hitting the powerful Cincinnati Reds, Wise also hit two home runs in the same game— a 2-way feat that no other pitcher has ever accomplished.

In 1974, Wise and Bernie Carbo joined the Red Sox in the controversial Reggie Smith deal. The normally durable Wise missed most of the 1974 season with a sore arm but rebounded with a career-best 19–12 record in 1975, though good run support covered up for a so-so 3.95 ERA. Wise won Game 3 of the ALCS against Oakland, clinching the series. He was also the winning pitcher, in an emergency relief appearance, of Game 6 of the World Series—though Carlton Fisk deserves credit for that one.

Wise had a solid year in 1976 (14–11, 3.53 ERA), but ran into trouble when Don Zimmer took over as manager in the second half. Their personalities clashed, and Wise joined the infamous "Buffalo Heads," a clique (led by Bill Lee, Fergie Jenkins, and Carbo) that openly mocked Zimmer. Wise only started 20 games in 1977, and went 11–5 despite a poor 4.77 ERA. Before the 1978 season, he and three teammates were traded to Cleveland for rising star Dennis Eckersley. Wise lost 19 games for the Indians in 1978, and ended his career in 1982 with a 188–181 record.

Smokey Joe Wood—a pitcher and outfielder who at his peak was one of the best pitchers ever. Wood first appeared for the Sox in 1908 and moved into the rotation as part of a youth movement in 1909, when the aging Cy Young was traded. An above-average pitcher for the next 2 years, Wood became a workhorse in 1911, when he went 23–17 in 275 innings, with 231 strikeouts and a 2.02 ERA. In 1912 Wood had one of the finest seasons ever for a pitcher, and one of the very best for any Sox pitcher. He went 34–5 in 43 games. He threw 344 innings that year and struck out 258. His 1.91 was only the third lowest of his career. (He managed an astonishing 1.49 ERA in 1915, when he was throwing on fumes.) The toll the 1912 season took on Wood's arm was severe; he pitched for 6 more years, but only appeared in 73 games over that span, including only 7 in the last 3 years. He continued to pitch well when he was available, though, winning the ERA title in his last full season as a pitcher in 1915, when he went 15–5 but could only start 25 games. Wood retired with a 2.03 career ERA (excellent, but not as astonishing as it would be today; the league average ERA was about 3.00 while he was pitching, while it's closer to 5.00 today).

Unable to pitch regularly after 1915, Wood resurrected his career as an outfielder and occasional pitcher for Cleveland, where he played until 1922. Wood finished his career with a .283 batting average. Wood's son, Joe Frank Wood, pitched briefly for the Red Sox in 1944.

John Wyatt—relief ace for the 1967 Impossible Dream team, Wyatt's career flamed out quickly at a time when almost all closers were overworked and ruined their arms in a few years (which is why people in the 1960s and 1970s used to complain about relief pitchers being inconsistent). Wyatt won 10 games as a Kansas City A's rookie in 1961, pitching mostly in relief. From then on he worked entirely out of the bullpen, saving between 10 and 20 games each year at a time when save totals were very low (since starting pitchers were expected to stay in games they were winning, even if they were tired), and leading the league in appearances in 1964, when he made the All Star team. He was traded to Boston after losing his first 3 games in 1966. As a 32-year-old in 1967 Wyatt had his best year, winning 10 games and saving 20 more while posting a 2.60 ERA. Although Wyatt didn't give up many hits he always struggled with his control. In 1967, however, he recorded the lowest walk total of any full season of his career. He blew a lead in Game 6 of the World Series, but won the game when the Red Sox rallied—becoming only the fourth black player to win a World Series game. The Sox sold Wyatt to the Yankees early the next season, his place in the bullpen lost to Sparky Lyle and Lee Stange, and Wyatt drifted to 4 teams over the next 2 years before retiring.

Carl Yastrzemski—in 1961, a year after the retirement of the immortal Ted Williams, the Red Sox turned to 21-year-old Long Island native Carl Yastrzemski, a second baseman in the minors, as the first candidate for the opening in left field. Yastrzemski had been signed by the Sox during his first year at the University of Notre Dame, and had put up explosive numbers at Raleigh and Minneapolis in the minor leagues.

Held up against nearly impossible expectations, Yaz's early performance was productive but not immediately reflective of his extraordinary predecessor, to whom he would be constantly compared. Both were sprightly lefthanded hitters who played left field and worked to adjust their swings and styles to the odd shapes and angles of Fenway Park. Yastrzemski was even assigned the number 8 by the Red Sox clubhouse manager because of its close association with Williams's number 9. But Yastrzemski's hitting style, with a sprawled crouch and the bat held straight up with the hands behind the head, was more unorthodox than Williams's was, and it took a few years for Yastrzemski to mature from a young hitting threat to a fearsome home run force (especially in the pitching-dominated 1960s).

Yaz did not play for numbers, but his hard work finally showed off in that column during the Impossible Dream season of 1967. After adopting a new training regimen, Yastrzemski launched 44 home runs to go with a .326 average and 121 RBI, becoming the last player of the twentieth century to capture baseball's triple crown (leading the league in average, home runs, and RBI). Yaz carried the team almost by himself offensively at a time when it seemed like the dream was about to end. He had an incredible September, and in the last 12 games of the season hit .523 with 5 home runs and 16 runs batted in. At the end of the season the Red Sox needed to win their final two games against the Twins to win the pennant and avoid finishing in a 3-way tie with Minnesota and Detroit. Yaz went 7-for-8 in the Sox 2 victories, including a home run and a terrific defensive throw that caught Bob Allison at second to end a rally.

He followed up his triple crown year by hitting a league-leading .301 (the lowest average ever to lead the league, in a year when the average hitter batted only .230). He would continue to hit well, but often sacrificed personal achievements for the good of the team. For instance, Yaz lost a batting title on the last day of the 1970 season because he refused to sit out the last game of a meaningless season, while California's Alex Johnson did sit out. Earlier in that strange season, Yaz became the only All Star to be named the game's MVP while playing for a losing team.

The key to Yaz's success was not so much a blessed ability as it was longevity, durability, and hard work. His 23 years with the Sox were the second most in baseball history for players who spent their careers with 1 team, behind only Baltimore's Brooks Robinson. As his hitting improved over his career, so did his defense in left field, one of Fenway's more demanding positions. Yastrzemski became known for some of his acrobatic catches he made in front of the Green Monster, despite the lack of modern finesse we see in some of today's highlight films. Because of his athleticism, Yaz was occasionally asked to fill in elsewhere, mostly at first base. In 1973 he made a valiant, but doomed, attempt to play third base, and as a 43-year-old he was forced to fill in briefly in center field. An aging Yastrzemski eventually moved to first base full time (and finally to designated hitter in the last years of his career) when Jim Rice emerged as a talented left fielder in his own right.

Yaz was a gritty, feisty player. Although he was outwardly stoic (part of his popularity, since it came off as New England reserve), Yaz on more than one occasion exploded at an umpire when he felt he had a legitimate complaint. A frequently replayed clip of Yaz during his playing days was of him being called out on strikes, never saying a word to or looking at the umpire, but dropping the bat at the plate, then bending down to cover the plate with dirt. He was thrown out of the game before he stood back up.

I became peripherally interested in the Red Sox during the '67 World Series, just listening to my high school classmates talking about the series. The following summer I was working a boring, lonely job on Sundays pumping gas at a station owned by my father. The only real entertainment available was a radio, and as I was not really a fan of any music that played on the stations, the only other choices were the three AM stations that carried baseball. The choices were the Red Sox, the Expos, and the Yankees. Because of my interest in the '67 series, I started listening to the Sox. Kind of scary to think how it might have gone, eh? A sign of my initial ignorance was me telling someone that Yaz had just hit a grand slam home run with the bases loaded. Anyway, I was soon hooked, and two years later being a Sox fan was one reason I went to college in Boston. That was followed for several years by twice-a-summer overnight ballgame trips with several family members, which are among my most cherished memories.

—Don Violette

In addition to being a fan favorite, Yaz was a favorite of owner Tom Yawkey. There was media criticism when Yastrzemski was suspected of having input on managerial decisions. Yaz was also criticized for being overpaid, at a time before free agency when baseball owners were notorious for underpaying players. (Highly paid players were frequently criticized at the time, since players were supposed to play for the love of the game, with money being secondary.) Like fellow Sox star left fielders Ted Williams and Jim Rice, Yaz often didn't get along with the press, which may have been related to his being so close to Yawkey.

The combination of longevity and hard work contributed to some outstanding achievements reached near the twilight of his career. He topped the 100 RBI mark five times, picked up seven Gold Gloves for fielding excellence, and was an 18-time All Star. He finished his career leading the majors in games played, and third in at-bats. In 1979 he became the first player ever to reach both 3,000 hits and 400 home runs. Hit number 3,000 came in September at Fenway against the Yankees, when the 40-year-old Yaz grounded a single past Willie Randolph that caused a frenzy in the stands. The game was halted for several minutes and a microphone was set up at first base for Yastrzemski to thank the Fenway crowd for their support—an unforgettable moment in Red Sox history.

Yaz retired after the 1983 season to another dramatic ovation; always reserved as a player, in his last game he trotted around the perimeter of the ballyard, greeting as many fans as he could. He repeated this ceremony when his number 8 was retired by the Red Sox in 1989, shortly after his induction into the Hall of Fame. His final totals included a .285 average (compiled at a time when pitchers dominated the game), 452 home runs, 1,844 runs batted in, and a countless number of thrills.

Rudy York—a slugger who spent most of his career with the Detroit Tigers. After playing first base for the 1940 and 1945 World Champion Tigers, York was acquired by the Red Sox before the 1946 season (in exchange for shortstop Eddie Lake) in order to bolster the team's lineup. Though his slugging percentage of .437 was a far cry from his peak years (.651 in 1937 and .583 in 1940), he hit 2 grand slams in the same game at one point during the season, and he drew enough walks that season to make up somewhat for his disappointing power numbers. In the 1946 World Series, York provided most of the power in the losing effort by the Sox, slugging home runs that led to wins in games 1 and 3. The next season, as the Red Sox slipped in the standings, York was traded to the White Sox for first baseman Jake Jones. A 7-time All Star, York played only 202 mediocre games for the Sox, but his contributions in that 1946 World Series still cause him to be fondly remembered by Sox fans.

Cy Young—righthanded pitcher whose career accomplishments became the standards by which pitching excellence is measured, and whose name graces the award bestowed upon the best pitchers in baseball each season. Denton True Young was nicknamed "Cyclone" in the minors because of how hard he threw, and the nickname stuck, and Cy is how he is known to all baseball fans. He spent 8 of his 22 years in a Boston uniform, from 1901 when he joined the Boston Pilgrims, through the 1908 season (the second year of the Red Sox.) He was one of the first big stars to make the jump from the established National League to the upstart, fledgling American League, and probably the biggest name.

The numbers that Young put up are difficult to comprehend for people watching today's game. He pitched in the dead-ball era, when players didn't hit home runs the way they do now. All of the pitching statistics from Young's era are incompatible to today's game. There was almost no such thing as a bullpen—pitchers finished what they started. In the last 3 years, there have only been 3 major league pitchers to complete more than 9 games, and the highest total was 15. From 1891 to 1898 Young averaged more than 41 complete games per season, with a high of 48. He did not lead the league in complete games in any of those seasons.In his career, he completed over 91% of the games that he started, starting 815 major league games and finishing a staggering 749.

But, while recognizing the context of his accomplishments, and the impossibility of comparing them to the pitching accomplishments of today, it is also important to recognize that, even in his own era, he stood out. Gehrig's consecutive games record, Cobb's hit record, and Ruth's home run record have all been broken, but Young's win record has never been challenged, even in the era when he set it. Second place on the all-time win record list is the Big Train, Walter Johnson—the only other man over 400, with 417 wins. Young had 511. His loss record is probably even farther out of reach, as he lost only 316 games.

Young owed a large part of his success to his control. In his 22 major league seasons, he led the league in fewest walks per 9 innings 14 times. 7 times he led in fewest baserunners (hits plus walks) per 9 innings. He believed that an arm only had a certain number of pitches, and never threw more than a dozen warmups before a game.

In Boston Young was the best pitcher on the staff of the first ever World Series champions (1903). In his 8 years with the Pilgrims/Red Sox, he won 192 games, while finishing 275 of the 297 games that he started. He was 41 in 1908 during his last season in Boston, and he was almost done. He won only 33 games in the three years before his retirement, spent mostly in Cleveland, with a partial season back in Boston playing for the Boston Rustlers (who, in 1912, became the Boston Braves). Cy Young was elected into the Baseball Hall of Fame in 1937. In 1956, Major League Baseball created an award for the best pitcher in baseball, and named it the Cy Young Award.

Matt Young—a Sox pitcher in the early 1990s who was plagued by inconsistent control. Following Bruce Hurst's departure after the 1988 season, Young cashed in on general manager Lou Gorman's desperation to acquire lefthanded starting pitching. Young had terrific talent, but in 1990 was coming off an 8–18 season with the Seattle Mariners in which he posted high totals in both walks and strikeouts. Nevertheless Gorman daringly signed Young to an expensive contract before the 1991 season, one of 3 handed out by the Sox that winter. Young's control problems with the Sox were no surprise, though he did show occasional flashes of dominance. His unpredictability made him unusually difficult to hit against, and he would frequently pitch himself both into and out of trouble, nervewracking as it was to watch.

Many critics felt that Young's control problems were psychological in nature, a theory that was supported by his erratic throws to bases. Most lefthanders, with first base in their line of sight when they prepare to pitch, are able to control baserunners more easily than righties. Young had an actual phobia about throwing the ball to bases, which led to horribly wild throws and baserunners taking advantage of him by confidently moving up. He experienced similar trouble whenever the ball was bunted or hit back to the mound and he had to throw out a runner. At one point he had regular consultations with a psychiatrist to help end this affliction, but it never led to any noticeable improvement.

Young's difficulties were epitomized in a heartbreaking game in Cleveland on April 12, 1992. Showing wild movement on his pitches, Young no-hit the Indians for 8 innings but allowed two runs as a result of seven walks, six stolen bases (four by speedster Kenny Lofton) and an error by shortstop Luis Rivera. Sox hitters were no help, leaving eleven men on base. The final result was an unbelievable 2–1 loss. (Because of a change in baseball rules, the game does not count as an official no-hitter.) It was only the second time in major league history that a pitcher lost a game without allowing a hit. The first came from the Yankees' Andy Hawkins on July 1, 1990.

Bob Zupcic—a young outfielder with strong defensive skills who spent parts of 4 seasons with the Sox in the early 1990s. While he hit 18 homers at AAA Pawtucket, his swing seemed to slow down upon reaching the major leagues, and he never exhibited the consistent power that his early performance promised. He did, however, hit 2 late-inning grand slams in the week following his callup to the Sox in 1992, tying the major league record for most grand slams in a season by a rookie.

QUOTES

Here are a few of the most interesting things said by or about the Red Sox over the years.

"We'll win more than we lose."
New Red Sox manager Dick Williams at the end of spring training in 1967. The Sox had been at least 18 games under .500 in each of the previous 3 years, and hadn't had a winning record since 1957.

"The sun will rise, the sun will set, and I'll have lunch."
Sox GM Lou Gorman on Roger Clemens walking out of training camp in 1987 as part of a contract dispute.

"That's what they get for building a ballpark next to the ocean."
Dennis "Oil Can" Boyd after the Red Sox win a fog-shortened game against the Indians at Municipal stadium in Cleveland, on the shores of Lake Erie.

"Will not play anywhere but Boston."
Text of a telegram from Babe Ruth as reported in the Boston Globe *by Ruth's agent Johnny Igoe. At the time, Ruth had already agreed to terms with the Yankees.*

"Blow it up. Blow the damned place up."
Red Sox first baseman Mo Vaughn, talking about Fenway Park in a 1995 interview.

"Hub Fans Bid Kid Adieu"
Title of an essay written by novelist John Updike upon the event of Ted Williams's final game. Updike was in the stands that day.

"What would we do with Willie McGee?"
Sox GM Lou Gorman during the 1990 season, when the American League West-leading A's picked up former batting champion Willie McGee.

"The price tag goes up every day."
Sox first baseman Mo Vaughn as he and the Sox were locked in a prolonged contract struggle during spring training of the 1998 season.

"My pitcher asked out of the game."
Red Sox manager John McNamara, following the sixth game of the 1986 World Series, about Roger Clemens who left in the eighth inning with a 3–2 lead. Clemens had a bleeding blister on his pitching hand, but denies that he asked to come out.

"A lyric little bandbox of a ballpark."
Novelist John Updike's description of Fenway.

"They killed our fathers and now the sons of bitches are coming after us."
Anonymous Sox fan after the 1978 playoff game loss to the Yankees.

"The twilight of his career . . . "
General manager Dan Duquette's assessment of pitcher Roger Clemens after the 1996 season when Clemens signed with Toronto rather than re-sign with the Sox. Clemens won the American League Cy Young award in both 1997 and 1998.

"If a frog had wings, he wouldn't bump his booty when he hopped."
Manager Jimy Williams at a press conference introducing him to the Boston media.

"Go crack me open a beer, I'll only be a minute."
Red Sox reliever Dick Radatz to starter Earl Wilson on the mound at Yankee Stadium. Radatz struck out Micky Mantle, Roger Maris, and Elston Howard on 10 pitches.

"There'll be no niggers on this ball club as long as I have anything to say about it."
Sox player, manager, and general manager Pinky Higgins.

"Good things happen to some people."
Earl Wilson, the first black player to pitch for the Red Sox, commenting on the death of former Sox manager and general manager Pinky Higgins.

"When Georgie-Porgie speaks, I don't listen."
Sox manager Jimy Williams after being accused by Yankee owner George Steinbrenner of "inciting" the crowd during the fifth game of the 1999 American League Championship Series.

"25 players, 25 cabs."
Description of the lack of clubhouse unity on the Red Sox teams of the early 1970s.

"I was worried about the horse."
Red Sox president John Harrington after being asked if he was concerned about seeing Mo Vaughn on a policeman's horse following the Sox clinching of the American League East in 1995.

"The kid's got ice water in his veins."

Red Sox manager Don Zimmer about rookie pitcher Bobby Sprowl before the fourth game of a crucial series against the Yankees in 1978. Sprowl faced only six batters and gave up four walks and a hit.

"Go, go, go!"
What Denny Doyle heard in Game 6 of the 1975 World Series from third base coach Don Zimmer before being thrown out at the plate in the last of the ninth inning.

"No, no, no!"
What Zimmer claims to have said.

"There are a lot of things that are a disadvantage to a family there."
Roger Clemens speaking of Boston in a live TV interview with Boston station WCVB in December 1988. Clemens was speaking in the wake of Bruce Hurst's decision to leave, and complained, among other things, of players having to carry their own bags through airports. It was the beginning of a big rift between Clemens and the Boston fans, and many still have not forgiven him.

"No one's worth that, but if they want to pay me, I'm certainly not going to turn it down."
Bill Campbell after the Red Sox made the reliever one of the first big money free agents in 1977 by signing him to a five-year $1 million contract.

"Pesky held the ball."
Johnny Pesky was said by broadcasters to have held the ball too long on Enos Slaughter's "mad dash" for home during Game 7 of the 1946 World Series.

"One of my superstitions is I'm not allowed to talk about them."
Nomar Garciaparra, who has a reputation for following many rituals to keep his game focused.

"Do they leave it there during games?"
Bill Lee the first time he saw the Green Monster.

"The worst curse in life is unlimited potential."
Ken Brett, a journeyman pitcher whose brother, Hall of Famer George Brett, said Ken was the best hitter in the family.

"A man has to have goals and that was mine, to have people say, 'There goes Ted Williams, the greatest hitter who ever lived.' "
Ted Williams.

"He has muscles in his hair."
Lefty Gomez, describing Jimmie Foxx's strength.

"I'm in the twilight of a mediocre career."
Red Sox pitcher Frank Sullivan.

"I loved the game. I loved the competition. But I never had any fun. I never enjoyed it. All hard work, all the time."
Carl Yastrzemski.

"The wrecking of this once famous ballclub is a crime and somebody ought to put an end to such methods."
A New York City newspaper in 1920 after the Red Sox kept selling players to the Yankees.

"Too much importance is placed on the starting pitchers. It's much more important to have a finishing pitcher."
Red Sox manager Joe McCarthy.

"I don't want my players to hustle too much in the spring."
Player/manager Joe Cronin, 1938.

"Bobby Doerr and not Ted Williams is the number one man of the Red Sox in my book."
Babe Ruth in 1946.

"He's an All Star from the neck down."
White Sox manager Eddie Stanky on Carl Yastrzemski in early 1967.

"I'll be back soon and make more money than all three of you together."
Ted Williams to taunting Red Sox players after being sent to the minors in 1938.

"All literary men are Red Sox fans. To be a Yankee fan in literary society is to endanger your life."
Author John Cheever.

"I still think neckties are designed to get in your soup."
Ted Williams.

"Left-handed pitchers are the only people in their right minds."
Bill Lee.

"If the Lord were a pitcher, he would pitch like Pedro."
First baseman David Segui, son of former Red Sox pitcher Diego Segui, discussing Pedro Martinez.

THE FENWAY EXPERIENCE

What is the Fenway experience? Perhaps it begins in the dark of the offseason, walking down Landsdowne street and looking up at the backside of the Green Monster, the looming, stretching images of the lights, darkened for winter, waiting for spring. The nightclubs and shadowed streets do their business even when there is no baseball, when the ballpark is quiet in its hibernation. Crowds ebb and flow through Kenmore Square without any thought or concern for the sleeping park off to the side. It is different in the winter, when a person traveling up Commonwealth Avenue does not occasionally hear the roar of the crowd even over the traffic, like a wave sweeping through the Fens.

Perhaps it begins with the opening of the box office, when people line the length of the street in the cold, the children restless and chilled but keeping warm with games of tag, their parents peering at schedules and murmuring questions about whether or not the Yankee games might be sold out by the time they get to the head of the line, and what other games they might want to get tickets to see.

But the Fenway experience is most fundamentally the experience of game day, the gathering of the people and the slow, graceful unfolding of the game of baseball. The Fenway experience is the snarl of traffic through the Fens, the group of twenty Cub Scouts with baseball gloves tucked under their arms occupying half of a commuter rail car until they're herded out onto the Yawkey Station platform by the tall form of their Scout Leader, the tight-packed clusters of people in their blue jackets with red lettering, their blue caps with the red B, exploding out of the green line trolleys and surging up the steps into the light of Kenmore Square.

The Fenway experience is climbing up over the bridge that spans the Pike and the rail line and being greeted by the vendors with their "Yankees Suck" T-shirts and baseball caps and the sound of the kid who turns over a few buckets and pans and beats on them with such skill and enthusiasm that the music is far more powerful than the fact that his materials are makeshift.

The Fenway experience is walking through crowds along Brookline Avenue, past fast-moving men with sharp eyes who bob alone through the traffic muttering, "Tickets? Tickets? Tickets?" and past kids trying to sell off tickets while terrified of being caught by a cop, and past people desperately trying to get tickets or sell them if the game is sold out (if the Yankees are playing, or if Pedro Martinez is pitching).

The Fenway experience is getting a ticket from one of those scared kids, and giving him more than he wanted because he couldn't make change, and because getting the ticket and getting in to the game mattered more than the extra few dollars.

The Fenway experience is going with a group of people who have scrounged their money from the seats of college dorm sofas to make the trip into Boston and getting tickets to claim a corner of the upper grandstand on a bright, sunny day in May.

The Fenway experience is getting tickets to an early game and huddling in the cold clear spot in Section 18 with a perfect view of the field.

The experience is in waiting for the gates to open among the bustle and activity of the other people waiting, the vendors, the scalpers, the casual passer-by. Perhaps it's waiting in a nearby bar until near game time; or then again perhaps it's browsing in the Twins store and prowling in among jerseys numbered 5 and 45 while being watched by the figures on the posters. It's in picking up the current copy of *Boston Baseball* to get the articles and have a new scoresheet for the game and hearing, down the way, the cry of "Pizza! Fried Shrimp! Fried Clams! Steak and Cheese!"

It's in turning up early and watching batting practice, with the stuff strewn across the field and each batter in turn popping a long sequence of baseballs across the field. Sometimes, they reach the nets over the Green Monster and earn a smattering of applause.

It comes in seeing the clusters of children pressed up against the wall near the dugouts, hoping that the players are coming out to sign their cards, their pieces of paper, their baseballs and gloves.

It comes in being there and pointing out the features of the park to someone who does not know them: the right-field foul pole? That's Pesky's Pole, named for John Michael Paveskovich, shortstop. That red chair way up there? That's where Ted Williams's home run hit the man in the straw hat. The bullpens? That's Williamsburg.

The Fenway experience is coming into the park with a love of the team and only knowing the name of one of the players, and discovering that that player is the starting pitcher for the day.

The Fenway experience is coming in to the park with a head full of stats and figures and making muttering noises at batters who are known to swing at balls far outside and continue to do so.

The Fenway experience is keeping score in a program with a pen that keeps running out of ink, and explaining to the nearby people what the arcane markings mean. It's keeping track of the gameplay for the other fans in the bleachers, and rattling off who the runners on base are when they've lost track, and how they got there. It's joining a section of some thirty people who are surrounding a visitor to the park who seems to speak not much English with what might be guessed is a French accent, and explaining to him what's happening in the game, listing off balls and strikes, the nuance of a foul ball after two strikes, the number of outs, the flow of the game: the entire group within earshot, not just the people who came with him, sharing the enthusiasm and the love of the game, sometimes in English a little too fast for him to follow.

It's in sitting in the bleachers up near the centerfield wall watching Pedro Martinez pitch against whatever team you hate most. It's in cheering the crowd of people wearing red—the K-Men—who post the big red Ks for Pedro's strikeouts, and after the first three are pressed up against the wall, and the stickum set by rubbing the corners with the end of a red umbrella, counting them off in a resounding chant that eventually is taken up by the entire upper bleachers: "One! Two! Three! Uno! Dos! Tres! Cuatro!"

It's in seeing the six guys without shirts, who have NOMAR painted across their chests and PEDRO painted across their backs, and who are painting a K on their remaining companion with each strikeout, as a living memorial to the game.

It's in watching The Wave sweep around Fenway until it stalls out in one strike against the Green Monster over in left field and just never makes the transition, or possibly even joining in. It's in seeing the signs that people make and wave at the cameras, the players, the other fans in the stadium.

The Fenway experience is meeting people one knows from elsewhere, finding them there for the sake of the game. Or coming with a friend (how better to get some hot chocolate in a cold April game than to send the other person in the party to go stand in line?) and rattling discussion back and forth about the progress of the game. Or coming alone and talking game with the people nearby.

The Fenway experience is razzing the Yankees fans who turn up—sometimes politely, sometimes not. The Fenway experience is being told to stop chanting at the Yankees fans because of the presence of kids.

The Fenway experience is taunting the players on the field with cries of "Bull-pen! Bull-pen!" when their pitchers struggle, or with the jubilant shout of "Wall ball!" when someone doubles off the Monster.

The Fenway experience is the howl of "Lou!" as Merloni comes to bat, or the rippling song of "Jose!" to the tune of the soccer anthem, "Alé," when Offerman is at the plate.

The Fenway experience is a double down the line to left, landing fair by a hand's breadth and rolling to the wall.

The Fenway experience is a Garciaparra leap to catch a ball that was surely gone otherwise, limbs windmilling, and a sudden, breathless landing.

The Fenway experience is a bang-bang double play, bases then mysteriously empty of runners, the pitcher on the mound catching his breath and going for the last out.

The Fenway experience is a ball lobbed into the triangle and barely caught, a foul into the right field stands chased by the right fielder like a heat-seeking missile, a skid on the grass and a three-base error.

The Fenway experience is a ball hit on what looks to be a perfectly straight line, rising, rising, rising, and barely dropping into the net over the Green Monster. The Fenway experience is a pitcher turning around with a look of dismay to watch that ball rise.

The Fenway experience is sometimes a blow-out victory, unadulterated triumph, glory for all told. Or perhaps it is an infuriating, heartbreaking loss, shut down by some pitcher who will never have a good game in the major leagues again. Or a game lost in a sudden implosion of defense in the eighth inning. Or a game won with yet another last-minute comeback—or lost because that comeback fell just a little short.

The Fenway experience is the ripples of "Dirty Water" played over the PA and sung, mostly on-key, by the fans as they file out and into the streets.

The Fenway experience is also silence, and tomorrow's game.

Getting to Fenway (and Parking)

Fenway isn't the most convenient place to get to by mass transit, but it is accessible. The parking situation around Fenway Park is hideous, however. The easiest way to get to the park by car is to park near a subway or trolley line and take the train to the park. The Red Sox also have a discount ticket arrangement with the Prudential Center parking garage.

By Car—Take the Mass Pike (Route 90) into Boston. Get off at exit 22 (Prudential Center/Copley Place) and follow the signs into the Prudential Center parking garage. If you park 2 hours or less before game time and show the attendant your ticket stub, you will get a discounted parking rate (currently $7.00). If you come earlier and want to check out the sights, expect to pay about 3 times as much to park, but at least your car will be safe and indoors. When you leave the parking garage, ask someone for directions to Massachusetts Avenue (it will depend on where you exit the garage). Turn right on Mass Ave. and then left on Commonwealth Ave., which will lead you to Kenmore Square. Follow the crowds to Fenway Park. Fenway is about a 10-minute walk from the parking garage.

By Train—On game days, certain trains on the Framingham/Worcester commuter rail line stop at Yawkey Station. This stop is well-announced by the conductors and located between the Back Bay and Newtonville stations. Yawkey Station is located between Brookline Avenue and Beacon Street right in front of Fenway Park. This line originates at South Station, which is on the Red Line of the MBTA, with stops at the Back Bay train station, in Newtonville, West Newton, Auburndale, Wellesley Farms, Wellesley Hills, Wellesley Square, Natick, West Natick, and Framingham; certain trains also reach Grafton and Worcester. In general, the two trains immediately before game time will stop at Yawkey Station, and the two trains after the projected end of the games will also stop there. Schedules for the trains can be picked up at South Station and the Back Bay, or accessed online at *http://www.mbta.com/text-only/schedmaps/comm/worcsc.cfm*.

By Bus—There are four buses that terminate in Kenmore Square: 8, 57, 60, and 65. Route 8 runs from the U. Mass campus at Harbor Point through the South End medical area and past Dudley Station. Route 57 originates in Watertown Square and runs through Newton Corner and Brighton Center, traveling the length of Commonwealth Avenue. The 60 comes from Chestnut Hill, goes through Brookline Hills and Brookline proper, and, in fact, follows Brookline Street directly in front of Fenway Park. The 65 bus begins in Brookline Center near St. Elizabeth's Hospital and follows Washington Street until it also picks up Brookline Street and does its final run towards Kenmore in front of Fenway. Bus fare is 75 cents.

By Subway—The nearest subway station to Fenway Park is the Kenmore Square station on the B, C, and D branches of the Green Line of the MBTA. E line trains do not go to Kenmore. The branch of the train is listed on the front and sides of the trolley; additionally, at the Park Street station (transfer point for the Red Line), westbound trains stop only at places marked for their branch. The Kenmore Square station has sign directions towards Fenway Park, and traffic flow will be moving in that direction near game time. It is a very good idea to buy a return token before leaving the station, as a large proportion of the people attending the game will be leaving by T, and a goodly number of those won't have gotten their tokens ahead of time. This makes for long lines.

All of the other subway lines intersect directly with the Green Line at at least one point. The Red Line intersects with it at Park Street, which is a very busy transfer station as the Red and Green Lines carry most of the MBTA's traffic. (The Red Line runs from Alewife through Somerville and Cambridge, under South Station, the terminus for the southern commuter rail lines, and splits, with spurs going to Ashmont and Braintree.) The Orange Line runs parallel to the green, sharing stations in the North End at North Station and Haymarket, and also is connected to Park Street via a walkway between Downtown Crossing and Park. (The Orange Line runs from Oak Grove and Malden to Forest Hills.) The Blue Line, serving Logan Airport and the North Shore out to Wonderland, transfers to the Green at Government Center. T fare is $1.00, except at the extreme southern end of the Red Line and the extreme western end of the Green.

By Air—There is a regular shuttle service between all terminals of Logan Airport and the Airport station on the blue line of the T. Visitors can acquire short-term T and bus passes at the Airport station, if they are interested in them. Logan is also well-provided with taxi stands and car rental agencies.

A Shameless Plug

If you would like to know more about Boston-area museums, the same editorial staff responsible for *The Red Sox Fan Handbook* has produced *The New England Museum Guide* (ISBN 1-931013-06-3), which contains information on hundreds of museums throughout New England, along with directions to all of them. Find it at your local bookstore, or visit www.swordsmith.com to find out more.

Where to Sit

There are good and bad things about sitting in a 90-year-old ballpark. All of the seats in Fenway are small and cramped, with metal armrests that may poke into you uncomfortably if you don't have the same dimensions as the typical World War I-era adult. On the other hand, most of the seats are close to the field and give you a better view of the game than in more modern parks, which are designed with more of an eye toward luxury box revenue than toward the needs of typical fans. And even though Fenway Park is close to full for most games, it's relatively easy to get good seats—without having to resort to ticket scalpers.

Most of the seats at Fenway are good, with the conspicuous exception of the right field box seats. Most of those seats face the right fielder, so if you sit in them you have to turn your neck to see the plate, and will have a stiff neck by the end of the game. During evening games, the setting sun will be in your eyes when you look toward home plate for the first few innings.

If you want the bleacher experience (the cheapest seats in the house) the best bleacher seats are in sections 34, 35, and 36. These seats look directly over the center fielder's shoulder and give a good view of all the action.

Getting Tickets

You can order Sox tickets by mail, fax, phone, through the team's touch-tone ticketing service, over the Internet, or in person. The best ways are usually by phone or in person—when you can talk to a staff member and ask questions about available seating before making your choice. Online, fax, and touch-tone tickets give you fewer options; you can pick an area of the park where you want to sit, but the team will assign you seats within that area, and you may end up with poor seats that you would not have chosen. For instance, if you're on the phone with a ticket agent and ask for a seat in section 15, the agent can tell you that the only seats left are obstructed view, and will suggest seats in another area if you ask. If you order online, by mail, or by fax, you will be assigned the obstructed view seats. Note that the Sox charge a $6 handling fee on phone, fax, and online ticket orders.

No matter how you order, you'll want to specify what section of the park you want to sit in. If you don't have a preference, you may be steered to less-desirable seats in right field. If you want seats against the Yankees, be sure to order early; Yankee games tend to sell out quickly. Tickets usually go on ale in early January.

Here's how to order Red Sox tickets:

> You can order Sox tickets by phone at 617-267-1700, or use 617-482-4SOX for the 24-hour touch-tone ticketing system (617-236-6644 is the TDD number). If you want more than 40 tickets, call 617-262-1915.

> You can fax a ticket order to the team at 617-236-6640. Download a ticket order form from http://www.redsox.com/tickets/buyingtickets.html#fax. Orders of 40 or more should be faxed to 617-236-6496.

> You can order tickets online at http://www.redsox.com/tickets/gateway.html.

> Tickets can be ordered by mail from Boston Red Sox Ticket Office, 4 Yawkey Way, Boston, MA 02215-3496.

> Disabled fans can call 617-267-1700 or can order in person at the ticket window. Tickets for fans with disabilities must be purchased at least 3 days in advance.

> Or you can order in person at the Fenway ticket window from 9:00 AM to 5:00 PM Monday to Saturday (617-267-1700).

Ticket prices for 2001 Red Sox games at Fenway Park are as follows:

upper bleachers	$18
lower bleachers	$20
outfield grandstand	$25
right field boxes	$30
right field roof	$30
infield grandstand	$40
loge box seats	$55
field box seats	$55
infield roof box seats	$55

Some discounted tickets are also available, mainly as part of package deals or special promotions. The team also sells gift certificates.

If you want to buy tickets on the spur of the moment for that day's game you should go to the ticket office. Often very good seats are available at the last minute, even for sold out games (usually from season ticket holders who are unable to attend the game). Be sure to check with the ticket office before buying tickets from a scalper, since the ticket office is likely to have better seats.

While the Boston police seem to tolerate some scalpers around the park, be very careful about selling tickets because of Massachusetts's strict ban on ticket sales by unlicensed agents. In one well-publicized case, a priest taking a youth group on an outing was arrested for trying to sell a spare ticket at face value. The DA's office usually won't prosecute these arrests, and they've been laughed out of court on the occasions they got that far, but you don't want to spend the game filling out paperwork at a police station.

The View Inside Fenway

Some of Fenway's legendary features are detailed below, along with a few snippets from the park's storied past.

The Green Monster
"The Green Monster," also known simply as "The Wall," is the 37-foot wall that extends from the left field foul pole to almost dead center field and is perhaps Fenway Park's most famous feature. It is topped by a 23-foot net that catches most home runs hit over it. The foul pole is marked as 311 feet from home where the wall starts in left field, but has been rumored for years to be even closer to the plate. The nickname "Green Monster" comes from the dark green paint that has nearly always adorned the wall.

The wall contains a real oddity in this day of multimillion-dollar electronic scoreboards: a simple scoreboard run by two people actually inside the wall. They keep score by listening to games on the radio and by looking through a small slit in the wall.

Another notable feature of the Green Monster is the ladder 13 feet up the wall in left center that is used by groundskeepers to retrieve balls hit into the screen during batting practice—during games, balls hit into the screen have been known to rattle around and confound outfielders. Very rarely balls will be hit off the ladder, causing wild bounces that fielders have no way to anticipate.

There is also a garage door in the center field area of the Green Monster. This door was once used by maintenance staff to drive a baseball-shaped golf cart onto the field and out to the bullpens to pick up and deliver relief pitchers to the pitching mound. This has been long since done away with, and relief pitchers now walk from the right field bullpens to the pitching mound.

Possibly the greatest myth about the Green Monster is that it creates many cheap home runs. While the occasional "normal fly ball out" does indeed drift over the wall, at least as many (probably several more, depending on the style of hitter) rising line drives will bang off the wall to become mere doubles, or even singles. What the wall does create is an unusually high number of doubles. As with Pesky's

Pole, the wall can work for or against the home team. And contrary to what has become a fairly widespread belief, there is no such thing as a ground-rule triple at Fenway Park.

Left Field Stands
About halfway between the wall and third base the stands jut out to just a few inches from fair territory. This not only gives fans sitting in this area a bird's-eye view but can become a nightmare for baserunners inexperienced in Fenway's many quirks. Balls are known to be called fair as they pass third base, but bounce off the stands afterward—thus caroming in reach of the left fielder faster than in other parks. This results in many runners being thrown out while going for seemingly sure doubles. Where the wall and the stands (which are by then as high as the wall) meet is also a problem for left fielders, as there is almost no room to catch balls hit down the foul line. Fan interference can also cause problems here.

Right-field Façade
Over the right-field grandstand, there is a façade on the roof where the retired numbers of past Red Sox greats are displayed. The numbers are red, like the numbers on the home uniforms, and displayed on circular fields of white. The team has specific rules on how numbers are retired. Players must be members of the Hall of Fame who played at least ten seasons in—and finished their careers with—the Red Sox. From the time that Williams's #9 was retired until 1997, the numbers were displayed in the order that they were retired. 9 (Williams), 4 (Joe Cronin), 1 (Bobby Doerr), and 8 (Carl Yastrzemski). In 1997, they were re-ordered numerically. The team denied that any superstition was involved with the re-ordering, but believers in the "curse of the Bambino" had long noted that the 9-4-1-8 on the façade was the eve of the last World Series win for the Sox (the 1918 World Series began on September 5, 1918—9-5-18.)

Also in 1997, number 42 was added to honor Jackie Robinson. Major League Baseball retired Robinson's number for all teams in both leagues upon the fiftieth anniversary of Robinson breaking the color barrier, though the twelve players wearing the number (including Boston's Mo Vaughn) were allowed to keep wearing it. Number 42 is numbered in blue, and slightly separated from the red numbers representing Sox players.

In 2000, the Red Sox retired Carlton Fisk's #27, bringing the total number of retired numbers on the façade to the current 6. In order to do this, the team needed to stretch the self-imposed rules somewhat, and Dan Duquette's hiring of Fisk as a special assistant was considered to meet the requirement that the career finish in Boston. If Jim Rice is elected to the Hall of Fame, his #14 will go up soon thereafter.

The Pesky Pole
One of Fenway Park's most legendary quirks, Pesky's Pole is the right field "foul" pole that stands a scant 302 feet from home plate. Though right field continues to arc deeper (thus the quirk) beyond the pole, fly balls that would be outs—or at least stay

in most parks—frequently curl around this pole for home runs that can be considered cheaper than those over the notorious "Green Monster" in left. Whether this pole has resulted in more "good" (i.e., by the Sox) or "bad" (i.e., by their opponents) home runs will be forever debated. The nickname for the pole comes from 1950s Red Sox infielder Johnny Pesky, who curled several of his rare homers around the pole.

Morse Code
On the scoreboard there are dots and dashes of green on two of the vertical white stripes. These are the initials TAY and JRY, for longtime owners Thomas A. Yawkey and Jean R. Yawkey, spelled out in Morse Code.

Duffy's Cliff
In the early years of Fenway Park, the 25-foot wooden wall in left field was fronted by a 10-foot slope. This feature was initially constructed to allow spectators to stand and see down onto the field over people in front of them. Sox left fielder George "Duffy" Lewis became adept at scrambling up the embankment to make plays. Cartoons of the day portrayed him as cavorting among mountain goats and snowcaps to field a fly ball; because of his prowess, the hill became known as "Duffy's Cliff." Unfortunately, Duffy's Cliff was flattened during the 1934 refurbishment of Fenway Park.

Williamsburg and the Center Field Triangle
In 1940 the team constructed new bullpens at Fenway Park, ostensibly for the purpose of giving the pitchers a better place to warm up. Prior to that, they had to use the meager foul territory or loosen up under the grandstand. However, the main purpose was rumored to have been to move the right field wall 23 feet closer to home plate as a target for Ted Williams. The new bullpens were unofficially dubbed "Williamsburg." One of the interesting eccentricities of the playing field was formed by the addition of the bullpens. The end of the pen slants back to a point where it meets the center field wall. The area formed by these two walls meeting is triangular in shape and thus called the Center Field Triangle, or just The Triangle.

The Red Seat
There is, in the sea of green seats in the right field bleachers, a red seat. This is the seat located at the spot, 502 feet from home plate, where Ted Williams is alleged to have hit a home run that ruined the straw hat of one of the patrons in June of 1946. Neither Williams—nor anyone else—has ever hit a ball over the roof above the right field grandstand, where the retired numbers of Red Sox greats are displayed.

Past Fires
Twice in its early years, Fenway Park suffered serious fire damage. In May 1926 the bleachers along the foul line in left field burned down and were not initially replaced. This actually allowed—for a brief time—left fielders to make plays on foul balls behind the third base grandstand. Then in January 1934, fire swept through the park

again, destroying nearly all of the construction then underway to refurbish the park. The refurbishment continued and the park reopened in April of 1934.

Where to Eat

There are dozens—if not hundreds—of restaurants offering everything from the latest in fusion cuisine, to whatever sort of ethnic food one might desire to New England staples such as Boston's famous clam chowder, to various fast food chains, both in Boston and around Fenway Park itself. The following is by no means a complete list (as restaurants go in and out of business, change personnel and/or menus, or are displaced by construction) of places to eat in Boston or the Fenway Park area— merely a few suggestions to get you started.

BOSTON BREW WORKS—located across the street from Fenway, Boston Brew Works boasts a large selection of specialty beers (some brewed on the premises) as well as an extensive menu heavy on appetizers and out-of-the-ordinary pizzas. The Brew Works is often very crowded before games with a correspondingly high noise level; IDs are stringently checked at the door. If you have to wait for a table, the staff will give you a beeper and let you roam the restaurant (or sit at the bar section and get a start on perusing the beer special board) until your table is ready. It's not the cheapest restaurant in the world, but it's a good one.

INDIA QUALITY RESTAURANT—located on Comm (Commonwealth) Ave. on the way to the ballpark, India Quality is open both before and after the game, and provides consistent if not extraordinary Indian food at a reasonable price for a Boston restaurant.

CASK AND FLAGON—a popular gathering spot game-goers will pass on the way to the ballpark; lines waiting to get in spill out the doors and mingle with the crowd heading for Fenway.

CROMWELL'S—also located on Comm Ave. on the way to the ballpark, Cromwell's is a traditional British-style pub with a great beer selection.

Outside Fenway Park—want roasted peanuts? Sausages? Kielbasa? Hot dogs? Buffalo wings? The various vendors set up permanently outside the park can provide all those and more if you want to sit or stand on the curb outside Fenway munching on your food of choice and listening to the program hawkers trying to outshout the cries of "Tickets? Anybody need tickets?"

Inside Fenway Park—if you don't want to sit in the stands and have bags of peanuts tossed to you by a vendor with a rifle arm or wait for his tireless leather-lunged cohorts to make their way up and down the ballpark with their cargoes of hot dogs,

Cracker Jack, cotton candy, cold soda, or ice cream, venture into the concourse inside Fenway and choose from a large array of foods. Legal Seafoods has a stand in Fenway, as do several other chains; if you're in the mood for pizza, hot dogs, fries, or Chinese, you can get it in the ballpark. Eating and drinking at the ballpark is not cheap, however. Beer drinkers should be aware that the only beers available (ID required; beer sales are cut off partway through the game) are domestic.

Souvenirs

TWINS STORES—a souvenir store monopoly across from the park (all 3 stores are owned by the same family). Ninety percent of the stores are reserved for Red Sox fan items (you name it, they have it), but there is a small corner with souvenirs for "other teams."

LANSDOWNE SHOP—the official Red Sox souvenir store located within Fenway (under the left field grandstand), the Lansdowne shop carries only merchandise that the team and league approves of, so don't expect to buy the infamous "1918 World Champions" t-shirts here. The shop doesn't open until shortly before games, and you can only use it from *inside* Fenway Park.

Street Vendors—vendors set up outside Fenway sell ballcaps, programs, and other baseball paraphernalia for the Red Sox as well as other teams. The prices are usually cheap, but the quality varies dramatically. If you really want a "Yankees Suck" T-shirt, odds are you can find it on the way to Fenway.

Other Things You Should Know

New England tends to be cool at night even during the summer. Daytime temperatures can be in the eighties and drop down to the fifties in the evening. It's wise to bring a sweater or light jacket if you're going to a night game—you'll be more comfortable in the late innings, and any non-fans with you won't be agitating to leave early.

As in any crowded surrounding, exercise sensible precautions: don't leave your wallet in a back pocket, keep an eye on your children and/or personal belongings, and be alert when using the ATMs on the way to, or inside, Fenway. There is a first aid station within Fenway; park personnel make periodic announcements as to where parents should look for lost children and/or where children finding themselves lost should go for help.

What Else to Do While You're in Boston

Boston, as a city, is probably best explored by the T. The subway not only has stations just about anywhere a person would want to go, but is a historical and cultural entity all its own; there are musicians frequenting a number of the major downtown stations and playing with a hat out; some of the stations are graced with art projects, and the system, while occasionally catankerous, is an excellent place for people-watching. Fare is a dollar a ride; however, at various central locations and access points (such as the Airport Station on the Blue Line) multi-day passes can be purchased for several days at a time, enabling a maximum amount of tourist exploration at a minimum cost.

Green Places to Visit

THE PUBLIC GARDENS (Arlington, Green Line): A pond and surrounding area, possibly best known for their role in Robert McCloskey's children's book *Make Way for Ducklings*. Statues of the famed Mrs. Mallard and her young march along beside one of the paths towards the pond. Small children may also want to ride on the Swan Boats—large, slow-moving man-powered boats adorned with a large sculpted swan; passage around the lake is moderately expensive, as is the mediocre popcorn to feed the local duck population.

BOSTON COMMON (Park Street, Green/Red Junction; Boylston Station, Green Line): Broad, open green space with a pond for winter skating; popular for such things as games of Frisbee and catch. Borders on the Boston Garden on the western side.

THE CHARLES RIVER (most direct access from Kendall Square and Charles/MGH, Red Line): The river is lined on both sides with bike paths and occasional benches, nice for a long, pleasant walk in good weather. Among other things to see in the city is the HARVARD BRIDGE, so named, apparently, because it goes from Boston proper into Cambridge, directly to MIT. The Harvard Bridge is somewhat infamous, as its length is measured in *Smoots*, a unit of measurement derived from the height of one Oliver Smoot, pledge at the Lambda Chi Alpha fraternity; the length of the bridge is 364.4 Smoots and one ear. (A Smoot is approximately five feet seven inches.)

THE BACK BAY FENS (nearest to Hynes Convention Center, Symphony, and Museum, Green Line): One of the Emerald Necklace parks designed by Frederick Law Olmsted, the Fens stretch between the BOSTON CONSERVATORY OF MUSIC and Simmons College, and are located behind Fenway Park. Originally a saltwater marsh and now a freshwater one, the region is a string of gardens that are impressive in bloom. (The other parks in the Emerald Necklace are Franklin Park, the Arnold Arboretum, Jamaica Park, Olmsted Park, and the Riverway. See *http://www.emeraldnecklace.org/* for details.)

Things to Do

THE MUSEUM OF FINE ARTS (Museum, Green Line): Collections of art from all over the world, with strong historical sections as well as modern exhibits. (See http://www.mfa.org/ for details.)

THE NEW ENGLAND AQUARIUM (Aquarium, Blue Line): A good-sized aquarium, with a wide variety of exhibits, including ecological studies and a recently installed habitat for a number of different species of penguin.(See http://www.neaq.org/ for details.)

THE MUSEUM OF SCIENCE (Science Park, Green Line): A bit run-down in places, but with interactive stuff here and there that has the potential to amuse. (See http://www.mos.org/ for details.)

THE BOSTON CHILDREN'S MUSEUM/COMPUTER MUSEUM (South Station, Red Line): Two museums located in the same building, across the Fort Point Channel from South Station.

THE ISABELLA STEWART GARDNER MUSEUM: Mrs. Gardner was a wealthy socialite who lived at the turn of the 20th century in Boston and gathered art from all over Europe. In the center courtyard of her "palace" is a plaza with fountain and Greek statuary. The stairways, ceilings and railings all came from various European palaces. Despite the loss of one of the most famous pieces, Rembrandt's *Storm On The Sea Of Galilee*, during a brazen robbery in 1990, it is still a marvelous sanctuary in the city, with fabulous works of art all around. For more information, see http://www.boston.com/gardner/.

THE FREEDOM TRAIL (Park Street, Red and Green Lines): This path meanders through historical Boston, to a number of Revolutionary War era sites. The truly devoted may wish to pick up the trail somewhere (near Park Street is one of the easy places to find it); alternately, a wander through the downtown area will almost inevitably cross the red line marked down the center of the sidewalk, and so those areas of historical interest are easy enough to find.

COPLEY SQUARE (Copley, Green Line): Home of TRINITY CHURCH and the BOSTON PUBLIC LIBRARY, both worth visiting.

Performances

THE THEATER DISTRICT (Boylston, Green Line): The theater district is adjacent to the Common; a number of Broadway shows make pre-Broadway runs through Boston before heading for New York. There are often seats available even on the day of the performance, though large parties may be split up, and many of those available seats have good odds of being restricted view.

Laser Shows/Omni Theater at the MUSEUM OF SCIENCE (Science Park, Green Line): The Museum of Science remains open after normal hours to keep the planetarium and theater open; the theater to show a selection of various, largely educational, Omni shows, and the planetarium for displays of laser art to music.

THE CHARLES PLAYHOUSE: One show that has taken Boston by storm is Blue Man Group, a surreal performance-art show currently running at the Charles Playhouse (74 Warrenton Street). The show features three bald men, spookily silent and covered with intense blue paint, engaging the audience in a flurry of wild multisensory trips involving sound, music, light, and classic comedy. Be forewarned that audience participation is a key component of the show. The result is an innovative collage of elements both stunning and hilarious, that will leave you breathless. The troupe occasionally rotates the themes of its shows, so if you like what you see, a return visit might be a good idea. The show is also running in New York, Chicago and Las Vegas. Tickets usually sell out in advance so grab them early. Call the Charles Playhouse at (617)931-2787 for more information.

Places to Shop

NEWBURY STREET (Hynes Convention Center, Green Line): A long path lined with new and used bookstores, assorted antique and generalized stuff shops, and restaurants, running from relatively prosaic at one end to fairly upscale at the other. An excellent meander, but food is probably better gotten elsewhere, as it is quite expensive.

HARVARD SQUARE (Harvard, Red Line): No longer the home of myriad different small shops, but still potentially worth visiting. Musicians often gather in The Pit, the space around the major exit from the T, as well as in the side streets and nearby Brattle Square. An excellent place for people-watching, with a few decent restaurants and small parks.

QUINCY MARKET (Haymarket, Green and Orange Lines): More a tourist trap than anything else, full of small booths selling kitsch at inflated prices and surrounded by chain stores. The food court has an excellent assortment of various food types, however, for about the prices to be expected of a food court.

Places to Eat Other Than Fenway Park

Again, this is by no means an exhaustive list of restaurants—just a few favorite places from some members of the editorial staff to give you a taste of the various restaurant options available in and around Boston.

BARTLEY'S (Harvard Square, Red Line): A few blocks walk down Mass Ave from the Pit exit to the Harvard Square T stop, Bartley's is a tiny, crowded, hamburger-and-good-food joint with personality; the walls are entirely covered with Boston memorabilia, peculiar posters, and plaques, in standard cluttered-bar style. An amusing menu with the odd political or social commentary in the burger toppings. Only accepts cash.

THE HARP (North Station, Green and Orange Lines): A pub and eating-house in among the crowded mess that is the street just outside of North Station. Tends to be a touch on the crowded side of an evening, but for a late afternoon lunch, a pretty good find. Moderately respectable dress required.

MARY CHUNG'S (Central, Red Line): An excellent Chinese restaurant on Mass (Massachusetts) Ave between Central Square and MIT. A bit out of the way for touristing, only accepts cash.

THE NORTH END (North Station and Haymarket, Green and Orange Lines): An exploration of the North End on foot will turn up about an Italian restaurant a block, varying in authenticity, style, and formality.

CHINATOWN (Downtown Crossing, Red and Orange Lines, Chinatown, Orange Line): As to be expected, quite full of Chinese restaurants, which vary greatly in quality; there are quite a few quick take-out places, and also some more formal.

MARCHÉ (Prudential/Hynes Convention Center, Green Line): Located near the Sheraton in the shopping center beneath the Prudential Tower, Marché is a unique dining experience. Patrons are handed a "passport" at the entry to the restaurant, and meander somewhat randomly among a number of booths—pasta, seafood, stir-fry, barbecue, crepes, soup and salad among them—selecting what they want to eat from a wide variety of options. At each station, the passport is stamped with information about what was acquired, and the entire meal is totted up upon departure. Each table has a small sign which can be flipped to one of three options—available, please clear, and reserved, so that other patrons do not take the table during any further explorations of the food available. The downstairs has a full bar with a variety of drinks and sometimes live music; below that is a market with fresh fruits, wines, chocolates, and newspapers. Open from 7:30 AM to 2:00 AM daily; middling to moderately expensive pricing, with the risk of major expense incurred by overly promiscuous exploration of the food available.

It started with baseball cards.

On Christmas Day 1987, when I was twelve, I came downstairs to find a baseball card starter kit. I had never asked for one; up until that point my experience with baseball had been limited to a few wiffle ball games with the neighborhood kids and one failed attempt at Little League when I was nine. (I bailed out on every pitch fearing the pitcher was more interested in killing me than getting me out. After three games I realized that no nine-year-old boy could throw a hard ball consistently for strikes. So I kept the bat on my shoulder for the remainder of the season and led the league in walks. "Good eye!" my coaches cheered, not realizing I had already given up on this confounding game.)

The kit itself was far from a gold mine, but it interested me enough to start buying baseball cards with my allowance. At the time most baseball cards came in wax-coated packages that gave off a sugary smell from the stale sticks of gum included inside. It didn't take me long to grow into the collecting habit; I eagerly memorized the information on the backs of the cards and organized them first by team then by player. Having gotten to know all about the players on the cards, I quickly yearned to see them in action, so I patiently waited for the baseball season to begin.

I already knew the basics surrounding the Red Sox. I knew that they had come astonishingly close to winning the World Series in 1986, and I knew all about Roger Clemens, Wade Boggs, Bob Stanley, Dwight Evans, Jim Rice, and Rich Gedman. Those guys had all been around a while so they needed little introduction. But as I watched more seriously I came across names that I had never seen before. They had just traded for a burly relief pitcher named Lee Smith. A lefthanded-hitting outfielder named Mike Greenwell got off to an early home run tear. By combining my fondness for underdogs and for players with interesting names, I settled my eyes on the team's starting shortstop, the light-hitting Spike Owen.

There was nothing dazzling about Owen's style of play, but that didn't stop him from becoming my favorite player. He wasn't very powerful but he ran pretty hard and was solid with the glove. While guys like Greenwell and Evans were hitting the ball all over the yard, I silently hoped for Owen to come up with some big hits on his own. Unfortunately, as the #9 guy in the order, he rarely got the chance.

For the Sox as a whole the 1988 season got off to a disappointing start. Oil Can Boyd went down with an injury early and much of the lineup struggled to hit in the clutch. At the All Star break manager John McNamara was fired and replaced by Joe Morgan.

The move took me by surprise for two reasons. For one thing, I didn't know that managers could be fired. I wasn't sure why they decided to blame the manager when the players weren't getting the hits and getting the other team out. As the season continued, however, I learned a great deal about the role of the manager on a baseball team. Under Morgan's command the Sox went on to have one of the more exciting halves in team history, winning twelve in a row and 24 straight at home en route to the division title.

As for Owen, he didn't get to play as great a role as would have happened had I written the season's script. He lost his starting shortstop job after Morgan was drawn to the play of Jody Reed, and was traded after the season. But he did have a couple of noted moments that year. Owen was the player Morgan pinch-hit for Jim Rice in a bunting situation during Morgan's first week as manager, leading to a shoving match between Rice and Morgan in the dugout. Spike also came through with a key late-inning pinch hit to win a game at Yankee Stadium in September that helped ice the division.

Sometimes I think I might have been spoiled a bit by Morgan Magic. After a season filled with improbable comebacks keyed by unlikely players like Todd Benzinger and Kevin Romine, I felt a little disillusioned in following years when the Sox didn't catch similar breaks. Now with over a decade's worth of seasons under my belt, and my baseball cards still hibernating in my bedroom closet, I think I'm better adapted to the emotional seesaw that comes with being a Red Sox fan.

—Neil S. Serven

THE MINOR LEAGUES

Who Are the Red Sox Best Minor League Prospects?

Here are some of the players you may see on the Red Sox in the next few years: young players working their way up through the minor league system who have the best chance of playing for the Red Sox—or of being traded for other players. Each player's age as of July 1, 2001, is listed in parentheses, along with how the Red Sox acquired him.

Why is age so important? The younger a minor leaguer is when he is good enough to play in the big leagues, the better his chances are of having a long career, since he will have longer to develop his skills before his reflexes begin to decline. Most players peak around age 27, and are out of the major leagues by their early thirties (so a player who doesn't make the majors until he's 27, like Lou Merloni, is likely to have a short career). Every once in a while a player peaks early and never gets any better (like Wil Cordero, who played briefly for the Sox), or shows a sudden improvement late in his career (like Dwight Evans did for the Red Sox). But most players continue to improve steadily until age 27 or 28 and then slowly decline. Of course, a superstar in decline may still be better than a younger—but less talented—player.

The Hitters
Rick Asadoorian, outfield (20; 1st round pick in 1999). Local product (Whitinsville, MA) who had a surprisingly difficult negotiation with the Red Sox. He signed too late to play in 1999, but had a decent debut in rookie league ball in 2000 (.264-5-31 with 22 steals in 55 games). Excellent defensive outfielder with good speed; scouts differ on his offensive potential.

Bryan Barnowski, catcher (20; 42nd round pick in 1998). Late-round pick who had an outstanding 2000 season in rookie ball (.291, 13 home runs in 55 games).

Tony Blanco, third base (19; free agent in 1999). Drew raves as the best player on Boston's Dominican Summer League Team in 1999, and followed it up with an incredible .384-13-50 season in rookie ball. Blanco tied the Gulf Coast League home run record, and *Baseball America* named him the circuit's top prospect. Blanco's swing has earned comparisons to Vladimir Guerrero, and one manager said he had the best infield arm he'd ever seen.

Juan Diaz, first base (25; free agent in 2000). Cuban refugee who was granted free agency after signing an illegal contract with the Dodgers. Started the 2000 season in A ball, but moved through Trenton to Pawtucket, hitting a combined .301 with 28 home runs and 82 RBI—in only 77 games! A foot injury ended his season before the Red Sox could watch Diaz assault the Green Monster, but the team has high hopes for his future.

Julio Guerrero, outfield (20; free agent in 1998). Brother of Vladimir and Wilton, and a highly touted teenage shortstop. Moves to third base and right field haven't awoken his bat or gotten him beyond short-season A ball, but Guerrero's youth and bloodlines still entice the front office.

Shea Hillenbrand, third base (25; 10th round pick in 1996). Drafted as a shortstop, Hillenbrand has also played catcher and first base. Surfaced on prospect lists in 1998, when he hit .349 with 19 home runs as a catcher at class-A Michigan. Injuries ended his catching days in 1999, but he rebounded in 2000 with a .323 average as a 1B-3B at AA Trenton. Hillenbrand doesn't draw walks or hit tons of homers, but he's always hit for high averages when healthy.

Carlos Leon, second base (21; free agent in 1997). Struggled in his first three years as a pro, but hit .305 with 13 steals in 2000, splitting time between A and AA. Never strikes out, but doesn't draw walks and has no power whatsoever.

Steve Lomasney, catcher (23; 5th round pick in 1995). Local hero (Melrose, Massachusetts) whose size, athleticism, and leadership has drawn comparisons to Carlton Fisk. Had a strong 1999 season in A and AA (.259, 20 home runs, 57 walks in 340 at bats). Injuries and strikeouts sidetracked Lomasney in 2000, but his power, defense, and high walk totals continue to impress the front office.

Angel Santos, second base (21; 4th round pick in 1997). Switch-hitter from Puerto Rico who had a quietly impressive 1999 season at class-A Augusta (.270, 15 home runs, 25 steals, 62 walks). Jumped to AA with mixed results in 2000 (.258, 3 home runs, 18 SB in 275 AB). A converted shortstop, Santos is considered a very good defensive second baseman.

Antron Sieber, outfield (21; 3rd round pick in 1999). Outstanding high school football player who had an excellent year in rookie and short-A ball in 2000 (.295, 23 steals in 55 games).

Dernell Stenson, first base/outfield (23; 3rd round pick in 1996). Big lefthanded hitter, with a physique eerily similar to Mo Vaughn's. Unfortunately, his glovework is also reminiscent of Big Mo, as he made a whopping 34 errors in 1999, after converting from left field to first base. Scouts love Stenson's swing, and he's put up solid offensive numbers at every level, despite consistently being one of the youngest players in his league. Stenson hasn't had a breakout year yet, but hit 23 homers in 380 at bats during the 2000 season.

The Pitchers

Brad Baker, RHP (20; 1st round pick in 1999). Drafted with a compensation pick for the loss of Mo Vaughn, this Leyden, Massachusetts, native showed great promise in his first full season. Armed with a 95 MPH fastball and a sharp curve, Baker went 12–7 3.07, with 126 strikeouts in 138 innings, in class-A Augusta. Still very young, Baker won't be rushed through the system, but is expected to be a major contributor by the middle of the decade.

Jin-Ho Cho, RHP (25; free agent in 1998). The first Korean to play for Boston, Cho made it to the majors during his first professional season. Despite excellent minor league numbers in 1998 and 1999 (a combined 17–6 2.96), Cho has been hit hard in his major league trials. Had an injury-plagued 2000 season, but finished strongly with Pawtucket.

Manny Delcarmen, RHP (19; 2nd round pick in 2000). Dominican who grew up in Boston and learned the game in the Red Sox–sponsored RBI (Revitalizing Baseball in the Inner City) Program. Will make his pro debut in 2001.

Justin Duchscherer, RHP (23; 8th round pick in 1995). Rail-thin Texan who came into his own in 1999, going 4–0 0.22 for class A Augusta—only allowing 21 hits and 1 run in 41 innings. That earned Duchscherer a promotion to Sarasota, where his 7–7 record and 4.49 ERA masked impressive peripheral stats. Pitching for AA Trenton in 2000, Duchscherer had an excellent 3.39 ERA (with 126 strikeouts to 35 walks), though his record was only 7–9.

Phil Dumatrait, LHP (19; 1st round pick in 2000). Threw a low-80s fastball in high school, but increased his velocity by 10 MPH after entering junior college in California. One of the 2000 draft's sleepers, Dumatrait was a surprise pick by Boston, but he had a 1.65 ERA in his brief professional debut.

Casey Fossum, LHP (23; "sandwich" pick between 1st and 2nd rounds in 1999). A star at Texas A&M, Fossum was put on the fast track to Fenway. Spent his first full season at class A Sarasota, where he went 9–10, with a 3.44 ERA. Fossum really heated up in the second half, which included a 16-strikeout no-hitter. Lauded for his composure and control, Fossum could see action in Fenway as early as 2001. Some scouts say he'll be a #3–5 starter, while others see him as a valuable lefty relief specialist.

Fossum and Richard Rundles were compensation picks for the loss of free agent Greg Swindell.

Eric Glaser, RHP (23; 2nd round pick in 1997). Spent his first three seasons in rookie and short-season leagues. Promoted to Augusta in 2000, where he pitched a no-hitter and finished 9–6, with a 3.33 ERA and 120 strikeouts in 124 innings.

Sun-Woo "Sunny" Kim, RHP (23; free agent in 1997). The hard-throwing Kim is generally considered the most talented of Boston's Asian pitching prospects, despite disappointing results in the minors. Kim pitched for Korea's 1996 Olympic team, and was MVP of the 1995 World Baseball Championships—in a game played at Fenway. Reportedly, Kim liked the park so much that he got Boston to give him an unofficial no-trade clause. Kim had 4.82 and 4.89 ERAs in his first 2 seasons, but had excellent strikeout-to-walk ratios. After an outstanding Arizona Fall League showing in 1999, Kim had a discouraging 6.03 ERA in Pawtucket last year.

Mauricio Lara, LHP (20; free agent in 1999). Signed out of Mexico, Lara spent the 1999 season with the Red Sox' Venezuelan Summer League Team, where he went 7–0 with a 1.71 ERA. He didn't miss a beat the next year in short-A Lowell (4–3 2.12, with 83 SO and 21 BB in 85 IP). *Baseball America* named Lara the fifth best prospect in the New York–Penn League.

Bryan "B. J." Leach, RHP (23; 14th round pick in 1999). Not to be confused with the NHL star, Leach was the NCAA Division II Player of the Year in 1999 (as a pitcher/second baseman at Florida Southern). Though a little old for his league, Leach was a dominating closer for Augusta in 2000, with 40 saves and a 1.62 ERA. He struck out 87 in 72 innings, while allowing only 45 hits and 20 walks.

Sang-Hoon Lee, LHP (30; free agent in 1999). Flamboyant Korean who wears his dyed-red hair like Dennis Eckersley and calls himself "Samson." Lee was a star pitcher in both the Korean League and the Japanese League and, like The Eck, he excelled as both a starter and reliever (when injuries made him unable to start consistently). Signed a lucrative contract with Boston before the 2000 season, but didn't make the team out of spring training. Spent most of his first year in Pawtucket, where he was a quietly dominant setup man (5–2 2.03, with 51 hits, 24 walks, and 73 strikeouts in 71 IP). Struggled in his first trial with Boston, but looked better in September. Expected to replace Rheal Cormier as the Sox' top lefty reliever.

Greg Montalbano, LHP (23; 5th round pick in 1999). New Englander who starred at Northeastern University after overcoming testicular cancer. Had a difficult negotiation with Boston, taking almost a year to sign a professional contract. Pitched only 22 innings, with a 2.82 ERA, in his first pro season.

Juan Peña, RHP (24; 27th round draft pick in 1995). Went 12–10 2.97 in his first full season as a pro (1996), and continued to pitch well as he moved up the ladder. Though he isn't blessed with great velocity, Peña's strikeout-to-walk ratios have been consistently good, and he threw a no-hitter for Pawtucket in 1998. He made the majors the following year, winning both his starts (1 run and 15 strikeouts in 13 IP) before an elbow injury cost him the rest of the season. Peña was in the running for a rotation job in 2000, but another elbow injury ended his season and put his future in some doubt.

Rick Riccobono, RHP (21; 6th round pick in 1998). New York prep star who nearly went to college instead of signing with Boston. Struggled in 1999, but his contract stipulated that he be invited to major league spring training in 2000. The Sox sent Riccobono to minor league camp almost immediately, and he came into his own at class-A Augusta (10-7 3.27).

Richard Rundles, LHP (20; 3rd round pick in 1999). Had ERAs of 2.13 and 2.45 in limited rookie league action. He and Casey Fossum were compensation picks for the loss of free agent Greg Swindell.

Seung Song, RHP (21; free agent in 1999). Talented Korean who made an impressive debut in rookie ball in 1999 (5–5 2.30). Led the NY-Penn League with 93 strikeouts in 2000, while going 5–2 with a 2.60 ERA. Only allowed 1 homer in 73 innings.

Visiting the Minor Leagues

If you're near one of the Red Sox minor league affiliates, or if you'd like to travel to watch some of the Sox players of the future in action, minor league games are a terrific value. Most games are inexpensive, with good seats and parking easy to come by. (Some minor league cities, like Trenton, are a hot ticket, so you'll want to call ahead to check availability.)

Pawtucket, Rhode Island
The Pawtucket Red Sox are the highest level team in the Red Sox farm system. This AAA team plays in McCoy Stadium in Pawtucket, Rhode Island, and competes in the Northern Division of the International League. You can contact the team by phone at (401) 724-7300, by fax at (401) 724-2140, and by e-mail at *info@pawsox.com*. Tickets can be purchased over the phone or through the team's website (*www.pawsox.com*). Parking is free. Directions to McCoy Stadium, taken from the website, are as follows:

From the North
Rte. 95 South to Exit 2A in Massachusetts (Newport Ave./Pawtucket). Follow Newport Ave. for 2 miles and take a right on Columbus Ave. Follow Columbus Ave. for 1 mile. Stadium is on right.

From the South
Rte. 95 North to Exit 28 (School St.). Take right at bottom of exit ramp. Go through two sets of lights and take first left onto Pond St. Follow to end of Pond (½ mile) and take right on Columbus Ave. Stadium entrance is on left.

From the West (Worcester)
Rte. 146 South to Rte. 295 North to Rte. 95 South and follow directions from the North.

From the East (Fall River)
Rte. 195 West to Rte. 95 North and follow directions from the South.

Trenton, New Jersey

After 22 years in Bristol and New Britain, Connecticut, the Red Sox moved their AA Eastern League farm team to Trenton, New Jersey, in 1995. The Red Sox initially planned to stay in Trenton for only a year or two, and reportedly eyed a move to Springfield, Massachusetts, but Trenton's state-of-the-art ballpark and sellout crowds prompted Boston to extend their arrangement with New Jersey's capital city.

Mercer County Waterfront Park was built in 1994, and the Detroit Tigers had their AA affiliate there for that season. The 6,604-seat stadium overlooks the Delaware River, and Pennsylvania looms just beyond the right field wall. It's a beautiful, immaculately clean ballpark with a large concourse, diverse refreshment stands, and a very nice souvenir shop with Trenton and Boston memorabilia.

Trenton prides itself on a family atmosphere, and there are plenty of activities to keep kids entertained. One lucky youngster wins a prize for racing the team mascot, Boomer, around the bases. Others compete in bat-spin races and the usual cornball minor league stuff. Kids and adults can even have their fastballs clocked by a radar gun behind the first base stands. Local restaurants and businesses give away prizes to lucky fans every inning.

Waterfront Park is a wonderful place to see a game, with one caveat: Virtually every game is sold out. Fenway-goers will be shocked at the low ticket prices (which range from $4.00 to $8.00 including discounts for kids and seniors). There is ample wheelchair seating, and some $4.00 standing-room-only tickets are made available as well. As with most minor league parks, every seat is excellent. Tickets are available on the team's website, *http://www.trentonthunder.com*, or by calling 609-394-TEAM. It's definitely recommended that you buy them in advance, though scalpers are known to frequent the parking lot (rarely charging more than face value).

The park itself is just off US-1 and I-95, and is officially located on One Thunder Road (a nod to Dan Duquette's hero, New Jersey's own Bruce Springsteen). Detailed directions are available on the team's website. The parking lot is large, cheap, and well-organized. Trenton isn't America's prettiest city, but Waterfront Park is located in a safe, quiet neighborhood.

As a AA team the Trenton Thunder (and their opponents) offer fans the chance to see players only a year or two away from big league stardom. The most famous and popular Trenton alum is Nomar Garciaparra. Nomar wowed fans with his defense in 1995, though he only hit .267 with 8 homers (and 35 steals). Other well-known alumni include first baseman Tony Clark (in 1994, when it was a Detroit affiliate), shortstop Adam Everett, outfielder Trot Nixon, infielder Donnie Sadler, and pitchers Tomo Ohka, Carl Pavano, Brian Rose, and Jeff Suppan. Top prospect Casey Fossum, a lefty pitcher, is expected to headline the 2001 Thunder.

Sarasota, Florida
The Sarasota Red Sox compete in the Florida State (A) league (one of the lower levels of the minor leagues). Ed Smith Stadium has a seating capacity of 7500 (with parking for 2000 cars). Tickets cost either $4 (grandstand) or $5 (diamond box). You can contact the club by phone at (941) 365-4460 and by email at *sarasox@acun.com*. Directions to Ed Smith Stadium are as follows:

From the North
Exit I-75 at University Parkway; go west on University to Tuttle; turn left and head south on Tuttle. Stadium is located on the right at the intersection of 12th and Tuttle.

From the South
Exit I-75 at Fruitville Road; go west on Fruitville to Tuttle; turn right on Tuttle to 12th; the stadium is on the left.

Augusta, Georgia
The Augusta Greenjackets play in the South Atlantic League (A) within Old Olmstead Stadium in Augusta, Georgia. They can be contacted by phone at (706) 736-7889. Ticket prices range from $5.00 to $7.00, with discounts to children, the elderly, and active members of the military. You can purchase tickets by phone or through the website tixonline.com. The team's website can be found at *www.greenjackets.net*.

Lowell, Massachusetts
The Lowell Spinners are a Boston Red Sox farm team in Lowell, Massachusetts. The Spinners are a short-season class A team, playing in the New York-Penn League. The Spinners derive their name from the major activity in the formation of Lowell, a Merrimack River Valley mill city. (The city also has a textile museum, celebrating that heritage.) Because it is so conveniently located (less than 30 miles from Boston), Lowell has been a good starting point for pitchers rehabilitating from injuries. In the last two years both Bret Saberhagen and Ramon Martinez have started games in Lowell. There are not yet any Lowell Spinners alumni in the major leagues.

The Spinners began play in 1996 at Alumni Field. In 1998 they moved to Edward A. LeLacheur Park (capacity 5,000), on the shore of the Merrimack River. Although a small city (and not a particularly attractive one), the Park is a beautiful ballpark, sitting on a lovely spot on the River.

Ticket prices range from $3.50 to $6.50. As with most minor league facilities, Lowell is very fan friendly, with a variety of entertainment going on between innings (some featuring the Canaligator, the Spinners' mascot). For any baseball fans in the area, a night at LeLacheur Park would be an evening well spent. Directions to the Park are as follows:

From 495 and Route 3, take the Lowell Connector. Follow the Connector to exit 5b, Thorndike Street. Follow Thorndike St. onto Dutton St. Go past City Hall and take a left on to Father Morrissette Street. At second set of lights take a right onto Aiken St. LeLacheur Park will be on your left.

In addition to the teams listed above, the Red Sox currently have two rookie league teams. One is the Gulf Coast Red Sox, a short-season rookie ball team located in Fort Myers, near the site of the Major League team's spring training facility. The other is the Dominican Summer League team, which is also short season rookie league, playing 72 games from June through August. The Boston Red Sox entry in the DSL plays in the San Pedro de Macoris division.

Visiting Spring Training

Since 1993 the Red Sox have held their annual spring training in the lush green surroundings of Fort Myers, Florida, on the southwest coast of the Florida peninsula. As part of the 20-team Grapefruit League, the Sox play an exhibition schedule of 32 games throughout the month of March (not including B-games and intrasquad games). The small season is usually kicked off with an exhibition contest against the Boston College Eagles. About 70 players show up for camp every year, hoping to impress team management with their skills and perhaps win a spot on the big league club (even though much of the roster is already determined before spring training starts). Nevertheless, the opportunity to be noticed is valued by an eager young player, since over the course of a long season an unexpected turn of events, such as an injury to a roster player or a subpar performance, may leave an opening for another player to be called up. (About 70 percent of major league players are injured at some point during the season.)

Red Sox spring training home games are played at City of Palms Park, at 2201 Edison Avenue in Fort Myers. Because the Minnesota Twins also hold their spring training in Fort Myers (on the other side of the city), they are scheduled as a frequent opponent for the Sox, to form a friendly series that the locals have dubbed "The Mayor's Cup." Spring training games are a popular attraction not only for local residents but also for fans from afar who want to see their Sox in a warm-weather environment without forking over the high price of admission to a major league park. Florida in March also serves as a warm, scenic, and life-affirming vacation spot for New Englanders who are tired of another arduous winter. In February the park also hosts the annual Red Sox Fantasy Camp, in which fans can fulfill their baseball dreams by receiving tips and coaching from some of the game's most renowned players. For more information on the Fantasy Camp call (888)901-PLAY.

Tickets for games at City of Palms Park can be ordered via phone, fax, or walk-up starting in the middle of January. Prices for the 2001 Spring Training season are $13 for box seats and $10 for reserved grandstand seating. Call the park's ticket office between 9:00 AM and 4:30 PM at (941) 334-4700 or toll-free at (877) RED-SOXX.

QUESTIONS AND ANSWERS

What are leagues, and which one do the Red Sox belong to? Are there big differences between the major leagues? Where do the minor leagues fit into things?

Major League Baseball is divided into the National League (NL) and American League (AL). The National League began play in 1876, and is regarded as baseball's first *major league*. (Some historians consider the National Association, which played from 1871–75, the first major league. Many of its teams and stars joined the National League in 1876.) The Chicago Cubs and Atlanta Braves (originally the Boston Red Stockings, before they changed their name several times and moved to Milwaukee and then Atlanta) are the only original National League teams still in existence. There were three other major leagues in the nineteenth century. The American Association lasted from 1882–91, and played World Series against the National League from 1884–90. (The National League had its top 2 teams play a form of the World Series from 1892–1900.) The AA is best remembered for allowing 2 black players, Moses and Welday Walker, to play in 1884—63 years before Jackie Robinson. Two other major leagues lasted a season apiece: the Union Association (1884) and the Players League (1890). As its name suggests, the latter was formed by players involved in a labor dispute with National League owners, who wanted to limit salaries. Some things never change.

The American League became a major league in 1901. It evolved from the Western League, a high-quality minor league created by Ban Johnson a year earlier. Johnson wanted to compete with the National League, and he moved some teams into bigger cities, while raiding National League rosters for stars like Nap Lajoie, Cy Young, and Jimmy Collins. In the minds of most fans, the American League truly gained major league status in 1903, when the first modern World Series was played—the Boston Pilgrims (soon to be the Red Sox) defeated the Pittsburgh Pirates. The loss so embarrassed the National League that the New York Giants refused to play in the 1904 World Series against Boston, but the Fall Classic resumed the following year. In 1933, the National League and American League began playing an annual midseason All Star Game, with the best players in each league facing off for bragging rights. (From 1959–62 the leagues played 2 All Star Games a year, but the experiment was a failure.)

From 1903–52, the National League and American League had the same 16 teams (none of them west of the Mississippi). In 1953, the Boston Braves moved to

Milwaukee, and the St. Louis Browns became the Baltimore Orioles in 1954. Later that decade the National League spread to the West Coast, with the Dodgers and Giants leaving New York City for California. In 1961 the American League added 2 teams, and the National League did the same in 1962. In 1969 both leagues expanded to 12 teams. Instead of having only 2 of 24 teams make the playoffs, each league split into an Eastern and Western Division, with the winners meeting in a playoff to qualify for the World Series.

The National League and American League played essentially the same game with the same rules from 1901–72, though players from different leagues only faced each other in the World Series and All Star Games. In 1973 the American League added the designated hitter rule (see page 230), changing its style of play dramatically.

The American League expanded to its current 14 teams in 1977, and the National League added 2 more teams in 1993. In 1994, a season ultimately ruined by a strike, baseball changed its playoff format. Each league went to a 3-division setup. The winners of each division made the playoffs, along with a wild card team (the team with the best record of the non-division winners). Another round of playoffs was added, so a team now needed to win 3 series to become World Champions. Though the 1994 playoffs were wiped out, the system went into effect in 1995, and remains the same today. For example, in 1999, the New York Yankees, Cleveland Indians, and Texas Rangers won the American League's 3 divisions. The Red Sox, who had the best record of the league's other teams, made the playoffs as a wild card team. It's not unusual to have a wild card team with a better record than one of the division winners, especially if one division has much stronger teams than the others.

In 1997 baseball made another radical change, incorporating some interleague games into regular season play. Traditionalists worried that interleague play would make the World Series less meaningful, while many others looked forward to new rivalries and the chance to see more star players. The next season, baseball added two more teams. Tampa Bay joined the American League, while Arizona entered the National League. To balance the schedules, the American League's Milwaukee Brewers moved to the National League.

Currently, the American League teams are the Anaheim Angels, Baltimore Orioles, Boston Red Sox, Chicago White Sox, Cleveland Indians, Detroit Tigers, Kansas City Royals, Minnesota Twins, New York Yankees, Oakland Athletics, Seattle Mariners, Tampa Bay Devil Rays, Texas Rangers, and Toronto Blue Jays.

The National League consists of the Arizona Diamondbacks, Atlanta Braves, Chicago Cubs, Cincinnati Reds, Colorado Rockies, Florida Marlins, Houston Astros, Los Angeles Dodgers, Milwaukee Brewers, Montreal Expos, New York Mets, Philadelphia Phillies, Pittsburgh Pirates, St. Louis Cardinals, San Diego Padres, and San Francisco Giants.

Each major league team has several minor league affiliates in smaller cities throughout the United States and Canada. The minor leagues are as old as the major leagues, and began as a series of independently owned teams. The best players, such as Baltimore's Babe Ruth, were sold to major league teams for big profits. Some major league teams owned minor league teams, but St. Louis's Branch Rickey invented the "farm system" in 1921, when he bought several independent minor league ballclubs—and the rights to many future stars. The goal of the minor league teams gradually changed from winning games to developing young players for the big leagues (though they still want to win).

Today major league teams generally have 6 minor league affiliates. Most affiliates are independently owned, but subsidized by major league teams, who stock them with players and instructors. The players are owned and controlled by the major league team,s though most will never reach "The Show." Each team has an affiliate in class AAA, which is one step below the majors. Many class AAA players have big league experience, and can be called up to the majors in case of injury. Other players are younger, and are getting seasoning to develop their big league potential. Each team also has a class AA affiliate, and generally 2 in class A. These leagues aren't as good as AAA, but are important steps in a player's growth. class A and AA teams are geared more toward development, and have very few ex-big leaguers or older players on their rosters. Big league teams typically have 2 more affiliates in short-season leagues (some are considered class A; others are called rookie league). These leagues only play from June to August, and consist of players just out of high school or college.

In the last decade several independent minor leagues have begun play, and some have been quite successful. These leagues have no affiliation with the majors, and their players aren't owned by big league teams. Their players are looking to gain the attention of big league scouts, and some, like Red Sox first baseman Morgan Burkhart and Texas relief pitcher Jeff Zimmerman, have been signed by major league organizations.

Why do runners go back to the base if there's a fly ball, but not if there's a ground ball?

Fly balls can hang in the air for a long time, and it would be too easy for runners to score if they could advance as soon as the ball is hit. So baseball rules require runners to go back to the base and "tag up" if fly balls are caught. If the runner doesn't get back to the base the defense can throw the ball to a player at that base, and the runner is out. If the runner tags up he can try to make it to the next base as soon as the ball is caught (if it's dropped, he can advance anyway). With fewer than 2 outs, runners on second or third often advance a base by tagging up after long fly balls. When a runner scores after tagging up, the batter is credited with a "sacrifice fly" and an RBI. Runners rarely tag up from first base (since it's a short throw from the outfield to second base). On long flies they generally run halfway to second base so that if the ball's caught, they can easily make it back to first. If it's not caught, they have a better chance of scoring.

On ground balls, runners on first base are "forced" to run to second. (If it's first and second, both runners are "forced" to advance, and all three must run if the bases are loaded.) A defensive player with the ball only needs to tag the base before the runner reaches it to get an out, instead of having to tag the runner (just like first basemen on groundouts). So the runner has little choice but to run to the next base, where he might be able to prevent a double play by distracting the fielder (Ty Cobb was notorious for sharpening the metal spikes on his shoes and trying to drive them into the second baseman while sliding, but umpires frown on that today), or be safe if the fielder drops the ball. If a runner is on second or third, and there's no one on first, he doesn't have to run on a grounder. He can safely stay on his base, or try to advance at his own risk, depending on where the ball is hit.

Can you explain the infield fly rule?

The *infield fly rule* only applies with runners on first and second, or with the bases loaded, when there are fewer than 2 outs. If a batter hits a high pop-up in the infield or short outfield, the umpire can (but doesn't have to, if he doesn't feel it's necessary) call "infield fly." This means that the batter is automatically out, whether or not the fielder catches the ball. (If the ball is foul, the infield fly rule no longer applies, but the batter is out if it's caught.) The runners can advance at their own risk. They can tag up if the ball is caught, or can run if it's dropped—but they can be thrown out. The reason for the rule? Without it, an infielder can purposely drop the pop-up, pick up the ball, and start an easy double play. The runners would be forced to advance, and it would be easy to get force-outs at two bases.

How does pinch-hitting work? What are double switches? What are some of the other kinds of in-game strategy I should look for?

Any players who aren't in the lineup—and haven't been used yet in a game—are eligible to *pinch hit*. A pinch-hitter bats in place of someone in the lineup. Unlike in football or basketball, a baseball player who is replaced for any reason *can't* come back into the game. In the National League (and the American League before the DH rule), pitchers have to bat. Since they're normally weak hitters, they're often pinch-hit for in close games but then can't pitch again. In the modern American League, pinch-hitting isn't nearly as common, but it still happens quite a bit in the late innings of tight games. Some regular players aren't good hitters, but start because of their fielding ability. If the team is behind, the manager often pinch-hits for those weak hitters. Sometimes, the opposing team brings in a tough righthanded pitcher to get a righty hitter out, and a lefty on the bench is summoned to pinch-hit. (There's a rule that says every pitcher brought into a game has to face at least one batter, so teams can't keep switching back and forth until they run out of players.) Pinch-hitting is difficult, since a player must enter a game cold, often facing a tough reliever in a crucial situation. Many great players have struggled in the role, while journeymen like Rick Miller and Manny Mota have been among the game's best pinch-hitters.

After a player pinch-hits, the manager has to change his lineup, unless the game ends during that half-inning. If the pinch-hitter plays the same position as the guy he hit for, then he normally stays in the game at that position. If not, the manager puts another bench player in, and the pinch-hitter leaves the game.

Sometimes a manager makes a *double-switch*, where a pinch-hitter stays in the game, but another change is made simultaneously. Let's say Jason Varitek is catching and batting eighth, while Darren Lewis is playing right field and batting leadoff (first). Suppose Trot Nixon pinch-hits for Varitek in the bottom of the eighth, and

Lewis makes the last out that inning. Since Nixon is also a right fielder, Jimy Williams might leave him in the game, batting in Varitek's old #8 spot. He still needs to bring a catcher in, so Scott Hatteberg enters the game and bats in Lewis's leadoff slot. Double-switches are far more common in the National League, where pitchers are often pinch-hit for. Some National League managers also make double-switches during a pitching change, to avoid having to waste a pinch-hitter the next time they bat (conserving spare players, since a manager usually has only 5 or 6 extra non-pitchers on his roster during a game).

In addition to pinch-hitting, managers can *pinch-run* for players who get on base. The same rules as pinch-hitting apply; the pinch-runner takes his predecessor's place in the lineup. Teams generally pinch-run late in games, when a faster player might be able to steal a key base, or score a run more easily. Managers also pinch-run for players who have minor leg injuries that prevent them from running effectively.

Though Red Sox fans haven't seen much of this over the years, the *hit-and-run* is a common baseball strategy. This occurs with a runner on first, or sometimes with runners on first and second. The baserunner will run with the pitch, as he would in a stolen base attempt. But the goal isn't a steal; instead, the batter tries to hit the ball to the area vacated by the fielder covering second base. When a hit-and-run works properly, the runner easily makes it from first base to third base, often leading to a big inning. But if the batter hits a fly ball or line drive, it could turn into an easy double play. The invention of the hit-and-run is often credited to the National League's Baltimore Orioles (1890s), but may have actually been invented by that league's Boston Beaneaters.

A variation of the hit-and-run is the *run-and-hit*. The difference is that the batter has an option. He can swing, like a hit-and-run, or he can let the pitch go, hoping the runner can steal second.

Managers often try to foil hit-and-runs, run-and-hits, and stolen bases by calling *pitchouts*. The catcher signals to the pitcher, who throws way outside, where the batter can't hit the ball. If the runner is on the move, the catcher has an excellent chance of throwing him out. If the runner isn't going, though, the failed pitchout increases the batter's odds of getting on base via a walk (because the pitchout counts as a ball, not a strike).

Another common managerial strategy is the *sacrifice bunt*, used with runners on base and fewer than 2 outs. The batter squares to the pitcher, puts the bat parallel to home plate, and taps the ball a short distance. The fielders can usually throw the batter out at first base, but a good bunt allows the other runners to advance a base. National League pitchers bunt frequently, since most are weak hitters. In the American League bunts are less frequent, and almost always occur with no outs. Studies have suggested that bunting increses a team's chances of scoring one run (because it moves up the runner) but *decreases* the chances of scoring two or more runs in an inning (because it gives up an out). For that reason, bunting is comparatively rare in today's high-scoring game, except in cases when one run may make the difference in the game (such as late in a close game, or in extra innings). In the 1960s, when games were much more low-scoring, there were many more bunts, because every run was more valuable.

A *squeeze bunt* is a sacrifice with a runner on third base. In a *suicide squeeze*, the runner breaks for home (as if he were trying to steal), and the batter tries to bunt the ball. As long as the batter makes contact, the run will almost always score, but if he misses, the runner is a dead duck. If the batter gives away the bunt too early, the pitcher will throw the ball where he can't bunt it, letting the catcher tag the runner. In a *safety squeeze*, the runner doesn't break for the plate until he knows that the batter has made contact with the ball. This makes it harder to score, but also cuts down on the risk.

In certain crucial situations, some managers opt to *intentionally walk* a batter. This normally occurs when first base is empty and a weaker hitter is on deck. The catcher stands up and puts his arm out, and the pitcher lobs 4 balls far off home plate. The idea is to prevent the tougher hitter from beating you, while hoping the pitcher can get the lesser batter out. It can also be used to set up a potential double play grounder. This strategy often backfires, as the Indians learned in Game 5 of their 1999 playoff series against Boston. Twice in that deciding game the Indians intentionally walked Nomar Garciaparra to face Troy O'Leary—who responded with a 3-run homer and a grand slam to help the Red Sox win, 12–8.

What is the designated hitter (DH)?

In American League (as well as minor league and most amateur) games, the designated hitter (or DH) is a player who bats instead of the pitcher. The DH doesn't play the field, and can stay in the game as long as the manager wants, regardless of how many pitching changes are made. The pitcher is not required to bat. (If the DH is forced to move into a defensive position, the pitcher is then required to bat, and the team loses the DH for the rest of the game.) The DH is fixed in whatever lineup spot the manager selects at the start of the game; unlike other positions, the manager can't move the DH around the lineup by using double switches (see page 228). A manager can pinch-hit or pinch-run for the DH, but the new player then becomes the DH; if the manager wants him to play a position in the field, the DH is lost and the pitcher will have to bat.

The DH Rule was adopted by the American League in 1973 as a response to the low-offense, pitching-dominated baseball of the 1960s and early 1970s. Fearful of losing popularity to football, American League owners decided that this radical change would spice up the game and add scoring. The National League decided against the rule, making the two leagues extremely different. The DH concept had been kicked around for decades, and was rejected at a National League meeting as far back as 1928.

Traditionalists were furious over the new rule, saying it tampered with the offense/defense balance of the game. Others disagreed, pointing out that it was a good way to let stars like Hank Aaron and Orlando Cepeda extend their careers. Early DHs tended to be that sort of player: slow, aging sluggers who could barely play the field. Later, teams were more likely to DH younger players like Jim Rice, or rotate several players in the role. The DH spot is also frequently used to keep an injured player who can still hit but can't field in the lineup, or to rest a player at a demanding defensive position without taking his bat out of the lineup.

The World Series presented a problem, however, since both leagues had different rules. In 1976 they decided to alternate years (DH in even years, no DH in odd years). This gave National League teams an advantage. In even years, they got to add a bat, and in odd years, the American League team had to bench one of their top hitters. In 1986 baseball changed the rule. All games in the American League park use the DH, but pitchers have to hit in National League parks. This compromise is also used in regular season Interleague games. The All Star Game uses a DH, regardless of ballpark, to make substitutions easier.

Explain to me about stats. What do some of the terms people throw around mean? Why can't everybody agree on which stats are important?

A single death is a tragedy, a million deaths is a statistic.
—*Joseph Stalin*

Most major newspapers, when listing players, sort them by *batting average*, from highest to lowest. Why is that? Is that the best way to rank players? Is someone hitting .314 necessarily hitting better than someone hitting .278? More importantly, is there any way to know for sure?

These questions are at the center of a debate that has raged for years. How do we measure performance on the baseball diamond? How do we determine which is the best *metric*, the best measurement, for identifying the activities that are valuable in assisting a team to win games? Answering these questions is one of the functions of the Society for American Baseball Research, or SABR. The general term for the mathematical, statistical evaluation of player performance has derived from this acronym, and is called sabermetrics.

It is easy to demonstrate the reasons why the traditional measures have fallen short of the mark when evaluating the individual contributions. Picture the following example:

> Player A leads off an inning with a walk. Player B follows with a ground ball. Player A is forced out at second, and Player B is safe at first. Player C then doubles, leaving men on second and third. Finally Player D hits a medium depth fly ball to right, and Player B scores.

So what has happened? Player A and Player C, the two players who really helped the team, get no statistical credit for the run. Player B gets a run scored and Player D gets an RBI, yet both of them made outs. It is frequently said that baseball is a game without a clock and that's true. But it does have a virtual clock, in the form of outs. Each team starts the game with 27 of them. As a general rule, hitters that don't use up those outs are more productive than players that do. So, for the most part, statistics which fail to take into account outs made are not truly helpful at measuring offensive performance.

Following is a brief glossary of the best-known traditional stats, and of some sabermetric tools for statistical evaluation:

Counting stats: statistics which consist of just raw numbers—hits, home runs, runs batted in, etc. on the offensive side and wins, strikeouts, etc. on the pitching side. They are strictly a measurement of events which happened, and are heavily influenced by playing time. For instance, Bill Buckner got 201 hits in 1985 (third in the league) because he played every game, never got hurt, and rarely walked, but he was not a very good player that year because he made almost 500 outs in the process of getting those hits. A very productive player who doesn't play as much may not have totals as good as a poor player who plays every day. That doesn't mean totals aren't useful and important—just that you have to look at them in context.

Rate stats: statistics which are adjusted for playing time. For instance, earned run average (ERA) is earned runs per 9 innings, batting average (BA) is hits per at bat.

Traditional statistics:

Batting Average (BA, AVG): Batting average is computed by dividing a player's hits by his total times at bat. Batting average is the most commonly mentioned stat, and one of the most useful. However, there are two weaknesses (from a sabermetric point of view) with batting average as a metric for performance—it fails to distinguish between singles and home runs, and it gives a hitter no credit for drawing walks. Fans therefore have to look at stats like slugging percentage and on-base percentage to tell how impressive a player's batting average really is. To go back to the previous example, Bill Buckner hit .299 (eighth in the league) in 1985, which would normally be a good average. However, he walked only 30 times in over 700 plate appearances. Despite his good batting average, he still made outs more than two-thirds of the time—which isn't very good. By contrast, Baltimore's Eddie Murray had a batting average 2 points worse than Buckner, but was on base over 50 times more than Buckner (because he walked a lot more) and made fewer outs!

Runs Batted In (RBI): Maybe the most maligned offensive statistic from a sabermetric point of view, RBI are still viewed as important in much of the baseball press. One of the most overused terms in baseball talk is "he's a big RBI man." The problem is that RBI are a heavily team-dependent stat. In other words, someone who plays for a team that puts a lot of players on base ahead of him will drive in a lot of runs, whether he's a good hitter or not. To once again pick on Bill Buckner in 1985, he drove in 110 runs that year (sixth in the league) while batting third in the Boston lineup. Does this mean he was a good RBI man, as he was called in the papers? Actually, no. Buckner batted third in the Boston lineup, behind Wade Boggs (best in the league at getting on base that year) and Dwight Evans (eighth in the league in on-base percentage). He had over 700 plate appearances with two of the best players in the league in getting on base hitting in front of him. For the number of outs he made, his RBI total is pretty ordinary. That same year Eddie Murray had an almost identical batting average to Buckner and played behind hitters who were much worse at getting on base than Boggs and Evans—but Murray drove in

124 runs, while making almost 300 fewer outs (or 11 complete games worth of outs).

Home Runs: A pure counting stat, this may be the least misleading of the traditional stats. A player who hits a lot of home runs is probably a useful player, unless his batting average and on-base percentage are truly awful. In the 1970s and 1980s, when offensive levels were lower, a player who hit 20 homers in a year was a pretty good power hitter. These days, with the surge in offense, 20-homer hitters are more common (although it's still pretty good), but a player who hits 30 or more in a year is definitely a power threat. Home run numbers can still be deceptive, however. Bill Buckner hit 16 homers in 1985 while Rich Gedman hit 18—comparable numbers on the surface—but Buckner took 673 at bats to hit his 16 (not a lot of home run power), while Gedman hit 18 in only 498 at bats (a pretty good total at the time). Also remember that some parks are easier to hit home runs in—like Coors Field in Colorado, because of the thin air at the park's high altitude. Fenway Park used to be a very good home run hitter's park, until the 1980s, when the 600 Club was built, cutting off wind currents that used to help the ball carry. Now Fenway is a little harder than average to hit home runs in (although it helps batting average).

Win-Loss Record (usually written as two numbers separated by a dash, i.e., 3–2 for 3 wins and 2 losses): A *win* is awarded to the pitcher who is in the game when his team takes a lead that it holds for the rest of the game. A starting pitcher has to pitch at least 5 innings to get a win, while relievers have no restrictions in how long they have to be in the game. Conversely, the pitcher who lets the other team take a lead that they never give up ends up with a *loss*. A few examples.

> Pedro Martinez pitches 7 innings and leaves the game with a 5–1 lead. The Red Sox eventually win the game 5–3. Pedro is given a win.

> Pedro Martinez pitches 7 innings and leaves the game with a 2–1 lead. Rich Garces comes in to pitch and gives up the tying run. Derek Lowe comes in with the game still tied and the Red Sox come back to win. Lowe is given a win.

> Hideo Nomo pitches 6 innings and leaves trailing 5–3. The Red Sox never catch up, and he is given a loss.

> Hideo Nomo pitches 6 innings and leaves trailing 5–3. The Red Sox catch up to tie the game, but Rod Beck later gives up the winning run. Beck is the losing pitcher.

Someone once, back in the murky depths of time, decided to award team victories to pitchers, based on a fairly straightforward set of rules. Unfortunately, this has misled generations of baseball fans on the relative quality of pitchers. There are two components that determine the outcome of a baseball game—the runs a team scores, and the runs a team allows. The pitcher has responsibility for only one of these and it isn't even solely his responsibility, as a bad defensive team can give up runs even if he pitches well. To award wins and losses to pitchers is so silly that no one would dare suggest it now if it hadn't been done for the last 120 years. But it has, and there's no getting away from it.

Why is it so silly? Here's an example. On May 6, 2000, Pedro Martinez pitched nine innings and gave up one run. That same day, Darren Dreifort pitched 5⅔ innings and gave up 4 runs. Who pitched better? Obviously Pedro did. He also got a loss, because the Red Sox didn't score at all against Tampa Bay. Dreifort, however, got a win, as the Dodgers scored 9 runs against Arizona. Probably the greatest pitching performance in major league history ended in a loss, as Harvey Haddix threw 12 perfect innings against the Milwaukee Braves of Joe Adcock and Hank Aaron, only to lose the game in the 13th inning when his defense fell apart, because the Pirates were shut out all night.

Does that mean won-lost records are meaningless? No, of course not. They just have to be taken with a grain of salt. Most of the time a pitcher wins games by pitching well. But sometimes people have great won-lost records even though they didn't pitch particularly well, because they play for great-hitting teams—or are just lucky. The opposite can happen as well. In 1987 Nolan Ryan was one of the very best pitchers in baseball, leading the National League in earned run average and strikeouts. His won-lost record? 8–16.

Earned Run Average (ERA): For starting pitchers, this is usually the best judge of quality. ERA measures how many runs a pitcher gives up per 9 innings—in other words, how many runs a game will be scored against your team with a certain pitcher in there. If a run scores as a result of a fielding error, it's called an *unearned run* and doesn't count toward a pitcher's ERA. Sometimes this leads to pitchers who play for teams that make a lot of errors looking better than they really are, since they give up a lot of runs that aren't counted against their ERAs. Another way that ERAs can be skewed is in the case of relief pitchers. If a reliever comes into a game with runners on base and allows those runners to score, they are charged to the starter (who originally let them get on base). A reliever who lets in a lot of other people's runs can have a good ERA, while a good starting pitcher can have a bad ERA if he plays for a team with poor relievers, who can't help him out if he starts to tire.

Before offenses were inflated like they are today, an ERA below 4.00 was considered average-to-good, while an ERA below 3.00 was excellent. These days, an ERA below about 4.50 is pretty good and below 4.00 is excellent. The league average is close to 5.00. Only *five* starting pitchers in the 2000 American League had ERAs below 4.00 (it takes 162 innings pitched to qualify for the league leaders), and only *one*—Boston's Pedro Martinez—was below 3.00. (Martinez's ERA was an astonishing 1.74, almost two full runs better than runner-up Roger Clemens).

Saves: Saves were officially sanctioned by Major League Baseball in 1969, to recognize that relievers had become an integral part of the game. (Before the 1960s, most relievers were broken down starters, and the few really good ones—like Boston's Ellis Kinder in the 1940s—were treated as flukes. You'll see saves from earlier years in stat books, but that's because they were figured out retroactively.) A save is awarded to a pitcher who finishes a close game (at the time he comes in his team has to be leading by 3 runs or less, or the tying run has to be on deck), assuming he isn't the *pitcher of record*—the pitcher who stands to be awarded the win or loss (a pitcher can get a win or a save, but not both in the same game). In other words, he saves a close victory for another pitcher.

The knock on saves is that a pitcher doesn't always have to pitch very well to get one. In the 1960s and 1970s, relievers tended to be used for two or more innings at a time, and the team's best reliever would be used whenever he was most needed, not just at the end of the game. A terrific reliever might have 20 saves in a season. In the 1980s and early 1990s, bullpens began to get much more specialized, with long relievers, middle relievers, and closers. Top relievers, now called a *closers*, usually were only used for an inning at a time at the end of a game. This led to huge save numbers for the top relievers, many of which were cheaply earned. In the last few years, the pendulum has swung back again. Because of the high levels of offense, a three-run lead is a much closer game than it was in 1985, so a closer's job is more difficult today. At the same time, the best relief pitchers are occasionally being used earlier in the game now.

Less Traditional Stats:

On-base percentage (OBP): A measure of the total times a runner gets on base, whether via base hit, walk, or being hit by a pitch. A .400 on-base percentage is very good, while anything below around .350 is not. A player with a .330 OBP may still be a useful player if he does other things well, such as hitting for excellent power, but he's going to make a lot of extra outs over the course of the season. A player who walks a lot may have a good on-base percentage even if his batting average is mediocre—and a player with a good batting average who never walks may not be a very good player. If you only had one stat available to judge players, in most cases, OBP is the most important one. Teams score runs by not making outs, and on-base percentage tells you how often a player makes an out and how often he gets on base. There are lots of people, iparticularly in the media, who talk about teams making "productive" outs, but in general, any out hurts a team's chances of scoring more runs. There are occasional times when a bunt makes sense, and with a tie game in the last of the ninth and a runner on third and less than two outs, a deep fly ball is as good as a hit, since either ends the game. But for the most part, trading sacrifice flies for walks would lead to a lot more runs.

Slugging Percentage (SLG): While batting average tells you what percentage of the time a player got a hit, slugging percentage tells you how much power a hitter has. It is calculated by dividing a hitter's total bases (a single is 1 base, a double is 2, etc.) by the total number of at-bats. A slugging percentage of .500 is good, even in today's high-offense baseball.

In general, on-base percentage is more important than slugging in winning games—even though home run hitters will appear more frequently in the highlight shows. A player who slugs .500 is good. A player who gets on base half the time (an OBP of .500) is outstanding. A guy who slugs .500 for his career is someone like Jim

Rice—a near Hall of Famer. Not even Ted Williams, the best player ever at getting on base, got on base at a .500 clip (though he came close). If you could slug .600 for a season you'd have had a really good season. If you could get on base at a .600 level, you'd have had the best season that anyone has ever had in the majors.

Because each point of OBP is that much rarer than each point of SLG, each point of OBP is more valuable. In heavy-slugging years, like the current era, with slugging at all-time highs, OBP becomes even more important in comparison—because it's easier to find a slugger who's good at driving in runs than it is to find people who are good at getting on base. And even without home runs, a team that gets a lot of players on base will score a lot of runs—because they aren't making as many outs they will have big innings. In low-scoring times such as the 1960s and the 1900s, the relationship comes pretty close to being even.

OPS: OPS is not really a statistic, but a simple addition of the two previous statistics, OBP and SLG. So what does OPS stand for? *On-base percentage Plus Slugging*. OPS does not correlate quite as well to runs as some other sabermetric measures, but it is very close, and has the advantage of being pretty easy to calculate, particularly as the SLG and OBP numbers have become more widely used. Ranking players by OPS gives you a list that is much closer to actual value than a list of batting averages. One of the problems with OPS, however, is that the relative value of OBP and SLG vary at different times. In a very low scoring environment, like the early 1960s, OBP is less valuable relative to SLG than it is in a high scoring era. In low-offense eras, the ability to drive yourself in (slugging) is more important, because your teammates are less likely to do it for you. In a high offense era, someone's going to get a hit, so just getting on base gives you an excellent chance to score.

Holds: A *hold* is designed as a way to measure the effectiveness of relievers who aren't closers. A middle reliever may come into a game when it is technically a save situation (for instance, when his team is nursing a two-run lead in the sixth inning), but he doesn't really have much chance to get a save. If he pitches well, the game will be turned over to the closer in the ninth inning (and the closer will get the save), but if he pitches poorly, the middle reliever is still charged with a blown save. So a hold is awarded if a reliever enters the game in a save situation and pitches effectively before turning the game over to another pitcher.

All right, I know there are some stranger statistics out there. What are some of the measurements that the "statheads" use, and where do I find out about them?

Linear weights: A method of evaluating a player's offensive contribution to his team run production, developed by John Thorn and Pete Palmer, the authors of *Total Baseball*.

Equivalent Average: Sabermetric evaluation of a player's offensive contribution, scaled to yield averages that look like batting averages. Includes adjustment for home ballpark effects. Developed by Clay Davenport, EQA reports are available at www.BaseballProspectus.com.

SNWL: Support-Neutral Won-Loss record. Developed by Michael Wolverton (and also available at www.BaseballProspectus.com) the idea behind SNWL is to take a bad metric (pitcher won-loss record) and massage it into something useful. Basically, SNWL looks at starting pitchers on a game-by-game basis and awards partial wins and partial losses, based on how often the average team could expect to win or lose with that pitching performance, assuming average run-support.

One of the keys to understanding SNWL is the concept that all runs given up are not equal. A pitcher who gives up 20 runs in 1 game and 0 in the next has got the same ERA as the pitcher who gives up 10 in each. But the first pitcher's team is likely to win that second game, and the second pitcher's team is very likely to be 0–2.

VORP: Value Over Replacement Player—attempts to value players against what a typically available major league replacement would be able to produce. Developed by Keith Woolner, VORP rankings can be found at www.stathead.com.

Pythagorean: Based on Pythagoras' theorum of the relationship of the sides in a right triangle, this was discovered by Bill James, the most famous of the modern sabermetricians. James was looking for the relationship between a team's runs scored and runs allowed, and its winning percentage. He discovered that the ratio of the square of the runs scored to the sum of the square of the runs scored and the square of the runs allowed, very closely approximates the winning percentages of nearly all teams. (Runs Scored^2) / (Runs Scored^2 + Runs Allowed^2).

And there are others. This is just a brief sampling of what's available out in the baseball research universe. But the things that you're most likely to see thrown around are still on-base percentage, slugging, and OPS.

What does it mean to score a baseball game? How is it done?
For some fans, *scoring* a game adds to their enjoyment and understanding; others prefer just to watch the game. Scoring a baseball game is more than keeping track of the number of runs each team has; it involves keeping track of the plays throughout the game to present a detailed picture of how each inning progressed. With even a basic record of the game it is possible to reconstruct how many hits each team had, which fielders made which plays, and some of the internal strategy of the game; more detailed scoring includes such things as pitch counts, distinguishing between a play made deep and a play made shallow, and other nuances. Game programs and some informational magazines sold at the park generally have scoresheets printed in them for the convenience of people who want to score games.

Basically a scoresheet is just a chart; a column runs down the left side for players' names, and then nine (and a few extra) columns that represent innings. Players are written down in the appropriate column, often by number and position. What each player does at the plate in each inning is entered in the appropriate place in a some-what standardized shorthand. There are two charts, one for each team, and therefore the fielding plays for one team are noted on the batting chart for the other.

The basic shorthand for fielding is also used by sports announcers, though it is rarely explained: each position on the field has a number. If the fielder touches the ball, his position number is part of the play. The pitcher is position number 1, the catcher 2; the infield is first base, 3, second base, 4, third base, 5, shortstop, 6; the out-field is 7–8–9 from left to right. Therefore, a ball hit to left field and caught is record-ed as "7"; a ball hit to the shortstop, who makes the successful throw to first, is recorded as "6–3." Strikeouts are recorded as a K, if the batter is out swinging, or a backward K for out looking; walks are recorded as BB (or IBB if intentional), and hit batsmen as HBP. If the batter-runner reaches on an error, the play is recorded with E-number; if a fly is bobbled by the center fielder, for example, it is E8. A double play is recorded with the addendum "DP," so a shortstop-second base-first base play is "6–4–3 DP." Sacrifice flies get scored as "SF" in addition to marking down the out, and bunts as "SH."

Hits are recorded with lines in the box on the chart; a clean single to center gets an 8 and a single diagonal mark, where a double to the same location would get an 8 and two such lines. The plays that allow the runners to advance are marked in the corners of the square that correspond to passage around the bases, with home plate at the bottom. For the abovementioned single an 8 and diagonal would be noted in the lower right hand corner, and if the runner later advanced to second on a wild pitch, the "WP" note would be written in the upper right hand corner, and so on around the bases. When the player has advanced around the bases, a run has scored, of course; at the bottom of the column on a pre-printed chart, there are sometimes boxes to check off runs scored, hits, and sometimes men left on base.

There are separate charts for keeping track of the pitchers; pitching changes are difficult to note on a lineup chart, especially if they happen frequently in a game. The pitching chart has columns for the player's number, name, and the game-related stats: innings pitched, hits and runs given up, earned runs given up, walks, and strike-outs. As many of these are cumulative stats that can only be written down conclu-sively after the pitcher is pulled from the game, they can be tabulated after he is relieved, or with tally-marks rather than numbers. You can make your own chart, or use one that comes with a program you buy at a game.

How does the manager decide on a lineup? What is platooning?

Several decisions go into a lineup, and a manager must ask himself a series of ques-tions: What kinds of hitters do I have? Who's healthy? Who needs rest? Who needs to get into more games? Who's on a hot streak, and who's cold? Do any of my hit-ters do unusually well or poorly against the opposing pitcher? Does my pitcher throw a lot of ground balls, necessitating better infield defense? Can I sacrifice defense for offense at certain positions?

Some managers, like John McNamara and Ralph Houk, are more apt to set a basic lineup in spring training and stick with it as long as possible. They prefer to let their best 8 regulars play nearly every game, while the bench players rarely appear. When Houk managed Boston in 1982, catcher Roger LaFrançois was on the roster all season, yet only played in 8 games, with 10 at bats. This runs the risk of tiring the regulars, or having an unprepared reserve if there's an injury. Other managers, like Jimy Williams, like to rest regulars and use bench players frequently. (Williams used 140 different lineups in 162 games during the 2000 season.) While this may keep the stars fresh over the long season, it can also backfire on a game-by-game basis—because the best players aren't on the field to help the team win.

In a traditional lineup, the leadoff hitter is someone who gets on base and has good speed, but lacks power. Speed used to be the primary qualification for a leadoff man, but many managers have learned the importance of on-base percentage (OBP). Players like Dwight Evans and Wade Boggs scored many runs as leadoff men despite little speed, thanks to high OBPs. Evans was a rare power-hitting leadoff man, but he drew lots of walks—and the Sox had plenty of power hitters to drive him in. Most managers prefer not to "waste" power hitters in that slot, since leadoff hitters often bat with the bases empty.

Traditionally, #2 hitters have been good bunters and hit-and-run artists, with the goal of moving the leadoff man into scoring position. But in today's high-offense game, many managers prefer a less passive, more skilled hitter in that slot. Many #2 hitters are similar to leadoff men (speed, high OBP), while others have more power. If the leadoff man steals lots of bases, a lefty hitter gains an advantage batting second. The first baseman holds the leadoff man on, opening a big hole on the right side of the infield for a lefty pull hitter (who is likely to hit the ball that way, toward right field).

The #3 hitter is generally the team's best: someone who hits for a high average, has power, gets on base, and drives in runs. The #4 (or *cleanup*) hitter typically has the most power, but isn't quite as good as the #3. The #5–6 batters are generally good hitters with power, but a notch or two below the #3–4.

The #7–9 slots are the best of the rest. In the National League (and the American League before 1973), the pitcher, almost always the weakest hitter in the lineup, customarily bats ninth—since the ninth spot will bat the fewest times. In the American League, the ninth hitter is usually the worst one in the lineup. But some managers like to make the ninth slot a "second leadoff," putting a fast player with some on-base ability in there. That way, if the ninth hitter leads off an inning, you have two speedsters setting the table for the #2, 3, and 4 hitters.

One of the oldest and most-criticized lineup strategies is platooning, where a lefty and righty hitter share playing time at a position. Since most lefties hit better against righties, and most righties hit better against lefties, platooning lets a manager combine the best skills of two flawed players. Some managers platoon at several positions, while others will only do so at one or two. It depends not only upon the manager's strategic bent, but also on the personnel. A star player like Ted Williams or Nomar Garciaparra will never be platooned. But lesser players (like Reggie Jefferson and Mike Stanley, or Rick Miller and Reid Nichols) have been very useful in platoon roles. Many young players (like Trot Nixon) begin their careers in platoons, and their managers are often urged to play them every day.

Some forms of platooning date back to the nineteenth century, but the practice was popularized by Boston's other team in 1914. The "Miracle Braves," a last-place club in July, won the World Series with platoons in all three outfield positions. Manager George Stallings was hailed as a genius, and many teams copied his strategy. The practice died down somewhat in the 1930s and 1940s, and Casey Stengel is credited with making it popular again.

As statistics have gotten more precise, some analysts have criticized the typical lefty-righty platoon system. They've urged managers to go deeper into the numbers, and select hitters based on such factors as players who hit better at home or on the road, during the day or at night, against fly ball pitchers or ground ball hitters, and other categories. (For instance, Red Sox catcher Scott Hatteberg hits much better during the daytime, while catcher Jason Varitek hits much better at night.) But managers have been reluctant to use this sort of complex platoons, and platooning remains largely a lefty-righty phenomenon.

What's a pitching rotation? What's an ace? How about a closer? What's more valuable, a great starting pitcher or a great reliever?

Unlike every other position on the field, the stress of pitching is such that no one can do it every day without significant damage to the shoulder and arm. There was a time in the late 1800s, the very early days of professional baseball, when the object of the pitcher was not to strike someone out, but rather to put the ball where the hitter could put the ball in play. Under these conditions, playing with balls that couldn't be hit out of the ballpark under most conditions (the so-called "dead ball era"), the stress on the shoulder and arm of the pitcher was significantly different than it is today, and many teams had just one starting pitcher. But starting shortly before the turn of the century, that changed, and teams began to have multiple starting pitchers, each of whom would start in turn. In other words, they'd "rotate" their pitchers from game to game. For most of the twentieth century a typical starting rotation consisted of four pitchers, pitching on about three days' rest. In the early 1970s the transition began to a five man rotation, each going on four days' rest. (In practice, the best starter gets more turns than the other pitchers, and the weakest pitcher gets skipped if there is a day off.)

As to what an "ace" is, there is no strict definition, but generally an ace is the best starting pitcher on a staff. However, some people think that an ace is a top-level pitcher, and that most teams don't have an ace at all. In the 2000 season Pedro Martinez clearly was an ace, and Randy Johnson, Kevin Brown, and Greg Maddux wouldn't draw much debate either. Beyond that, people disagree, based on different usages of the term. Broadcasters typically use the looser definition, defining the best starter on a team, or sometimes even the best over the last couple of starts, as the "ace of the staff."

A closer is a relatively new phenomenon, not seen much before the 1960s, and assuming its current form and stature within the past decade or so. The closer is a pitcher who starts the game in the bullpen and is brought into a game as a reliever, when the team is leading by a small margin late in the game, to close out the game.

The typical manager brings the closer into the game in situations where the closer is eligible to receive a *save*. That ordinarily means to pitch the last half-inning with a lead of three runs or less.

As to which is more valuable, there isn't any real debate over that. A great starting pitcher is of more value to a team than a great reliever, simply due to the number of innings pitched. Derek Lowe, who generally pitches more than a typical closer, pitched 91 innings in 2000, while the Red Sox had 4 starters with more innings pitched, and a fifth that racked up 71 in only 2½ months with the team.

While it is clear that a great starter is the more valuable commodity, there is some debate over the actual value of a closer. Some think that anyone can pitch the ninth inning, and that there isn't any reason to designate someone for that job. In addition, there are people who believe that closers would be more valuable to the team by pitching more innings—either starting the game, or coming into games earlier and being available out of the bullpen less often. On the other hand, there is a case to be made for having a great or near-great pitcher available to pitch in situations where the outs are determinative—that is, when a perfect inning guarantees a victory. But the exact value of the closer is still unclear, and frequently debated.

How can I tell a good defensive player from a bad one when I'm watching a game? Why do people say defensive stats are unreliable?

How can I tell a good defensive player from a bad one when I'm watching a game? The short answer is, you can't. A trained scout who has been watching for years can make a guess, but the reality is, no one can actually tell from watching a game whether someone is good, bad, or indifferent. There are certain aspects of defensive baseball that we can evaluate, but the bottom line on defense is this—the goal of position players is to turn batted balls into outs, and there is no way to say for sure who is good at it, and who isn't. There are some exceptions, mostly on the downside, where it is obvious that a player is just incapable of getting to balls, or incapable of fielding them. But at the typical level of major league competence (even the worst major leaguer is one of the top 1,000 or so baseball players in the world), it is just not possible for human beings to make the comparisons that a rigid assessment of defensive abilities would require.

Scouts certainly want to see how fast a player is. They want to know how well a player catches the ball and throws it. There are drills that they'll watch and things they'll look for in games to try to make a judgment on how well the player reacts to a batted ball. How quickly does he react? Does he go in the right direction immediately? Every time? How do his reactions compare to the other players in the game? How do his reactions compare to the other players available to the team? One of the biggest things that is tough to quantify is instinct—was the player standing in the optimal spot when the pitcher released the ball?

All of these questions are useful criteria in trying to determine a player's potential. They are things that a scout with a stopwatch and some time to observe and interact with a player can use to perform some high level evaluation. Unfortunately for the fan in the stands, the human brain is not constructed to make rational assessments and comparisons between two similar events separated by time. Observation can make you think that two events are similar, but can't quantify the similarities and differences. Consider, for example, that a ball is hit to a Red Sox second baseman's left and he handles it. A similar ball is hit to an Indians second baseman 2 weeks, or 2 days, or even 2 innings, earlier. Were the balls hit at the same speed? Were the second basemen playing at the same spot on the diamond? Did the balls spin off the bats the same way? Was the terrain the same? There just isn't any way to tell by observation.

Frankly, the same holds for offense as well. If you only watched games and didn't take numbers into account you'd look at what happened and form opinions, but very possibly those opinions would cause you to think that Garret Anderson is a better hitter than John Olerud, or Sammy Sosa is more valuable than Barry Bonds. But how a player looks at bat or in the field doesn't always reflect how good he really is. It is only by objective analysis of what they've accomplished in their at-bats that we know that Anderson doesn't compare to Olerud over time, and that Sosa's home runs don't match up to Bonds's overall offensive game. Sometimes scouts *do* make judgments based on this sort of appearances, and they can lead to disaster; for instance Wade Boggs was stuck in the minor leagues for years because he didn't fit the perception of what a good hitter should *look* like, even though he hit well every year. Similarly, Phil Plantier wasn't given much of a chance as a major league hitter because he had an unorthodox batting stance, and scouts decided that he couldn't hit that way, instead of paying attention to his actual results.

When the same comparisons come up while talking of defense, there is no objective standard to fall back upon to measure the actual accomplishments of the defensive players. The one standard that is typically used is one of the most misleading statistics of all—fielding percentage. Fielding percentage is a simple rate statistic, where the number of errors that a players has made is divided by the total number of chances that the player has. (A *chance* is any time a player handles the ball during a play.) The problem with fielding percentage is that it's only half of fielding, and doesn't tell you anything about a player's range—how many balls a player gets to. An outfielder that stood in one place would be a horrible defender, but wouldn't ever make an error. By contrast, Nomar Garciaparra gets to a lot of balls that other shortstops wouldn't, but makes an above-average number of throwing errors on those balls. None of this is going to be discernible by someone watching a single game, or even several.

One way to try to judge a player's range is to see how many total chances he has per game—does he make a lot more plays than his peers at that position? This is useful in figuring out what kind of range players have, but it's not infallible. A team whose pitchers yield a lot of ground balls will inflate the stats of the infielders, while a team with a lot of flyball pitchers will make the outfielders look better. Different ballparks can affect range as well; for instance Fenway Park left fielders always seem to have terrible range, because left field in Fenway is small, and many potential outs in other parks turn into hits off the Green Monster.

Frequently, defensive skills are judged much as figure skating is judged—people watch and assign higher rankings to the people that look the smoothest. There is also often a mental "bonus" applied to players who make spectacular plays, diving to the left or the right. A player will get praise for making a play with a diving catch that a faster, or more reactive, or better positioned player will make standing upright. But there has not yet been, despite some very good attempts, an objective means of rating defense.

There are currently a couple of sabremetric attempts to quantify defense. Project Scoresheet has observers at every single major league game, tracking the balls that are hit. They divide the fields into different areas, and every batted ball becomes the responsibility of a fielder. They compute a Defensive Average, which is analogous to batting average—every fielder gets a DA, computed by dividing outs produced by total opportunities. STATS, Inc. also has observers, whose data they use to compute a rating called Range Factor. Range Factor is similar to DA but does not have zones overlapping, so there are balls in right field that are no one's responsibility, while every ball has a zone of responsibility for DA. But while each has adherents in parts of the "stathead" or sabermetric community, neither has been embraced by the mainstream yet.

How much effect does Fenway Park have on the Red Sox players' stats? Do other parks have the same kind of impact?

Fenway has always been known as a park that greatly favors hitters, leading to more runs and home runs. Since the late 1980s Fenway has actually hurt home run hitters, but most media members still think of it as a "launching pad," because of its long-time reputation. In terms of overall offense, Fenway isn't as much of a factor as it once was, but it still favors hitters.

As any fan or player can attest, Fenway has the oddest dimensions of any big league stadium. For one thing, there is almost no foul territory. This is to the hitter's advantage, since popups that would be outs anywhere else fall harmlessly into the stands. (By contrast, Oakland has acres of foul ground, helping its staff's ERAs and saving them from throwing a few extra pitches.)

For example, the Green Monster is an inviting target in left field, and several righty hitters (Bobby Doerr, Felix Mantilla) tailored their swings to loft flies into the screen. On the other hand, hitters like Nomar Garciaparra and Jim Rice lost several homers a year, since the Wall turned their long liners into singles and doubles. What's worse, some righty batters try too hard to hit homers at Fenway, ruining their swings (and batting averages) in the process. Because of the Monster, managers have been reluctant to use lefthanded pitchers at Fenway, since righty batters can turn mistakes into homers. The stereotype isn't entirely true, however, since Lefty Grove, Bill Lee, and Bruce Hurst all pitched very well at Fenway.

Right field is another story, however. Once you get past Pesky's Pole, it takes a monstrous shot to hit a homer to right (before the bullpen was installed in 1940, it was even tougher). Lefty pull hitters routinely lose home runs at Fenway. Most of the Red Sox best hitters, however, have been lefthanded line drive hitters who learned how to hit to the opposite field (including Fred Lynn and Mo Vaughn, both of whose stats declined tremendously when they moved to the Angels).

In 1988 the Red Sox added the 600 Club seats behind home plate, a huge structure that is widely believed to have cut down the wind that normally blew out to left field—thus reducing homers. The statistics clearly indicate that Fenway is now one of the more difficult parks to hit a home run in. (In 2000 only Detroit's new Comerica Park was less homer-friendly.) Other teams have moved into smaller parks that favor homers, and this makes Fenway look like even less of a launching pad—while also reducing the overall offensive impact of the ballpark.

One of the charms of baseball is the uniqueness of its stadiums; each park has a different effect on statistics. Coors Field, in the Mile High City of Denver, increases offense more than any park in baseball. The thin air makes the ball carry about 10% further than it does at sea level. The park has deep fences to compensate, but this results in more base hits—since there is more area for the ball to drop in where an outfielder can't reach. The Astros' new park, Enron Field, is also known for helping batting stats, but their old home, the Astrodome, was the best pitching park in history. Shea Stadium (Mets), Dodger Stadium, and the Tigers' Comerica Park are other parks that help pitchers. On the other hand, some parks favor certain types of players. Yankee Stadium has a very short right field, but a deep left field. Lefty hitters who master the art of pulling fly balls hit more homers there, but righties are often frustrated by the deep fences in left-center.

What happens if the umpires can't agree on a call?

The umpires will privately huddle and discuss the disputed play. Each ump will discuss what he saw, and they'll try to come up with the most fair (or foul) solution. The umpires usually let the one who had the best view make the final decision. For example, umpires are often blocked by fielders on tag plays, and another ump may have a better angle. Umpires are divided into 4-man crews who work together all season, so they usually communicate with each other pretty well. But if they still can't agree on a call, the crew chief (generally the one with the most experience) has the final say.

One frequent complaint of Red Sox manager Jimy Williams is that major league umpires frequently don't ask for help from another umpire if they don't have a clear view (and umpires almost never overrule calls once they have been made—even if they realize the call was wrong). Once in a while the crew chief will overrule another member of the crew on a call.

Are players allowed to steal the other team's signals? How about doctoring the ball or the bat? What's considered legal and illegal?

Players, coaches, and managers have stolen signs from opponents since the game began. Though it may not be ethical, certain kinds of sign-stealing are condoned as "part of the game," while more blatant efforts have been outlawed. Runners on second base have a great view of the catcher's signals, and often try to relay them to the batter. The catcher, in turn, will frequently send bogus signals to the pitcher, to trip up the baserunning spy. This is considered fair, but if a batter turns around to peek at the catcher's signals, the pitcher will sometimes throw the next pitch at his head. People in the dugout can try to decode the third base coach's signs, but other forms of spying are big no-nos. Several teams have been accused of putting hidden cameras in the center field scoreboard (monitored from within the clubhouse behind the dugout), in order to decipher the catcher's signs. This is completely illegal, though most of these allegations are never proven.

Other forms of cheating include spitball pitching and a corked bat. Before 1920, pitchers could put spit, grease, and other substances on the ball. This made pitches move sharply and unpredictably, and drove hitters crazy. After the 1920 season baseball made rules to increase hitting (due largely to the fallout of the 1919 Black Sox gambling scandal, and also the popularity of Babe Ruth's homers). The spitball was outlawed, but 17 known spitballers were allowed to keep throwing it until they retired. Though illegal today, many pitchers (most notably Hall of Famer Gaylord Perry) have used it, or been accused of using it. If caught, spitballers are ejected and suspended.

The hitting version of the spitball is the corked bat. Some batters have been known to drill holes in their bats and fill the holes with cork or rubber. This makes the ball go further than it would when hit by an unaltered wooden bat, but the illegal contents are easily revealed if the bat breaks. Players caught with corked bats are also ejected and suspended. One famous incident occurred in the Red Sox–Indians playoff series in 1995. Manager Kevin Kennedy accused Cleveland slugger Albert Belle of corking his bat. After a home run, Belle taunted Kennedy by pointing to his muscles. At another time, earlier in Belle's career, his bat shattered during a time at bat and a bunch of rubber balls fell out.

What is salary arbitration? How does it work?

All but a few players with less than three years of service time have to play for whatever salary the team wants to pay them. Teams will negotiate to a certain extent, because they don't want their players to be unhappy, but players have very limited leverage until after their third year in the big leagues. After a player has about three years of major league service time (the top 17 percent of players with more than two years are included as well) he is eligible for *salary arbitration*. If a player with three or more years of experience and his team can't agree on a salary, the team can offer arbitration. If the player accepts (and players with less than six years of service time don't have a choice), he is considered signed to a one-year contract. Teams can also offer their own free agents arbitration. If a team refuses to offer arbitration to an unsigned player who is eligible, he becomes a free agent. (This is common when a team wouldn't mind signing a player at a low salary, but doesn't think he is worth the high salary an arbiter would award.)

Before the arbitration period in February, the team and player exchange salary figures. If they can't compromise before the hearing is held, each side gets a chance to argue before an arbitrator why their figure is more in line with the major league salary for comparable players. The argument often centers on whom the player in arbitration is most comparable to. The arbiter can pick either the team's proposed salary or the player's proposed salary—he is not allowed to compromise. Often arbitration is offered because if a player declines arbitration and signs elsewhere, the team who loses him may get up to two high-round draft choices, depending on how good the player is. Every once in a while a team offers arbitration to a player it doesn't really want for this reason and gets burned when the player accepts.

Because even players who lose generally get huge raises (and players who win increase the salary scale to which other players in arbitration are compared) arbitration was seen as a huge factor in driving up player salaries in the 1980s and early 1990s, and was a major sticking point in the negotiations to end several strikes. More recently owners have reacted by either signing young players to long-term contracts before they are arbitration eligible (as the Red Sox did with Nomar Garciaparra) or releasing arbitration eligible players who they feel can be replaced more cheaply. (Many of these players then have to sign more cheaply elsewhere or settle for minor league deals, so the effect has been mainly to increase the salary gap between the stars and the lesser players.)

How many times can you send a player to the minor leagues? What does it mean to "option" someone? What are waivers?

When a player is first signed the club who signs him gets 3 *options*, each one good for a year. If the player is under 19 when first signed, he needn't be protected from the Rule 5 draft (see page 251) until 4 seasons after he signs. If he is over 19 he must be protected by being placed on the team's 40-man roster after 3 seasons or the Red Sox risk losing him. As long as a player has options remaining, the team can call him up and send him down as much as they want (although a player who is sent to the minors can't be recalled for 10 days, to keep clubs from shuttling different pitchers through their roster every night, which would make the 25-player roster meaningless). A player who isn't ready for the major leagues is usually optioned to the minors at the end of spring training. That uses up one option, but he can be recalled and sent back to the minors any number of times during the year that option is in effect. Remember that most players who make the major leagues spend about 5 years in the minors. The option rule is designed to allow teams to send players back and forth for a reasonable amount of time while they are developing, but not to keep them indefinitely in the minor leagues when they could be playing in the majors somewhere else.

After the three options are used up, a player has to pass through *waivers* to be sent down to the minors, meaning that any other club can put in a claim for him, and if the team doesn't pull the player back off waivers, the claiming team gets him. They get his salary, too, so you don't want to claim an overpriced player whom you don't want. You have to pass a player through waivers for certain kinds of trades, too—about half of major league players are put on waivers every year. The list is supposed to be secret (so players don't feel like their teams are trying to get rid of them).

When the Red Sox send down a marginal veteran player like Andy Sheets, for example, any other team can claim him. If nobody wants him, he is sent to the minors.

After you have 5 years in the majors, you can refuse an assignment to the minor leagues and become a free agent if the team tries to send you down, even if you still have options. Once a player passes through waivers (it takes 72 hours) and is officially released, any new team that signs him only has to pay the major league mini-mum salary (or a prorated portion of it). The rest of his contract is paid by the team who signed him to the contract. So in 2000 the Red Sox only paid Pete Schourek $200,000. The rest of his $2 million salary was being borne by the Pittsburgh Pirates, who had released him in spring training.

When does a player become a free agent?

After six years of major league service a player whose contract expires can become a *free agent,* and is free to sign with any team in baseball (including his current team). Players who are released and clear waivers also become free agents, as do players who have been in the minor leagues for 6 years and are not put on a team's 40-man major league roster (these players are usually called *minor league free agents*).

Sometimes players become free agents for other reasons, such as when a team breaks a rule. The Red Sox lost Carlton Fisk to free agency (and would have lost Fred Lynn if they hadn't quickly traded him for much less than his true value) after the 1980 season when they didn't mail them contracts by the deadline. The Red Sox signed minor league first baseman Carlos Diaz in 2000 after he was made a free agent because the Dodgers went into Cuba to sign him, violating the American embargo on Cuba.

A team can offer arbitration to a player eligible for free agency, but players—who want the security of a guaranteed contract lasting more than one year—seldom accept.

Star free agents command the highest salaries in baseball, but they aren't always a good deal. It may be popular with sportswriters and casual fans when a team signs a big-name player for millions of dollars, but when Red Sox general manager Lou Gorman signed a bunch of pricey free agents in the late 1980s and early 1990s it led to disastrous teams filled with old, frequently hurt players.

Remember that baseball players typically make the major leagues when they are 23 to 25 years old, and don't become free agents until they have 6 full years of major league experience. As a group, baseball players peak around age 27 (some say a little older), and start to decline rapidly after age 30. While there are exceptions to this (and a few players have played into their fifties), most major league players end their careers before they are 35. So as a general manager, you have to think long and hard about whether you want to sign a superstar player to the 7-year contract he wants when he may only have 2 or 3 good years left.

If a Red Sox player signs with another team as a free agent, do the Sox get any kind of compensation for losing him?

It depends. Each year, the Elias Sports Bureau ranks all players based upon their stats in certain categories over the past two seasons. Many statisticians ridicule these results, which even Elias admits are pretty arbitrary, but they're used by major league baseball to determine free agent compensation.

The top 30% of all players at each position are classified as Type A. If the Red Sox lose a Type A free agent, they get the other team's first or second round pick in the next draft. If the other team has one of the 15 best records in the major leagues, it must surrender its first rounder. If they're one of the bottom 15 teams, they can keep their #1, but must give up their #2. In addition, the Red Sox would get a "supplemental" pick between the first and second rounds. For example, when Mo Vaughn left Boston in 1999, the Sox got the Angels' first rounder (used to select outfielder Rick Asadoorian) and a supplemental pick (pitcher Brad Baker).

Players ranked in the 31–50% range are Type B. If the Red Sox lose a Type B free agent, they get the other team's first or second round pick (same rules as Type A). However, they do not get the supplemental pick. In 2000, Type B Rheal Cormier signed with the Phillies, so Boston gets the Phillies' second round pick (the Phils were one of the bottom 15 teams, so they keep their first rounder).

Players ranked in the 51–60% range are Type C. If the Red Sox lose a Type C free agent, they get a supplemental pick between the second and third rounds. Type C free agents are very rare. Tom Gordon, who signed with the Cubs in 2000, is the first Type C free agent the Red Sox have lost in recent years.

Any players ranked in the lowest 40% do not require compensation as free agents.

Also, before a team can get compensation, it must formally offer arbitration (see page 245) to a free agent by an early December deadline. If the player accepts, he is considered signed, and returns to his original team at a salary determined by an arbitrator. If a team doesn't offer arbitration to a free agent, it doesn't get compensation if he leaves—even if he's a Type A, B, or C player. Since draft picks are involved, one might think teams that would always offer arbitration. But sometimes they're afraid that other teams won't make good offers, forcing the free agent to accept arbitration and return. If the team doesn't want to get stuck with a big contract, or just wants the player gone at any cost, they might decide to play it safe and not offer arbitration.

I've heard people say that big-name free agents don't like to sign with the Red Sox. Why is that?

Boston has a poor reputation with many athletes who grew up in the Southern or Western United States or the Caribbean (as the majority of them do). It's about as far culturally from what they are used to as can exist in the United States. Besides, Boston's climate is cold in April and May and too overcast and rainy for many Southern, Western, or Caribbean athletes' taste all year round—especially for those players who have grown up in a hot climate and would prefer to play and live somewhere warmer than New England.

Whether it fully deserves it or not, Boston has a reputation as a snooty, academic town with its share of racism, which alienates many ballplayers. The Boston Red Sox were the *last* team in major league baseball to have a black ballplayer on their roster (the very limited Pumpsie Green). They passed on signing both Jackie Robinson and Willie Mays. Despite the current team administration's systematic eradication of the Sox racist legacy, the reputation persists to a certain extent even though Boston fans of all races and creeds have welcomed Pedro Martinez, Nomar Garciaparra, Rich

Garces, Troy O'Leary, Carl Everett, Sang-Hoon Lee, Hideo Nomo, and Tomokazu Ohka—to name just a few players who happen not to be white. In fact, Manny Ramirez was advised by friends and family to sign with the Red Sox in late 2000 in part because of Boston's thriving Dominican population and friendliness to Dominican athletes. He also shopped in the Dominican areas of Boston for years when he came to town on road trips and so already had first-hand experience with the community.

Unfortunately, despite Fenway Park's fabled history, it has some of the worst major league clubhouse and ballpark facilities in baseball, especially when compared to sleek new corporate parks in other cities. (Talks about building a new Fenway Park are in process—a very *long* process involving complex multiparty negotiations between the club, the state, and the city of Boston, which do not appear to be immediately resolved at this writing.) For instance, the clubhouse is small, cramped, and visited by the occasional rat. Boston traffic—including traffic to and from Fenway Park—is infamous for its frustrating density. Therefore a multimillionaire free agent, given the choice, might pick a team with more modern clubhouse and ballpark facilities over the quirky and historical but aging Fenway Park.

The good news and the bad news is that Red Sox fans are passionate about their team. Since Fenway Park is tiny, the fans are very close to the playing field. A player on the field can hear everything some drunk fan is shouting from Section 14—which makes for an unpleasant working environment for a personally struggling player or a struggling Red Sox team. (Ted Williams once tried to silence a heckler by repeatedly pulling the ball foul to where he was sitting, for example.) There is really no designated place for players' families to sit and watch a game without sitting in the stands and hearing often-obscene, often-personally vitriolic tirades directed against their loved ones by aggravated and sometimes inebriated fans (despite Fenway Park staff's diligent attempts to curb boorish fan behavior). This can make a free agent concerned about not only his own working environment at Fenway but the safety of his family in the stands. And like anyone else, ballplayers prefer a pleasant working environment.

In terms of media relations, the Boston media is very intense and actively investigative in its coverage of the Red Sox. Some players are happy with this and some players find this intensely uncomfortable, depending on what kind of relationship they have traditionally had with media as well as their own communication style. Players who are not natural communicators can get themselves into trouble with the Boston media through simple misunderstandings on both sides. Some players also might prefer not to be put under the enormous combined media and fan pressure of decades and decades without a World Series title and would rather sign with a team that has had a World Series win more than 82 seasons ago.

There is also the issue that the Red Sox are owned by a trust. And a trust can't buy a player a drink and put its arm around a player and say "No matter what happens, if you sign with my team, I'll always treat you and your family right. You have my sacred word on that." Since the Red Sox are up for sale, it's an open question as to who the new owner (or ownership group) will be. Does a free agent want to sign a long-term contract and then find out that he doesn't fit well with the new owner or ownership group—and that contract might be in jeopardy? Perhaps . . . or perhaps not.

These are a number of potentially daunting negatives to work against, and agents aren't above bringing up any or all of them during negotiations. While most teams start at zero, and a few teams—like the Yankees, the Giants, the Diamondbacks, and the Braves—may start on the plus side, the Red Sox have to start at a minus on the player likeability scale.

To sum up: Boston is not an ideal place to play as far as many baseball players are concerned. And, some things—like the weather, the traffic, and the culture—the Red Sox general manager can't do much about. So the general manager may end up over-paying for a lot of Grade B free agents and having to acquire most of the best play-ers through the system (Nomar, Nixon, Hatteberg) or in trades (Pedro, Everett, Lowe, Varitek). The general manager may give former lesser stars second chances (Saberhagen, Beck, Fassero) which they appreciate and find young players who've had arm troubles (Pichardo, Garces) and give them a chance. The general manager may go to the Frontier League and find a Morgan Burkhart or give career minor lea-guer Brian Daubach a last shot. In short, the Boston Red Sox general manager will do the best he can. That may not include being able to sign big-name free agents.

How does the amateur draft work? What happens if a player doesn't want to sign with the team that drafts him? How do players from foreign countries get signed by teams?

The Amateur Draft was created in 1965. Baseball wanted to stop big-budget teams from signing the best amateur players, while giving the worst teams the first shot at top prospects. The draft is held every June. (There was once a January draft too, but it was discontinued.) Picks are alternated between American League and National League teams, in reverse order of their records the previous year. If a team loses 100 games, they'll have one of the top picks in each round, while the World Series win-ner will have one of the last picks. The draft generally lasts about 50 rounds, though very few late-round picks make the major leagues.

Only players born in the United States, Canada, and Puerto Rico are eligible for the Amateur Draft. All high school seniors are eligible, as are all players at two-year "junior" colleges. Players at 4-year colleges are eligible if they turn 21 within 45 days of the draft.

Not all drafted players sign right away, especially if they're picked in later rounds. High school players often choose to go to college, either for an education or to increase their value in future drafts (for example, the Mets drafted Roger Clemens in 1981, but he decided to go to the University of Texas, and was redrafted by Boston). College players sometimes return to school (an example is Red Sox catcher Jason Varitek, who refused to sign with the Twins in 1993) if they don't like the team's offer and think they will be able to get more money later—although this is risky, since a player who gets hurt or plays badly may see his value go *down*. If a drafted player goes to (or returns to) a four-year college, the team loses their rights to sign him. But if a drafted player goes to (or returns to) a two-year college, the team can still sign him up to a week before the next Amateur Draft. Teams often let late-round picks from high schools play a year at junior college before deciding whether to sign them; this practice is called *draft-and-follow*.

Amateur players from other countries (again, except for Cuba, because of the United States' embargo on Cuba) can be signed as free agents by big league teams as long as they're at least 16 years old. The Dominican Republic, despite its tiny size, has produced some of the game's greatest stars, including Pedro Martinez, Manny Ramirez, and Vladimir Guerrero. Other foreign sources of big league talent include Venezuela, Mexico, Japan, Korea, and Australia. Many Cubans have signed with major league clubs in recent years *after* defecting to the United States.

What is the Rule 5 Draft? Is it good or bad for a player to be selected?

The Rule 5 Draft is held every December at baseball's Winter Meetings. Teams must submit a 40-man major league roster by a certain date in November. Minor leaguers who have played more than three professional seasons (four if they were signed before age 19) who are not placed on the 40-man roster can be lost in the Rule 5 Draft. Since there are only 40 roster spaces available, including 25 major leaguers, only the most promising minor league players can be protected from the Rule 5 Draft. Hundreds of minor leaguers are eligible, but few are strong candidates to be drafted.

Like the Amateur Draft, teams pick in reverse order of their records. Teams can only select players in the Rule 5 draft if they have an opening on their 40-man roster. They can take any eligible player from any organization (they pay $50,000 to the team who loses the player). But there's a big catch: whomever they select *must* be on the major league roster for the entire season. Before a Rule 5 draftee can be sent to the minor leagues, he must be offered back to his old team for $25,000. (The original team usually takes the player back.) Relatively few players are selected in the Rule 5 draft, which usually lasts one or two rounds—and all but a handful are given back to their old clubs by the end of Spring Training. In 1999 17 players were taken in the draft (16 in the first round and 1 in the second round), and none of them had an impact on the major league team who selected him. The Red Sox lost two players in 1999 (pitcher Chris Reitsma, who was returned, then later traded to Cincinnati, and pitcher Marty McLeary, who was also returned) and none in 2000. The last Rule 5 selection to play for the Sox was Vaughn Eshelman from 1995–97. Other recent Sox Rule 5 players include John Trautwein and Mike Trujillo, neither of whom went on to have successful careers.

Although Rule 5 players have a golden opportunity to make the majors ahead of schedule, the draft is often bad for their careers in the long run. Most Rule 5 players are very raw (often coming from Class A ball) and far from ready for the majors. Big league teams are often forced to bury these players at the end of the bench, depriving them of valuable at bats or innings pitched. After a season in the majors, many Rule 5 players go back to the minors, and most are never heard from again. Notable exceptions include George Bell and Kelly Gruber, two Rule 5 selections by Toronto who became stars in the 1980s, and current Detroit shortstop Deivi Cruz. Fortunately for the Red Sox, Wade Boggs was never lost in the Rule 5 Draft; he was eligible in 1980 and 1981, but 25 teams passed him up twice.

How do trades work? Why is there a trading deadline? What's the 10-and-5 rule? Are there other ways that teams or players can block trades?

Trades can occur during the season (pending some deadlines and rules), or in the off-season (usually during the December Winter Meetings). Sometimes teams don't get a player in return right away; instead, they'll trade someone for a "player to be named later" or "future considerations," and the deal is completed within six months. Teams can also trade players for cash, but baseball (unlike other sports) does not allow teams to trade draft picks.

Broadly speaking, there are three types of trades. Teams with bad records and/or payroll restrictions often trade high-priced players before they can declare free agency. The idea is to get some young, cheap players in return, instead of losing the player for draft picks. The Red Sox did this in 1997, getting Derek Lowe and Jason Varitek for Heathcliff Slocumb. Other times teams do the opposite, trading young players for veterans they hope can get them into the playoffs, as the Sox did in the Pedro Martinez and Carl Everett deals. Or a team might have a surplus at one position, but a weakness at another. They'll try to find a team with the opposite problem, and work out a deal to help both teams. The Red Sox did this in 1989, trading Lee Smith—one of two good closers—for outfielder Tom Brunansky, who the Cardinals easily replaced.

During the season, there are two main trading deadlines. From Opening Day through July 31, teams can freely trade players. After July 31, only players who have cleared waivers (see page 246) can be traded. Because of this rule, teams often put players on recallable waivers (if the player is claimed, the team can pull him back) before July 31, hoping to sneak them through and make them eligible for a trade. August 31 is, for all intents and purposes, the second trading deadline. After that date, players acquired in trades aren't eligible for the playoffs (see page 253). So playoff contenders tend to make deals in late August to firm up playoff rosters, but trades after September 1 are rare.

Players have some control over whether they're traded. The "10-and-5 Rule" gives all players with 10 years of big league service, the last 5 on their current team, the right to veto trades. (No current Red Sox player is a "10-and 5-Man," but John Valentin could become one when he reaches 10 years, in July 2001.) Other players negotiate no-trade clauses in their contracts (the Red Sox have a club policy prohibiting this). Some no-trade clauses give the player veto power on all trades. Others specify teams the player can or can't be traded to. Trades can also be vetoed by the commissioner if he feels they violate "the best interests of baseball." In 1976, the Red Sox gave Oakland $2 million for Rollie Fingers and Joe Rudi, but Commissioner Bowie Kuhn overturned the deal, essentially banning the longtime practice of poor clubs selling their stars to better-off teams for quick cash.

What's the difference between the 25-man roster and the 40-man roster? How about the playoff roster?

During the offseason teams are required to set a 40-man major league roster. All players with three or more years in professional baseball (four years if they signed before age 19) must either be placed on the 40-man roster, or else be subject to the Rule 5 Draft (see page 251). The 40-man roster will have established big leaguers, several players from the AAA team, and a few other prospects. Teams often leave a few spaces open for free agents or players acquired in trades. By spring training, the 40-man roster is usually completely filled.

Players on the 40-man roster and selected minor league invitees fight for spots on the 25-man roster during spring training. From Opening Day to August 31 big league teams carry 25 active players. During spring training, some players from the 40-man roster are sent to the minors or released, and the active roster is cut to 25 before the regular season begins (with the other players on the 40-man roster playing in the minor leagues).

If a player on the 25-man roster is hurt, he can be placed on the disabled list. Most injured players go on the 15-day DL, meaning they can't play for a minimum of 15 days and are temporarily off the 25-man roster. During this time the team can call up a replacement from the minors. When the injured player returns, someone must be taken off the 25-man roster (usually by sending them to the minors). Seriously injured players often go on the 60-day DL. Players on the 60-day DL are also taken off the 40-man roster until they're reactivated, so they're easier to replace.

Any player on the 40-man roster can join the 25-man roster without any problems. Sometimes players who aren't on the 40-man roster are called up. If there aren't any vacancies on the 40-man roster, someone must be taken off. Any player taken off the 40-man roster goes on waivers, giving all other teams the right to claim him for cash. For example, Troy O'Leary was removed from the Brewers' 40-man roster at the end of 1995 spring training. He went on waivers, and the Red Sox claimed him.

On September 1 teams can expand their 25-man roster to 40 players, and they bring up several minor leaguers (generally 5–8 players, rather than the maximum 15). Teams in contention call up players to fill specific roles (pinch-runner, extra lefty reliever, third catcher). Teams lower in the standings like to give minor leaguers auditions for the following season. Most callups are already on the official 40-man roster, so they can be easily added to the active roster. If not, they can only join if there's a vacancy on the 40-man roster, and the same waiver rules apply.

If a team makes the playoffs it submits a 25-man roster prior to each round. Only players on the 25-man roster or the DL on August 31 are eligible for the playoff roster (so a team can have a few more than 25 players available). Players acquired in September trades—and those still in the minors on August 31—are ineligible, unless the league grants special permission. However, the team can submit a different roster before each playoff round, provided they have more than 25 eligible players. Sometimes a team omits a player from the first round roster, but decides he'd be a better fit than someone else in the next round.

How do the playoffs work in baseball? How many games do the Sox have to win to become world champions?

Four teams in each league make the playoffs. The three division winners (East, Central, and West) qualify, as does a *wild card* team (the non-division winner with the best record). The first round of playoffs is a best-of-five (called the Divisional Series). The division winner with the best record plays the wild card team, and the other two division winners play each other. (If the wild card winner is in the same division as the team with the best record, the team with the best record plays the division winner with the worst record.) The winners of the first round play each other in a best-of-seven League Championship Series (LCS). The winner of the LCS goes to the World Series, where it plays a best-of-seven against the other league's champion.

If the Red Sox make the playoffs, they'll need to win 11 games to be World Champions. (They'll probably need to win at least 90 regular season games first!)

What does "games behind" mean? What's a "magic number?"

Games behind (sometimes abbreviated GB in newspapers) is a way of measuring how hard it is to catch up to a team that's ahead in the standings. A team gains a game in the standing anytime it wins and the team in first place loses (meaning that each win or opponent's loss is worth half a game). So if the Yankees are 54–47 and the Red Sox are 51–50, the Sox would be 3 games behind—meaning that the Sox need to win 3 games while the Yankees lose 3 for the Sox to catch up (at 54–50). If teams have played different numbers of games, the number of games behind may not be even. For instance, if the Sox are 88–60 and Baltimore in 85–60, Baltimore would be 1½ games behind the Red Sox.

It's not unusual for a team to come from 6 or 7 games behind at midseason, but late in the season it's hard to make up more than a few games in the standings. It does happen, though. In 1949 the Sox were 12 games behind the Yankees in July, but came back to pull a game ahead on the last weekend of the season—only to lose the last 2 games to the Yankees and finish a game out of first place. In 1978 the Red Sox were in first place by 14 games at midseason, only to fall hopelessly behind the Yankees amid a string of injuries and mismanagement—and then stormed back into a short-lived tie for first by winning 8 games in a row at the end of the season.

Toward the end of the season people will start talking about a first-place team's *magic number.*That's the combination of wins and opponent losses that it will take to clinch the division title. For instance, if the Red Sox are 98–58 and the Yankees are in second place at 95–61 (3 games behind, with 6 to play in the 162-game season), the Sox magic number is 3. Any combination of Boston wins or Yankee losses totaling 3 will guarantee at least a tie for first in the division. (If the Sox win 3 games, the Yankees can only tie them at 101–61, even if New York wins all 6 of its remaining games. Another Boston win or New York loss would guarantee an outright win for the division title.)

How do you get into the Hall of Fame?

Practice, practice, practice.

The most common route to induction to the Baseball Hall of Fame is via election by the Baseball Writers Association of America (BBWAA). In order to be elected, a player must be selected on 75% of the ballots cast by the writers during the annual voting. During the voting process, each member of the BBWAA (active or honorary) who has at least 10 years experience may submit a ballot naming up to 10 eligible players. (Most writers name fewer than 10 on their ballots.)

To be eligible for election by the BBWAA, a player must have played parts of at least 10 seasons in the major leagues (at least some of that time during the previous 20 seasons), and must have been retired for 5 seasons. No player who is listed on Major League Baseball's permanently ineligible list may be selected—with the two best-known names on that list being "Shoeless" Joe Jackson and Pete Rose. In addition, any player failing to receive at least 5% of the BBWAA vote during any voting year ceases to be eligible for selection by the BBWAA. In other words, a player with at least 10 years in the major leagues goes on the ballot after being retired for 5 years (usually 20 players or so each year). If he gets 75% of the votes (like Carlton Fisk did in 2000), he is elected to the Hall of Fame. If he gets fewer than 75% (but more than 5%), he stays on the ballot and has another chance. (Jim Rice and Luis Tiant are former Red Sox stars who are currently in this sort of holding pattern). Players who aren't elected can stay on the ballot for up to 15 years. Many players are not selected the first time they are eligible, since some sportswriters think only the most elite players deserve a vote in their first year of eligibility.

The other route to the Hall is via the Baseball Hall of Fame Committee on Baseball Veterans (affectionately known as the Veterans Committee, the source of many of the least qualified members of the Hall). The 15-member Veterans Committee, made up of Hall of Fame players, baseball executives, and/or broadcasters, has the ability to address players that the BBWAA chose not to induct, as long as they meet certain requirements. The first criteria for Veterans Committee selection is that the players have been retired for over 23 years and played in at least 10 seasons. Because there was a perception that Veterans Committee members were selecting their old cronies to the Hall based on marginal qualifications (such as Phil Rizzuto), the rules for who the Veterans Committee can select were recently tightened. Players whose careers started after 1945 must have received at least 60% of the BBWAA vote or received at least 100 votes in the one season's BBWAA voting. The Veterans Committee may also consider players who played 10 years in the Negro Leagues prior to 1946, or whose service in the Negro Leagues prior to 1946 and in the Major League from 1946 on totals at least 10 seasons. Unfortunately, this means that the Veterans Committee can't do what it was originally created for—select players for the Hall of Fame whose greatness only becomes apparent after a number of years have passed, or who are deserving but unpopular with the BBWAA. For instance, under the current system, Dwight Evans will never be eligible for selection to the Hall of Fame, despite his long and excellent career—because he was overshadowed and never received 100 votes from the BBWAA, the Veterans Committee can't consider him.

In addition, the Veterans Committee may consider the selection of managers, umpires, and baseball "pioneers/executives" who have been retired for five years. The five-year waiting period is reduced to six months after the persons in question reach 65 years of age. Over the years, the Veterans Committee has selected 147 members of the Hall of Fame, as opposed to only 93 selected by the BBWAA. However, as mentioned, the Veterans Committee selections include all of the managers, umpires, executives, and broadcasters in the Hall, in addition to most of the Negro Leaguers. Today, any player not elected during his period of BBWAA eligibility is extremely unlikely to get in.

From 1971 through 1977, there was also a Negro League Committee that elected nine players to the Hall, including Satchel Paige, Josh Gibson, and Cool Papa Bell.

How does a player get put onto the permanently ineligible list? Can players be banned from baseball for committing crimes or having drug problems, or only for gambling?

In theory, the Commissioner of Baseball has wide-ranging powers to act for the "good of the game." Practically speaking, the commissioner isn't generally going to do anything without fairly widespread support among the owners (who hire and pay the commissioner). While it is theoretically possible that a player could be put on the list for committing crimes, or repeated drug suspensions, in reality it is only gambling that has gotten players into trouble. In the early days of baseball there were many gambling scandals, and the game itself, at the professional level, was endangered by the perception that the games were not honest. This culminated in 1920 when eight members of the Chicago White Sox team that lost the 1919 World Series were put on trial for intentionally throwing the series in exchange for payoffs from gamblers. The eight have been known as the "Black Sox" ever since. Though eventually acquitted (largely due to the fact that signed confessions disappeared from the courthouse), Judge Kenesaw Mountain Landis, hired by the owners as Commissioner of Baseball, banned the eight (including Joe Jackson and former Red Sox pitcher Ed Cicotte) permanently from major league baseball. Since then gambling on baseball games has been expressly forbidden.

While players have been suspended for up to a year for drug-related offenses, the commissioner is very unlikely to ban a player permanently for personal problems that don't affect the integrity of the game (even in cases where the player commits a violent crime, as with Wil Cordero's spousal abuse). This is partly because the Players' Association would be likely to challenge such a suspension through arbitration or in court, and would probably win, undermining the commissioner's power. In a similar case in the 1980s, the Chicago White Sox tried to void the contract of pitcher Lamarr Hoyt who was caught selling drugs, based on a standard good conduct clause in his contract—and lost the case.

Why do people say there's a curse on the Red Sox?

Baseball is a game of both superstitions and traditions. The influence of fate is given great weight in the game and its legends, and there are speculated theories, supernatural and otherwise, about many of the trends and patterns in the history of the game.

One of these traditions is that of the Curse of the Bambino, which is the supposed reason that the Red Sox have not won the World Series since 1918. This supposed curse is the lasting influence of the departed Babe Ruth. As legend tells it, the team which sold him would never win again, where the team he was sold to—the New York Yankees—presumably was given his lasting blessing.

Ruth was only one of a number of Red Sox players who eventually turned up in pinstripes, and an alternate history could well look at the Yankees rosters of the beginning of their dynasty and see a golden age of Red Sox championships. It is commonly said that Harry Frazee, then owner of the Sox, sold Ruth to finance his Broadway productions, specifically *No, No, Nanette*, but this is not precisely the case; Ruth was a discipline problem who was demanding to have his salary literally doubled (he *was* being dramatically underpaid), and Frazee was still financially strapped from his purchase of the ballclub. Frazee, in justifying the sale, blamed Ruth's boisterous and difficult behavior on the team's failure to follow up on their championship year with anything better than a sixth-place finish. Ruth was sent south in 1919, and *No, No, Nanette* didn't hit the big time until 1925.

The years after the Ruth sale and the other departures of players to the Yankees were dark ones for the Red Sox, especially as many of the transfers were cash sales rather than trades, so comparatively unskilled, or at least untried, players needed to be brought up to fill out the Boston roster.

In fact, the Red Sox did not appear in the World Series again until 1946. It was after 1946, in fact, that the notion of "the curse" first appeared. With World War II over, the Sox war heroes came home again, and baseball as it was meant to be played lived in Boston again. Ted Williams, Dom DiMaggio, Bobby Doerr, Johnny Pesky, and a number of other players came back from the war, and it seemed the Red Sox dynasty was finally back on track. In 1946 the Sox had never yet lost a World Series, and they were favored to win it all over the Cardinals.

It came down to a seventh game, though. Dom DiMaggio came out of the game with a limp in the eighth inning, and Leon Culberson had to go into center field. Enos Slaughter led off the bottom of the eighth with a single, and was on first with two outs—and then Harry Walker popped a shot into left center field, which was chased by the backup fielder and relayed in a lob throw to Johnny Pesky. The shortstop turned in short left center, prepared to throw the ball into the infield so it wouldn't be mishandled, and saw Slaughter a few strides from home plate, scoring from first on the double.

"Pesky holds the ball" became the anguished cry after the Sox failed to rally in the ninth, despite mounting a threat. Accused of hesitating on the throw, of losing Bobby Doerr's call of "Home" in the crowd noise, or of losing the runner in the sunglare, Johnny Pesky was the goat of the 1946 Series. After the loss in the "sure thing" World Series win, rumors of a curse inflicted by the loss of Babe Ruth began to surface.

In 1948 the Red Sox tied the Cleveland Indians for first place on the last day of the season, but lost a one-game playoff when manager Joe McCarthy inexplicably started journeyman Denny Galehouse instead of one of his four stronger starting pitchers.

The next year the Sox went into Yankee stadium with a one game lead and two games to play, and 20-game winners Mel Parnell and Ellis Kinder on the mound. They lost both, and the Yankees went to the World Series.

In 1967 the Impossible Dream team, which had come out of nowhere to win the closest pennant race in history, also stretched a World Series to seven games—and lost in heartbreaking fashion. The team's rising young star, Tony Conigliaro, was hit in the head by a pitch that year and was never the same player. After the season, pitching ace Jim Lonborg destroyed his knee in a skiing accident. The team was no longer a contender the next season.

In 1972 a players strike caused the season to start a week late, and the missed games were not replayed. The Red Sox missed seven games, and the Detroit Tigers six. When the dust cleared, the Red Sox lost the division title by the margin of of that single game that they weren't allowed to make up—85–70 to the Tigers' 86–70.

Boston was forced to play the 1975 World Series without rookie star Jim Rice, who'd had his wrist broken by a pitch the month before. What's been called the greatest baseball game ever, the legendary Game 6 of the 1975 World Series, was won by Carlton Fisk's wave-it-fair home run off the left field foul pole. These explosive heroics were followed by yet another Game 7 loss, reinforcing the highs-and-lows feel of Red Sox championship hopes.

In 1978 Boston held a fourteen-game lead in the American League East before the All Star break. However, Rick Burleson, the shortstop cited as a sparkplug for the team, injured his ankle just before the midseason. There was a strong hierarchy in the clubhouse between the regulars and the backup players. The team lost nine straight after the break, but their lead was so strong that not many people worried— especially as the Yankees weren't doing well either, their lineup and pitching also full of injuries.

By the end of the season, however, the Yankee team was cobbled back together, and a number of injuries struck the Sox. The Boston pitching staff, perhaps frustrated by manager Don Zimmer, seemed almost to implode, and major players—including Carl Yastrzemski—were disabled. After several series between the two teams, the Yankees were up three and a half games in the division, and the Red Sox needed to win twelve out of the thirteen remaining games to make the postseason.

The last day of the season, the Red Sox won, the Yankees lost, and a tie was forced: another single-game playoff, just like in 1948, to be held in Fenway Park (the Red Sox won a coin toss). Down by two in the seventh, two outs, two on, Yankee short-stop Bucky Dent came to the plate. He fouled the second pitch off his shin, replaced his cracked bat in the pause in game play, then lofted a perfect Fenway Park home run over the Green Monster, aided by a shift in the wind.

Bucky Dent had four home runs and a .243 batting average on the season, and had previously been 0-for-2 that game.

After being one pitch away from elimination in a hard-fought and dramatic competition against the Angels, the 1986 Red Sox managed to stage a comeback, claim the pennant, and get into the World Series, where they faced the New York Mets. Boston won the first game in a 1–0 duel, the second handily, and then dropped the next two to New York before winning Game 5. There was a theory that the jinx had been broken; the Sox, after all, were one game away from victory and their rings.

The game was knotted at two by a Mets rally in the fifth, but the Sox took a one-run lead in the seventh. In the eighth, Roger Clemens, who had torn a blister in the fifth and ripped a fingernail in the seventh, was pulled for a pinch hitter, who struck out. A left-handed pitcher was brought in to face Bill Buckner with the bases loaded, and Don Baylor, who was told to be ready to pinch hit, was not called in. Buckner flied out, and then took his place at first base for the bottom of the eighth.

Calvin Schiraldi was brought in to pitch and seemed rattled, rushing a throw and failing to get an out, throwing balls, and eventually blowing the save. The game went into extra innings as neither team scored in the ninth.

In the tenth, Dave Henderson led off for the Sox with a home run. After two strike-outs, Wade Boggs got a double and scored on a following single, pushing the score to 5–3. Buckner was hit by a pitch, but Jim Rice lined out, leaving him stranded on first. With victory seemingly assured, Buckner (who'd had ankle problems all year) stayed at first for the bottom of the tenth rather than giving up his place to the defensive replacement, Dave Stapleton.

Unlike the previous two innings, Schiraldi managed to get two outs fairly quickly in the tenth, not letting the first two batters reach. The third batter reached on a single. The fourth, a pinch-hitter for the pitcher, also reached. The next Mets player, Ray Knight, took a called strike and fouled the next pitch off; the following pitch was blooped off his handle into short center. A run scored, 5–4, runners on first and third, two outs.

A new pitcher was called in to face Mookie Wilson: Bob Stanley—the Red Sox career saves leader. Wilson fouled it off, took two pitches for balls, and fouled off another, leaving the Sox again one strike away from winning the Series. Two more foul balls heightened the tension, then a wild pitch allowed the runner on third to score. Tie game.

Wilson fouled off two more balls before hitting a tapper down the first base line. Buckner moved to intercept the ball, as Stanley moved to cover the bag. The ball took a bounce, slipped under the first baseman's glove, and rolled through his legs into right field. Ray Knight rounded third, saw the error, and ran home. Game 6 was over, with the Mets winning.

The Sox had a three-run lead in Game 7, but eventually lost, 6–3.

In both 1988 and 1990, the Oakland Athletics swept the Red Sox in the American League Championship Series. Ace Roger Clemens was inexplicably rattled in 1988, negating the Red Sox strong starting pitching. He was even thrown out of one game for reportedly cursing at an umpire whose calls he disagreed with.

In the 1998 Division Series manager Jimy Williams chose to start sore-armed Pete Schourek in the crucial fourth game, despite fan clamoring for ace Pedro Martinez (Boston needed to win two in a row to take the series). Schourek pitched very well, but Tom Gordon—who'd been the best reliever in baseball all year—blew his first save since May, and the futility continued.

The 1999 American League pennant came down to a competition between the Red Sox and the Yankees after the Sox posted a stunning comeback against the Indians in the Division Series. The games were plagued by controversy, as a single umpire botched several calls around Yankee second baseman Chuck Knoblauch—in one case calling Jose Offerman out to end a rally when Knoblauch missed the tag by six inches—cutting short potential Red Sox rallies in very close games. When another bad call in the fourth game had Nomar Garciaparra out at first, the crowd at Fenway bordered on riot, sensing another chance at a pennant cut short by perverse circumstance.

From the sixth game in 1986 until the first game in 1998, the Red Sox lost 13 consecutive postseason games. Assuming that they had a 50–50 chance of winning any one of them, the odds of randomly losing 13 in a row is 1 in 8,192. Even if you only assume a 45% chance in any game (and remember, these are all teams that were good enough to make the postseason) the odds are still 1 in 2,372. It isn't surprising to see Red Sox fans seeking supernatural explanations.

People point to language and symbols as evidence for the curse. Bruce Hurst is an anagram for *B Ruth Curse*, and Peter Schourek can be rearranged as *Ruth Keep Score*. The retired numbers 9–4–1–8 on the facade in right field were also the date of the eve of the 1918 World Series. On 9/5/18, Babe Ruth shut out the Cubs to begin the last victorious World Series for the Sox.

In the half-century since the notion of the curse was spawned, in the 80-odd years since the last World Series Champions in Boston, the notion of the afflicted has become part of the culture of baseball fandom in New England. Fans who were merely thought of as long-suffering in 1946 are now seen as profoundly afflicted by their cross to bear, this long drought in championships. It is almost a badge of pride, to carry on in loyalty despite the lack of consummation.

The feeling of almost supernatural persecution has also flavored individual games. A short series in the middle of the summer may be charged by one incredible come-from-behind win, as if in tribute to Carlton Fisk and the good Game 6, and then let down again by a late-innings squander. There is always the hope that somehow, someway, the Sox will pull something out of a hat and come back to win, and always the fear and (sometimes the conviction) that something will go wrong, somewhere, leaving the team and its fans let down again.

People in other parts of the country point to Cleveland, and the Cubs, and other teams that are perpetually bad, and say that Red Sox fans shouldn't complain, but they miss the key feature of the curse. It isn't that the Red Sox are always bad. On the contrary, the focus of the curse is that the Sox have frequently been good or very good, and found excruciating ways to lose. 1986 stands alone, but Bucky Bleepin' Dent, losing the 14½ game lead in 1978, losing to Gibson three times in 1967, Pesky held the ball, Parnell and Kinder losing in Yankee Stadium in 1949, Aguilera giving up the Belle home run, then losing on the Peña home run—the particular magic of the curse is to turn well-earned victory into heartrending loss.

It's tradition, it's superstition; it's part of the flavor of Red Sox fandom.

I grew up in Maryland, a long way from Fenway Park. I had gone to minor league games with my father and brother, watching the Carolina League teams play through their seasons in their appearances about an hour's drive north of our house. I did not see a game at Fenway before I was eighteen and in college.

I was a Wellesley chick. Wellesley, being a women's school, was not exactly chock-full of diehard baseball fans, but I knew one. Her name was Leanne, and her team was the Padres. The year was 1996, which was, I seem to recall, not a good one for San Diego. She did, however, acknowledge the Red Sox as a poor American League substitute for her team, and in the late spring organized a trip to Fenway.

It was the eighteenth of May. A cluster of us Wellesley chicks headed into town and took the T to Kenmore Square: Leanne stubbornly wearing her Padres cap, me eagerly preparing to take notes and score the game (as is my tradition), and the others along for the ride and the social expedition.

We got our tickets at the gate, and filed into the depths of Fenway, the shadowed corners, the booths and gates. Our seats were, of course, obstructed-view, in the grandstand probably at about Section 19—I could see the pitcher's mound, and the batter if I leaned.

"Who's pitching?" That was what I wanted to know.

The answer, as it happened, was Roger Clemens.

Roger Clemens!

My first game at Fenway, and I was going to see Roger Clemens pitch. My brother was the person who knew the stats, the names of the players—I was a Red Sox fan then, but a fan of the team, not someone who knew who was playing on it in any sort of useful way. That came later. But even I knew the name of Roger Clemens. Roger Clemens!

And, to make this even the more sweet, he was pitching against Oakland—Oakland, my brother's team, Oakland, which shall live in infamy in my heart forever for 1990 and the sweep to take the pennant, Oakland, whose players I knew because my brother recited their names to me: Giambi, McGwire, Canseco.

Except Canseco was . . . playing for Boston. A name I knew.

With Roger Clemens!

I kept score—in the basic way that I still do, though my scoring is slowly evolving to complexity—scrawled in my program. In between pitches, I explained what I was doing to people next to me, though I have no idea how much of it was retained or even interesting to them.

Boston got a run in the second.

Then Oakland racked up two in the third. It was a horrible sight to see.

Then Roger Clemens began to pitch like Roger Clemens could: he sent men down in rapid succession. I do not recall a man from the Athletics reaching base for three, maybe nearly four innings.

And Boston racked up three runs in the fourth. 4–2.

Seven and a third innings into the game, Roger Clemens sat down. I don't know why, if he was hurt, if the manager saw something I didn't see: I just know that he had been unhittable since the unfortunate third inning, with a number of Ks to his credit, and he went and sat down. I seem to recall as well that the crowd applauded Roger, and hissed at the manager.

McGwire was one step from on deck when the manager sent out the new pitcher. I looked up at the scoreboard to see who this person was who was coming in to replace Roger Clemens.

Gunderson, the name was.

ERA: 0.00. Not bad.

Except that. . . . Innings pitched: 0.

Gunderson lasted a third of an inning. He got the guy he came in to face, and gave up a home run to Giambi.

Slocumb came in then, and got McGwire. Phew.

The score was 4–3. It was a narrow margin, but it could hold. Only one inning left to go.

The Red Sox did not score in the bottom of the eighth.

Stanton pitched the top of the ninth. Got Plantier. Got Berroa.

Gave up a home run to a pinch hitter.

4–4.

The Red Sox did not score in the bottom of the ninth.

Garces pitched the tenth. And gave up two runs to go with his three strikeouts.

The Red Sox scored in the bottom of the tenth.

One run.

Final score: 6–5. In 10 innings.

There are times when one comes to a visceral understanding of what it can be to be a baseball fan in general, a Red Sox fan in specific. What if Clemens had pitched through the eighth? What if one or another of those nail-biting scoring opportunities had come through? What if, what if, what if. There are times when one knows in one's heart that that game could have been won, if only if a little more prayer had been applied, a little more hope, a little less that-ump-is-blind, a little more hey batter batter and a little less wind blowing out.

There are times when one packs up the scoresheet, puts it in one's pocket, and goes home in shock and denial.

Maybe next game.

—Heather Anne Nicoll

A Red Sox Bibliography

Here is an annotated list of some of the best and most interesting books written about the Red Sox over the years, along with a few key reference books about baseball. Many of the older books are out of print, but used copies are readily (and usually inexpensively) available through search services such as www.bibliofind.com or www.half.com.

Babe: The Legend Comes to Life, by Robert Creamer. One of the best sports biographies ever, it gives excellent info on Ruth's years with the Red Sox (1914–19, including 3 championships). There's a lot more to Ruth's story, of course, and the whole book is a must-read.

The Ballplayers, edited by Mike Shatzkin. A mammoth book containing brief biographies and essays about more than 6,000 players, teams, leagues, and other baseball topics. The book appeared in 1990; a slightly updated version is available online at *http://cbs.sportsline.com/u/baseball/bol/ballplayers/*.

The Baseball Encyclopedia, published by Macmillan. This is "the complete and definitive record of major league baseball." Includes the record of every player in all major leagues (including Negro Leagues and the All-American Girls Professional League), a season-by-season record of the major leagues, and appendices of trades and other useful information.

Baseball Scoreboard, from Stats, Inc. This yearly publication is a very accessible look beyond the traditional statistics. There is an essay for every team in the game, as well as sections on offense, pitching, and defense. This is a very enjoyable resource for fans at almost any level of understanding.

Baseball's Greatest Rivalry, by Harvey Frommer. A pretty good book about, yes, the Red Sox and Yankees. Most of it will be pretty familiar stuff to diehard fans, but there's some good info on the early days of the rivalry.

Beyond the Sixth Game, by Peter Gammons. This book shows why Gammons built a reputation as one of the finest local sportswriters in the country, long before he moved to TV and became an ESPN "personality." Gammons uses the 1975 Red Sox as a microcosm of how baseball changed in the free agency era. The descriptions of the great 1970s teams and how the team lost its way in the early 1980s is one of the clearest accounts of a confusing time.

The Boston Red Sox, by Donald Honig. A coffee table book with lots of great photos and a basic history of the team.

Boston Red Sox: The Complete Record of Red Sox Baseball, with historical text by Henry Berry and Harold Berry. A 1984 version of *The Baseball Encyclopedia* specific to Red Sox teams and players, with short (and excellent) accounts of each season, along with complete team, player, and manager stats through 1983.

The Bronx Zoo, by Sparky Lyle with Peter Golenbock. This diary of the infamous 1978 season is a must read for masochistic Sox fans, though it's told from the perspective of the hated Yankees. We're not crazy about the ending, but Lyle's candid descriptions of clubhouse pranks and fights are often hilarious. Lyle briefly discusses his days as a Red Sox reliever, prior to his disastrous trade for Danny Cater.

The Catcher Was a Spy, by Nicholas Dawidoff. A biography of Moe Berg, the brilliant Red Sox catcher who also served as a World War II–era intelligence agent.

The Curse of the Bambino, by Dan Shaughnessy. A dark and pessimistic, but funny, history of the Red Sox. Includes a lot of gossip about who was sleeping with whom on the 1980s teams.

Fenway, by Peter Golenbock. Entertaining team history, aided by many interviews of players and fans. Very similar to the author's acclaimed histories of the Yankees (*Dynasty*) and Brooklyn Dodgers (*Bums*). Unfortunately, Golenbock is notorious for careless editing, so nitpickers may be distracted by the occasional typo.

Fenway: A Biography in Words and Pictures, by Dan Shaughnessy, with photographs by Stan Grossfeld, and introduction by Ted Williams. A history and commentary on the ballpark, with some tremendous photographs.

The Girl Who Loved Tom Gordon, by Stephen King. A short novel about a girl lost in the woods who depends on the Red Sox pitcher—listened to over her Walkman— for support. A novel written as a tribute to the Sox by one of the team's greatest fans—even if catcher Jason Varitek's name is misspelled throughout the book.

The Glory of Their Times, by Lawrence Ritter. Many say it's the best baseball book ever written. The book is made up of interviews with a wide variety of players from the early twentieth century, told in the first person. This style has been copied many times, but there's something magical about the way Ritter edited the players' stories; you feel like you're on the field with them. Two Red Sox greats are included, Harry

Hooper and Smokey Joe Wood, so you'll learn a lot about the old-time teams. Frankly, each player's story is a great read.

Lefty Grove: An American Original, by Jim Kaplan. An excellent biography published by the Society for American Baseball Research in 2000.

Lost Summer, by Bill Reynolds. The story of the 1967 "Impossible Dream" season.

One Pitch Away: The Players' Stories of the 1986 League Championships and World Series, by Mike Sowell. The history of the events leading up to the World Series, as well as accounts by the key players involved, drawn from records and interviews.

The Progress of the Seasons, by George Higgins. Covers the years 1946–86.

Real Grass, Real Heroes, by Dom DiMaggio with Bill Gilbert. Light, but very interesting look at the last prewar season, 1941, written by the man who was a teammate of Ted Williams and the brother of Joe DiMaggio. Less than $5.00 at Amazon.com.

Red Sox Century, by Glenn Stout and Richard Johnson. Comprehensive account of the team's first 100 years, written by two prominent sports historians. Gained attention for exposing the truth about Babe Ruth's sale and Boston's delay in signing black players.

The Red Sox Reader, edited by Dan Riley. A cross-section of articles about the team through the years, including the famous John Updike piece on Ted Williams.

Red Sox Triumphs and Tragedies, by Ed Walton. Last published in 1980 and full of quirky anecdotes and stats. Walton used to be the Sox publicist, and a lot of his stuff is still in the team's media guide. It's not an extremely well-organized or brilliantly written book, but it's fun and useful.

A Rooter's Guide to the Red Sox, by Harold Kaese. An odd 1974 collection of facts and tidbits compiled from 41 years of the longtime sportswriter's notes.

Tales from the Red Sox Dugout, by Jim Prime with Bill Nowlin. A collection of anecdotes and strange stories, with something of a greater focus on recent players. An overview of the historical and current wackiness of the team.

Ted Williams: The Seasons of the Kid, by Richard Ben Cramer. Large format coffee-table book, featuring a fabulous collection of photos with relatively brief biographical text. Currently out of print and hard to find, but well worth having if you can track it down.

The Science of Hitting, by Ted Williams and John Underwood. Possibly the best book ever written about hitting a baseball. First published in 1971.

The Sports Encyclopedia: Baseball, by Neft and Cohen. Unlike its more comprehensive competitors, this annual reference book doesn't arrange stats by player. Instead, it compiles each team's stats year-by-year, with brief but informative summaries of each season. If you need information on a particular season (rosters, who led a team in homers, etc.), *The Sports Encyclopedia* is a great resource. Unfortunately, it doesn't include year-by-year stats for the nineteenth century, and it lacks the extras that make *Total Baseball* so valuable.

This Time, Let's Not Eat the Bones, by Bill James. A best-of compilation culled from books and articles by a writer who redefined baseball analysis with his *Baseball Abstract*. There are articles on a number of Red Sox players and teams included, as well as many other fascinating bits (including what may be the best and clearest article ever written about the salary arbitration process). James's *Historical Baseball Abstract* is a terrific study of how the game, teams, and players evolved over the years, and his *Whatever Happened to the Hall of Fame* is a fascinating look at the players who were selected (as well as many who weren't) and the shifting politics of the Hall of Fame. Actually, anything by Bill James is worth reading. Don't be put off by the stathead reputation; James is one of the liveliest and most incisive sportswriters around today.

Total Baseball, edited by John Thorn, Pete Palmer, and others, is the official encyclopedia of Major League Baseball, and a relatively recent competitor with *The Baseball Encyclopedia*. Like *The Baseball Encyclopedia*, *Total Baseball* has a complete record of major league players, but instead of a season-by-season record of teams, the book has a more anecdotal approach to each season. *Total Baseball* also includes essays on key players and topics, and features many newer statistical categories.

The Wrong Stuff, by Bill Lee with Dick Lally. A quirky autobiography from one of the Red Sox's quirkiest players.

Yaz: Baseball, The Wall, and Me, by Carl Yastrzemski with Gerald Eskenazi. Better than most "as told to" sports autobiographies, with some good insights on what it took for Yaz to play so well for so long. Has some interesting anecdotes about Yaz's relationship with Ted Williams, Tom Yawkey, and many of his teammates.

The Year of the Gerbil, by Con Chapman. About the 1978 season.

THE RED SOX ON THE INTERNET

The Internet Revolution of the mid-1990s has been a wonderful development for baseball fans. Instead of waiting for the morning paper or the 11 o'clock news, fans with Internet access can click their mouse for instant boxscores, game broadcasts, stats, news stories, rumors, and just about anything else they want to know. Here are a few of the Net's best resources for Red Sox fans:

General Baseball Information

Major League Baseball (www.majorleaguebaseball.com): Baseball's official website. In addition to the standard news, scores, and stats, this site lets fans listen to teams' radio broadcasts. Also features lots of officially licensed baseball merchandise.

ESPN (www.espn.go.com/mlb): Probably the most popular baseball website. Features instant updates of game action, and columns by Peter Gammons, sabermetrician Rob Neyer (who's writing a book about the 2000 Red Sox), and others. Its writers also have frequent chat sessions with fans.

CBS SportsLine (www.cbs.sportsline.com): Information-heavy site similar to ESPN, but with more of a focus on Rotisserie Leagues. Also features an excellent historical section, with profiles of former big league players.

Fox Sports (www.foxsports.com): Another good source of baseball info. Particularly good on business-related issues. Lots of columnists, including Keith Olbermann.

CNN/Sports Illustrated (www.sportsillustrated.cnn.com/): Combines two excellent resources, giving fans lots of content, including top columnists and a fine historical section.

The Sporting News (www.sportingnews.com): No longer "The Bible of Baseball," but the website is very attractive, and features outstanding team-by-team coverage.

USA Today: (www.usatoday.com/sports): Lots of info, including team updates and articles from the Baseball Weekly newspaper. Good resource for Rotisserie players.

Baseball America (www.baseballamerica.com): Online version of the newspaper, which is the top source for information on the minor leagues and amateur baseball. In addition to many articles, its minor league and winter league stats are updated daily.

RotoNews (www.rotonews.com): A must click for Rotisserie players, but also an excellent source for all fans. Has links to every team's local newspapers, and up-to-the-minute reports on injuries, trades, and rumors.

John Skilton's Baseball Links (www.baseball-links.com): Extemely well-organized warehouse of baseball sites, divided by categories. Great starting point for web-surfers.

Sean Lahman's Baseball Links (www.baseball1.com): Not quite as extensive as Skilton's site, but probably the best source for baseball stats and analysis. Fans can download Lahman's free database, which has stats on every big league player.

Baseball Reference: (www.baseball-reference.com): outstanding statistical resource on teams and players. Includes conventional and sabermetric stats, plus the addictive "similarity scores," which tell you which players have had the most comparable careers to your favorites.

Yahoo! Sports (sports.yahoo.com/mlb/players/): Includes 3-year stats on players as well as useful splits (how they perform at home and on the road, lefties versus right-ies, etc.).

Baseball Contracts (www.bluemanc.demon.co.uk/baseball/contracts.htm): updated information on salaries and contracts of all big league players.

Red Sox Sites

Official Site (www.redsox.com): Not as flashy or comprehensive as some teams' sites, but still one of the best sources for Red Sox information. Features full game-day coverage, minor league information, player bios, historical information, and official press releases that make even the worst utiltyman seem like a future Hall of Famer.

The Boston Globe (www.boston.com/sports/redsox) and *Boston Herald* (www.bostonherald.com) both post each day's stories and columns, and are great resources for out-of-town Sox fans.

Providence Journal-Bulletin/Off the Wall (www.projo.com/redsox): The best newspaper site for Sox fans, ProJo has three things the others don't. First, it also covers the nearby Pawtucket Red Sox, so it's a great source on prospects. Second, it features "Art's Notebook," a regular column by ProJo's Sports Editor, Art Martone. Martone is a gifted writer who interprets stats well, yet also conveys a fan's passion for the game. He doesn't buy into the conventional "wisdom" of his peers, but makes his points with reason rather than sarcasm. Finally, Projo includes a "Your Turn" forum for fans to debate the team and Martone's columns.

Boston Baseball (redsox.rivals.com): Provides Sox-oriented news and chat rooms. Affiliated with *Boston Baseball Magazine.*

The Sox Media Review (members.dingoblue.net.au/~mcgerty/SoxMR/) is a very valuable resource that keeps track of current news stories from a variety of sources.

A few visionary players, like Detroit pitcher C. J. Nitkowski, created their own quirky, unique websites in the mid-1990s. Former Red Sox coach Wendell "Wave 'Em In" Kim began The Coach's Box (www.wk20.com) in 1995, but time constraints have forced him to stop updating it. Today, most official player sites are pretty generic, and are usually under the umbrella of a bigger web company, aiming to sell memorabilia and adspace. The most prominent is AthletesDirect (www.athletesdirect.com). Nomar, Nomo, O'Leary, Saberhagen, and Varitek have official pages on this site, and periodically post their thoughts and answer fan e-mail. Another is Bigleaguers.com, featuring a John Valentin page, which he's put some effort into (players.bigleaguers.com/John_Valentin.html).

Three former Sox greats have official sites. Ted Williams's website (www.tedwilliams.com) includes career highlights, memorabilia, and information on his museum in Florida. It might be most interesting for its coverage of Teddy Ballgame's other careers—as a military man and fisherman. Carl Yastrzemski's site (www.yaz8.com), has solid info on his career, and seems to be maintained by his rep or agent. Roger Clemens has a very good site (www.rocketroger.com), which includes pitching tips, start-by-start analyses, e-mail Q-and-As, and merchandise.

Many fans have created Internet tributes to their favorite players. These sites aren't always kept up-to-date, and most of the content is readily available elsewhere. As a result, the best fan-run sites are often the ones that pay homage to lesser-known players. Some of the better fan-run sites include:

Morgan Burkhart (www.morganburkhart.com).

Nomar Net (www.nomar.net)

Ari's Nomar Page (members.nbci.com/AriMunky/NGP.html).

The Pedro Martinez Bible (hometown.aol.com/bmastersock/index.html).

Pedro Martinez: Strikeout King (cal-ripken-jr.com/pedro).

Hideo Nomo: Tornado Boy (www.st.rim.or.jp/~k_ono/tornado/). Japanese site with English translations. Totally out-of-date, but the translations and hyperbole are often amusing.

Jose Offerman Tribute: (www.geocities.com/SunsetStrip/Underground/8288/)

Manny Ramirez: (www.anythingbaseball.com/manny)

Keep Manny!: (www.keepmanny.com). Desperate plea by Indians fans to re-sign Ramirez.

Other recommended fan-run sites include:

Red Sox Nation (fwp.simplenet.com/redsox/): About 3 million people visited this terrific site in the past year. Includes stats, detailed info on each player, extensive audio/video, a chat room, games, and much more.

The Buffalo Head Society (www.ultranet.com/~kuras/buffalohd.htm): Excellent articles on Red Sox players past and present, including an outstanding piece on Tony Conigliaro.

Red Sox Uniform Numbers (www.ultranet.com/~kuras/soxunis.htm). Archive of every Red Sox uniform number, past and present.

A Haven for the Diehard Sox Fan (http://www.redsoxdiehard.com/): A comprehensive site with history, information, articles, a near-complete links list, and a message board, maintained by a fan in Atlanta.

Darkhawk's Boston Red Sox Page (http://aelfhame.net/~darkhawk/baseball/): A personal site with essays and commentary and a little bit of creative work.

Christine's Red Sox World (www.fenwayfaithful.com): Unlike the more information-heavy sites, Christine focuses on more "fannish" features. You wouldn't go here for research, but it's fun to browse through, with lots of great sound files.

Newsgroups and Mailing Lists

Red Sox Newsgroup (alt.sports.baseball.bos-redsox): Forum for fans to post their thoughts on the team, analyze stats, argue about the manager and GM, and reminisce about Sox history. Like many unmoderated Usenet newsgroups, it has its share of "flame wars" between overzealous Red Sox and Yankees fans, but there's plenty of intelligent, provocative discussion. Regular posters include statistical guru Eric M. Van; a poet named hytem, who posts in haiku; the infamous Gnorkmeister; and most of the contributors to this book. Newcomers are welcomed, provided they participate in a reasonably intelligent fashion.

Red Sox Mailing List (www.best.com/~kwoolner/redsox/list/): Created in 1991 and currently operated by Keith Woolner. Same basic idea as the newsgroup, but the Mailing List keeps discussions more focused by discouraging off-topic posts and "flame wars." Members can follow a simple procedure to subscribe (there are about 600 subscribers), and the list is received via e-mail. The site also includes a FAQ (Frequently Asked Questions) section on the Red Sox.

I was born in Brooklyn, NY, to a father who was a rabid Yankee fan despite growing up a few blocks from Ebbets Field. Even as an infant, there are photos of me wearing baby Yankee hats and outfits, and by the time I was 4, he started taking me to games. The Yankees played at Shea Stadium in 1974–75, and I kept thinking it was weird to see them play in the Mets' park. Due to his talent and TV commercials, I had become interested in Tom Seaver, and kept begging my father to take me to a Mets game. He hated the Mets but relented, and I saw Seaver lose a brilliantly pitched 2–0 game to San Diego in 1975. Much to my father's dismay, I became a stone cold Mets fan.

Meanwhile, I had also become a baseball card collector. The Topps cards back then had little banners to signify All Stars, and I used to put those cards in a special place—thinking they were more important than the others. I immediately noticed how many Red Sox players were All Stars: Fisk, Lynn, Rice, and this guy with a long, weird name. I asked my father about him, and was told that everyone called him "Yaz." I loved that nickname and the stories of his defense and Triple Crown, and Yaz began to rival Seaver as my favorite player. The Sox of 1977 had weak pitching, but the lineup was loaded, and while the Mets were slipping, these guys were hitting homers at a near-record pace. Their ballpark was more interesting than dumpy old Shea, they had more history, and I learned that they were much bigger rivals with the Yankees.

So from May 1977 until June 15, my loyalties were divided. I was still more of a Mets fan, but began following the Red Sox day-by-day. Then, on that fateful day, the Mets traded my two favorite players: Dave Kingman (at age 7, I didn't understand that he only had one skill) and Tom Seaver. Had it only been Kingman, I would've been able to handle it. But Seaver's departure was too much to take, and from that moment on, the Mets were on the back burner. Needless to say, it was an incredible thrill to see

Seaver, even as elderly 6-inning pitcher, play for Boston in 1986. I still follow the Mets and go to many of their games, but it hasn't been the same. As for the Sox, I managed to survive Bucky Dent (naively thinking, "We'll get 'em next year")—and all the taunts from Yankee fans. If you can make it through that, and 1986, you're a fan for life.

Living in New York City, I don't get to see many Sox games. I used to call "Sports Phone" for in-game updates, go to the library for day-old *Boston Globes*, and manipulate my radio to get WTIC-AM in Hartford (its signal faded every half hour or so). Today, with more cable coverage and the Internet, it's easier to follow the team. There are a few thousand Sox fans in NYC, including my younger brother, and while many people around here think we're crazy, the effort we put in just makes our loyalty stronger. And going to Fenway is like a religious pilgrimage for us. I first went in 1978, seeing Boston beat Chicago, and have been fortunate enough to watch 15–20 games there since.

—Dave Bismo

My love of the Red Sox begins with my dad. My dad grew up in a very small town in Maine. Because Maine has no professional sports teams of its own, my dad became a fan of the nearest teams: in football, the New York Giants, and in baseball, the Boston Red Sox.

By the time I was born, my dad had become a dyed-in-the-wool Red Sox fan. He'd gone to high school in Philadelphia, college in Massachusetts, and returned to his high school to teach math. He'd suffered through the mediocrity of the 50's, the lousy teams of the early 60's, and had gone nuts (as all other Sox fans had) with the Impossible Dream team of '67. These trials and tribulations forged a strong bond between the team and my dad, as is to be expected, and so when I finally came around, I really had very little choice about my rooting interests.

Parents know that the oft-feared rebellion of the teenage years is preceded by a miniature version around third grade (a first foray into the joys of testing parental limits and boundaries). One of my small acts of rebellion was to decide that I wasn't just going to root for the Sox, but I was also going to root for the Yankees since they at least always won. I keenly remember the day that I told my dad all this. He reacted calmly. He told me to get out of the car. And I walked the rest of the way to school.

I have many memories of the Sox from my formative years. Living in Philadelphia, it was hard to follow the Sox. I remember having to be very quiet at night when the radio was on as Dad tried to listen amid the static (lots of static) to the Sox broadcast out of Hartford. Typical car-ride home from a youth soccer game . . .

Radio: "Bzzzzzzzzzzz . . . Rice . . . Bzzzzzzzzzzzz . . . double . . . Bzzzzzzzzzzz." Me: "What happened?" Dad: "Shh." Radio: "Bzzzzzzzzzzzz" Me: "I can't hear through the static. Double or Double play?" Dad: "Shh!" (He adjusts the radio dial). Radio: "Bzzzzzzzzzzzz . . . can't . . . Bzzzzzzzzzzzz . . . Sox . . . Bzzzzzzzzzzz." Dad: "We missed it! Dammit. You've got to be quiet!" Radio: "Bzzzzzzzzzzzz"

I remember being told about the gods of baseball. Not an obviously religious man, my dad however strongly believes in divine retribution when it comes to Sox fans. It's not that he believes in "The Curse," but he definitely believes that the gods of baseball punish the impious. The gods of baseball (always the full title—it's not "God" or "the gods" or "the fates" but "the gods of baseball") make Sox fans jump through hoops of superstitions and jinxes; moreover, they will continue to make us do so until the Sox finally win. For instance, whenever my dad is watching the Sox on tv, and they mount an offensive rally, he will not change positions on the couch, no matter how uncomfortable or hungry he is. Nor will he let anyone else in the room move. I can recall going to bed at night with the radio on, lying on one side and then another, trying desperately to figure out whether one side was good for the Sox and the other good for the opponent, or whether perhaps on this particular night one side was good for offense (for both teams) and one side good for defense. Needless to say, I did not sleep much until the game was over.

Just as the Baby Boomers have '67 and '78, their children have '86. That was a glorious summer. Away on a class trip, I found out about the 20 strikeout game upon my return, and that the Sox had taken over first place. First place! I'd yet to know the joys of that within my conscious following of the Sox. This was my first real taste of it and I was thrilled by the way it felt. I remember listening to the 3-game sweep of the Yankees in early summer and falling in love with Don Baylor as a player, both for the stories I heard of his kangaroo court and for the way he seemed to hit well in the clutch. I remember the Oil Can Boyd nonsense and how half the teams in the East (the Orioles, the Yankees, the Blue Jays) drew close at various points in the summer, only to fall back (but not before making Sox fans, mindful of '78, nervous).

I remember the playoffs. I remember being distraught by the fact that the Sox were down 3-1 (how could this be? this was clearly the Sox's year!) I remember racing home to watch the last innings of Game 5 of the playoffs. I remember the ecstasy of Henderson's homerun (and thinking how this too was fate, since it was he who had allowed a ball to bounce off his glove and over the fence for a homerun in that game— the gods of baseball were allowing him to redeem himself). I remember being incredulous and distraught that Crawford was in the game (he was my least favorite pitcher of that year and the one in whom I had the least confidence) and yet even he was allowed to escape being the goat (well, sorta, he gave up the tying run, but not the winning run—I felt that this was as much as anyone could hope for from Crawford).

The Sox advanced to the World Series and I walked on air. At school, some girl who didn't even follow baseball asked me why I was so happy—I answered her that I was happy because the Sox had made it to the World Series. Quick to punch a hole in my happiness, she said, "Yeah, but the Mets are going to beat them. So . . . so what?" I, mindful of how the gods of baseball punish hubris, admitted that the Mets were the better team, but that anything could happen. She taunted me, without really knowing anything about either team, and she bet me that the Mets would win. Knowing that this wasn't something I should necessarily be doing, I took the bet. (In my defence, I still do not think that betting on the Sox is inexcusable in the eyes of the gods of baseball—I did not bet out of any sort of misplaced faith in my team, but merely to uphold their honor. No, the bet was not the reason why the Sox lost). Still, when they did lose, not only to I have the sorrow of defeat hanging over me, but I had to pay this girl $3, adding pecuniary insult to spiritual injury.

Not that I didn't offend the gods of baseball. I did, to my shame. After winning the first two games, I offered to let the girl who had bet me pay me now—this was inexcusable for the gods of baseball and when the Sox lost the next two games I knew it was my fault. Also, when the Sox won Game 5, I asked my mom if we'd open up a bottle of champagne if the Sox won the World Series. This was not a horrible jinx, since I said "if the Sox won" and not "when the Sox won" but Sox fans really have no business talking about champagne when any little capriciousness on the part of the gods of baseball can mean waiting for the better part of another century. Finally, I fell asleep during Game 6. I don't remember any of it. I'm not sure that this is something for which the gods of baseball punished me, but it's still not something of which I'm proud. I stayed up as long as I could, I watched as much as I could, but the excitement of the Series, the long school days, and the numerous soccer teams left me too exhausted and, though I tried to stay awake, I konked out midgame. My dad, not sure whether to wake me or let me sleep (for the purposes of the jinxes) let me sleep where I lay on the floor. Having taped the whole Series (and so knowing that I could watch the actual events afterwards), he was getting ready to wake me up when the Mets' rally started occurring. Still not sure whether the Sox were destined to win or not (would waking me change the fate of their winning? of their losing?) he let me sleep. Even through the error. At that point, neither of my parents had the heart to wake me up to see the Mets' celebration. I didn't find out until early the next morning when I woke up on the floor of the tv room and rewound the last few minutes of the video tape. Only later did I find out that NBC had gone to congratulate the Sox before the final out was recorded and the game officially over. (My family has still not forgiven NBC for that, which surely cost the Sox the Series far more than the passed ball or Buckner's atrocious hitting). The rain which postponed Game 7 for a day, allowing Bruce Hurst to pitch, was just a cruel twist by the gods of baseball, who allowed hopes to raise, only to have the Sox lose with their best pitcher of the postseason on the mound. For all the year-long feelings that this was The Year, it wasn't the year. I cried.

There have been other memorable moments. Sam Horn. Morgan's magic. Nick Esasky. Brunansky's catch. Wakefield in '95. Rallying to beat the Indians in 5 games. But though my passion for the Sox has increased in many ways, though I now spend much more time and energy following the Sox, thinking about the Sox, worrying about the Sox than in my early youth, I've never had quite the same excited feeling. Like first love, 1986 taught me how great life could be when the Sox win, and it taught me never to forget that it could all come crashing down in the blink of an eye. Since 1986, there have been few seasons in which I did not have an unusually optimistic view of how good the Sox were going to be in the coming season, and yet I've never let my hopes get too high because I remember how horrible it is to realize that this year isn't really The Year. The gods of baseball are evidently not yet done testing my faith, but I am quite hopeful that I will prove worthy, that the Sox will win (and perhaps someday soon, if we're all lucky), and then, oh how glorious that day will be!

—Robert P. Machemer

TELL YOUR OWN STORY

Do you have your own story that you'd like to see included in the next edition of this book? Is there something you'd like to see added to a player entry, or a piece of history that you'd like to clarify? Is there a question you've always been dying to ask? Do you think it's a travesty that Scott Fletcher and Randy Kutcher aren't included in the player entries? Or would you just like to comment to the people who worked on this book? To reach the editors, e-mail soxfan@swordsmith.com, or write to:

Swordsmith Productions
Attn: Red Sox Fan Handbook
PO Box 242
Pomfret, CT 06258

Updated information, new questions, and players who didn't quite make the cut will be posted on the Swordsmith Productions website, www.swordsmith.com. (You can also order books from the website.) Feel free to visit and to comment on this and other Swordsmith Books.